ELECTORAL POLITICS IN THE MIDDLE EAST

ELECTORAL POLITICS
IN THE
MIDDLE EAST

Issues, Voters and Elites

EDITED BY

JACOB M. LANDAU, ERGUN ÖZBUDUN
FRANK TACHAU

CROOM HELM LONDON
HOOVER INSTITUTION PRESS
Stanford University, Stanford, California

© 1980 Jacob M. Landau, Ergun Özbudun and Frank Tachau
Croom Helm Ltd, 2-10 St John's Road, London SW11

British Library Cataloguing in Publication Data

Electoral politics in the Middle East.
1. Elections - Near East
2. Comparative government
I. Landau, Jacob M   II. Özbudun, Ergun
III. Tachau, Frank
329'.023'5604   JQ1758.A95

ISBN 0-7099-0454-1

Hoover Press Publication 241
© 1980 by the Board of Trustees of the
Leland Stanford Junior University
All rights reserved
International Standard Book Number: 0-8179-7411-3
Library of Congress Catalog Card Number: 80-8333

Printed and bound in Great Britain

CONTENTS

ABBREVIATIONS

DMC	Democratic Movement for Change
DP	Democratic Party
Ind.	Independents
JP	Justice Party
MK	Member of the Knesset
NAP	Nationalist Action Party
NP	Nation Party
NRP	National Religious Party
NSP	National Salvation Party
NTP	New Turkey Party
RP	Reliance Party
RPNP	Republican Peasant Nation Party
RPP	Republican People's Party
RRP	Republican Reliance Party
SPO	State Planning Organisation
TLP	Turkish Labour Party
TUP	Turkish Unity Party

PREFACE

When the editors of this volume first met in 1974 to discuss the project of analysing and comparing elections in competitive political systems of the Middle East, they were particularly attracted to this joint project. For, they soon found out, in Oscar Wilde's words, that they could resist everything but temptation.

Preparation of this book has required an intensive collective effort and considerable patience—even more than was anticipated. Every one of the nine contributors to this volume, including the three editors, has written a chapter in his field of expertise, incorporated in one of the three sections on electoral issues, voting behaviour, and the selected elites. In addition, each editor has tied up the functional section he was mainly responsible for with a concluding chapter for that section. All three editors share equally in the responsibility for the whole volume, and have also jointly prepared the introduction and epilogue. No less than in other joint products of this nature, collaboration has not always been easy, particularly as the contributors have resided in four lands—Turkey, Lebanon, Israel and the United States. The civil war in Lebanon, particularly, hindered communication and delayed the completion of the whole book. The editors are grateful to the New York office of the American University of Beirut for its assistance in maintaining contact, and to Professors Crow and Khalaf for persisting in the face of awesome personal and professional obstacles.

Despite the sustained efforts of the editors, these events have perhaps served to accentuate some differences of emphasis among the contributors. Hopefully, most of the remaining differences result, rather, from the varying essence of research in the functional topics selected for analysis. One such consequence has been that the use of certain terms—such as 'left,' 'centre,' 'right' and some others—has not been identical, but generally reflects their bearing within a given situation in place and time. The editors have not always smoothed out such variances, since they do not believe that glossing over real differences would serve any constructive purpose. They are ready to assume the blame of omission and commission, wherever this has inadvertently occurred. Meanwhile, they enjoyed the time which they shared with one another and in addition with the other contributors in preparing this book.

INTRODUCTION
Comparative Electoral Politics in the Middle East

This book emerged because of the need for comparative research on significant issues of contemporary Middle Eastern politics. Up to the Second World War, despite rising interest in the Middle East, the lack of a sufficient body of scholarly publications about it made serious comparative research unfeasible. Since then, so much has been published on almost every country in this area, that comparative political study can be readily envisaged, in order to provide scholars with an additional dimension of understanding of the area's complexities. That comparative political analysis on the Middle East has started relatively late was due, also, to the fact that the modern study of comparative politics is rather recent.[1]

Several distinguished investigators have perceived this possibility and have enriched the body of published research by their studies. Methodologically, however, their approach has been, almost without exception, to discuss the subject of their choice, country by country, then to reach some comparative conclusions in a final chapter. This has been the case, for instance, when comparing one Middle Eastern country to another outside this region, such as Turkey and Japan (in what are otherwise excellent functional 'case studies').[2]

The same has been the practice when dealing, on a general level, with the politics of several states in the Middle East,[3] or with a more specific subject, such as elites.[4] In these cases, the search for excellence has led the editors of such tomes to recruit the best authority on the state discussed. However, even when one single author considered himself qualified to write about such a topic concerning different countries, for instance on political leadership in three Middle Eastern states,[5] he still adhered to the same method—a separate discussion of leadership in each state, building up to a comparison in the concluding chapter only. The foregoing are, consequently, more in the nature of strictly parallel rather than analytically comparative studies.

1

Whilst there is still great merit in state-by-state research, for a thorough understanding of each political entity, we feel that a comparative approach may well afford a better opportunity for grasping and assessing the essentials, and for acquiring a truer insight. A comparative approach needs no apology, as it has already been employed to good purpose and seems well established in the field of political science.[6] Not coincidentally, studies dealing with contemporary European politics have pioneered the comparative approach, as one facet in a policy-oriented search for solving common problems by co-operation. The wonder is why the same has not occurred in current research on Middle Eastern politics.

But perhaps there is less to wonder about this than one might assume at first sight. The Middle East, although geographically one area with a largely common past, is less integrated now than either Western or Eastern Europe, respectively. It does not possess a common heritage as, say, Latin America does, in culture and religion. Students of the Middle East encounter much that baffles them with what not only appears paradoxical, but really is so. In addition to a great deal that is common, they find at least as much, probably more, that is disparate and conflicting—due to differences in the socio-cultural and religious background inherited from such ancient civilisations as the Jewish, Arab, Turkish, Iranian, Armenian and others. The multilingual situation is another obstacle for the comparativist who wants to base his research on primary sources.

A recent book by Bill and Leiden[7] is however a breakthrough, in many respects, in the study of comparative politics in area studies, in this case the contemporary Middle East. The two authors, both political scientists at the University of Texas, Austin, treat, comparatively, political development, the politics of social stratification, leadership, bureaucracy, the role of the military and ideologies. In this they have broadened the scope of a study by Halpern,[8] which dealt chiefly with social structure and social change, and they have made politics their main frame of reference. Written with expertise and acumen, the main merit of this work is that Bill and Leiden have succeeded in presenting comparatively and analysing some of the major issues in the contemporary Middle East, from Iran to Egypt (and, to a lesser extent, North Africa). Not surprisingly, even though they have analysed in depth stratification and patrimonialism, their approach has led them to focus keenly on those political processes and phenomena which seemed to them more immediately significant and relevant to large parts of the area, that is, the ones connected with the politics of violence and repression. In consequence, competitive democracy has perhaps received less than its due.

One such aspect, with which they have not dealt at all, is political elections, which Bill and Leiden have not considered an important phenomenon of participation, in the Middle East context. They argue that 'Legislatures often promote under-representation, pseudo-representation, and misrepresentation'.[9] Even were this the case throughout the whole area, there would nevertheless be some lesson in this. Moreover, elections and their parliamentary outcome are of little relevance in those states where they mean little or nothing, for instance in one-party and no-party political systems. However, in multiparty states, in which active political competition thrives, elections are—no less than coups and revolutions elsewhere—among the most prominent modes of manifesting political participation and, specifically, of bringing about or legitimating change in political regimes. In other words, in the Middle East there exist, side by side, some regimes ruled by the military; others with 'old-fashioned' patriarchal governments; and yet others which essentially are parliamentary multiparty states. In the last mentioned, the salience and functions of political elections may, and do, vary; but then again, this is the added incentive a student of comparative politics may well be looking for.

A careful analysis of elections in competitive political systems of the Middle East can provide a better understanding of the political cultures of these systems as well as of important parts of the region. This appears particularly applicable to an understanding of the interrelation of situational factors and basic factors—an interrelation frequently highlighted by elections. For this purpose, although laws and mechanisms are relevant, the character, attitudes and behaviour of the voters and the elected have been considered as much more so, especially when the latter are juxtaposed with the former. In order to cope with the task in one volume, the editors decided to concentrate on parliamentary elections and to discuss these under three main headings—electoral issues, voting behaviour and the selected elites. Naturally, the issues lead up to the elections; the voters decide the outcome; and those selected embody the consequence of the vote. In other words, the ballot box processes the votes and transfers 'inputs' into 'outputs'. As the issues are, at least partly, 'elite-made', the relationship of the factors to one another is, needless to say, more complex. It has been assumed that each of the three factors would reveal something about the political culture in at least one of the states chosen for the purpose; their general interrelation ought to characterise the political system in each state.

Then, the interrelation of each factor, in all the states chosen, on the one hand, and of all three factors combined, on the other hand, should provide the comparative basis for the conclusions of the study as a whole.

The three states chosen—in alphabetical order, Israel, Lebanon (prior to April 1975) and Turkey—are the only competitive political systems in the Middle East. Parliamentary democracy is deeply rooted in all three and has shown that it can weather dangers and crises. In Turkey there was apprehension in some circles, after the military 'Memorandum' of March 1971 and the proclamation of martial law, lest parliamentary elections might be postponed; however, martial law was lifted and elections were held on time, on 14 October 1973. In Israel war broke out on 6 October 1973, and the 30 October elections had to be postponed—but the postponement was as brief as possible; the elections were held on 31 December of the same year, even while a renewal of the fighting still seemed imminent. In Lebanon, the bloody internecine strife in 1975-6 prevented the smooth functioning of parliament; but it frequently convened, amidst snipings and bombings, to reach important decisions and to elect the State President (which, in Lebanon, is a prerogative of parliament).

In addition, Israel, Lebanon and Turkey offer enough similarities and dissimilarities to warrant their selection, in an attempt to account for their characteristics comparatively. All three share certain common attributes. Their politics are reasonably well institutionalised, open and non-violently competitive. In other words, political power is exercised through recognised institutional channels; parliaments, parties and elections have a meaningful significance in the national consensus, based on a sense of balance and toleration (which recently suffered a grievous blow in Lebanon, yet without, however, being shattered totally). Actually, the three republics boast of multiparty parliamentary systems, distinguishing them from most other states in the Middle East. Their political culture is imbued with constant, articulate interest in the political process.

All three have a common geographical setting and occupy important geopolitical positions. They are relatively young states—with republican Turkey being the oldest, having just passed the half-century mark; the other two obtained independence in the 1940s. Also, all three held general elections at about the same time: Lebanon in June 1972, Turkey in October 1973 and Israel in December 1973.[10] Our analysis will be chiefly of these three general elections, with earlier ones also being discussed in order to provide an added, dynamic dimension and a better frame of reference for comparison. The elections of May and

June 1977 in Israel and Turkey, respectively, could not be fully considered, in part because Lebanon has not had an election since 1972, thus hampering comparative analysis. None the less, the 1977 elections have been referred to when appropriate. In this context, it is worthy of note that Turkey and Israel—and, to a slightly lesser degree, Lebanon—have active and well-established institutes of statistics, whose careful official publications supply much of the data for an analysis that is intended to be precise rather than impressionistic. This is not necessarily the situation regarding data availability throughout the rest of the Middle East.

Yet, there is much that is different in the basic data, the political systems, attitudinal values and organisational styles. Taking the three states, again, in alphabetical sequence, one finds some striking dissimilarities. The State of Israel, established in 1948, is a small country. Not counting the Israeli-held territories beyond the 1967 borders, it has an area of 8,017 square miles and, at the end of 1973, a population of 2,810,400 Jews and 497,100 non-Jews.[11] The former originate from many lands and display numerous features of an immigrant society; about half are of Afro-Asian origin. The latter are mostly Arabs and include the inhabitants of East Jerusalem, annexed to Israel in June 1967. Literacy is very high, but Israel's people are not literate in one and the same language: in addition to the two official languages, Hebrew and Arabic, many Jewish immigrants still speak their mother tongue also, and some read newspapers which appear in Israel in those languages. Although unemployment is virtually non-existent, an inflationary economy has increased the material problems of a part of the population.

Lebanon, an independent state since 1943, has almost the same number of inhabitants as Israel (precise population data are not available), in an area of 3,950 square miles, or approximately half of Israel's.[12] The population, almost evenly divided between Christians and Muslims, is made up of a mosaic of religious communities, none of which has an absolute majority. The Maronites, Sunnites and Shiites are the largest numerically. In many crucial decisions of a political nature, the religious communities, rather than the political parties, have the final say. Lebanon has the highest literacy rate among all Arab countries, apparently over 75 per cent; while Arabic is the official language, French still predominates among many intellectuals, particularly (but not exclusively) the Christians. While Lebanon has the highest per capita income of Arab countries—excluding the oil-producers of the

Persian Gulf—wealth is very unevenly distributed. Inflationary trends and unemployment have been growing in recent years.

Turkey, established as a republic in 1923, is easily the largest and most populated of the three states selected. With an area of 311,780 square miles, its population reached about 38,500,000 at the end of 1973.[13] The population is quite homogeneous, practically the whole of it being Muslim. The only major ethnic minority is the Kurds in the country's south-east; other minorities, such as the Greeks, Jews and Armenians, number only several tens of thousands each. The official language is Turkish and literacy is the lowest of the three states under consideration, about 60 per cent. Increasing unemployment and rising expectations have driven many Turks in recent years to emigrate from village to town and even seek employment abroad; Turkish *Gastarbeiter* are the largest contingent of foreign workers in Western Europe, reaching 786,471 at the end of 1973.[14]

Further, the nature of the major problems facing these three states, both internal and external, varies considerably. This is not merely an outcome of the physical differences alluded to above. In all three, the role of religion in politics is important, but its character differs. Conflict levels are high, but they, too, vary among the three cases. Survival as a separate entity is crucial for Israel, a Jewish-majority state with an Arab minority of its own, and still in armed conflict with most of its neighbouring Arab states. So it is for Lebanon, where the delicate equilibrium between its present slightly larger Muslim majority and somewhat smaller Christian minority has been shaken visibly by political ideologies to an extent that endangers the state's very existence. No such emergency currently faces Turkey. However, in Turkey, modernising is a more immediate concern than in Lebanon; and in Lebanon more than in Israel. These and other points of resemblance and differentiation find expression in the electoral laws and campaigns, as well as in the composition and character of the elected assemblies. While the bicameral parliament in Turkey somewhat resembles those of the West, Israel's and Lebanon's are influenced in some degree by the British and French prototypes, respectively. Each, however, has largely developed in its own way, under the impact of local traditions and of particularistic ideologies and views.

Finally, special emphasis has been given to modernisation, whose challenge is ubiquitous and inevitable. Although the impact of modernisation varies in the three states selected—or, perhaps, due to this difference—modernisation may well serve as a unifying theme for all the chapters. This is evident when discussing competitive electoral systems which provide for mass participation on the Western model; obviously, it is no coincidence that all three states are among the most modern in the Middle East. The theme of modernisation, in particular the interaction of political institutionalisation and expanding participation, is highly relevant to each of the three cases before us and, indeed, in many other developing societies as well. Moreover, concern with these processes is currently widespread in the scholarly community.[15] The Epilogue of this volume will attempt to take up this theme again.

Notes

1. Details are in H. Eckstein, 'A Perspective on Comparative Politics' in H. Eckstein and D. E. Apter (eds.), *Comparative Politics : A Reader* (The Free Press, New York, 1963), pp. 3-12.

2. R. E. Ward and D. A. Rustow (eds.), *Political Modernization in Japan and Turkey* (Princeton University Press, Princeton, New Jersey, 1964).

3. For example, T. Y. Ismael *et al.*, *Governments and Politics of the Contemporary Middle East* (The Dorsey Press, Homewood, Illinois, 1970); A. A. al-Marayati *et al.*, *The Middle East: Its Government and Politics* (The Duxbury Press, Belmont, California, 1972).

4. F. Tachau (ed.), *Political Elites and Political Development in the Middle East* (Wiley, New York, 1975); G. Lenczowski (ed.), *Political Elites in the Middle East* (American Enterprise Institute, Washington, DC, 1975).

5. J. Dekmejian, *Patterns of Political Leadership : Egypt, Israel, Lebanon* (State University of New York Press, Albany, 1975).

6. J. Blondel, *An Introduction to Comparative Government* (Weidenfeld and Nicolson, London, 1969), pp. 3ff.; J. A. Bill and R. L. Hardgrave Jr, *Comparative Politics : The Quest for Theory* (Merrill, Columbus, Ohio, 1973), pp. 229-38; R. L. Merritt, *Systematic Approaches to Comparative Politics* (Rand-McNally, Chicago, 1970), pp. 3ff.

7. J. A. Bill and C. Leiden, *The Middle East: Politics and Power* (Allyn and Bacon, Boston, 1974).

8. M. Halpern, *The Politics of Social Change in the Middle East and North Africa* (Princeton University Press, Princeton, New Jersey, 1963).

9. Bill and Leiden, *The Middle East*, p. 20.

10. See J. M. Landau, 'The 1973 Elections in Turkey and Israel', *The World Today*, 30 (April 1974), pp. 170-80.

11. *Statistical Abstract of Israel 1974* (Central Bureau of Statistics, Jerusalem), 5, 21.

12. 'Lebanon', *Encyclopaedia Britannica* (1974), vol. 10, p. 764.

13. *1973 Statistical Yearbook of Turkey* (State Institute of Statistics, Ankara, 1974), 3, 29.

14. N. Abadan-Unat *et al.*, *Turkish Workers in Europe 1960-1975 : A Socio-Economic Reappraisal* (Brill, Leiden, 1976), p. 7.

15. S. P. Huntington, *Political Order in Changing Societies* (Yale University Press, New Haven, Conn., 1968); R. W. Benjamin *et al.*, *Patterns of Political Development: Israel, India, Japan* (McKay, New York, 1972); S. N. Eisenstadt, *Tradition, Change and Modernity* (Wiley, New York, 1973).

PART I

Electoral Issues

1. TURKEY

Doğu Ergil

Elections in Turkey date back to the First Constitutional Assembly of 1877-8. However, until 1946 the electoral system had many limitations that denied free participation in the political process. There were limitations of age, sex and literacy in the electoral system that went into effect in 1877 and prevailed during the second constitutional period and in the first decade of the republican era. Those under 30, females and those illiterate in Turkish were barred from the Assembly. The result of these provisions was to deny candidacy to approximately 90 per cent of the population. The electorate was required to be male, over 25 years of age and to pay property tax. One year's local residence was also mandatory.

Until 1946 the electoral system was indirect. The registered voters chose secondary electors who, in turn, selected the actual deputies. The candidates had to be male, over 30 years of age and own property.

Law No. 320 which was passed in 1923 extended the franchise to all males over 18 years of age. The taxpaying requirement for first and second electors was lifted. In 1934 the word 'male' was dropped from the necessary qualifications of both electors and deputies (Law No. 2598). As a consequence the Fifth Assembly, elected in 1935, included 18 female deputies.

In 1946 Law No. 4918 changed the electoral system from a two-stage process to a single-stage process. But, perhaps more important than that, formation of political parties other than the Republican People's Party was legalised.

These changes paved the way for competitive and free elections which, in turn, brought plurality of ideas, expression of different interests and organisation of interest groups into the Grand National Assembly.

What are the main electoral issues that were voiced by the political parties since 1920? I believe that electoral issues can be analysed in the context of ideologies. In fact, they are expressed in the framework of ideological tendencies.

11

Ideologies can briefly be described as (i) forms of perception of the world, and (ii) socio-political responses of various social groups to the conditions that they experience in specific historical periods. According to this characterisation, ideologies can and do change over time (they are time-specific) and they appear in different forms due to diverse socio-structural circumstances.

The national liberation struggle following the surrender and partitioning of Ottoman Turkey was strongly supported by the ideology of liberation characterised by nationalism, anti-imperialism and national-bourgeois revolutionism. The latter component embodied the missions of replacing the theocratic Ottoman monarchy with a secular modern republic and the predominantly pre-capitalist economy with transforming contemporary capitalism. This, of course, meant the elimination of several classes and social institutions which upheld them and the elimination of direct foreign influence in the economy such as the Ottoman Public Debt Administration and the Capitulations.

The 1924 Constitution laid down the foundation of legal institutions that aimed at centralising power by which social change could be engineered. Followed by the adoption of the Swiss Civil Code and other bodies of law of Western origin such as the penal and commercial codes, the 1924 Constitution provided the legal framework for creating a modern secular state. The military-civilian bureaucracy which controlled the state apparatus took on the inevitable mission of nation-building which meant reinforcing central control over local authorities and diverting all loyalties to the state. This endeavour culminated in a single party, the Republican People's Party, the programme of which was symbolised by six arrows representing: republicanism, nationalism, populism, statism, secularism and reformism.

Nationalism was the uniting force among all social groups and the governing elite. Secularism was the instrument of rebuilding a traditional society based on rational and contemporary principles which would allow scientific evaluation of worldly affairs and dynamic policy-making. Republicanism served two purposes: (i) to dismantle the old traditional authority and replace it with a new secular elite, and (ii) change of governing cadres through popular election. Populism meant the support of the ruling elite by the majority of the people. The bureaucracy established the material basis of populism by using the state apparatus. It created the necessary infrastructure, found jobs and provided consumer goods, and at the same time supported the private sector.

Needless to say, this mission gave the bureaucracy a central role in every aspect of daily life. This included planning for the future and directing social change. It was no coincidence that the sixth principle of the RPP was reformism. In more contemporary terms, the ruling Kemalist elite symbolised revolutionary change 'from above'. It was a directed change and the ruling cadres were to be the 'managers' of change (modernisation). The direction of change is evident from the reforms they introduced. Starting with the traditional attire, they changed many things including the script used for centuries. Eastern traditions, values and institutions were dropped in favour of Western ones. This was Westernisation, and Westernisation meant modernisation.

The state or the Kemalist cadre who controlled the state apparatus was the driving force behind this scheme of modernisation. In the absence of a modernising bourgeoisie, the bureaucracy had shouldered the task of nation-building, that is, creating a new nation state out of a traditional monarchy. The programme of the state party (RPP) embodied all aspects of national solidarity, centralisation of power, and directed change, in short, the ideology of nation-building. The ingredients of this ideology were reflected in the party's documents until 1950. That year was a turning point in Turkish political history in that multiparty politics became an integral part of political life.

The Democrat Party's accession to power and the *laissez-faire* economic policy it advocated and supported opened the phase of competition of development ideologies. This competition was further exacerbated by the failure of the *laissez-faire* policy towards the end of the 1950s.

The 1961 Constitution, approved by popular vote, contained new principles aimed at obtaining social welfare and policy-making for developmental purposes. First of all, it was established that 'Economic, social and cultural development is based on a plan. Development is carried out in accordance with this plan' (Article 129). Considering that the Turkish economy is a 'mixed' one comprising both state and private sectors, the plan would be binding on the state sector and regulatory for the private.

A Central Planning Organisation was created directly attached to the Prime Minister's office. The first Five-Year Development Plan issued by this organisation bears the date of 1963 to cover the period from this year until 1967. The plan initiated debates over the issue of whether a state-directed economy was better suited to Turkey's conditions or development through supporting the private sector was a better solution. The RPP, still representing the central authority's predominance in public and economic affairs, was inclined to support the first thesis. The Justice Party and other liberal parties all of which claimed that they had inherited the defunct Democrat Party's platform were firm believers in the virtues of the private sector. For them, private enterprise was the very foundation of human liberties.

On the other hand, the democratic nature of the new Constitution provided the legal basis for the formation of new political parties giving voice to different social groups in the society. The Turkish Labour Party was the most prominent among them.

It is appropriate to say that formation of a socialist party such as the Turkish Labour Party and free discussion of socialist ideas in Turkey were not primarily due to the more permissive nature of the 1961 Constitution. General economic growth since 1950 and accelerated industrialisation since 1960 brought qualitative changes one of which was the growth of a working class. This class was continuously fed by migrating masses from the mechanising countryside. On the other hand, it was legally shielded by new laws and regulations providing new opportunities such as collective bargaining, forming trade unions, striking and full coverage by social security.

The character of political debates had drastically changed when the Turkish Labour Party brought 15 MPs to the National Assembly following the 1965 general elections. It is during this period that the RPP, in spite of the later danger of losing its right-wing supporters, adopted a left-of-centre programme. The RPP's social-democratic stance was assumed at this stage. The year 1965 was a turning-point in the progress of Turkish politics towards a more crystallised political and ideological polarisation, augmented not only by limited develop-ment, but also by the incongruity between economic growth and the relatively equitable distribution of national wealth on the one hand and rapidly rising political consciousness or expectations that surpassed it on the other.

The period following the 1965 general elections was also fertile for the formation of many professional and political organisations which performed the duty of bringing together new pressure groups. This development may be deemed as the formation or organisation of the 'civilian society' outside the state apparatus. The initial proliferation of left leaning organisations was observed by both the Justice Party government and private enterprise with dismay. As a precaution, rightist youth organisations, some of which have been transformed into armed groups, began to be formed and trained in special para-military camps.

The ensuing economic difficulties and the inevitable clashes between the extreme left and the militant right left no chance for conciliation between the two sides. The military intervention of 12 March 1971 was the result of this clash which rapidly turned into a large-scale political vendetta.

The so-called 'intervening regime' under martial law ended with the general election held in 1973. Since this date two further elections have been held, namely the 1975 partial elections for the Senate and the 1977 general elections. Since there were few changes in the platforms, slogans and views advocated by the existing political parties no periodisation will be attempted between the elections held since 1973.

Electoral Issues Since the 1973 General Elections

Since 1961 Turkey's parliament has been made up of two houses, the National Assembly, with 450 seats, elected every four years; and the Senate, with 150 elected members (in addition to life Senators and those appointed by the State President), of whom a third is elected every two years for a six-year term. Representation is based on population and the elections are held by provincial constituency. Only electoral issues voiced by those parties large enough to have a group, i.e. ten members, in the National Assembly will be scrutinised. There are now only four such parties: the Republican People's Party (RPP), the Justice Party (JP), the National Salvation Party (NSP) and the Nationalist Action Party (NAP).[1]

Issues to be discussed can best be grouped under four headings: issues of economic development; issues of internal peace and political stability; issues of national security and foreign policy; and attitudes towards social change.

Issues of Economic Development
The RPP Platform. The democratic left or social democratic programme of the RPP is intended to begin national development in the countryside, where the majority of the Turkish people still live. This policy is aimed both at ending the existing inequality between urban centres and the villages and also creating the necessary capital to support growing industry. If the envisaged transfer of surplus value from agriculture to industry can be accomplished through this scheme, then reliance on foreign capital will be reduced and so will Turkey's overall economic dependence, evinced by snowballing deficits in the balance of payments.

Development of the agrarian economy must be based on rural enterprises, such as modern operations engaged in animal husbandry, poultry, fisheries and mechanised farming. These newly established enterprises must be helped to support themselves and compete both in the internal and external markets. To achieve this, they should be united in co-operatives to which the state makes financial and technical contributions. This programme will hopefully put an end to the small, non-competitive and stagnant private agricultural operations and create rational enterprises with increasing production capacity and marketing facilities. For the RPP, this is the only sound way to transform the subsistence economy which characterises the Turkish agrarian sector.

There are two complementary schemes of achieving the desired transformation in the countryside: (i) formation of agro-towns; and (ii) formation of production co-operatives. The first scheme is aimed at creating central dwellings and production units out of nearly 65,000 rural settlements dispersed throughout Anatolia. For example, one central village may be chosen out of ten, and government aid, including public utilities, may be directed to this centre. This means one school, one doctor, one power plant etc., instead of ten. These centres are expected to grow into communities which will also be the medium for industrial investment. The industrial plants envisaged will utilise excess labour power freed from subsistence farming. Similarly, local raw materials, now cultivated in greater quantities in nearby co-operatives, will be utilised in the factories installed in such centres. Co-operatives will be voluntary unions of farmers formed to overcome problems of finance, marketing and technical aid. The rationale behind agricultural co-operatives is not collective ownership but collective production to surmount the difficulties of subsistence farming and inefficiencies of rural artisanship (manual industry). This is also the basis of a land and agricultural reform programme proposed by the RPP.

The rural community project also envisages halting the flow of population from the countryside. This flow may not be important for the increasingly mechanised rural economy, but it imposes heavy burdens on the urban economy in several respects. First of all, the infrastructural capabilities of Turkish cities are insufficient to absorb a continuously migrating rural population. The rings of squatter houses swelling around urban centres symbolise a process of pseudo-urbanisation rather than a healthy transformation from an agricultural economy into an industrial society. These communities would diminish imbalances between geographical regions. Thus the continuing traditional socio-economic structure, especially in the countryside, will be transformed by means of a novel model and without coercion.

In the industrial realm, the RPP has another solution which proposes to combine economic development and social equity. This project is called the creation of a 'People's Sector'. The People's Sector (PS) is a combination of both small and medium-scale and large-scale enterprises. The first section will be composed of existing viable craft industries financially supported by small savings which presently flow to big enterprises. The shareholders may be workers employed in the very enterprise in which they invest their humble savings. Thus they gain the privilege of participating in the management of the enterprise. In the case of large enterprises there will also be individual investors whose volume of shareholding will be limited in order to curb monopolisation of management rights. But mostly popular large-scale organisations like social security institutions, confederations of co-ops, labour unions, business or investment firms created by domestic or migrant workers abroad will provide the much-needed large-scale financial resources. In fact, firms of a competitive scale can be created by persuading such institutions to invest in the PS. But for the popular control and management of the PS enterprises these large-scale institutions/organisations must be structured democratically.

The existing state sector will aid the PS to develop, but will not form partnerships or invest in any private enterprise (private sector).

The JP Platform. For S. Demirel, leader of the JP, 'the aim of development is to end poverty'.[2] This aim is symbolised as creating a 'grand Turkey', in which not only increases in the GNP are expected, but also equitable distribution of national wealth. In other words, the aim of development is the widening of social security. But how is development to be achieved?

The JP finds the method to be adopted in the Turkish Constitution (in Articles 40, 41 and 129). For this party the driving force of development is the private sector and the state provides the necessary conditions for safe investment and stability of the market. The role of the state is not limited to be only a protector of free enterprise but it also invests in areas which private entrepreneurs deem unprofitable or too expensive, such as public transportation, energy and heavy industry. Thus the structure of the economy advocated by the JP is a mixed one, but without any doubt the leading sector is the private one.

The JP believes in the planning of national development, but this must not be an obligatory and central plan. Five-Year Development Plans must be hortatory not obligatory. The plans must delineate the areas in which entrepreneurs should invest, which products should be subsidised, and what lines of production should be protected. Choice and implementation must be free and individual. If this scheme is implemented, then the concepts of freedom and planning can be united.

Industry will be the leading force in economic development. But this does not mean that agriculture will be neglected. On the contrary, it will receive more aid than in the past. Both in agriculture and industry the guiding principle will be increasing efficiency and aid to those lines of production in which more output can be obtained. Otherwise this country cannot compete in international markets.

Indeed, free enterprise is the key concept in the economic dictionary of the JP. Without free enterprise there can be no freedom and, for that matter, no democracy. The role of the state is to safeguard the economy built around this principle. The free will of the entrepreneur is matched by the free will of the worker. Both sides conciliate their interest in the legally established collective bargaining system.

The JP platform is very open to foreign capital. In fact, it sees foreign capital as a necessary tool to develop the country and to provide jobs.

In summary, the JP is a classical liberal party in its programme and world view. Its basic principle in the economic realm is to increase efficiency and profitability. It envisages land reform as a form of land distribution to the landless rather than a tool of transforming the agrarian society. It advocates amelioration of the unjust tax system but does not put forth concrete ways to change from dependence on indirect taxes. This vagueness may be due to the party's philosophy which favours investment and efficiency over social justice.

The JP's programme aims at transforming artisans and craftsmen with limited opportunities into medium and big industrialists through a more favourable credit system. These strata are to be tied to a social security and pension system called the Bağ-Kur (which already exists) independent of the workers and government officials.

Similar to the RPP programme, the JP wants to start economic development from the village, but disagrees with those past governments which looked down upon the villagers as inferior citizens and as a result neglected the countryside. The JP proposes concrete improvements in the life of peasants, such as reducing the villagers' share of the cost of the extension services brought to the countryside by the central administration. The JP is also a firm supporter of the policy of subsidising agricultural products (mostly industrial cash-crops) and inputs necessary in the agrarian production cycle.

The NSP Platform. Development is perhaps the most frequently used word of NSP spokesmen. But for them development has two aspects, material and spiritual, and they cannot be separated from each other. Spiritual development is necessary to develop the ideal human being who is the embodiment of Islamic ethics. Material development is to provide such citizens with the comforts of the contemporary world.

The NSP's key slogan is to 'Recreate Great Turkey'. Unlike the JP, which deems the present as the best period of Turkish history, NSP members argue that Turkey was once a great world empire; therefore, the target of all Turks must be to reconstruct that glorious past. The method chosen to realise this end is to open the phase of heavy industry in Turkey. In the words of the NSP election platform, investments so far implemented in Turkey are of a 'colonial' nature in that they aim at assembling prefabricated parts and bottling bubbling soft drinks. The NSP's investment should be of a kind which will create a 'leader' country, and this can only be done by investing in heavy industry.

For the NSP, previous governments have accomplished certain things with goodwill; however, these are insufficient. In order to recreate Great Turkey, and to make a leading country out of her, factories must be erected in every provincial capital. More of what has been accomplished in the past fifty years must be realised in the coming five years. It is only through this programme that Turkey can break through from the bonds of being a satellite underdeveloped country.

The development model proposed by the NSP is described by its leaders as 'national, rapid, substantial and widespread'.[3] For the party, only through this scheme will the GNP increase, balance of payments improve and unemployment be curbed.

The NSP intends to disperse the newly established industries to every corner of the country so that the existing imbalances between regions may be eliminated. These large-scale industries will create a new and modern division of labour by giving birth to auxiliary industries. This scheme is the only way out of the present assembly kind of industry which perpetuates the country's dependence on developed economies. Imitation will be over and the 'national doctrine' will take its proper place.

For the NSP, 'the debate over progressivism and obscurantism is over. The progressives are the believers.' 'Now the reign of the bureaucracy is ending, the era of the national doctrine is starting.'[4]

Considering that the NSP receives most of its votes from Anatolian towns where small business and small-scale agricultural and craft industries are lingering on, how would this party reconcile its programme of heavy industry which means instant death for these strata? The

NSP, although vague in many of its documents, envisages a scheme of making the 'peasant, worker, civil servant, the artisan and the limited income earner shareholders (or partners)'[5] in the newly established industrial complexes. How this mechanism would work is not clear, but the historical task of transforming the economy from its traditional structure based on small-scale production to heavy industry of a competitive scale is as presented above.

The NSP is cognisant of the fact that the era of small production and strata engaged in such activities is gradually waning. The 'future shock' or the feeling of insecurity felt by these strata can be curbed by reinserting them into the economic process which is ousting them. In the psychological realm, religion is seen as the necessary pacifier. For the Believers there is no defeat. The NSP is the instrument of Salvation.

The party is also aware of the fact that a part of its constituency is the body of small businessmen and rising petty capitalists of Anatolia. For this reason, it has several proposals to divert government services and supportive programmes in favour of these strata. The most important among these is to put an end to lending money at interest. For the NSP, interest is one of the worst forms of sin; a medium through which man exploits man. Islam does not allow such exploitation. If there is something to be claimed for the money lent, it must be a fair share of the profit earned. The abolition of interest will be remedied by the establishment of government financial or credit organisations. These new institutions will provide credits for agriculture, craft industries, housing and education. All of these credits will be given without interest.

The NSP also envisages the reorganisation and updating of animal husbandry. The party documents assert that what was once the Ministry of Agriculture has been transformed into a Ministry of Food, Agriculture and Husbandry during their administration as coalition partners.

It seems that the NSP economic development programme is based on two focal points: (i) redistribution of government facilities from big business to medium and small business; and (ii) absorbing the vanishing small proprietors and traditional commodity producers either as workers or shareholders, preferably in both ways, into the industrial complexes of scale which the party claims to be the creator of.

The NAP Platform. The NAP, like the NSP, is a latecomer on the Turkish political scene. Both parties are products of the great split on the political right represented primarily by the JP, which ruled the country single-handedly until the 1971 military intervention. Up to that point the JP served as a mass party embodying many interest groups. However, insurmountable difficulties arose out of the JP's policies which could not freely meet emerging economic and social demands. Nevertheless, the extent of the JP's loss of popular support only became evident after the 1973 general elections. Two parties which especially benefited from the JP's losses were the NSP and NAP.

The NAP's general programme is based on a doctrine called the 'Nine Lights'. Each 'light' as it is called represents a separate ideal or target of the party to be achieved.

These are: nationalism, idealism, moralism, communalism, scientism, liberalism, ruralism, developmentalism/populism and industrialisation/technology. It can be surmised from this combination of principles that, like the NSP, the NAP also wants to combine the spiritual with the material. But the spiritualism envisaged by the NAP is worldly (although utopian) and pragmatic rather than religious.

The economic structure to be created around the Nine Lights, in the words of NAP's leader, Alparslan Türkeş, is as follows:

> Our model is national and social. In this model we will organize the six social categories. The first form of organization is legal. We will form six national organizations out of workers, peasants, artisans, civil servants, members of free professions and employers (entrepreneurs). Each citizen will register in the appropriate organization which corresponds to his activity. There will be obligatory Savings and Investment Funds... If every member of each category saves, say 10% of his salary... this will reach enormous amounts. Unable and inept governments for years have begged equivalent amounts from other nations...Thus we will bring not the egg, but the hen into our country. At the end, our homeland will be full of national factories and machines.
>
> In the new order of the Nine Lights, the means of production will be owned by the worker, peasant, artisan and the civil servant because these are built with his savings. Thus national wealth and economy will belong to all the members of the Turkish nation. There will be no exploitation, blackmarketeering, middlemanship and usury in such a system.[6]

These organisations are in reality production corporations. Each corporate body will produce different commodities and services. Thus a new sector will be born in the economy, namely the national sector.

The relationship of this sector to the other two sectors, state and private, will be arranged[7] by the state which is the symbol of power, dignity, and trust for the Turks. 'The state is an iron fist in a velvet glove.'[8]

As regards the agrarian sector, the NAP has similar projects to the RPP's scheme of transforming the present structure of the countryside. Just like the agro-towns of the RPP, the NAP proposes agro-towns (*tarım kent*) to perform almost the same functions. These agro-towns will be centres of economic and social attraction that will curb the drain of both capital and manpower from the countryside. Agro-towns will be local centres of industry that will utilise the raw materials produced in the villages, but also provide industrial inputs such as farm machinery produced in the factories established with the contribution of Village Production Corporations and Savings Funds. Thus villagers will be the owners of the newly instituted industries in the developing agro-towns.

Another aspect of rural development is land and agricultural reform. For the NAP, an efficient size of farm operation is 100 dönüms for irrigated land and 300 for dry land (1 dönüm = ¼ acre). Division of farm lands beyond these limits will not be permitted. The NAP calls this process the 'consolidation of farm lands'. The party also proposes an amendment in the inheritance laws in order to halt the fragmentation of lands beyond those limits. One of the points which makes the NAP's programme attractive to big landlords is that any expropriation of land for distribution to the landless peasants is to be by compensation to its present proprietors. But, following the Japanese model, the reimbursement payments of expropriated lands will not be allowed to go to consumption. Shares of existing state factories will be given in return. Moreover, land distributed to the needy will be sold to them for a price which will be paid in instalments.

The necessary credits for technical and operational expenses of the farmers will be provided by Village Farming Co-operatives. The organisation of the villagers in co-operatives is obligatory. But according to Türkeş, this corporate body is qualitatively different from the communistic collective farms.[9] In the Soviet type of collective farms there is no private ownership of land. In the NAP's project, formation of co-operatives will be based on production not ownership. 'Rare minerals will be nationalized. The internal and external private sector will not be allowed into mining.'[10]

It can be understood from this programme that the NAP wants to create a corporatist society. The existence of classes is denied. There are only functional categories with non-antagonistic interests. What the state must do is to organise these social/professional categories and monitor the division of labour between them from above. Each category has its own rules of conduct, and, like all corporate bodies, can interact with another social category through the mediation of the state or the central authority. This, indeed, is an authoritarian conception of society.

Issues of Internal Peace and Political Stability
As regards social peace and political stability each party has both similar and different solutions and ideas that are consonant with its world view.

The RPP Platform. Solidarity is the precondition of a just and free society. For the realisation of solidarity, the primacy of labour must be accepted. Labour *per se* must receive its material and spiritual returns without any discrimination between manual and mental products. Labour's satisfaction on these principles will contribute to equality, social balance and political peace. Both working conditions and allocation of material wealth must be decided upon by the labourers themselves. It is through this process that the working person will develop his potential fully.

In a society which has accepted the principle of the primacy of labour, employment is every individual's prerogative. So every individual must be provided with an appropriate job. Unemployment must be curbed by the state.

For the RPP, development is a combined process of economic, social and political transformation. If the real target of development is the well-being of the individual, this must not be postponed to a period after a certain phase of economic growth. Existing imbalances and inequalities may then become insurmountable. The only safe way to evade this danger is to maintain the principles of freedom, democracy, equality and the primacy of labour in every phase of economic advancement. These principles can be put to work through a system of self-management. Self-management means solidarity and conciliation of antagonistic interests in the management of work and daily life.

Self-management is a form of democratic government proposed to cover all aspects of social life, including local administrations and the state apparatus. Increasing areas of popular organisation will obviate monopolisation of political power by a wealthy minority which may come to control the state apparatus. Augmentation of economic power of the working population will provide the material basis for establishing democracy.

For the enhancement of democracy, equality between man and woman must also be implemented. The right to vote and to stand for election must be reduced to 18 and 21 years, respectively. Migrant workers abroad must be given the opportunity to vote and/or be candidates in Turkish elections while they are still in foreign countries.

Students and other personnel must take their part in the administration of universities. In the state sector, participation of workers in the management of enterprises should be ensured. Civil servants must be given the freedom of forming or entering trade unions which perform the function of collective bargaining until self-management is realised in the state sector.

Popular participation will be provided in national planning.

Political capabilities of labour unions will be increased.

All limitations on freedom of thought, belief and expression will be purged. Thus, for the RPP, there will be no 'crimes of thought'. Similarly, the party proposes the abrogation of restrictions on basic freedoms and rights under Martial Law. The same is proposed for the amendment of legal restrictions on printed matter or censorship.

In sum, the RPP does not see realisation of social peace and political stability as an outcome of successful administrative control of deviance. Rather, the party wants to widen the base of popular participation in both economic and social life in the framework of self-management. It is through this model that the RPP hopes to reduce the existing hiatus between the rich and the poor as well as between the rulers and ruled.

The JP Platform. The JP's election platform and other documents on the party's political philosophy unanimously state that internal peace and political stability will be achieved through 'a powerful and efficient State'. But, despite its power, this state apparatus will not endanger democratic institutions and free enterprise. On the contrary, it will reinforce these sacred institutions and also spread social security, free unionism, collective bargaining, the right to strike and other governmental services to the working population.

Development must be achieved not by reducing the existing life-standard of the Turkish people or by hampering their existing freedoms and legal rights. This point is stressed despite the fact that such a policy may reduce the rate of economic growth. Thus, the JP puts personal freedom ahead of economic gains obtained through coercion. In this respect its programme differs from that of the NAP which advocates obligatory organisations and savings.

JP documents advance the following solution to social peace and political stability: the working population must receive an equitable share of the rise in standards of living made possible by economic development; at the same time, there must be contributions to the developmental process in accordance with individual capacities; such a combination of principles will curb clashes of interest between social strata of an antagonistic nature.[11]

Equitable and balanced distribution of increasing national income among citizens will be aided by a new tax and fiscal policy as well as a balanced distribution of public services throughout the population. The state structure that can implement this is the Social Welfare State which the JP intends to create in the near future. The basic principle or task of the Social Welfare State is to offer the nation's population social services that will free them from anxiety about the future. If this end is achieved, accumulation of differences between individuals and social strata that cause animosity and hostile competition will be reduced, if not eliminated altogether.

The NSP Platform. The NSP on every occasion repeats that 'Our homeland and nation are an indivisible entity. We 43 million are all brothers.'[12] Differences of thought must not lead to accusations and division. 'An idea must be met with another idea.'[13] Party leaders believe that the anarchic milieu inherited from previous governments is due to the materialist administration of the leftist and liberal doctrines. They assert that 'Realization of brotherhood, internal peace and tranquillity is [their] duty. Materialists disturb public peace...Spiritualism is the foundation of internal peace and tranquillity. Political parties must give up bickering, exploitation and imitation [of Western ways and habits].'[14]

Another precondition of stability is 'harmony between the State and nation... [This can be achieved by] adoption by government officials of [the NSP's] national and spiritual values and carrying in their hearts not seeds of oppression but love of service. The State must be kind, just, protective and guiding to its citizens.'[15] For the realisation of such an ideal programme there must be no discrimination based on colour, religion, race, language and class. But for the NSP, 'the leftist doctrine values the society and neglects the individual. The liberal doctrine values the individual and neglects the society and it is exploitative by nature. Thus, none of these doctrines can fulfil the necessary harmony between the State and society. ...Salvation lies in the NSP world-view.'[16]

Party documents and spokesmen often boast about the NSP accomplishments between 1974 and 1977 (as partners in coalition governments) in order to achieve internal peace, brotherhood and political stability: ethics courses have been included in the curricula of primary and middle schools; overall combat has been waged against pornographic publications; pressure previously put upon national and 'ethical' publications has been abolished and their reading is no longer prohibited; the civil servant is perceived as a part of the nation; appointment of administrators devoted to ethical and spiritual values has been realised; better living conditions have been provided for peace-keeping forces (police and army personnel); great stress has been put on moral and spiritual education, and many educational institutions have been initiated to further this end.

What still remains to be done is as follows: in the educational realm all of the children of the country must be familiarised with the national targets; new efforts must be brought into the battle against corruption and blackmarketeering; all laws and legal restrictions which oppress freedom of belief and religious conviction must be abolished.

It is necessary to point out that after so much propaganda for freedom of belief and conviction, most of the NSP deputies voted against the release of leftist prisoners when the RPP-NSP Coalition Government declared a general amnesty in 1974. This occurred despite the bargaining of both sides for the release of both incarcerated religious-minded and political prisoners. The RPP could secure the release of the latter only through court action.

In summary, the NSP has one main solution to anarchy and political instability in the country: cleansing the soul of the people and making them better citizens or, in their own words, 'brothers'.

The NAP Platform. The NAP takes the 'nation' as the indivisible unit of social organisation: 'For us, the Turkish Nation is composed of distinct qualities such as a common language, race, ideal, culture and historical unity and is a collection of human beings who have reached the consciousness of living together.'[17]

The sacred entity which is called the 'nation' can be protected in two ways. Externally, the state must be protected from the incursions of imperialism, especially communist Russian imperialism. Internally, all conflicting interests which set one part of the nation against another must be reconciled. The most significant scheme to achieve this end is to formalise the existing functional division of labour in the society by creating estates out of six socio-economic categories. These categories are workers, peasants, artisans, civil servants, free professionals and employers (or entrepreneurs). The nation will be a corporate body comprised of these social estates whose duties, rights and administration will be determined in detail. NAP documents declare that this will be a democratic administration; however, there is no hint in all of their political literature about the democratic aspects of this corporate administration. Rather, there is evidence to the contrary.

For the NAP, the main principle of social well-being is proprietorship. This right is limited in both capitalist and communist systems. In the first system a handful of capitalists expropriate most of the national wealth, leaving little to the working population; in the latter, the Communist Party bureaucracy controls everything. But in the system of Nine Lights every corporate estate will build its own means of production—means of livelihood—and at the same time have a share in their ownership. Thus, there will be no exploitation and oppression. Capital will not be able to subdue and exploit labour. No class differences will arise in such a system. National development will be rapid, balanced and equitable. The NAP calls this process 'integration of labour and capital'.

With the achievement of this integration a new phase will begin for the Turkish nation. In the words of Türkeş, 'The new age is the age of nationalist action. In this age, the principle "Everything is for the Turk, according to the Turk and by the Turk", and the National Doctrine will be dominant.'[18]

There seems to be a similarity between the NAP's and NSP's election declarations in that both parties advocate a strong administration. In fact both parties prefer the presidential to the parliamentary system. They want to abolish the Senate and reduce the number of deputies. Both parties have no tolerance for other ideas, especially of the political left. This is no coincidence, because both parties appeal to petty businessmen, farmers, craftsmen and the traditional middle class of Anatolian towns and cities. These are social strata which are experiencing great stress and insecurity in the face of rapid social and economic change. The relations of production and cultural values to which they have been socialised, the whole frame of reference which has delineated their lives, is waning. This fact makes it easier for them to support a strong administration which may halt the disintegration of the world around them. Similarly, both parties offer them new opportunities of making a great leap over ages and social categories to gain a new identity in the industrial society in the making. Moreover, these insecure and baffled individuals are invited to take part in the determination of their own future. In this future there will be the most significant symbol of security: private ownership. Enlarged social security facilities will provide services which have heretofore been denied to them.

Despite the attractiveness of this programme it is still too grandiose and too obscure for a people whose practicality is their predominant virtue. However, both the NSP and NAP offer something also which makes their propaganda more convincing, at least more convincing than that of the RPP which offers a similar programme, and, furthermore, dressed with a more democratic garb. For the NSP it is religion and for the NAP it is Turkish nationalism. Both ideologies are solidarist, apt to de-emphasise social and economic differences between social classes, and call for obedience to a transcendental authority, namely God or the nation. Both concepts carry cultural legitimacy and deep-seated links with the prevalent value system of the society. Once this legitimacy is utilised to rally people, whether the platform it accompanies is realistic or not, it still may have some success in attracting voters.

Considering that nearly 60 per cent of the Turkish population is still toiling on the soil at or below the subsistence level, that migration and constant population increase (2.5 per cent annually) swell the number of the unemployed, that inflation is undermining humble income, social change to a large number of people may seem a dreadful process which ought to be stopped. Both the NAP and the NSP offer to their constituencies the ideal of a rather stable society where there is no internal strife and where there is no crisis of deciding what to do next. What is to be done is either offered as a religious edict or by the corporate government symbolised by a fatherly leader at the top, whose orders are unquestionably correct.

Issues of National Security and Foreign Policy

With increasing polarisation of the society due to a clearer crystallisation of social classes in recent years, foreign policy, which was once the prerogative of the political leaders, has become subject to public debate.

The RPP Platform. The RPP favours foreign policy which will contribute to international peace as well as secure Turkey's independence. This aim can be achieved by (i) equal partnership in international mutual defence organisations of which Turkey is a part, (ii) establishing Turkey's control over mutual defence bases and installations or other military material on its soil, (iii) developing good relations with all states, especially with neighbouring countries, (iv) supporting detente between superpowers or even contributing to this process but with an eye on its own national security, (v) refusing to be left out of diplomatic negotiations which involve its allies, and (vi) rejecting a drastic cut in the military manpower of the security system it belongs to but at the same time supporting a balanced and mutual reduction of arms and armed personnel. Furthermore, the RPP proposes to advance good relations and cooperation between the nations of the Balkan Peninsula and of the Middle East. Diplomatic relations must be established and advanced with nations which have recently won their political independence.

The RPP offers three principles to guide its foreign policy:

We will not be emotional in our foreign policy.
There is no place for ideologies in foreign policy.
We will not attach more weight to our country's economic interests than to national security.[19]

As regards the Cyprus problem, the RPP favours the 'establishment of an independent federal Cypriot State that will guarantee the Turkish population's land ownership, participation in administration and opportunities for economic development as equal citizens'.[20] This excerpt is taken from the 1973 election platform. Today only one clause is added to the party's understanding of the issue, and it is 'an independent federal State based on two geographic regions'.[21]

For the RPP, national security and foreign policy comprise an inseparable whole. Planning for one must cover and support the other. Since national security can be achieved through independence, strategic industries in arms manufacturing like electronics and engines will be developed. Moreover, the concept of national security will be brought into harmony with the country's economy and geographic position.

As regards Turkish ethnic groups living in other countries, the RPP will try to secure them opportunities to preserve their culture and to receive an education befitting this end; that their rights are observed as guaranteed by international agreements; and that the necessary permission be obtained from their respective governments if they want to migrate to Turkey.

The RPP desires to continue relations with the EEC. The party considers full participation of Turkey in the EEC economically and politically beneficial. Turkey must take its place in the process of European integration if it wants to have progressive and balanced relations with the West. On the other hand, the RPP deems it undesirable both for the Common Market and for Turkey to be a burden on each other. But it seems that the RPP means the second: 'Concessions given by Turkey concerning industry have reached a level that will hamper Turkey's advancement to the rank of an independent industrialized society.'[22] The RPP believes that unequal relations also prevail in the agricultural sector. Turkey's full partnership in the EEC may be endangered unless these adverse conditions are ameliorated.

The JP Platform. The JP evaluates foreign policy as a tool of 'procuring external security and developing [the country's] international relations according to a balance of interests'.[23] The JP announces that its foreign policy is guided by the principle set forth by Atatürk that domestic tranquillity depends on international peace.

Today, nations having different political regimes are seeking co-operation and are signing agreements for peaceful coexistence while at the same time respecting their differences. Turkey too has to find its proper place in this changing world.

The JP also wants Turkey's relations with the EEC to develop into a closer collaboration in the social, economic and financial fields.

As regards the Cyprus issue (1973), the JP election platform proclaims that the party will defend the legitimate rights of the Turkish community on the island in the most suitable way befitting Turkey's national interests. In any case, this way will be a peaceful one. There are no further details in JP documents on these issues.

The NSP Platform. The NSP sources introduce the subject by criticising previous governments. For this party, the JP and the RPP have applied a foreign policy dependent on external powers. Turkey has been made a slave and open market of the EEC. Turks are turned into servants of Western tourists. The outcome has been colonisation of the country. Previous administrations could not strike a balance between gains and losses within NATO. They have repulsed all friendly appeals from brotherly Arab countries. 'The only direct airline out of Turkey to the Middle East is to Tel Aviv... Turkish delegates have attended Islamic Conferences as tourists... They have claimed that we cannot be members.'[24] Finally, the NSP criticises the zeal for imitating the West in spite of a glamorous history with the honours of which Turks are proud.

What had to be done in the 1973 elections was expressed by the party as follows: an independent, nationalist and stable foreign policy must be implemented. The main principle in this policy will be defence of basic rights and justice. The party claimed that it would never allow the application of a belligerent policy while on the other hand appearing as a symbol of peace. 'We will institute closer relations with nations with which we have geographical, cultural and historical affinity.'[25]

There is no opinion of the NSP on the Cyprus issue in 1973, but following the Turkish military intervention in 1974 during the RPP-NSP Coalition Government, the pronouncements use very belligerent language on the subject. NSP leaders are presented as saviours of the Turkish Cypriot community by forcing their partners, when a few hours after the operation had started the RPP wanted to stop the successful advance of the troops. Similarly, NSP leaders claim that they prevented their partners in the following coalition governments from giving concessions on the territorial gains. They go on relating their successes as follows: we staged a dignified policy in the Aegean Sea to protect our national interests. We went on with oil explorations in spite of the Greek threat; we shut down the bases in Turkey as a warning when the US imposed an arms embargo on us; another significant decision concerning this matter is that we initiated the rapid installation of a national war industry; we convened the Conference of Islamic Countries in Istanbul; we became a full member of the Conference of Islamic Countries and signed separate economic, commercial, technological and cultural agreements with many of the Islamic countries; we rendered the agreement signed by the RPP and JP with the EEC ineffective, thus we opened the way for the establishment of our national heavy industry.

It can be inferred from the statements above that the NSP is vigorously against Turkey's entry into the Common Market. There are four reasons why the party opposes membership in the EEC: (i) national, moral, cultural and ethical values will degenerate when we mix with foreigners; (ii) the advanced industry of the EEC will crush the nascent Turkish industry; (ii) entry into the Common Market will facilitate settlement in Turkey of many foreigners who will in turn buy property and create a cosmopolitan society; (iv) following economic integration there will be political integration which will reduce Turkey to a mere province of Europe.

This evaluation clearly reveals that the NSP wishes to preserve the country's traditional culture which is to a great extent alien to the West but has more in common with the Middle East with which it shares a common history and religion. Despite its very conservative recipe, the NSP's protectionist attitude for small-scale industry that exists in Turkey appeals to smaller businessmen and leftist intelligentsia alike.

The NAP Platform. The NAP's foreign policy is intended to be nationalist and determined to preserve Turkey's sovereignty by remaining in the present alliance system. This does not mean, however, acceptance of the obligations of this alliance as a mechanism of pressure. The NAP is in favour of close relations with European nations in all fields including the economic, but it is vigorously opposed to 'the slavery of the European Common Market'.

The NAP is against any form of concessions on the Cyprus issue. In fact, this party believes that all of Cyprus should be Turkish. It holds the same attitude on the Aegean islands on the Turkish continental shelf. The NAP also declares that the Aegean is not a Greek sea, but an international passageway. Thus it deems Greece's policy in this sea as belligerent and imperialistic. Notwithstanding the hostile attitude of the other side, the NAP favours friendly relations and collaboration with Greece. This alliance is directed against Soviet incursion into the region.

Consonant with its utopian programme of uniting all the Turkic peoples of the world, the NAP promises to work toward securing civil rights for Turkish populations in Eastern European and Asian countries. This motif is one of the most frequently used in the documentation prepared for the party's youth organisations.

The NAP also calls for a realistic integration of Islamic countries on the economic front. This move will be reinforced by the common past, culture and religion shared by all the nations involved. Such an alliance is seen as the formation of a defensive front of regional countries between big power blocs. In fact, the NAP favours participation in the Western alliance because it is anti-communistic, but its nationalist politics further alienates its parochial constituency from Western culture. Furthermore, the NAP is not very sympathetic to democratic politics in Europe which it evaluates as a part of Western degeneration. In any case, the NAP's foreign policy is based on extreme anti-communism on the one hand and strong pan-Turkism on the other.

It seems that there is a split among the parties on the issues of Turkey's political commitment to the West and economic integration with Europe. Politically, the RPP and the JP are committed to the West; the NSP is openly against becoming a part of the Western world; the NAP, due to its great fear of communism, wants to stay in the Western alliance. However, while the NAP wants an autarkical economy through the forced savings of the people, the NSP sees salvation in a common market of Islamic countries. In the NSP's scheme, Turkey will be the leading country in terms of manpower and technology. This potential must be combined with the Arabs' petro-dollars to create a new and formidable international economic power centre. If and when this plan works, not only will the underdeveloped nations of the Middle East prosper, but they will also close the region to foreign influences which disrupt peace and cultural (Islamic) integrity under the cover of economic aid.

The RPP and JP both desire economic integration with the West. However, the RPP is more cautious in this respect. The latter party wishes to be a part of the democratic Western community but not its economic colony. Its expressed desire for integration is more political than economic until economic problems between the EEC and Turkey are solved. The JP, on the other hand, sees Turkey's membership in the Common Market as inevitable. This stance is seen by some observers simply as due to big business which is behind the JP and is in so many ways linked to Western capital that their severance means the death of Turkish entrepreneurship with its present structure mainly based on assembly type of industry.

Various approaches to the issue of national security are also reflected differently. The RPP and JP envisage democratic societies in which the state is not the symbol of brute force. The reflection of this view in foreign policy is the search for conciliation in the international arena through arms reduction. But the NAP and NSP see the world from a conspiratorial point of view. The NSP wants an army which will make Turkey a world military power. This army will not only be equipped with the most modern weapons manufactured in the country, but also with nuclear capability. The NAP, on the other hand, envisions a militaristic society. The slogan 'One Leader, One Nation' is often used by the NAP's youth organisations. The NAP has organised its youthful followers in semi-military camps for the purpose of using them as combat forces against the growing left in Turkey. Military training and use of arms in those camps have been reported by police authorities.[26] More evidence is revealed by police investigation and proceedings. While the immediate duties of these militants are to combat 'international communism' in Turkey, they are indoctrinated for saving the so-called 'enslaved Turks' living especially in countries ranging from the Soviet Union to Bulgaria and China.

In the light of this information, of the two parties which dream of Turkey becoming a superpower, the NSP's rationale seems to be defensive while that of the NAP is belligerent. But whether this belligerence is internally oriented to subdue democratic forces, or is planned to be externally used later, is a question that remains to be answered.

Attitudes Towards Social Change

One of the most painful aspects of social change is the alteration of the value structure that gives meaning to the individual's life. His roles, status, rights and obligations are all defined in the frame of reference delimited by the value system of a given society. In the face of rapid change, which in fact means formation of a new frame of reference, the individual finds it difficult to adapt to a new lifestyle, function and demeanour that comes with social change. It is no coincidence that in underdeveloped societies which are undergoing such rapid social change, the major ideology that accompanies the creation of the new social structure has been religion. This was the case in many societies ranging from Algeria to Libya and to Iran as the most recent case. Why religion?

First of all, the predominant ideology in pre-capitalist societies is religion. Retarded development and the slow pace of social change are not strong enough to transform the society from its traditional format. Thus religion lingers as the legitimising value system of the existing social, economic and political structure. If this structure is transformed by force, for example through revolution, the same super-structure may conveniently be utilised to legitimise the new institutional network created by the new elite. Otherwise the outcome can be chaos. Hence it is no coincidence that combined concepts like Islamic socialism are contrived.

Religion, however, is not the only ideology prevalent in a post-colonial society. Nationalism often accompanies religion. Nevertheless, this is a different kind of nationalism from that which emerged in Europe with the rise of the bourgeoisie. In colonial societies either there is no national bourgeoisie or it is very weak. What does exist is a dependent entrepreneurial class born out of the relations with external capital or created by it. In any case, they are still organically linked together. Hence it is impossible to expect the bourgeoisie of post-colonial societies to be the driving force of independent development and, as a result, rapid social change. This vacuum is often filled by middle-class elements of bureaucratic origin. It is this stratum that shoulders the mission of a revolutionary bourgeoisie to modernise their country and mobilise its human and material resources. Such a large-scale mobilisation of traditional masses requires a transformation which in turn calls for a uniting factor that can rally most members of the society. Nationalism provides the necessary spiritual medium and collective conscious-ness.

Both religion and nationalism as political ideologies conveniently serve the following ends. First, they disguise class differences. Second, the differences between the ruled and the ruler remain intact. Indeed, Islamic religion speaks about equity but not equality. Moreover, obedience to one's superior is an obligation as long as the superior cares for and protects his inferiors. Similarly, there is no explicit reference to the hierarchic nature of society in nationalism. On the contrary, nationalism advocates unity, solidarity, respect for one another and for a strong central authority which everyone would obey equally. Third, both nationalism and religion are ideologies which are exclusive. In other words they function as barriers against external/foreign incursion. It is very easy to mobilise the masses against external enemies on the grounds of protecting both the nation and religious community.

Sometimes nationalist elites or governments use religious symbolism in reform movements. This is because reference to a familiar traditional value or belief while building a new institution or implementing a reform reduces the chance of popular resistance. Religion clearly plays a legitimising role here, but of a new order under the leadership of a nationalist elite. Additionally, this elite benefits tremendously from religion as an established system of social justice to be materialised by a programme proposed by the new ruling elite (or a group within it).

Whether religion or nationalism will play a larger role in the nation-building process of post-colonial societies depends on who the leaders are and their class alliances on the one hand, and on the level of development of the society on the other hand. By development here I mean organisation of the civil society outside the state apparatus.

There are also cases where religion and nationalism may be used as escapist ideologies. In fact, how these ideologies or value structures are used by two Turkish political parties may be unique examples.

The National Salvation Party abstracts religion from its ecclesiastical and moral function in society and tries to administer daily life in accordance with religious rules. Despite its moral purity, the picture of the society presented by the NSP is still hierarchical. Furthermore it is based on existing relations of production. The only difference is that the NSP's economic programme seems to be more supportive of smaller capitalists. The vagueness of the party's economic programme is camouflaged with a concept of 'spiritual development' which amounts to more religious education and a devoutness combined with realisation of Islamic brotherhood (both among individuals and Islamic societies). A strange example of spiritual development boasted by the NSP is the opening of Saint Sophia to Islamic praying.

A secular example of escapist ideologies is that of the Nationalist Action Party which in documents other than election declarations proposes to recreate pre-Islamic empires. Unlike the NSP, which wished to create 'Turkey, the leader' by uniting all Muslims in an international community headed by Turkey, the NAP strives to unite all peoples of Turkic origin under one flag. The geographical area thus gained, the human and material resources thus assembled, will be so great that all of Turkey's present problems will be overcome. Conveniently, the NAP does not forget to put a pinch of religion into this scheme in order to attract the children of conservative Anatolian families.

The outcome of these programmes has been to rouse the religiously devout on the one hand, and the passionate militants who are made to believe that they will deliver the 'Last Turkish State' from the assault of the communists on the other hand. As stated previously, both parties appeal to social strata who are anxious to find a new identity in a modernising society in the making. This means a decent job, educational opportunities and a new status based on modern skills. Any social organisation which cannot offer in reality a desirable future to its constituency will offer either unrealistic hopes or the glories of the past. In the case of the NSP, it is the religious community of Muslims which will live and toil in harmony and solidarity and in turn be rewarded by God for obeying His orders. Needless to say, these orders are or will be delegated to the Believers by a new elite represented by the NSP.

In the case of the NAP, the primary calling is to render the present Turkish society as strong as it was in days of Jenghiz Khan, Attila the Hun or Süleyman the Magnificent. Only a very strong government can achieve this end.

Both of these social programmes reflect solidaristic and authoritarian societies recreated in the industrial age.

The Republican People's Party sees the driving force of history in the antagonistic nature of social groups. But this antagonism is not of an insoluble kind. In the long run, inequalities that create antagonisms can be eliminated by the betterment of the conditions of the oppressed and exploited groups. Solutions in this direction are stepping-stones for societal development and modernisation. This in itself is a continual process. The most sacred social value is human labour and reform policies must start from this assumption. The ultimate goal for the RPP is the establishment of the self-managing society which solves emerging problems through democratic ways.

The Justice Party, on the other hand, believes that free enterprise and the profit motive are the driving force of social progress. This instinct must be supported by the state and its gains must be protected. Accumulation of more wealth will bring prosperity to the society. Modernisation is the evolution and accumulation of the fruits of private enterprise. This explanation is almost verbatim that of classical liberalism. In fact, the JP differs very little from classical liberals of the past century in its world view.

Conclusion

This analysis was intended to deal with some of the major issues in recent Turkish elections. Issues which were not salient during the 1973 election campaign, such as political violence or policy on Cyprus, have not been emphasised, even though they may have assumed considerable importance at a later time. I have also omitted the study of issues voiced by socialist parties. Inclusion of these would do injustice to the aforementioned parties, each of which received one million or more votes. The existing five socialist parties could attract only a minute number of votes in the past three elections. None at present has an elected representative in parliament. Nevertheless, their programmes are not substantially different from similar parties in Europe. Despite the attractiveness of their programmes for the working population, these parties have failed to establish mass constituencies. One reason for this is that the RPP stood as the first target on trial with a 'leftist' platform. If radicalisation is the outcome of the failure of more moderate programmes, then the RPP's failure may drive the 'left' votes closer to the more radical parties. This shift may signify the passing of social democracy and the beginning of socialist politics in Turkey. However, there is as yet no clear evidence of such a change. The RPP still claims credit for having established the Republic of Turkey.

Notes

1. Although there were other parties which emerged with more than ten seats in the 1973 election, these four are the only ones of importance which survived.
2. S. Demirel (edited by U. Gümüştekin), *İktisadî Büyüme* (Economic Growth) (2 vols., Gümüş Tekin, Istanbul, n.d.), vol. I, p. 21.
3. Millî Selâmet Partisi (MSP), *5 Haziran 1977 Seçim Beyannamesi* (National Salvation Party (NSP), 5 June 1977 election manifesto), p. 49.
4. Ibid., p. 47; MSP, *İnanç ve Hamle* (Belief and progress) (Gaye, Ankara, n.d.).

5. MSP, *İnanç ve Hamle*.

6. A. Türkeş, *Millî Doktrin: Dokuz Işık* (Nine lights: the national doctrine) 21st edn (Kutluğ, Istanbul, n.d.), pp. 47-9.

7. Ibid., p. 49-50.

8. Ibid., p. 44.

9. Ibid., p. 57.

10. Ibid., p. 58.

11. Adalet Partisi (AP), *1973 Seçim Beyannamesi* (Justice Party (JP), 1973 election manifesto) (Adalet Partisi, Ankara, 1973), p. 30.

12. MSP, *1977 Seçim Beyannamesi*.

13. Ibid.

14. Ibid.

15. Ibid.

16. Ibid.

17. Türkeş, *Dokuz Işık*, p. 41.

18. Ibid., p. 110.

19. Cumhuriyet Halk Partisi (CHP), *Ak günlere, 1973 seçim Bildirgesi* (Republican People's Party (RPP), Towards the bright days: 1973 election manifesto) (Cumhuriyet Halk Partisi, Ankara, 1973), p. 220.

20. Ibid., p. 222.

21. Premier Ecevit's various radio and television speeches.

22. CHP, *Ak günlere*, p. 224.

23. AP, *1973 Seçim Beyannamesi*, p. 27.

24. MSP, *1977 Seçim Beyannamesi*, pp. 81-2.

25. Ibid., p. 88.

26. Radio and television announcements about the existence of a police intelligence report completed and circulated in 1970 by both the Minister of Interior, Irfan Özaydınlı, and by Premier Bülent Ecevit, in early 1979, were promptly denied by both JP and NAP leaders, despite the fact that the leader of the former had his initials on the circulation list as Prime Minister of the time.

2. LEBANON

Ralph E. Crow

This chapter attempts to provide a brief introduction to the Lebanese political system and to identify the major issues which have dominated the political scene, both as a background to the analysis of political elites and of the politics of elections which follow. The treatment of the material here may differ somewhat from that given to the two other countries dealt with in this volume, first, by relying on material drawn from a longer period of time, and second, by describing issues which arise in a wider context than that of the electoral arena itself. The main reason we have expanded the scope of our enquiry in the case of Lebanon is that the expectation that the major issues of a political system will emerge from the electoral process is based on assumptions which are not fully met in the Lebanese case. These include the assumption that the basic framework of society is at least roughly worked out and that, although subject to change, there is a widespread agreement about the nature of the society, i.e. enough common ground to permit the political system, especially through elections, to provide the basis for the development of a common policy and to establish priorities for society. As we hope to show, some features of the Lebanese system are designed to prevent this from taking place, and for other reasons the Lebanese system fails to produce a common policy or set of programme priorities.

Many countries of the world do not meet these conditions, and many polities do not sustain electoral politics at all. Particularly where political integration is low, only a few highly fragmented societies have struggled to do so, although with great difficulty and not always with success. There is a growing literature about the politics of fragmented or pluralistic society. Indeed, the widespread assumption of twenty-five years ago among students of politics that political development or modernisation depended on the homogenisation of political culture and the decline of parochial social institutions is being questioned. The idea that modernisation is not necessarily incompatible with primary social organisation is also being given increasing attention.[1] Not only do developing nations find that traditional communities and affiliations are stubbornly persistent but even some 'modernised' societies of Europe are experiencing a resurgence of communal forces such as Scotland and Wales in Great Britain and Brittany and Corsica in France. Recently it has been suggested that for culturally fragmented developing states (whether on the basis of ethnicity, religion, language or race) political integration is not always possible or necessary in the modernisation process. Instead, the concept of 'consociational democracy' has been proposed which emphasises the mechanisms and skills of conflict management as a means to bridge differences among communities.[2] A more realistic position is that of 'national accommodation' which recognises and accepts the reality of entrenched communities within the political system, but stresses that national integration should be the goal, and that the gradual development of a supra-communal bond is possible.[3] We will be interested to see how far this reasoning applies to the Lebanese case.

Impact of Environment on the Electoral Process

The problems of national consensus and of nation-building are considered central to political modernisation and development, and this certainly applies to the Lebanon. We can approach these related concepts in the Lebanese context through a discussion of the communal structure of the society and its relationship to the political process. The fact that Lebanese society is composed of over a dozen major religious communities which are basic to the organisation and conduct of society, and the fact that these communities are officially recognised and institutionalised in the political system, is well known. We will not provide any systematic description of the history, characteristics or values of the various communities which are available elsewhere, but will confine our attention to the role these communities play in generating and resolving the 'issues' in Lebanese politics.

National Consensus and Nation-building

First, the term 'religious community' is used rather than religion or religious sect, in order to emphasise their social and political functions and significance. It is not so much the theological differences (the faiths) that matter. Rather, it is the fact that they are religious communities which act as social reference groups. Functionally, for many Lebanese the religious community is his nation, that is the people to whom he belongs and with whom he identifies.[4] There is no lack of nations in

Lebanon, the problem is that there are too many of them and that they are already well built. But national consensus, that is, a single Lebanese nation—this is certainly lacking.

It is because the Lebanese body politic is so deeply fragmented by the historical cleavages of religious communities that I feel that we can best discuss the issues of Lebanese politics by relating them to this fundamental, primary reference group and the differences which are generated by these conflicting loyalties. Let us call the bedrock issue the 'crisis of identity', which as our central theme will provide a focus for a discussion of the variety and various levels of other differences within the Lebanese political system.

It may be helpful to briefly cite the deep historical roots of religious communalism (often referred to as 'sectarianism' or 'confessionalism'). For several centuries religious communities (especially Christians and Jews) were granted religious community autonomy for their spiritual and personal affairs by the Sunnite Muslim rulers of the Ottoman Empire. So the practice of being allowed to regulate much of their personal and community affairs according to their own religious law and under their own leaders had deep roots. In addition the Maronite and Druze communities of Mount Lebanon enjoyed a *de facto* political autonomy for long periods of that time. In the seventeenth century the Mountain was brought into a single political unit, the *Imāra*, under the supremacy of the Ma'nī family and later under the Shihābīs. By the eighteenth century the previously efficient Ottoman provincial administration was losing its effectiveness, and communal loyalties were strengthened; within the Lebanon this eventually led to the demise of the *Imāra* with the Egyptian invasion of 1831-2. Following Maronite-Druze clashes in 1841, the *Qā'im-maqāmiyya* (as an administrative unit) was established with two districts, each based on one of the two religious communities. After further communal clashes in 1860, a single government was established for Mount Lebanon under a *Mutaşarrif* served by an administrative council on which by 1864 each of the major religious communities was represented proportionally.[5] After the First World War, under the French mandate, the institutionalisation of religious communalism was further elaborated in the political and administrative system by the Constitution of 1926, and in 1943 with independence, it was sanctioned in the National Pact in a form which has essentially continued (with minor adjustments) until the present. We can say then that the religious community has been the basic reference group for centuries and that it has been recognised as a basis for political organisation for over a hundred years.

There is some evidence that over the past thirty years there has been a gradual transcending of the communal loyalties and viewpoints.[6] However, for many (maybe most) Lebanese, deep in their hearts, if not explicitly in their minds, their first loyalties and strongest attachments remain with the religious community. All of the religious communities (to different degrees) have tended to develop a strong 'in-feeling'. Individuals tend to live within the community; marriage, residence, school, social activity, business partner and for some even political party. There are institutions in the country which are multicommunal or universal in their membership such as the market, army, public bureaucracy (and one or two political movements), but they do not provide strong substitutes for one's community. Each community tends to develop its own world view and images of itself and of the other communities. It is difficult (not impossible) for individuals immersed in their communities to gain a very objective view of society, since the religious community plays such a dominant part in the political socialisation process. On the contrary, there is considerable evidence to show that the processes of urbanisation and modernisation have heightened communal loyalties, at least in their initial phases.

Socio-economic Structure

The last fifty years have seen the Lebanese economy transformed from a largely rural peasant-run agricultural sector plus a small but important urban commercial and shopkeeping element, into a highly complex mixture of financial, commercial, service, tourist and light industry. A significant proportion of non-Lebanese entrepreneurs and capital participated in this process. Development after the Second World War has centred in and around Beirut and has been undertaken largely through the private sector (even in such areas as education and hospitals) with less participation or assistance of the government. It is therefore not surprising that the process has been largely unplanned and unco-ordinated, with little or no concern for its long-run implications or its social or political consequences. The impact of this rapid economic growth has been very uneven. Largely concentrated in Beirut, investment and job opportunities outside the capital have been minimal, and cities like Tripoli and Sidon have felt slighted and many rural regions, particularly in the south and north-west of the country, have hardly benefited at all. It is only since the quasi-partition of the country and the destruction of the central business district of Beirut in 1975-6 that some development of regional centres has occurred, with the exception of the extreme south which has been largely destroyed by Israeli bombardment.

While the gross figures of economic growth have been impressive and the per capita income of roughly $900 (in 1975) was well above the average of developing countries, the unequal sharing in these benefits has been dangerously large. While a significant proportion of the rural and urban population continued to live at subsistence level and in extremely sub-standard conditions, a wealthy few lived ostentatiously at a level hardly surpassed elsewhere in the world. Even the larger, less wealthy, upper-middle and professional class took for granted a standard of living above the average in Europe and North America. These discrepancies were exacerbated by the inflation which occurred in the early 1970s, when prices increased to the point that one could maintain one's standard of living only if one had a non-Lebanese income, that is, if one was a wealthy non-Lebanese (for example from the Persian Gulf), or a Lebanese who worked abroad at salary levels well above those in Lebanon, or was involved in foreign business, commerce and the like. The Lebanese who worked in Lebanon, at a Lebanese salary, found that he could barely afford to live in Lebanon. Rents on new housing soared to levels which almost exceeded a lower and middle-class income.

Even educational levels reflected this social and economic disparity. While the literacy rate is relatively high (probably above 75 per cent), and although a variety of educational alternatives are available, the government schools have not been among the best. And so to enjoy the advantages of higher educational standards one had to be able to afford to attend private institutions—many of which were religious or foreign in nature. Ironically, what is certainly an advantage (i.e. a relatively highly educated population) was achieved in a manner which contributed to cleavages in society. Those with better education and at least a baccalaureate degree (and possibly a university degree) were eligible to live in the professional 'modern' world, while those with less or no education were restricted to semi-skilled or technical jobs and therefore lower incomes and social status. Education fragmented society in another sense, namely by the gap between those educated in government schools where foreign languages were not well taught, and those who could attend private schools and learn a foreign language well and, in an astonishing number of cases, go on to qualify professionally in the finest universities in France, Switzerland, Germany, Great Britain and North America.

Although a description of the political system follows below, something about the nature of the government and administration should be mentioned here as a contrast to the freewheeling, dynamic (if somewhat unstable) economic and social structure. The public bureaucracy (with a few exceptions) was antiquated in its structure and procedures, given over to serving its own interests more than any other, and largely incapable of meeting public needs. It neither regulated the private sectors of society nor provided compensating services itself. In the 1960s, during President Shihāb's regime, efforts were made to increase governmental support for education, health, social security, public utilities, roads and port facilities. But, commendable as these intentions were, they were so ineffectively pursued that they failed to improve the situation significantly.

The Political System

While our main concerns with the political system are the political parties and electoral system, brief consideration must be given to the other institutions so as to appreciate these two subsystems. The Lebanese have attempted to operate according to the Constitution (originally adopted in 1926 during the French mandate) since independence in 1943, and have done so despite some brief but serious interruptions, namely in 1952 when the President was forced out of office and in 1958 when civil law and order broke down, as has occurred again more recently in 1975-6. In addition the Syrian Social National Party has twice attempted *coups d'état* (1949 and 1961-2) which failed. But despite these incidents, and until 1975, it seems fair to say that on the whole there has been a broad commitment to constitutional government, when compared with most developing countries during the same period. It might also be claimed that the alternatives for the Lebanese are not very attractive, for almost everyone in Lebanon agrees that they are not willing to allow any one of the factions or communities to dominate the system on their own terms, and the military being a microcosm of the country as a whole does not offer the alternative which armies do in many other countries.

Before discussing the political institutions let us consider the importance of the scale of the system. Lebanon is a small country with a population of approximately three million and a size of 3,950 square miles (half the size of pre-1967 Israel and only a tiny fraction of Turkey). The small scale of the state and its people has a political importance which is often overlooked. The Lebanese government is scarcely bigger than that of one of the world's larger municipalities. Each sector of Lebanese society (government, business, banking, syndicates, academia and each profession) has a very 'personal' character about it. The leading figures in each sector know each other well and know the leaders of all the other sectors at least by reputation.

Given the importance of traditional family affiliation one can usually recall the religion and the family relationships of any person simply by knowing his name. As a result, all activities, and especially administrative and political activities, are highly personal affairs. There are both advantages and disadvantages to this, but one of the disadvantages is that political and administrative activities cannot be conducted on the basis of impersonal rules and procedures. An unpleasant decision is a personal affront. As a result, public officials can seldom refuse a request (although they may not always follow through on a promise to help).

Another repercussion of the size of the community is the centralised character of the political process. All of Lebanon is within half a day's drive of the capital, Beirut, and, as a result, government (like most other small countries) is highly concentrated in this one city. So the physical concentration of government and society in Beirut further contributes to the intimate character of Lebanese politics.

This personal aspect of public activities resulting from the overlapping of the personal and public arenas has the effect of reducing the choices, options, procedures and time available for the pursuit of the public interest. (Take, for example, the proportion of the life of a public figure spent in attending funerals.)

On the surface, Lebanese governmental institutions appear to constitute a typical representative parliamentary system, characterised by a universally elected Chamber of Deputies for a four-year term with legislative functions which in turn elects the President of the Republic for a six-year non-renewable term. The President designates the Prime Minister, who, along with the Ministers of the Cabinet, must receive and maintain the confidence of the Chamber of Deputies and of the President. However, two features of this arrangement deserve special comment. The first is that the executive power is largely in the hands of the President. He nominates the Prime Minister and has a large say in the designation and dismissal of the Ministers; the formal Council of Ministers meets under the chairmanship of the President (while cabinet meetings are presided over by the Prime Minister) and all of the highest administrative decrees (marsūm-al-jumhūriyya) and laws must be signed by the President (as well as the Minister concerned). In addition the President is the Commander-in-Chief of the Army and at times has had direct or indirect control of the internal security forces. He also is granted the powers of conducting the foreign affairs of the government and may negotiate treaties which must be approved by the Chamber of Deputies. But with all of this it is the Prime Minister who is politically responsible to the Chamber of Deputies and who must resign if its confidence is not forthcoming, or if the Cabinet disagrees among itself. So executive responsibility is not very clear, nor is it wholly responsible to the legislature as is often assumed in the case of the European type of parliamentary systems. This has led some to consider the Lebanese system as being essentially presidential rather than parliamentary.

The second feature which requires comment is that the Chamber of Deputies is elected according to a system which prescribes the religion of each of the presently 99 seats of the chamber and so its religious composition is determined by law and not by the electoral process. The number of seats allocated to each religious community is supposedly in the same proportion as that community's proportion of the population, as reflected in the census of 1932. There is serious discontent about the present division of the seats which in fact is the result of a political compromise rather than of a current census of the population. The electoral law (in effect for the four elections from 1960 to 1972) provides for a total of 26 electoral districts, all but one of which (Sidon) are multimember (averaging about four per district and ranging from two to eight). Sixteen of the 26 have mixed religious population and representation. All voters of all religious communities in a voting district vote for all of the seats, whether of their own religion or not (a single electoral college for a multiconfessional list). The result is that all electoral contests are among coreligionists, and that in the multimember districts intercommunal lists must be formed.

When this type of electoral system operates in a political environment in which political parties (although numerous) are weak, the electoral process and the composition of the Chamber of Deputies is rather amorphous. At no time in the history of the Lebanese Republic have a majority of the members of the Chamber of Deputies been party members, and no one party has ever been able to elect more than ten members to the chamber at one time, and although electoral alliances among two or more parties do take place they are not long lasting. They are never large enough nor enduring enough to provide the political base for an ideologically consistent Cabinet or programme, nor an effective opposition.

Lebanese political parties could be classified in a number of ways, one of which would be on the base of the support they seek and receive. There are personality-based blocs like the National Bloc Party (Ḥizb al-Kutla al-Waṭaniyya) and the Constitutionalist Party (Ḥizb al-Ittiḥād al-Dustūrī), both Christian. The more recently established National

Liberals Party (Ḥizb al-Waṭaniyyīn al-Aḥrār) of Camille Shamʿūn began as this type of organisation. These blocs or parties have little in the way of a national organisational base, formal membership or specific programmes but they do command considerable support and have significant symbolic meaning for sections of the population. The Muslim counterparts of these organisations are traditional Sunnite and Shiite leaders from long-established families, who together with the members of the blocs, constitute the largest group of representatives in the Chamber of Deputies. Since 1975-6, these groups have declined in importance, but should not be entirely discounted in the near future.

A second category of political groups are the 'Lebanese political parties', which are typically sectarian in orientation, although this is officially denied. Two of these developed in the 1930s as paramilitary youth organisations and are characterised by formal membership, specific programmes, and a degree of discipline largely lacking in other political groups. The largely Christian Phalanges (Katāʾib) and the largely Muslim Najjāda have had little representation in parliament. The more recently established National Liberals Party (Ḥizb al-Waṭaniyyīn al-Aḥrār) of Camille Shamʿūn evolved into this category. Recently, the Phalanges have been able to gain several seats in the Chamber while the Najjāda, never very strong, has declined.

The third category of political groups in Lebanon are what amount to branches of political parties which have a wider concern and membership beyond Lebanon. Although they may have considerable membership in Lebanon itself, their strength is seldom sufficiently concentrated in one district for electoral success. Examples of this type of party would include the Lebanese Communist Party, the Independent Communist Party of Lebanon, the Iraqi Baathists, Syrian Baathists, and the Syrian Social National Party.

Almost in a category by itself is the Progressive Socialist Party (al-Ḥizb al-Taqaddumī al-Ishtirākī) founded and led by Kamāl Junblāṭ until his assassination in 1977 and led since then by his son Walīd. Socialist by doctrine, and attracting a number of educated members from all religious communities on ideological grounds, it also benefits from the important traditional status of the Junblāṭ family (among the most important of the notable families of Mount Lebanon) and from the ardent devotion of many Druze who saw Junblāṭ as their communal leader. Equally important has been the fact that although Junblāṭ's National Struggle Front (Jabhat al-Niḍāl al-Waṭanī) had only a few members in the Chamber of Deputies, Junblāṭ has acted as the chief representative of radical elements and organisations which are not represented in parliament. This gave Junblāṭ a greater role in the official organs of government than his electoral position would indicate, and led to his position of leadership of the leftist elements during the 1975-6 civil war.

Lastly, there are political groups, entirely extraparliamentary, which usually draw their support from a single leader and/or region. They have their impact on the political process through the threat of force and undermining of security, law and order. Since they played significant roles in the fighting during 1975-6, they gained *de facto* access to the national political process and in some instances actually assumed peace-keeping/security roles in the absence of effective central government. Their future in the political process is not clear, but it is unlikely that they will disappear from the political arena. Examples of these groups would include Fārūq Muqaddam's 24th October Movement (Ḥarakat Arba' wa-'Ishrīn Tishrīn) and the Independent Nasserist Movement (Ḥarakat al-Nāṣiriyyīn al-Mustaqillīn) of Ibrāhīm Qulaylāt. Among the more important of this type of group but clearly distinguished by its religious character was the Movement of the Deprived (Ḥarakat al-Maḥrūmīn), organised and led by the Shiite Imam Mūsā al-Ṣadr, which became a powerful non-parliamentary force for mobilising the heretofore quiescent Shiites. For example, in March 1974 the Imam addressed a crowd of an estimated 75,000 people in Baalbek, vowing to redress the wrongs of his community by force if the government failed to do so. Since the Imam disappeared in August 1978, the movement has been dormant. Shiite spokesmen claim that their people are the most economically and educationally deprived among the Lebanese and that they do not receive an equitable share of governmental services and employment.

Some observers hold that Lebanese society, despite the lack of a national consensus, was able to operate because of a consensus among the establishment, which included the leading and conservative figures of all of the religious communities, and of the leading traditional families and economic interests in the country. Co-operating across communal lines, this group of traditional leaders was able to manage the major conflict areas and to provide at least minimal responses to societal demands which in turn enabled the more traditional political figures and interests to survive.[7]

Four sets of tensions had to be managed simultaneously. First, the tensions among the religious communities were primarily dealt with by the provisions of the National Pact by allocating the major political offices to the three major religious communities (President to the

Maronites; Prime Minister to the Sunnites and Speaker of the Chamber of Deputies to the Shiites). The communities are also balanced off by the provisions of the electoral law which provides for a number of deputies (variously 44, 55, 66, 77 and presently 99), so that Christians can be represented by six deputies to every five of the non-Christian deputies. This supposedly proportional representation of the communities has been a continual source of difficulty as we shall see below. The other community-balancing provision has been that stemming from Article 95 of the Constitution which allocates positions in the public service and in the Cabinet according to their proportion of the population. This self-styled 'provisional' arrangement has continued to operate for over thirty years and, although it has been modified somewhat, continues to be the source of much controversy today.

The second set of tensions which had to be managed was that among the 'factions', i.e. among the notables of the establishment, frequently referred to as the *Zu'amā'*. Within any one religious community and among the various regions of the country there were a number of rival families or clans and considerable competition existed among them for positions in Parliament and in the Cabinet. As a result, the political process which centred around the continual flux of changing alliances and coalitions was largely orchestrated by the President of the Republic.

The third area of tension requiring political attention was that between this establishment group of traditional leaders and public office-holders on one hand, and, on the other, the forces outside the formal political arena which were not strongly represented in the official organs of government, such as some of the newer ideological political parties or the labour syndicates, or from professional and intellectual critics who were calling for reforms and change, and occasionally from sections of an outraged public when public utilities or services broke down. These groups were kept at bay by a combination of incremental change: initiation of projects or programmes, many of which were never completed; of promises seldom kept; and of changing the Cabinet and avoiding the problem for another year or so. These techniques of handling tensions were never very satisfactory and just barely kept the level of violence and discontent below the surface. In retrospect it is not surprising that civil politics broke down entirely in 1975, and one wonders that things had gone on in this style for so long.

The last area of tension management confronting the Lebanese political system is that between Lebanon and other Middle East countries, that is the other Arab states and Israel and of course the

Palestinians and their organisations, who in Lebanon have constituted a number ranging from 6 per cent in 1950 to possibly 16 per cent today. In addition, there have been the strong currents of the cold war (and even of detente). As we shall see, the difference of attitudes of the various communities within Lebanon makes this a particularly difficult task, because the religious communities react differently to many international events, depending on how each community sees them as supportive or non-supportive to their own vision of Lebanon. That these tensions caused the Lebanese government difficulties is not surprising. On the contrary, one notes the progress made over the first thirty years of Lebanese independence. But as Michael Hudson has commented:

> In all these areas Lebanese ingenuity is readily apparent. It is easy for a political scientist to admire the techniques of bargaining and coordination that maintain domestic tranquillity; but, ingenious as these techniques may be, they are inadequate to surmount the basic dilemma. Without strong institutions Lebanon must count upon extraordinary good luck.[8]

By definition, no one always has good luck, and neither has Lebanon. Observers tend to agree that Lebanese political institutions are primarily designed and operated for the purpose of preventing communal conflict. Instead of using political institutions to resolve conflict, primary concern is given over to preventing conflict from destroying the institutions.[9] Kerr has expressed it somewhat differently by suggesting that Lebanese political leaders act as trustees and brokers, not political decision-makers. Hence the executive branch of government behaves more like judicial and administrative agencies, adjudicating claims and maintaining services to which their communities are entitled.[10]

Lebanese politicians were reasonably adept at managing the first two tension areas, namely among the religious communities and among the political factions. They were much less attentive to the increasing problems and demands emanating from the third tension area, particularly the political forces outside the formal political arena, the non-establishment interests. Growing dissatisfaction among these groups along with the overload of problems from the fourth area, that is non-Lebanese pressures (especially Palestinian) were more than the system could bear. The failure or inability to successfully manage the latter two tension areas led to the events of 1975-6.

Given the increasing urgency of the social and economic problems facing the country and the increased tension developing from the unresolved Palestine problem, the warning set forth by the French research organisation IRFED of Father Lebret in a study conducted for President Shihāb in 1960 seems prophetic. It included the following paragraph:

> If the status quo does not undergo early changes—if the more privileged classes do not voluntarily tighten their belts through more honesty in tax payments, if an intellectual moral revolution led by a devoted core of selfless citizens is not mounted, if an efficient state administration does not start inducing an intercommunal pattern of living and spreading development to cover all Lebanese regions—Lebanon can expect a 'revolution which would plunge it into chaos and place it at the mercy of its neighbor's ambitions.'[11]

The Issues

The 1972 Elections and Parliament

We have seen how the fundamental issue of Lebanese politics—the identity of the nation—is muted in the political process through constitutional provisions and electoral laws. By reserving each of the major executive offices to a particular religious community and by predetermining the religious composition of the Chamber of Deputies and by requiring that electoral contests must be within religious communities, the electoral process cannot directly confront the identity problem. Further, by recognising that because of the weakness of political parties and of the continued strength of loyalties to traditional leaders, who trade in various forms of patronage,[12] much of the electoral process is personal and factional rather than over programmes, projects or 'issues'. Ordinarily, Lebanese elections do not develop into a single national campaign. Instead there are several campaigns going on independently, or at least only loosely connected. To begin with, this is partly the result of the scheduling of elections on three successive Sundays (in 1972: Beirut and North Lebanon on 16 April; the Biqa' and South Lebanon on 23 April; and Mount Lebanon on 30 April). This is done to ensure the availability of adequate security forces to maintain law and order. So, if we cannot say that there are three separate campaigns, we can say that the campaign occurs in three phases. But more important than the fragmentation in time is the lack of an overall nationwide co-ordinated effort due to the lack of truly national political organisations. In a sense, there is no overall electoral strategy, only a series of tactical moves which vary from one electoral district to another.

We can hypothesise that in general electoral politics raise and settle basic political issues only in systems that have achieved a reasonable degree of consensus on the problem of national identity. Where this is lacking (as in Lebanon) then one finds that elections are not held at all, or, if held, they are 'managed' so that the basic issues do not arise and become disruptive.

However, in the 1972 election there were some secondary issues of a national character which, although not explicitly at stake in specific electoral contests, did have electoral overtones. The most general of these was the claim by Kamāl Junblāṭ and his allies that the whole political system needed changing because it did not reflect current social and political tendencies in a country which had altered significantly during the previous ten years. They charged that the upcoming election could not help meet this clash of the old and new tendencies because the existing electoral system would only reflect the will of about 25 per cent of the population. Opponents of the left and especially the Ṣā'ib Salām Government countered that of course political systems must not be static and should evolve to meet the needs of the time—but (the emphasis was here) change must not be by violence, implying that the change would have to come through existing institutions.

Somewhat more specific was the debate triggered off by the government-sponsored draft law regulating the authorisation or licensing of political parties and associations on 1 March 1972. The government sent the bill to the chamber as an 'urgent' measure, which meant that if the chamber had not acted on the bill within forty days the government could issue it as a law by decree. Understandably, in view of the upcoming elections, deputies for and against the bill joined in requesting the government to withdraw the 'urgent' procedure proposed and to allow the bill to go through the normal legislative procedure. This the government agreed to do on 10 March.

However, the substantive issue at stake was that in 1970, as Minister of Interior, Kamāl Junblāṭ had issued licences to some parties previously prohibited from operating (including some leftist parties) on his own authority as Minister. The government-sponsored bill provided that this action would require the approval of the Council of Ministers with the implication that the parties licensed by Junblāṭ would have to reapply and then operate under tighter controls (if relicensed). The issue actually dragged on long after the election until it was clear by the middle of June that a majority of the deputies were against the government's bill and so it dropped the proposal.

Another issue that surfaced at the same time was the dispute between the political allies, the Phalanges and Armenian Tashnaq parties, over who should be allotted the Protestant seat in Beirut's 1st electoral district. The question was eventually resolved through the mediation of former President Sham'ūn, who recommended that since the Armenian Protestants constituted one-fourth of the Protestant community and the non-Armenian Protestants had held the seat for the last three elections, therefore in 1972 it was the turn of the Armenians. This seems to be a case of extending the Lebanese principle of allocation of seats one further dimension from among religious communities to among ethnic groups within communities.

Issues Revealed in Investiture Debates: 1973 and 1974
Between the 1972 elections and the events of 1975 two new governments were confirmed in office, that of Taqī al-Dīn al-Ṣulḥ (June 1973 to September 1974) and that of a distant relative, Rashīd al-Ṣulḥ (October 1974 to May 1975). In each case a debate in the Chamber of Deputies prior to the vote of confidence took place over a period of several days in which a large number of deputies set forth their views about what they expected of a new government and about the situation in the country at that time. It might be instructive to look at the issues as they were revealed in those debates.

The circumstances leading up to the resignation of Ṣā'ib Salām in April of 1973 were dominated by increased Palestinian raids into Israel and of Israeli retaliations and especially the bombing of Shiite villages in the south of Lebanon making thousands of people homeless and refugees within their own country (most of them flocking to Beirut to join the dispossessed in the slums around the city). On 10 April Israeli commandos landed in Sidon and Beirut attacking Palestinian and pro-Palestinian targets and particularly killing three Fatah leaders in their homes in Beirut. Because of the inability of the Lebanese security forces to prevent such incidents and because, according to his own account, he was overruled in his efforts to use the security forces, Ṣā'ib Salām resigned and eventually, after three months, during which time serious clashes between the Lebanese army and Palestinians occurred, a new government was installed under the Premiership of Taqī al-Dīn al-Ṣulḥ.

Thirty-one of the Deputies of the Chamber participated in the debates leading up to the confirmation of the new government. A count shows that they raised a total of 42 different issues, ten of which were mentioned only once. Of the remaining 32 issues raised, seven were emphasised by several speakers. Two of these seven issues concerned specific (one-time) events, namely demands for the reinstatement of several hundred government public-school teachers who had been dismissed because of an illegal strike, and a call for the reopening of the Lebanese-Syrian border, which Syria had closed because of its displeasure with the use of the Lebanese army against the Palestinians. The more long-standing issues raised were:

1. Demands for greater participation in the processes and benefits of government.
2. Economic reforms.
3. Pros and cons concerning the Palestinian presence in Lebanon and what Lebanese policy should be on this issue.
4. Deficiencies in water supplies throughout the country.
5. Complaints about government neglect of 'my district'.

In September of 1974 Prime Minister Taqī al-Dīn al-Ṣulḥ resigned after a serious deterioration of the situation in the country. Soaring prices and increased corruption led to labour and student strikes. Increased Israeli raids in the south contributed to the increased voicing of Shiite grievances. A weakening of traditional Muslim leadership accompanied growing demands for Muslim participation in the centres of power. There was a growth in support for the 'Rejection Front' (consisting of Arab governments who refuse to negotiate with Israel) and a discernible merging of the Palestine Liberation Organisation in Lebanon with the Lebanese left and the Nasserite movements. And two internal power figures moved closer to the centre of the political stage, Imam Mūsā al-Ṣadr and Kamāl Junblāṭ as leader of the National Movement (al-Ḥaraka al-Waṭaniyya). This time the debate showed a somewhat different pattern. The 32 deputies who participated in the debate raised 50 different issues of which 22 were mentioned only one time. The nine issues which received most attention included three from the list of five longer-run concerns of 17 months earlier, namely the questions of participation, economic reforms and the complaints about the neglect of 'my district'. The newer issues were:

1. Defence of the south against Israeli attacks.
2. Need to check the drift into anarchy and to establish internal security.
3. Need for drastic administrative reform.
4. Extension of citizenship to permanent residents long excluded.
5. The problem of the relationship between the power of the Prime Minister and the President of the Republic.
6. The oligarchic character of the regime and need for constitutional change.

It is clear that by the end of 1974 the most basic issues had emerged and even penetrated that supposedly most unrepresentative body, the Chamber of Deputies. It is equally clear that in this form, the issues are not much more than complaints—rather than issues to be resolved by the political process. Perhaps it is unrealistic to expect the normal political process to solve basic issues about the nature of the body politic and the character of the regime as a whole. For this reason we believe that fundamentally there is one issue underlying Lebanese political problems, namely the issue of national identity and that as long as this issue goes unresolved the political system will not successfully solve its other problems.

The Identity Crisis at Various Levels of Politics

The process of explanation often involves considerable simplification, and we choose to use the concept of identity as the focus for our explanation of the issues in Lebanese politics, since it is at the base of most other issues or at least closely related to them. It may help to understand the pervasiveness of the identity crisis in Lebanon if we look at it on three different levels: the system level, the institutional level and the event level. (Since we have already mentioned the international forces at work in the Lebanese political system, we shall not deal with them again here.) It is somewhat artificial to treat these as entirely separate for they spill over and interact. The events often occur within or in relation to institutions, and they in turn go a long way to shape and give character to the system as a whole. Nevertheless, they will be dealt with one at a time if not altogether independently.

The Scope and Character of the Political System
In the short span of our individual lives we tend to take for granted the extent and domain, and the character or national identity, of political systems. However a glance at a pre-1939 world map will remind us how many states have undergone important changes in the past forty years. Lebanon throughout history has expanded and contracted and the ethnic and religious composition (always mixed) has also undergone frequent changes. The questions 'what is Lebanon?' 'who are the Lebanese?' 'should there be an independent Lebanon?' 'what is Lebanon's national identity?' have never been settled for any length of time. Lebanon's day-to-day and decade-to-decade politics have wrestled with this problem. It is not much of an exaggeration to say that Lebanon has lived in a continuous identity crisis.

In terms of the physical scope of Lebanon, history has already provided several versions including the Mount Lebanon of the Ottoman Empire with its Druze and Maronite population; the Syria and Lebanon of the French mandate (quickly divided); the Greater Lebanon (*le Grand Liban*) proclaimed by the French (an enlargement of the Mount Lebanon to include its Muslim coastal areas) the extent of which still constitute the borders of Lebanon; Greater Syria, the geographical expression referring to the entire Fertile Crescent and regarded as the natural extension of the Syrian nation by the Syrian Social National Party; the entire 'Arab World' and the Arab nation (including Lebanon); and recently, the *de facto* partition of 1975-6.

More important for our purposes, however, are the self-perceptions of Lebanese people as to the character of the Lebanese nation, and how they conceive themselves in and what they expect from their 'homeland'. Several self-images have been held by different Lebanese groups, some of which correspond roughly to the attitude of one or another of the religious communities. However, it is important to stress that when one refers to the attitudes or outlook of any community, many of its individual members have not shared that view and even among those who do, it is with varying degrees of intensity. So in effect 'the Maronite view' or 'the Sunnite view' is not the viewpoint of all Maronites or Sunnites but those members of that community who have chosen to speak out as Maronites or Sunnites. Hereafter, reference to the viewpoint of a community is made with the above qualification.

Among the more important views of Lebanon's identity are: Lebanon as a Christian state; an Arab state; a Christian-Muslim partnership; a Phoenician state; a secular state; and a refuge or haven for minorities. A brief examination of each of these reveals how incompatible some of them are and how difficult it would be for Lebanon to operate as a single political community if no reconciliation of these differences was achieved.

The concept of a Christian Lebanon is of course one held only by Christians and particularly by the more ardent members of the Maronite community, although there has been some sympathy for this point of view among other Christian communities as well. To fully appreciate this view one should recall the historical minority status of the Maronite community. As the first Catholics in the Middle East in communion with Rome they were a Christian minority among the Christians of the Middle East ('My rose among the thorns,' as one Pope was reported to have said), but in a more important sense Christians throughout the four hundred years of the Ottoman Empire lived under Muslim rule and felt that they had suffered unfairly. But in Mount Lebanon and especially during the nineteenth century the Maronites developed a feeling of separateness which they came to identify with the mountain itself. To many of them, a century later, the establishment of the French mandate appeared to be the realisation of their growing hopes for an independent Lebanon (Greater Lebanon) with a Christian majority, under European (Christian) protection. This was particularly important for those among them who felt they had more in common with Christian Europe than with the Muslim Arab world. This attitude was exemplified by a phrase still current, 'We are the front line of Christendom.' They further argued that an independent Christian Lebanon was necessary to protect the interests of all the Christians in the Middle East, not only of those in Lebanon itself. These attitudes add up to something very close to a religious nationalism which asserts a claim for a state of its own. To Christians who shared this view, the quasi-official phrase 'Lebanon's Arab face' was interpreted to mean a facade to placate the Muslims in the country and Lebanon's Arab neighbours. Christian interests in a sovereign independent Lebanon would be guaranteed by special provisions in the political institutions which (while recognising the right of non-Christians) would ensure Christian control and dominance of the system. This 'separatist' position in its extreme form was willing, if faced with the choice of losing its dominance of the state or of retracting the state territorially until it coincided with a Christian community, to opt for the latter and to withdraw into a Christian mountain redoubt maintaining its identity if not all of Lebanon. The events of 1975-6 revealed all too clearly the depth and extent of these feelings. Speaking of the role of religious fears among Lebanese, one commentator observed, 'Unfortunately, the grimmest nightmares of these people became self-fulfilling prophecies as they acted on the basis of their worst assumptions.'[13]

The second major identity considered here is that of an Arab Lebanon. In the larger sense Lebanon has always been a part of Arab history over the centuries and gradually has assimilated the language and culture of the Arabs. While some Lebanese will claim that they are Arabic-speaking people but not Arabs, this fails to acknowledge the strong cultural content of language or the degree to which language is the carrier of culture. An Arab identity for Lebanese is for the Muslims of Lebanon or Druze and many non-Maronite Christians, the natural evolution of historical forces but most especially the outcome of the necessity of redefining their identity at the end of the nineteenth and early twentieth century with the decline of the Ottoman Empire.

Ottoman society was an Islamic society in which many non-Muslims lived but its official and dominant norms were Islamic. At the end of the nineteenth century, as emphasis was placed on the Turkish aspect of Ottoman society, the non-Turkish Muslims and the non-Islamic Arabs sought a new basis for the organisation of their lives. The so-called Arab awakening was a reflection of this and affected both Muslim and Christian Arabs. In fact Christians were prominent among the Arab intellectual leaders and early Arab nationalists. So in the immediate post-1918 period, when Arab hopes for the establishment of one or more independent Arab states were high, the Muslims of Lebanon were apprehensive about being cut off from the Arab peoples of Syria and incorporated into what appeared to be a non-Arab Lebanon dominated by a European power. The history of the Middle East for the last fifty years has been dominated by the struggle of Arabs to gain their independence and live according to their own and not foreign (European) values. For the Arabs in general, and Muslims and some others in Lebanon, it was natural that Lebanon should be a part of this process, either as an independent Arab state or as part of a larger Arab union. Christian opinion has feared that the concept 'Arab' carried heavy Islamic overtones and that acceding to this version of identity would be another form of Muslim dominance resulting in the loss of their special character and freedom to live by values which they maintain were distinguishable from those of the Muslim Arabs.

Three other perceptions of Lebanon have attempted to avoid the tensions inherent in the two views described above by defining identity in non-religious terms. The first envisions the Lebanese as being culturally if not ethnically the neo-Phoenicians of the Eastern Mediterranean. This view emphasises the mobile, energetic, entrepreneurial, commercial nature of the society, the bridge between the peoples and cultures of the Mediterranean and the Levant, the people of the sea (now the air), not the people of the desert, a special people set off in spirit and destiny from those of their hinterland of the Middle East. This view has never had a very convincing ring about it and is viewed by its critics as an evasion of the issue of identity, another version of separateness and not one which had a realistic prospect of being broadly accepted. It does not offer an identity of consensus, especially for those Lebanese (probably a large majority today) who feel themselves to be part of the Arab world. There are a number of 'Phoenicians' in Lebanon today, but the Lebanese are not on the whole Phoenicians.

The concept of Lebanon as a 'refuge' or a 'haven' has a historical basis and suggests that there should be a place where persecuted minorities can have some hope of surviving without being submerged in another culture. Hence the Druze and Shiites of Lebanon, as well as the Maronites and the Armenians, found that the mountains of Lebanon offered their communities opportunities to survive. Critics of this point of view today characterise it as a fossilised view of society preserving the traditional characteristics and resisting the reforms and advantages of modernisation. To describe Lebanon as a 'refuge' is to identify one of its functions, but not its identity.

A view which gained support from elements among all of the religious communities in Lebanon over the past twenty-five years is the view of a secular, modernising, socialist society in which the parochial differences of the religious communities will be replaced by a homogeneous, industrial, socialist society. Despite the increasing support for this perspective of society, the religiously oriented elements in all of the communities resist it still and fear that the most basic values of their lives would be in jeopardy if there were a sweeping and fundamental secularisation of society. This may be the *vision* of the future but it is not yet the *view* of Lebanon today.

This leaves the last perception of Lebanese identity, that of a Christian and Muslim partnership, which would ensure the preservation of the values and identity of each community and bring them together into a working political system as envisioned in Lijphart's concept of consociational democracy. It is possible to interpret the 1926 Constitution and the National Pact of 1943 (and the customary practices which developed about the relations of the religious communities in government) as being an expression of this version of Lebanese identity. All communities participate proportionally and share proportionally in the processes and benefits of government and society through the equitable allocation of positions and authority in the public institutions. The community leaders representing peoples with different values and priorities would bridge these differences or make them compatible by agreement among themselves. It envisions a partnership in which nothing fundamental has to be surrendered and much could be gained by all of the partners. It is a vision recognising existing differences, accepting them as legitimate, exercising restraint in maintaining them, and a determination to cap them with an intercommunal arrangement which would bring greater benefits to all. It is a very attractive vision, but one which even with the best of will and a minimum of outside interference would be difficult to execute. But as we shall see in the actual practice of the Lebanese system, not everyone was committed to making it work.

The most explicit formulation of the partnership version of Lebanese identity was set forth in the unwritten National Pact at the time of independence in 1943, by agreement between the Maronite President and the Sunnite Prime Minister. It enunciated the principles upon which the state was to be based and seemed to provide some guidelines toward a common view of the Lebanese identity. Its two main provisions involved a commitment on the part of the Western oriented Christians to abandon their reliance on European protection and especially that of France, and a commitment by the Syrian and Arab oriented Muslims to abandon their claim for union with Syria or some larger Arab entity. But, as George Naccache has been quoted as saying, 'Two negatives do not make a nation'.[14] The implication was that having agreed on what they did not believe in was not the same thing as stating what the new identity was to be. Subsequent statements by Prime Minister Riyāḍ al-Ṣulḥ in Parliament and by President Bishāra al-Khūrī made clear their understanding that the pact was designed to achieve national unity rather than to institutionalise religious differences or feelings. Riyāḍ al-Ṣulḥ called for the abolition of confessionalism and stated that Lebanon is a nation with an Arab face that selects what is good and useful from Western civilisation. Bishāra al-Khūrī advocated the merging of all communities in Lebanon into one Lebanese nation, so that there will be no Muslims or Christians in the new Lebanon. 'We are Lebanese: national, independent and Arab.'[15]

However, not all Lebanese shared Bishāra al-Khūrī's interpretations and many more paid little attention to them over the next thirty years. Instead of producing a single Lebanese nation, the guarantees of communal rights which were adopted in order to provide the security necessary to develop confidence in the new Lebanon came to be institutionalised differences regarded as privileges attached to the communities.

It must be remembered that the National Pact was a compromise, falling short of the full aspirations of the parties to the agreement. During the first twenty-five years of independence the partnership was not an equal one in Muslim eyes because of what they saw as Maronite dominance, and because of demographic changes which indicated a growing preponderance of Muslims over Christians. Later still the Maronites themselves were uneasy about the pact because of their fears that large numbers of Palestinians would become permanent residents in Lebanon, thereby altering the ratio of Christians to Muslims upon which their privileged position depended.

The Institutional Level

We have identified some of the most important views of the Lebanese identity. But views of identity do not often compete directly in the political arena, although in Lebanon they do permeate most political institutions, some of which will be examined here to see how they reflect this underlying issue.

Perhaps the core of the matter is in the distribution of the executive authority between the President of the Republic and the Prime Minister. As we have seen the Lebanese pattern is perhaps closer to that of the French Fifth Republic than to either the classical parliamentary or presidential models. A President elected for a fixed term holds most of the power and a Prime Minister with less independent authority is responsible to Parliament and to the President. This problem of the relationships of the two executive authorities is complicated by the fact that the presidential post is reserved by custom to the Maronite community although the President as the Chief Executive is supposedly the custodian of that power for the whole nation and all of its communities. And the Prime Ministership being the reserve of the Sunnite community is as close as any Muslim comes to the centre of power. The Maronite Christians claim their right to the predominant position on the basis that they are the largest community, and justify the 'imbalance' of power by what they see as the necessity of a strong executive in a country with such a weak consensus. Every time a dispute arises over the exercise of executive power between these two executive officers there are overtones of communal rivalry of the two largest communities. If, as is usually the case, the President's will prevails, then the Prime Minister can do nothing but resign in order to preserve his honour (and that of his community). An effort was made to alter this situation in 1955 when leading Muslim dignitaries of the nation gathered and signed the 'Muslim Pact' which sets forth the Muslim demands for what they felt were equitable claims of their community especially in the institutions of government.[16] They insisted that meeting these demands should be a condition for forming a government and that if they were not fulfilled by the President then the Prime Minister should resign and all other candidates for the office should refuse to accept the nomination, thus making it impossible for the President to rule. It has not been possible in practice to enforce this pledge. Retiring Prime Ministers often publicly complain as they leave office that the President has not given Sunnite leaders just opportunities to participate in power, but they seem unable to resist the temptation to assume the office at the outset even if these conditions are not met. Muslims complain that the President's ability to play one candidate for the office of Prime Minister against another has the effect of weakening the influence of the community as a whole. There is nothing in the constitution to prevent the President from giving a much greater role to the Prime Minister in practice, to co-operate with him fully, and to act in a manner clearly perceived as being in the interest of the nation as a whole. Some Presidents have come closer to this than others, especially Bishāra al-Khūrī and Fu'ād Shihāb. Others have given the impression that they were more of a Maronite President than a Lebanese President.

The confessional ratios are also of major importance. To allocate public offices and seats in Parliament on a proportional basis among the communities requires some notion of their relative size, if not the actual number of each. Many critics call for the taking of a census which, aside from the possible results of the count, raises a number of questions about whom to count: all residents in Lebanon, including the Palestinians, or all Lebanese in Lebanon and abroad? This is often stated as the problem of whether or not there is a Christian majority. More to the point than the ratio of Christians to Muslims are the ratios among the Maronites, Sunnites, Shiites, Greek Orthodox, Greek Catholics, Druze, Armenian Orthodox and the minorities. For it is decided on this basis how many of the major offices of state, how many of the seats in the Chamber of Deputies, and what percentage of positions of the civil service will be allocated to each of the communities. There is a great deal of dissatisfaction with the ratios which have been employed for many years. As an example, the Shiites, who are officially ranked as the third largest community, claim to be the second largest and possibly the largest. If this were so and if the size of the community continues to determine who holds the office of President, Prime Minister, and Speaker of the Chamber, one can readily see the implications of re-adjusting the ratios. The same can be said for the membership of the Chamber of Deputies and for the civil service.

There are two types of demands made about the problem of ratios. One is that they be made much more equitable, that is, in keeping with the actual distribution of the population among the communities. The only area in which some progress has been made is in the civil service, where Christians and non-Christians now share the positions on a 50-50 basis. However, the issue has more recently changed from the numbers of positions to the importance of positions. Recently an attempt has been made to break down the custom that certain positions 'belonged' to certain communities and could only be filled by their members, through a system of periodical rotation of top administrative posts. One can see the significance of who occupies what position when one recalls the size and the personal nature of the political and administrative process in Lebanon. The second kind of claim being made about community ratios is the call for the total abolition of political sectarianism. The leaders of the Muslim communities have emphasised their desire to see 'political confessionalism' abolished, thereby removing consideration of religion from all public bodies and offices. However, Muslim religious officials insist that the personal status religious law should be retained, meaning that religious communities would continue to be officially recognised. In contrast, political parties like Junblāṭ's Socialist Party and the Syrian Social National Party along with most of the more radical groups call for the total abolition of the communal structure of society and government, and advocate a completely secular society and regime. In response the leader of the Phalanges Party agrees on the objective, but insists that confessionalism must first be erased from the hearts and minds of people before it can be removed from the legal and social system. Most observers believe that had the sectarian requirements been removed from the political system ten or even twenty years ago, the pattern of development would not have been significantly different because of the strength of traditional and communal ties. The events of 1975-6 have strengthened the determination of both the more radical elements to abolish sectarianism entirely, and of the more traditionally sectarian groups to cling even more tenaciously to their religious identity.

In February 1976 President Franjiyya announced a so-called 'New Lebanese National Covenant' usually referred to as a constitutional document. Its long-run status and significance cannot be predicted, but it deserves our attention because it was the product of the leaders of all of the major communities in Lebanon and represented an unusual consensus. Among its provisions are a number which bear on the distribution of power among the communities and on the ratios of representation in public offices. While maintaining the traditional practice of allocating the three highest public positions (the presidency for the Maronites; the presidency of the Chamber of Deputies to the Shiites; and the prime ministership to the Sunnites) it departs from the tradition of the six to five ratio of Christians to non-Christians in the legislature by adopting a 50-50 distribution.

The covenant also addresses itself to the relationship between the President and the Prime Minister by assigning the function of conducting the parliamentary consultations for the formation of the Cabinet to the Prime Minister (in consultation with the President). Similarly, it requires that all decrees and draft laws shall carry the signature of both the President and the Prime Minister.

Significantly, it envisions the abolition of sectarianism in the public service (except in the top category) and sets criteria of merit as the basis for recruitment into government employment.

Command of the army and the internal security forces (Gendarmes) has caused friction among the communities for some time. The army has never been given the men or equipment necessary to defend the country from foreign attack. Israeli aircraft penetrate Lebanese air space regularly and Israeli ground forces cross into Lebanon to attack Palestinian positions and adjacent Lebanese villages. Instead, the Lebanese army has been used, along with the security forces, for internal security purposes, controlling demonstrations and strikes which threaten to get out of hand, and restoring order where violence threatens to take on political importance. The top command positions of both the army and security forces have been dominated by Christian officers and especially by Maronites. Over time, the traditional 'neutrality' of the army became eroded in the minds of the Muslim communities and of the more radical political movements who were often the object of the army's attention. During the Presidency of Shihāb (previously Chief-of-Staff) the Intelligence Bureau of the army took on a political role and in the years that followed gradually gave the army and internal security forces a communal tinge. The controversy was made worse by the fact that on several occasions the Prime Minister (who is often also the Minister of Interior) found that his instructions to the army and security forces went unheeded and that his orders were countermanded by the Commander-in-Chief—the President of the Republic. This resulted in strong opposition to the use of the military for internal security purposes, particularly at a time when they seemed unable to protect Lebanon from Israeli attacks. In addition to pressures to have certain officers transferred, there has been a strong move to have the army under the control of a joint military council which would not be the preserve of one political tendency or religious community. Before a decision on this issue could be taken, the events of spring 1975 deteriorated so fast that it was pushed into the background. One of the repercussions of the feeling on the part of Muslims that the army was a partisan instrument of the 'Christian right', was that the Muslim community began viewing the increasingly well-armed Palestinians as their armed protection.

This issue has continued as a contentious issue, and a bill to re-organise the Military Command, proposed by the Ḥuṣṣ Government in 1978, was debated in the press and the Defence Committee of Parliament for months, and was finally passed into law in March 1979 (unanimously, without debate). In outline, it provides for the restriction of the previous direct control of the armed forces by the President and his Maronite Chief-of-Staff by requiring that they work through the Cabinet and a Higher Defence Council made up of the President (Chairman), the Prime Minister (Vice-Chairman), the Deputy Prime Minister, and the Ministers of Defence, Foreign Affairs, Finance and Interior, with the Chief-of-Staff participating as an adviser. In addition, a 'Military Chamber' and the 'Military Command' would be clearly under the Minister of Defence. The overall effect of these changes imply a reduction of the Maronite control of the armed forces, the reduction of the political role of the Chief-of-Staff of the armed forces and an increase in the control of the military by the Cabinet (especially the Prime Minister and the Minister of Defence).

The impact of the Palestine problem on the Lebanese identity crisis has been so strong that it requires separate treatment. Debarred from their homes in Palestine since 1948, the Palestinians sat hopelessly in their camps waiting for the Arab governments to help them recover what they considered their legitimate national rights. But, after the 1967 Arab-Israeli war, there seemed little prospect of Arab governments being able to do anything effective, and the Palestinian commando forces became more active, after 1970-1 especially on the southern border of Lebanon. Increased Israeli retaliations struck innocent Lebanese just as hard as the Palestinians and this had a series of internal political repercussions: namely that the Muslim Lebanese, feeling close to Muslim Palestinians, were very unhappy that the Lebanese government and army would not actively support the Palestinians and prevent Israeli attacks. The result was a drawing together of Muslim Lebanese and Palestinians, and increased disaffection from Lebanese authority. However, since the events of 1975-6 have settled nothing internally in Lebanon, and near anarchy continued for some years, a coolness between some Muslim leaders and the Palestinians has set in. Furthermore, Lebanese leftists drew closer to the Palestinians because of their strong Arab bond and because of ideological affinity with some of the more radical Palestinian groups and their rejection of the Lebanese political system. The Christian rightists (not all the Christians) saw the presence and activities of the Palestinians as a threat to their existence and identity. The increasingly well-armed Palestinians began to look

like a state within a state, not subject to Lebanese authority but preci-
pitating Israeli attacks on Lebanon, and alienating significant proportions of the Lebanese population from the Lebanese system. So the
Palestine problem and the Palestine people became enmeshed in the
communal relations of the Lebanese, and the Palestinians became *de
facto* actors in the Lebanese political process.

The Event Level

Even at the level of specific public events the identity issue is present.
Since every public official is also associated in people's minds with a
particular religious community and some position on the identity
problem, and since every major public office is associated with a
religious community and plays a role in asserting and achieving the
interest of that community, there are obvious identity overtones to
everything public officials do. Communal and identity problems seem
to leap unspoken from the daily newspaper headlines. It is sufficient to
mention only the bare outlines of specific events in order to appreciate
the difficulties and implications which stem from them. Some examples:

1. The first graduates from the new and unauthorised Faculty of Law
of the Egyptian sponsored Arab University of Beirut sought admission
to and recognition by the lawyers' syndicate.

2. Armed Palestinians were ambushed as they returned from Damascus
bearing the body of a martyr.

3. Beirut Muslim dignitaries went to Damascus to greet President
'Abd al-Naṣīr.

4. Several Shiite villagers were taken hostage by Israeli troops, while
Lebanese army troops clashed with Palestinian commandos.

5. A Maronite member of Parliament slapped a Druze district officer
who had refused to execute an irregular request.

6. A former Sunnite member of Parliament was wounded by army
shots while leading a demonstration of Sidon fishermen protesting the
granting of a fishing monopoly to a large company headed by a leading
Maronite politician.

7. The Prime Minister resigned when his orders to dismiss the army
commander who had not followed his orders were countermanded by
the President.

8. The President of the Republic conferred with the Papal Nuncio
and the French Ambassador.

9. The Cairo Agreement restricted armed Palestinian commandos to
their camps where they, and not Lebanese forces, would have full
authority.

Conclusion

The 1975-6 war in Lebanon has identified the limits of the capacity of the Lebanese political system. During the previous thirty years that system had demonstrated some of the qualities which Lijphart ascribes to his 'consociational' democracy. While there were always difficulties in reconciling the demands and expectations of the various communities, and while successive governments were barely able to provide a minimal level of security, or of economic infrastructure, or social services, or restraint to individual efforts to pursue their own interest at the expense of others, still one may say that in this imperfect world Lebanese governments seemed able to provide the overhead connecting links which made one political system out of several incompatible communities. But the different visions of Lebanon, particularly the visions with different external links, meant that outside forces were always present by implication and involved directly in crises. Before the Lebanese state had developed the capacity to fully overcome the internal contradictions, the system was required to bear a heavy load of external pressures.

It is still not clear whether the guarantees to the various communities and the legal institutionalisation of the communal system account for the partial success over the past thirty years, or whether on the contrary it was this institutionalisation which itself brought about the catastrophic events of the recent past. But it is clear that the conditions necessary to maintain Lijphart's 'consociational' democracy were not present, and the growing consensus overriding communal differences did not develop rapidly enough to merit the application of the Smocks' concept of national accommodation. The problem facing the Lebanese in the 1980s is, again, how they will conceive of their identity? Will they attempt to impose an identity as envisioned by one or another of the communal viewpoints; or will they attempt the partnership formula with a serious effort to use it as a means of rising above communal horizons to a national Lebanese level; or will they attempt to build a truly secular New Lebanon? Or will there be a Lebanon at all?

Notes

1. S. Khalaf, 'Adaptive Modernization: The Case for Lebanon' in C. A. Cooper and S. S. Alexander (eds.), *Economic Development and Population Growth in the Middle East* (American Elsevier Press, New York, 1972).

2. A. Lijphart, 'Consociational Democracy', *World Politics*, vol. 21, no. 2 (1969), pp. 207-25.

3. D. Smock and A. Smock, *The Politics of Pluralism: A Comparative Study of Lebanon and Ghana* (American Elsevier Press, New York, 1975).

4. A. Hourani, *A Vision of History: Near Eastern and Other Essays* (Khayats, Beirut, 1961).

5. K. Salibi, *The Modern History of Lebanon* (Weidenfeld and Nicolson, London, 1965).

6. Smock and Smock, *Politics of Pluralism*.

7. M. Hudson, *The Precarious Republic* (Random House, New York, 1968), p. 161; E. Salem, *Modernization Without Revolution* (Indiana University Press, Bloomington, 1973), p. 138.

8. Hudson, *Precarious Republic*, pp. 125-6.

9. L. Binder (ed.), *Politics in Lebanon* (Wiley, New York, 1966), p. 291.

10. M. Kerr, 'Political Decision Making in a Confessional Democracy' in Binder, *Politics in Lebanon*, pp. 188-90.

11. *Monday Morning* (a Beirut weekly), 17 November 1975.

12. Khalaf, 'Adaptive Modernization', p. 23.

13. Hudson, *Arab politics: the search for legitimacy* (Yale University Press, New Haven, Conn., 1977), p. 294.

14. *L'Orient—Le Jour*, 10 July 1975.

15. *al-Nahār*, 5th August 1975, quoting a statement made at the time of independence.

16. M. Dannāwī, *al-Muslimūn fi Lubnān* (The Muslims in Lebanon) (Beirut, 1973), pp. 123-8.

3. ISRAEL

Jacob M. Landau

Introduction

Israel's most pressing national problem remains the continuing conflict
with the Arab States. On the one hand, the conflict—which offers a
threat to Israel's very existence—makes for a large measure of national
consensus within the Jewish majority. On the other hand, it necessarily
excludes from this consensus the Arab minority,[1] part of which harbours
irredentist feelings concerning a future Arab Palestine. Again armed
conflict has drawn heavily on Israel's Gross National Product. Equally,
however, it has prodded Israel's economy towards self-sufficiency and
has aroused world Jewry to assist Israel financially. Although there was
hardly any unemployment in the 1970s and the standard of living of all
strata rose markedly, inflation increased the gap between the rich and
the poor. Sizeable subsidies and welfare payments notwithstanding, in
the 1970s large families complained increasingly of difficulties in
making ends meet. Common causes of complaint are the high cost
of living and the difficulty of obtaining reasonably priced housing.

These factors and others have contributed to a noticeable awareness
of politics amongst large segments of the population, both Jews and
Arabs. Israelis are avid readers of the press and constant listeners to
radio and television. Many argue endlessly about politics and econo-
mics. Electoral campaigning is taken very seriously and voting participation has been among the highest in multiparty states: with the
exception of 1951, when it was merely 75.1 per cent, participation in all
seven parliamentary contests, between 1949 and 1969, was between
81.6 and 86.9 per cent. The 120-member Knesset, elected for a term of
four years, is chosen by proportional representation, the whole country
being considered as one constituency.[2] Conceivably, this system
heightens interest and participation even further, since every single
vote is added to the total and weighs in the final count. However, this
system also causes every member of the Knesset to feel allegiance to his
political party, without any ties to a particular district.

Parties and Candidates

Parties are so much a feature of Israel's political culture and socio-
economic pattern (most parties are in business, at least to some extent),
that it was natural to establish the electoral system on the basis of interparty competition. Indeed, this system was inherited from the internal
election system of the Jewish community in British-ruled Palestine, in
pre-independence days. Then, as now, no single party had an absolute
majority and the national affairs of the community—later of the state—
were administered by coalitions of parties. In the quarter-century from
1948 to 1973, the comparative strength of the parties in voting terms
has not varied substantially, despite major changes in the composition
of the voting population, mainly as a result of large-scale immigration.
Even those differences become less significant, when related, separately,
to the three major 'camps' of parties—the labour, the centre (or rather
right of centre) and the religious parties.[3] These, by and large, preserved
their electoral strength, in comparative terms, in the seven Knessets,
which were elected as follows:

1st Knesset—1949
2nd Knesset—1951
3rd Knesset—1955
4th Knesset—1959
5th Knesset—1961
6th Knesset—1965
7th Knesset—1969

In Israel it is quite easy to draw up a slate of candidates and run for
the Knesset. All that a group, not a part of the outgoing Knesset, needs
is 750 signatures and a deposit. Although the latter was tripled in 1973
to IL 15,000 (at the time $3,571), this did not prevent quite a number of
groups from joining the contest. Twenty-one slates of candidates,
representing a wide spectrum of parties and groups, ran in 1973,
notably more than the 16 which had competed in 1969. Only once, in
the 1959 elections, had there been more; in 1949, too, the number had
been 21. The large number of slates in 1973 indicates the great interest
in the Knesset elections, the concern for the issues at stake, the desire to
be involved closely in parliamentary decision-making, and the fragmentation of some groups into splinters representing varying political and
socio-economic ideologies. Actually, although several slates were of
established political parties, others were set up by *ad hoc* groups.

Several of the competing slates were made up by parties that had sat
in the outgoing 7th Knesset. Some of these had, however, formed

parliamentary blocs, while others had changed their name. The largest outgoing group was the Alignment of the Israel Labour Party and Mapam. The former was a slightly left-of-centre party; its moderate policies in both internal and external affairs had enabled it to obtain mass support, thanks to which it succeeded in maintaining itself as the core of all Cabinets since Israel's establishment. The latter, much smaller, had a philosophy combining socialism with Zionism. The second-largest outgoing group—and the Alignment's main competitor— was the Likkud (i.e. United Front), made up of several centrist (or right-of-centre) parties, which claimed they were not anti-labour, but rather nationalist; its most vocal component, Herut (Freedom) was the most activist, even aggressive, in matters of foreign policy. There were two 'religious' groups, the National Religious Party, and the bloc of Agudat Israel—Poalei Agudat Israel, each of which claimed to speak for orthodox Jews; they were both dedicated to furthering the position of religion in all aspects of public life—but with a difference. The latter was committed to Zionism and the State of Israel, and had served as a coalition partner in most Cabinets. The former was avowedly non-Zionist and ultra-orthodox.

There were, also, two communist parties, the New Communist Party and Moked (or 'Focus'). The former was a dogmatic Marxist group, toeing Moscow's line, and enjoying marked support amongst Israel's Arabs; the latter, with which the Israel Communist Party had fused, indicated repeatedly a commitment to the State of Israel and its few members and supporters were mainly Jews. The Independent Liberals were a small group, which declared itself committed to individual liberties and to progressive, non-socialist policies. Another, even smaller, group was named Meri (an acrostic meaning 'Israeli Radical Centre'), which had previously been called Haolam Hazeh (or 'This World'). This had a typically oppositionist character, advocating better public administration and smoother relations between Jews and Arabs; in the main it had shown itself to be a maverick group.

Among the new slates of candidates, one should mention the Movement for Citizen's Rights, which called for economy and efficiency in the administration and for fair treatment by the bureaucracy of the individual citizen. There were separate slates of Arab candidates, mostly communal or regional; a Beduin group was running for the first time. Two of these slates were allied with the Alignment, one with the Likkud, and another was leftist and independent. Several slates purported to champion underprivileged Jews, including the Black Panthers and its rival, the Blue and White Panthers.[4] A few slates appealed to certain specific Jewish communities, such as the List of Yemenites in Israel. Several tiny groups manifested extreme left tendencies; while, at the other end of the spectrum stood the Jewish Defence League, which had both a chauvinist and ultra-orthodox character.

The number entitled to vote in elections to the 8th Knesset in 1973 was 2,037,778, including 17,782 who were granted the franchise shortly before election day: these were youngsters who were to be 18 years old before that day (formerly, they had to be several months over 18 on election day). Voting took place at 3,928 polls—and special measures were taken to ensure that the large number of men and women still serving in the military forces would be able to cast their votes.

Long before election day there unfolded a heated campaign in which a number of issues were at the centre of public attention. While the smaller political formations could select a positional issue and build up their whole electoral campaign around it, the larger ones were in some difficulty in this respect; as 'catchall parties', the latter had to steer clear of policy choices that would alienate their own supporters (and the larger the party's following, the wider the variations of outlook within it, of course) and still take such positions on issues, which would appeal to the mass of uncommitted voters. In Israel, as in other democracies, those registered as members of political parties form only a minority among voters—and it is the majority, the uncommitted, that the competing slates sought to attract. The three largest blocs—the Alignment, the Likkud, and the National Religious Party—came close to breaking up several times, on the eve of and during the election campaign, because of intraparty disagreement on policies, and the resulting specificity in the choice of issues and on how they ought to be presented to the electorate.

Issues in Earlier Elections

Before considering and analysing the major issues of the 1973 electoral campaign and indicating the stand of the political parties and groups on each, a few comments are necessary on the major issues of the previous seven electoral contests. As one would expect, the issues of earlier elections reflected the changing conditions of state and society. They may be arranged in two disparate groups: questions of social and economic interest, and matters related to security and foreign affairs. One notes a sort of see-saw between these two groups of issues: rarely balanced, usually one or the other preponderates in the issues presented by the parties and argued by the public.

In 1949, with war still seeming around the corner, the issues of security and foreign affairs overshadowed all others in the electoral campaign.[5] In 1951, with the ceasefire agreements secured, the issues of inflation, food-rationing and the social problems of the numerous immigrants (the number of those having the right to vote had increased by 70 per cent, chiefly through immigration) prevailed. Religious education, especially for the immigrants, was also ardently debated. In the 1955 electoral contest, military considerations played a greater role, due to an increase in violent infiltration across the borders. However, the problems of Israel's economy and society, too,[6] appear to have occupied the voters' attention in particular—for instance, the *modus vivendi* between the public and private sectors, or the integration of immigrants into Israel's society. In 1959 there was a lull on Israel's borders, following the Sinai campaign three years previously. However, labour unrest, allegations of discrimination against Jewish immigrants from Afro-Asian countries, and complaints by the Arab minority[7] attracted considerable attention amongst the voters. In 1961 issues with internal and external appeal were more or less evenly balanced in electoral propaganda. This was also the case in 1965, when the argument about foreign affairs centred on Israel's relations with Federal Germany; while internal affairs debated were the economy and the status of religion in the state. The Knesset elections of 1969 highlighted a wholly new situation. Israel, victorious in the June 1967 war, held extensive Arab territories; its policies on the future of these territories would be decisive for the state's destinies. Not surprisingly, then, considerations of security and foreign affairs prevailed over socio-economic issues.[8]

The 1973 Electoral Campaign

The 1973 general elections in Israel were set for 30 October, and campaigning started in earnest two months earlier, at the beginning of September—before the elections to the Histadrut (General Federation of Labour), scheduled for that month. However, on 6 October came the Egyptian and Syrian attacks on Israel and the Yom Kippur War started. The elections were postponed until 31 December, and electoral propaganda was renewed by the parties early in November, after the ceasefire on both fronts. Not unexpectedly, many issues had changed almost completely, due to the Yom Kippur War; or, at least, the emphasis had shifted markedly. While in the electoral campaign of September and early October socio-economic issues occupied a central position, in late November and December public interest focussed on matters concerned with security and foreign affairs. Insofar as socio-economic issues were raised in the electoral debate during the second stage, it was only on a minor scale.[9] Not surprisingly, perhaps, this had an adverse effect on the fortunes of most groups which campaigned mainly on a socio-economic platform, without having anything original to offer on security and foreign affairs.

The changed attitude was not only a consequence of the shock many had experienced as a result of the surprise attack on Israel and of the initial successes of the Egyptians and the Syrians. It was also connected with the fact that many Israelis had been called up for long periods of military duty, which they were serving during the weeks preceding voting day and on it as well. All things considered, these were most unusual general elections for Israel.[10] A parallel may be found only in Israel's first electoral campaign, early in 1949, when the whole country was still on a war footing, at the end of Israel's war of independence.

For purposes of our analysis, we have examined the propaganda materials of the parties, the speeches of their leaders and the contents of readers' letters published in the daily press. Israeli parties, no less than political parties elsewhere, not only attempt to 'sell' their respective platforms to the voter, but also take time to emphasise matters of concern to him. In the Israeli context, much of each party's electoral campaigning, on the one hand, is directed at its own members and sympathisers and at the uncommitted voter; and, on the other hand, is a direct response to the campaigning of its rivals. Consequently, the issues which one or more party estimates are of concern and interest get even greater attention, with particular emphasis on issues having a broad appeal. This is especially true of the Alignment-Likkud electoral contest, each of which also had to take into consideration differences of opinion among its own factions.

Here one should observe that the Alignment was supported in the Histadrut daily, *Davar,* and in Mapam's daily *Al Hamishmar.* Most other parties had newspapers or periodicals involved in the electoral campaign: the National Religious Party, Agudat Israel, Poalei Agudat Israel, Moked, the New Communist Party and Meri. The notable exception was the Likkud, with no organ of its own. Consequently, it had—along with the Independent Liberals, the Movement for Citizen's Rights and many others—to solicit support by advertising in the independent press, chiefly in the daily *Haaretz* and the evening news-papers, *Maariv* and *Yediot Aharonot*.

In the following pages, we shall attempt to estimate the various issues, not excluding those which indicate less emphasis. The intensity of the debate on the issues, and to some extent its nature, are coloured by the moods of the period, which had a strong impact on this unusual electoral contest.

Socio-economic Issues

The first set of issues of major importance are those relating to econo-mics and welfare. Israel resembles developed states in some political and cultural aspects, but economically still has many of the charac-teristics of underdeveloped states. According to various public opinion polls in Israel, over the years this peculiar combination has raised considerable dissatisfaction with the general economic and financial situation, and with its consequences for the individual. There has been a growing feeling that, although many have never had it so good, quite a few others have become increasingly poorer, and that the gap between the haves and have-nots has been widening.

These worries, and the ensuing criticism, found substantial scope in the elections to the leading bodies of the Histadrut, or General Federa-tion of Labour, held on 9 September 1973. Because of its large member-ship (at that time it had 1,159,852 enfranchised members) and its substantial share in Israel's economy, the Histadrut elections have often been seen as an indicator of the general trend of opinion towards Knesset elections. In the present case, the Histadrut elections of September 1973 clearly indicated the rise of protest groups and of organisations with a radical-leftist socio-economic message. An example is the Black Panthers' group, claiming to represent the interests of the underprivileged, chiefly among the poorer Jews of Afro-Asian origin; the leaders of the group and the first candidates on its slate to the Histadrut elections were themselves from this background. Although the Black Panthers obtained a mere 1.63 per cent, or 12,638, of the valid votes in the 1973 Histadrut elections, the result was generally considered a signal success, in view of the tough competition in the campaign, and the fact that the group was running for the first time.

It was natural, therefore, that socio-economic issues were at the centre of the electoral campaign for the 8th Knesset, at least in its first stage, during September and early October 1973. However, the situation changed materially with the Yom Kippur War. In the first stage, the arguments were markedly indicative of the hopes and fears of Israelis in this sphere. Few points of significance were left out by the electoral propaganda. Some of the main ones were as follows.

The Alignment took credit for the rapid growth of the Israeli economy—as asserted by Pinhas Sapir, Minister of Finance.[11] It prided itself on the fact that, even during the grim weeks of the Yom Kippur War, there had been no shortage of food, no rationing of basic commodities, no lines in the shops, no recession and no unemployment.[12] Nevertheless, the Alignment could not simply ignore the problems besetting the Israeli economy, nor could it deny the seriousness of the recent war's effects on the state's finances. Soberly enough, Alignment leaders—such as Shimon Peres, Minister of Communications, and Haim Gvati, Minister of Agriculture—pointed out these factors and called on Israelis to limit their consumption to essentials, to save, work harder, agree to forgo wage increases, and plan ahead better.[13]

The activities and attitudes of the Alignment in economic affairs were attacked, with varying intensity, by almost all its competitors. While the National Religious Party called for the better use of Israel's manpower and for the increased mobility of workers,[14] Moked demanded heroic measures. Meir Pail, a retired colonel and ex-instructor in history at Tel Aviv University, who headed the Moked list, demanded the instituting of a state of emergency in the state's economy. This would involve a more equitable division of the burden imposed by defence expenditure, a total freeze of prices and earnings (along with stiff penalties on speculators and profiteers), and a ban on all imports of luxury goods.[15]

The Independent Liberals, although identified in the public mind as a close coalition partner of the Alignment for many years, spoke up against the Alignment's economic and fiscal policies—probably in order to erase some of the impact of this identification with the Alignment in voters' minds, and to offer a more independent image. Anyway, spokesmen of the Independent Liberals—like Moshe Kol, Minister of Tourism—came out for greater opportunities for the private sector, alongside the state and the Histadrut sectors, in Israel's pluralist economy.[16] Other party leaders, like Yehuda Shaari, demanded state-sponsored insurance of health services and of retirement pensions, as well as of adequate housing for everybody.[17] They also criticised what they considered inequities in the country's taxation system.

Taxes were a favourite target for Likud spokesmen, also, as part of their overall attack on the Alignment and of their effort to present themselves as a feasible alternative to form the Cabinet. The Likud's propaganda advertisements[18] emphasised distortions in the manner of calculating the fringe benefits of many salaried people and in calculating their income tax. It strove to demonstrate that, with the tacit approval of the government, numerous categories of salaried people were granted permission to cheat on their income tax ('90 ways'). The Likkud demanded the overhauling of the whole tax system, so that, without diminishing the individual's net income, everything should be above board. Honesty would go hand in hand with increased productivity and the stabilisation of prices needed to curb inflation.[19] Such issues were stressed even more by the Likkud after the Yom Kippur War, when it loudly called for the eradication of the corruption it claimed to see everywhere—in government-sponsored companies, in public housing, and in the whole bureaucratic system.[20]

Security and Foreign Affairs

Other issues in the electoral campaign of 1973 were closely connected with war and peace. As we have said, these were particularly highlighted in the second stage of the campaign, after the Yom Kippur War. We shall discuss them under four main headings: the Yom Kippur War, the peace settlement, the approach to territorial issues and the Geneva Peace Conference.

The Yom Kippur War. That the Yom Kippur War—with its heavy loss of life—had left a trauma on many Israelis became evident in the prominent part it played in the electioneering. The war put the Alignment, more so than other political formations, in a difficult position. As the major party of the government which had been taken almost completely by surprise, the Alignment could hardly shirk its responsibility. It decided to acknowledge it and try to put it in a more favourable perspective. Shimon Peres argued for the Alignment that the Yom Kippur War ought to be regarded as a chapter in the war which had been fought since 1967[21] and that Israelis should look to the future, not to the past.[22]

Other parties and groups, however, took a diametrically opposed view; they addressed themselves to public feeling on the matter, and attempted to channel it into an anti-Alignment vote by 'punishing' the Alignment.[23] The New Communist Party was apparently the first opposition party to express its opinion in this respect—as early as the fourth day of the war. In an advertisement,[24] the party's Political Bureau published a policy statement, in which it put the whole blame for the new bloodshed on the Israeli government. As the New Communist Party phrased it, this government had failed to strive sufficiently for peace and, by keeping the Israeli-held territories, with Washington's consent, it had brought about yet another war.

Other parties did not see matters in that way at all. They blamed Egypt and Syria for starting the new war, but accused the Israeli government of a terrible *mehdal* ('blunder'). Bitterest was the tone of the Likkud, which accused the Alignment-led government not only of leading Israel into a social, economic and moral crisis, but also of failing to watch over its security. As the Likkud put it, the government, despite advance warning of the Egyptian and Syrian offensive build-up, failed to call up the reserves and move the Israeli forces nearer to the front in time. The almost fatal *mehdal*, it maintained, had rendered the government unworthy of the people's trust.[25]

The Independent Liberals reacted differently still. They maintained that the Alignment had been at fault in the recent war by its actions, just as much as the Likkud had been wrong in its general approach on the ideological level. Their party held that the war had proved that the status quo was not a satisfactory alternative to peace; it had demonstrated, also, serious misjudgements in decision-making. The Independent Liberals, as a party of peace, strove to play down their responsibility in the Coalition Cabinet preceding the Yom Kippur War, and claimed that they ought to be the obvious voters' choice. The same attitude, by and large, was adopted by Mrs Shulamit Aloni, leader of the Movement for Citizen's Rights.[26]

The Peace Settlement. Notably, peace was the magic slogan with which all competing groups hoped to convince both their own adherents and the floating voters. As a result of the recent war, the clamour for peace was loud. The dilemma of each grouping was how to impress the voters that it—rather than anybody else—had hit on the proper formula for achieving peace. The Alignment leaders frankly admitted that there was no easy option for securing peace. Further, they acknowledged that decisions were very difficult, as the government's wish for peace was tempered by suspicion as to the real intentions of the Arab states; the risks Israel ought to take should be calculated ones.[27] However, both Golda Meir and Yigal Allon, then respectively Prime Minister and Deputy Prime Minister, claimed in their election broadcasts that the chances for peace had never been so good.[28]

Others approached the peace settlement differently, be it from a dovish or a hawkish point of view. The former was reflected, for instance, in a speech by Meir Pail of Moked.[29] According to Pail, the hawkish conception of moving towards peace had been proved bankrupt in the Yom Kippur War. The dovish approach ought to be given a chance, and Israel should take the initiative for a peace plan of its own, lest it be pressured in discussing plans prepared by others. His own peace plan was that Israel should propose a withdrawal in stages from the Israeli-held territories, each withdrawal to be in exchange for Arab concessions towards peace—such as Israeli navigation in the Suez Canal, cessation of the Arab economic boycott, and the establishment of some sort of diplomatic relations. Another small group, Meri, maintained that it understood the Arab mind better than others, that it had already initiated peace plans, and that it ought to be given an opportunity of obtaining a fair peace that would be in Israel's best interests.[30]

An almost diametrically opposed attitude was exhibited by the Likkud. It had, first and foremost, to persuade the voters of its moderateness, i.e. that it was *not* a party of war, as asserted by the Alignment. True, some of the groups making up the Likkud were known for their extreme hawkishness. Menahem Begin and Shmuel Tamir, each the leader of component groups of the Likkud, refuted, in separate public meetings, the charge that their grouping was 'a war party'. On the contrary, they maintained, the Alignment, although having headed Cabinets for a quarter-century, had failed to secure peace for Israel, succeeding only in bringing about a series of wars.[31]

The Approach to Territorial Issues. The issue of peace, thus, was hardly a real issue in itself, since everybody agreed on its desirability. The polemic centred on the best way of securing peace. The crux of the issue was whether to relinquish all or part of the Israeli-held, Arab-populated territories, and, if so, in exchange for what. No political and military issue was more bitterly argued in the 1973 electoral campaign as was to be the case in 1977, too. These territories were four different areas, all taken over by Israel in the June 1967 war. They were the Golan Heights, the West Bank (Judaea and Samaria), the Gaza Strip, and the Sinai Peninsula. The first had been part of Syria, the second of the Kingdom of Jordan (which had annexed it in 1949), the third had been administered by Egypt (since 1949) and the fourth had been a part of Egypt. Only the second and third had been within British-mandated Palestine, in the thirty years after the First World War.

The response of the competing parties and groups as to the disposal of the Israeli-held territories was most varied. The continuum of views ranged from the extreme dovish to extreme hawkish or, in operative terms, from a minimalist to a maximalist stance. While the New

Communist Party recommended[32] Israeli withdrawal from all these territories, other parties, like the Independent Liberals, favoured more gradual or partial withdrawal, conditional on the negotiation of peace. The religious parties were more attached to the West Bank, the area of religious shrines and historically hallowed sites, than to the other territories. The Likkud did not declare outright against an Israeli withdrawal and denied that it was intransigent;[33] but its spokesmen asserted that this could be brought about solely in exchange for a secure peace, only to the extent that the security of Israel's borders would be fully assured; this was taken to mean only minimal concessions. Most extreme in this context was Rabbi Meir Kahane's Jewish Defence League, which frankly proclaimed[34] that not an inch of land should be given up by Israel.

In all this complex array of arguments and counter-arguments, the Alignment found itself in a difficult dilemma, largely due to the divergent views of its varied membership and the changed situation.[35] Early in September 1973, i.e. before the Yom Kippur War, the Secretariat of the Israel Labour Party—the major component of the Alignment—had approved the 'Galili Document' (so called after Israel Galili, Minister without Portfolio, who had done most of the drafting). This declaratory statement purported to determine the party's policy towards the Israeli-held territories for the following four years. Generally speaking, the document demonstrated a new tougher attitude in the party, approving—among other things—more extended, even though controlled, settling of Israelis in those territories. After the Yom Kippur War, the Israel Labour Party had to retreat on the Galili Document, in order not to appear in too extreme a position in view of the approaching Geneva Peace Conference and in the electoral campaign. Another document, the 'Fourteen Points', was adopted as a substitute, after much debate in the party's bodies.[36] This was basically a compromise between hawks and doves in the party, between those who insisted on security frontiers and those who were ready to take risks insofar as boundaries were concerned, as part of a peace settlement. The final version envisaged ceding territories without prejudicing Israel's security frontiers.[37] The views of Mapam, generally more inclined to compromise on the boundaries,[38] naturally weighed too, since it was running in the Alignment with the Israel Labour Party. All in all, the Fourteen Points provided a broad umbrella and served the Alignment excellently to defer decisions until after election day. Briefly, it was a relatively dovish programme: although emphasising the Alignment's concern with security (to satisfy the demands of the hawkish wing within the Alignment), the Fourteen Points dealt mostly with its readiness for peace and concessions, based on co-operation with the United States and on the support of world Jewry. This was, actually, a unique occurrence, for a major political party in Israel, to backtrack and change direction, on a cardinal point of policy, in the midst of a tough election campaign.

The Geneva Peace Conference. The change of direction was closely connected with the impending Geneva Peace Conference on the Middle East. During the second stage of the electoral campaign, the planned conference became one of the trump cards in the government's hand.[39] The leaders of the Alignment maintained that, despite the risks involved, a negotiated settlement in Geneva, even if not complete, would ultimately lead to a fully fledged peace.[40] Time and again, they drove home the point that it was to the Alignment's credit that the Arab states had, at long last, agreed to talk with Israel, as an alternative to the option of making war.[41] True, the conference was not yet peace, but, rather, 'a laboratory for peace'.[42] Speeches by Golda Meir[43] and Peres[44] warned that peace depended on willingness on the part of *both* sides to the conflict, and that, while Israel was prepared for give-and-take negotiations, it would never neglect its own basic interests. A similar view was voiced by Moshe Dayan, Minister of Defence, who asserted that, while the Arab states still desired Israel's destruction, the confer- ence held hope for some sort of peaceful settlement.[45] On the other hand, Abba Eban, Minister of Foreign Affairs, called the Geneva Peace Conference 'an opportunity—not a danger'.[46]

Although the Alignment seemed united on Israel's active participa- tion in the conference, it was divided as to its estimate of the chances of success. Most of its spokesmen, however, seemed to adopt a sober attitude, based on cautious optimism, as expressed in Golda Meir's speech in the Knesset announcing Israel's agreement to take part in the conference. The Mapam component of the Alignment took the same view and emphasised that, however slim the chances of success, Israel ought to participate.[47] Mapam spokesmen, like Victor Shemtov, Minister of Health, were optimistic and expected more from the conference, which they regarded as 'an historic event'.[48] All in all, Mapam's spokesmen were no less divided about the peace plans[49] than were those of the Israel Labour Party.

The above arguments and others were designed to persuade the voter that here was a most unusual opportunity, which ought to be grasped, and that the Alignment alone was capable of so doing—despite differ-

ences of opinion in the matter among its own members.[50] It was maintained that all the other parties, particularly the Likkud, would merely
torpedo the conference, if granted the power to do so. The Alignment's
propaganda claimed that the Likkud had persistently opposed earlier
peace initiatives and that it could not be trusted with the delicate negotiations in Geneva,[51] especially since the Likkud opposed the moves of
the United States.[52] The message was loud and clear: the Likkud could
not obtain peace and would lead Israel into war.

This line was emphatically rejected by the Likkud, which supported
Israel's attending Geneva, but demanded a strong stand there.[53] In his
reply to Golda Meir's statement in the Knesset announcing Israel's
participation in the Geneva Peace Conference, Menahem Begin, the
Likkud's leader, took quite a different approach.[54] As Begin phrased
this, it was libellous on the part of the Alignment-led government to
divide Israel into a peace camp and a war camp; the Likkud was as eager
as the Alignment for peace and as ready to attend the Geneva Peace
Conference. Other Likkud leaders, like Elimelech Rimalt, asserted that
the Likkud would do this better, since it would represent Israel 'with its
head held high'.[55] In the same tone, Shmuel Tamir maintained that
only the Likkud would preserve at Geneva those parts of the Israeli-
held territories which were essential for securing Israel's continued
existence.[56]

After the Geneva Peace Conference was convened, the Likkud
published its views in an advertisement.[57] It warned in no uncertain
terms that the Arab statements at the conference indicated a clear
intention of breaking up Israel in a successive series of steps. The
advertisement was so designed as to cast heavy doubts on the government's chances of success at the conference, on the one hand, and to
present the Likkud as the true defender of Israel's basic interests.

All other parties and groups taking part in the 1973 electoral
campaign favoured Israel's participation in the Geneva Peace Conference—generally in a dovish spirit. The variations were chiefly a matter
of the gradation of their support and the arguments they listed for it.
Thus, the Independent Liberals approved participation, considering
the conference a unique opportunity for peace-making, for the sake of
which Israel should be prepared to cede some of the Arab-inhabited
territories it was holding.[58] The party's election advertisements
repeated this approach, adding that Israel ought to strive for a complete
normalisation of the relations in the area at all levels.[59] Gideon
Hausner, head of the party's parliamentary group, speaking at a public
meeting, warned however that the United Nations' involvement in the

conference—presumably through Waldheim's official presence—endangered the proceedings, since the United Nations was not impartial.[60]

Israel's two communist parties expressed an even stronger commitment to the Geneva Peace Conference. While Shmuel Mikunis, of Moked, pressed for the application of the UN resolutions at the conference,[61] the advertisements of the New Communist Party went further. They cited the Soviet Union's participation in the conference as an omen for peace, and called on Israel's delegates to the conference to give up all the territories and recognise the rights of the Palestinians, in exchange for Arab recognition of Israel's sovereignty and of its rights of navigation—equal to those of all other states.[62] While the above was claimed to represent a balanced approach, it was indeed quite extreme, both in urging the government to give up *all* Israeli-held territories, occupied in June 1967, and in demanding that it recognise the rights of the Palestinians—a vague formula which many Israelis suspect means, in fact, the end of Israel as a Jewish state.

Other groups, like Meri, called for sending to Geneva Orientalists and experts in Arab thinking, rather than career diplomats,[63] while a leader of the Black Panthers, Saadia Marciano, although not opposed to the conference, alleged that the whole matter was largely a vote-getting trick of the Alignment-led government.[64] This fitted in with the emphasis put by the Black Panthers' campaign on socio-economic issues.[65]

State and Religion

Another issue or, rather, set of issues, had to do with the interrelation of state and religion. The status and function of religion in the State of Israel is of absorbing interest, not only to the religious parties, but also to many of the other political parties, albeit for different reasons. It has been a constant issue in Israel's electoral contests[66] and has been argued heatedly in several of them.[67] Although overshadowed by the acrimonious debate on security and foreign affairs, particularly in the second stage of the 1973 electoral campaign, this issue was also much debated. The religious parties were very strongly committed to the proposition that although a minority cannot impose its views on the majority and set up a theocracy in Israel, still much could be done to further the standing which religion deserved in law, society and education. In addition to a systematic campaign in their own periodicals and newspapers, these parties published many advertisements in the uncommitted press, seeking the support of floating voters.

The National Religious Party was particularly active in this respect, and one of its first advertisements was characteristic of the rest of its campaign. This went as follows: 'The main point is: Will the State of Israel be a state of the Jews and Judaism, or merely a secular state whose citizens are of Jewish origin? Join those who are defending the Jewish character of the State of Israel!'[68] This party was known for its hawkish attitude on Israel's frontiers, and particularly for its reluctance to give up any part of the West Bank, so intimately associated with Jewish tradition. Nevertheless, the party openly proclaimed that the spiritual integrity of the nation was as important for the state's future as the frontiers of the state.[69] On more specific points, the National Religious Party insisted in its electoral campaign on the need for a specifically orthodox definition of Jewishness, with respect to the Israeli Law of Return, which allowed any and every Jew to come to Israel and become a citizen, if he so wished.[70] The point was to prevent those who had not been converted properly from claiming to be Jews.

Naturally, other political parties regarded the whole issue differently. The Alignment, which included a section for religiously observant workers, took the view that religion was not the exclusive prerogative of the religious parties. On the contrary, the Alignment camp—it argued—could further the cause of religion more because of its power to implement policies.[71] The leftist parties devoted hardly any attention to the issue of state and religion. Their views in the matter ranged from indifference to anti-religiousness. As such they well knew that they could not hope to attract new votes from those committed to furthering the stand of religion; nor did they try to do so. Actually, the only parties—besides the religious ones and the Alignment—involved in this issue in the election campaign were the Independent Liberals and the Movement for Citizen's Rights, both of which held quite a different position from that of the religious parties. The Independent Liberals had fought in the outgoing Knesset for liberalising the marriage laws in Israel, intending to restrict the exclusive jurisdiction of the Jewish rabbinical courts in certain hardship cases. Although it had failed in this, the party promised to persevere and to watch over the civil rights of the individual against what they considered the encroachment of the religious authorities.[72] The Movement for Citizen's Rights took basically the same approach.

The Moods of the Period

More than the specific issues of the electoral campaign, what characterised it most was the moods of the period. The issues debated in the two stages of the 1973 electoral campaign were highlighted by the general trends peculiar to this campaign, especially those in its second stage. The moods reflected the widespread malaise inherent in the post-war atmosphere and revealed a general consensus that Israel's troubles were far from over and that hostilities might break out anew at any time. A desire for change—some change, any change—was voiced by many people.[73] None the less, political analysts warned against an unbridled witch-hunt for those responsible for the *mehdal*,[74] and the warning was heeded, at least by some of those involved.

The argument over the formation of a Cabinet of National Unity, proposed by those who wished a stronger government, stirred many passions. Two parties, the Likkud and the National Religious Party, championed the idea, while the Alignment and practically every other group vehemently opposed it. The reasoning of the former parties was that the national emergency facing Israel was so serious that a broadly based coalition was absolutely necessary for survival.[75] The latter parties argued that a Cabinet of National Unity would be virtually paralysed in any important decision-making by the very divergent approaches of its components.

In more detail, the Likkud maintained that only a strong government, with broad popular support and made up of Israel's best brains, would succeed in resisting pressures.[76] Begin reminded his listeners, in a mass meeting in the town of Bnei Brak, near Tel Aviv, that his party had been a partner in a former Cabinet of National Unity for three fateful years, from June 1967 to July 1970; and that the party had left it not because they had opposed peace, but because they had rejected the proposals for a new partition of the country, embodied in the so-called Rogers Plan.[77]

The Alignment answered this charge by asserting that it alone could lead Israel to peace via the Geneva Peace Conference, while the Likkud—with its record of opposing peace initiatives and rejecting territorial concessions—would only cripple the Alignment's peace moves, if allowed to participate in the government.[78] Peres argued in an election meeting that while a Cabinet of National Unity was sometimes desirable on the eve of war, it was not at all so on the eve of peace negotiations.[79] Allon warned that a Cabinet of National Unity, including the Likkud, would be regarded abroad as a stiffening of Israel's positions and annoy Israel's friends.[80]

These arguments of the Alignment were countered by the Likkud, which reiterated that its aim was *not* to participate in an Alignment-led government, but to form and head a Cabinet of National Unity which other parties would be invited to join.[81]

The attitude of the National Religious Party on this point was closer to that of the Likkud. Its strong emotional commitment to the preservation of the West Bank within the State of Israel in any future settlement caused it to promote and support the concept of a Cabinet of National Unity, in which the Likkud would participate. Consequently, the National Religious Party urged the voters to enable it to bring about the formation of such a Cabinet; the party held that it was the only political force able to bring together both the Alignment and the Likkud.[82] Since the NRP could hardly expect to obtain sufficient votes to head the following government, it could still foresee a situation in which the Alignment and the Likkud would be almost evenly matched within the Cabinet, in which case it would hold the balance of power—yet another reason for its attitude.

Another lively argument, indicative of the moods of the post-war period, had to do with the elections themselves. After the war there seems to have been a rather widespread feeling that both the programmes of the parties and the composition of the slates of candidates had become outdated.[83] Various small parties and groups demanded a further postponement of the election as well as an opportunity for drawing up new candidate slates, in which new names could be inserted. The leader of one of these groups, Shalom Cohen of the Black Panthers, even took the case to the Supreme Court, but lost.[84] Cohen's argument was that too many youngsters were serving at the front to allow balanced, well-thought-out campaigning.

The Movement for Citizen's Rights called for a postponement of the elections to 1 March 1974, and for the submitting of new slates in order to include more youngsters among the voters, and new, abler men among the candidates, instead of those responsible for the lack of preparation for war.[85] The Independent Liberals adopted a similar stand, pointing out that the shock of the Yom Kippur War had made changes in the slates of candidates imperative.[86]

However, the two largest parliamentary groups, the Alignment and the Likkud—which between them easily constituted a majority in the Knesset—had jointly approved 31 December as the election day. The smaller parties clamoured against what they regarded as an unholy alliance.[87] None the less, the two largest parties, in a classic example of elite accommodation, campaigned as energetically for that day's retention as the others argued for its postponement. The Alignment was the main opponent of such a postponement, perhaps due to the reluctance of its leadership to reopen the debate over factional differences. Although some of its members differed,[88] a majority of the party's functionaries held that elections were feasible while there was no fighting; even necessary, for the government needed a renewed mandate from the electorate.[89] Such a government, maintained Alignment MK Haim Zadok, would then negotiate for peace from a stronger position.[90] The Likkud, although less articulate in this matter, took a rather similar approach.[91]

The whole argument about the postponement of the election and the redrafting of slates of candidates ought to be viewed in the proper context of the mood of doubts in, and criticism of, the public order as such. The performance of the national leadership during the crisis of the Yom Kippur War was seen by many as faulty—not merely by itself, but as part and parcel of a deeper *mehdal,* which concerned the whole structure of Israeli life. Claims for greater democratisation within the parties and a larger say for the individual members, on the one hand, and for changes in the electoral system, on the other, were only part of the overall picture.

More so than in previous electoral campaigns, the parties demanded reform in the general political and socio-economic system. In addition to what has already been mentioned, various parties spoke up against Israel's extensive red tape, its tax system, the overlapping of government offices with ill-defined powers and neglect of the individual by those in authority. They promised reforms in the constitutional definition of individual rights, giving the public all the information it was entitled to receive, instituting national health insurance and a more equitable retirement pensions system, devoting more attention to ecology and establishing a National Security Committee and a National Committee for Social Problems.

Conclusion

Generally speaking the 1973 electoral campaign was much more heated than that of 1969; in some ways, it was reminiscent of the *Sturm und Drang* of the campaigns for the Knesset elections in the early years of the state. The Yom Kippur War was considered by many as 'an earthquake' (in Hebrew, *reidat adama*). There was a widespread—even if not general—public feeling that Israel's very existence as a state, which had been taken for granted formerly, was at stake.[92] Indeed, there was somehow a feeling of destiny in the second stage of the electoral campaign, and the competing groups worked at intensifying this feeling and trying to use it to their advantage, in the manner they related to the main issues. Concerning security and foreign affairs, in particular, each party made a particularly determined effort to persuade the voter to participate, and give it his support.

Most issue areas raised in the 1973 electoral campaign were the same as those of previous years, and some were to come up again in 1977, but the concrete issues and emphases were different. Some issues which had occupied electoral interest formerly had lost the interest of the general public, almost to the extent of becoming non-issues. Two examples suffice. First, the grievances of the Arab minority in Israel, which had been given space in early electoral contests[93] as its number grew and its leaders became more vocal,[94] were hardly mentioned in 1973. The last obstacle to their full political integration, the military administration, had been done away with in December 1966, and their economic situation was thriving. True, the New Communist Party did appeal to the nationalist sentiment of the Arab minority (and benefited as a result), but this was a different matter from appealing to grievances.[95]

Secondly, the issue of discrimination against Jews from Afro-Asian countries (whatever the objective situation in this matter) was rather limited in the electoral propaganda—especially in the second, decisive stage of the campaign. The fact that, on the one hand, all the large and middle-sized parties virtually ignored it and that, on the other hand, none of the small groups running on a platform of protest against discrimination of Afro-Asian Jews won a single seat in the Knesset, is indicative of the limited concern of voters for this issue. Many voters probably regarded this issue as inappropriate for public argument then, due to its dangerous conflict potential. In other words, the 1973 campaign was unique in Israel's electoral history in that the issues (particularly in the second stage of the campaign) focused sharply on one set—those closely bound up with the survival of the state.

Notes

I am grateful to my assistant, Mr Meir Nitzan, who has helped me to scan the Israeli newspapers for material bearing on the 1973 elections.

1. The inhabitants of the Israeli-held territories are not discussed in this chapter, as they did not participate in Israel's parliamentary elections—not being Israeli citizens. (They have preferred to remain citizens of Jordan, Syria etc.).

2. A. Zidon, *Knesset* (Herzl Press, New York, 1967).

3. M. Sharett, 'The Multiparty Democracy of Israel' in J. M. Landau (ed.), *Man, State and Society in the Contemporary Middle East* (Praeger, New York, 1972), pp. 189-95; A. Akzin, 'The Role of Parties in Israeli Democracy', *Journal of Politics*, 17 (November 1955), pp. 507-45; E. Gutmann, 'Das politische System' in J. M. Landau (ed.), *Israel*, 2nd edn (Glock und Lutz Verlag, Nuremberg, 1970), pp. 101-8.

4. Blue and white are the national colours of Israel.

5. A. Arian, *The Choosing People: Voting Behavior in Israel* (Case Western Reserve University Press, Cleveland, 1973), pp. 15-17.

6. S. N. Eisenstadt, *Israeli Society* (Weidenfeld and Nicolson, London, 1967), pp. 154ff.

7. J. M. Landau, 'Les Arabs Israéliens et les élections à la quatrième Knesset', *International Review of Social History,* 7 (1962), pp. 1-32.

8. E. Torgovnik, 'The Election Campaign: Party Needs and Voter Concerns' in A. Arian (ed.), *The Elections in Israel—1973* (Jerusalem Academic Press, Jerusalem, 1975), pp. 25-37; E. Torgovnik, 'Election Issues and Interfactional Conflict Resolution in Israel', *Political Studies,* 20 (1972), pp. 79-96; E. Stock, 'Foreign Policy Issues' in A. Arian (ed.), *The Elections in Israel—1969* (Jerusalem Academic Press, Jerusalem, 1972), pp. 43-60; J. M. Landau, 'The Arab Vote' in Arian, *Elections—1969,* pp. 253-63.

9. Torgovnik, 'Election Campaign', p. 83.

10. J. M. Landau, 'The 1973 Elections in Turkey and Israel', *The World Today,* 30 (April 1974), pp. 170-1.

11. *Haaretz* (Israeli newspaper), 12 December 1973.

12. Ibid., 20 December 1973.

13. *Davar* (Israeli newspaper), 15 November 1973.

14. Ibid., 13 November 1973.

15. *Haaretz,* 24 December 1973.

16. Ibid., 20 September 1973.

17. Ibid., 21 September 1973.

18. Ibid., 4 September 1973.

19. Ibid., 21 September 1973.

20. Ibid., 26 December 1973.

21. *Davar,* 30 November 1973.

22. *Haaretz,* 15 November 1973.

23. *Maariv* (Israeli newspaper), 27 December 1973.

24. *Haaretz,* 9 October 1973.

25. Ibid., 30 November, 4 December 1973.

26. Ibid., 10 December 1973.

27. *Davar,* 15 November 1973.

28. Ibid., 13 November, 16 December 1973.

29. *Haaretz,* 22 November 1973.

30. *Maariv,* 5 December 1973.

31. Ibid., 10 December 1973; *Haaretz,* 12, 18 December 1973.

32. *Maariv,* 28 December 1973.

33. Ibid., 25 December 1973.

34. Ibid., 30 November 1973.

35. Y. Arnon, 'Petihat hareshimot—derisha demokratit' (Opening the slates of candidates—A democratic request), *Davar,* 22 November 1973.

36. *Maariv,* 29 November 1973.

37. G. Yaakobi, 'Hanhaga umediniyut' (Leadership and policy), ibid., 26 November 1973.

38. H. Knaan, 'Shalom nusah Mapam' (Peace as Mapam sees it), ibid., 13 December 1973; *Haaretz,* 5 December 1973.

39. *Maariv,* 19 December 1973.

40. Y. Tadmor, 'Habehirot, havikuakh hapenimi uve'idat Jeneva' (The elections, the internal argument, and the Geneva conference), *Davar,* 4 December 1973.

41. See the speech by Shlomo Hillel, Minister of Police, in the Arab village of Umm al-Fahm, reported in *Haaretz,* 16 December 1973.

42. Ibid., 19 December 1973.

43. Ibid., 14 December 1973.

44. Ibid., 30 November 1973.

45. *Davar*, 29 November 1973.
46. Ibid., 12 December 1973.
47. See Mapam leader, Yaakov Hazan, reported in *Haaretz*, 21 December 1973.
48. *Davar*, 29 November 1973.
49. Knaan in *Haaretz*, 5 December 1973.
50. *Davar*, 14 December 1973.
51. *Haaretz*, 13 December 1973.
52. Ibid., 16 December 1973.
53. *Maariv*, 10 December 1973.
54. Summarised in *Haaretz*, 21 December 1973.
55. Ibid., 20 December 1973.
56. Ibid., 21 December 1973.
57. Ibid., 24 December 1973.
58. Ibid., 3 December 1973.
59. Ibid., 13 December 1973.
60. *Davar*, 12 December 1973.
61. *Haaretz*, 21 December 1973.
62. Ibid., 20, 25 December 1973; *Maariv*, 28 December 1973.
63. *Haaretz*, 12 December 1973.
64. Ibid., 18 December 1973.
65. *Maariv*, 18 December 1973.
66. Arian, *The Choosing People*, pp. 61-7, 130-2.
67. E. Gutmann, 'Religion in Israeli Politics' in Landau, *Man, State and Society*, pp. 122ff.
68. *Haaretz*, 14 September 1973.
69. Ibid., 14 December 1973.
70. *Davar*, 23 September 1973.
71. *Haaretz*, 14 December 1973.
72. Ibid., 23 December 1973.
73. M. Bruno. 'Tzelilut da'at ve'arafel habehirot' (Clear-mindedness and the fog of elections), Ibid., 23 December 1973.
74. Y. Ezrahi, 'Lekahim o tzeid mekhashefot' (Drawing lessons or witch-hunting), *Maariv*, 7 November 1973.
75. Ibid., 11 November 1973.
76. *Haaretz*, 12 December 1973.
77. Ibid., 12 December 1973; *Davar*, 12 December 1973.
78. *Haaretz*, 11 December 1973.
79. Ibid., 12 December 1973.
80. *Davar*, 14 December 1973.
81. *Haaretz*, 14 December 1973.
82. Ibid., 6, 19 December 1973.
83. D. Bloch 'Ein manos mikiyum habehirot behekdem' (The elections have to be held soon), *Davar*, 7 November 1973; H. Bartuv, 'Haim nealetz lehatzbi'a baraglaim?' (Shall we have to vote with our feet?), *Maariv*, 14 November 1973.
84. *Davar*, 26 November 1973.
85. Ibid., 8 November 1973.
86. Ibid., 27 November 1973; *Haaretz*, 2 December 1973.
87. D. Golomb, 'Eikh lehahazir et emun hatzibur' (How to restore public confidence), *Davar*, 28 November 1973.
88. *Maariv*, 25 November 1973.
89. *Davar*, 11 November 1973.
90. Ibid., 12 December 1973.
91. Ibid., 26 November 1973.
92. S. H. Rosenfeld, 'Be'ad mi lo lehatzbi'a' (For whom not to vote), *Maariv*, 28 November 1973.

93. M. M. Czudnowski and J. M. Landau, *The Israeli Communist Party and the Elections for the Fifth Knesset, 1961* (The Hoover Institution on War, Revolution and Peace, Stanford, California, 1965); J. M. Landau, *The Arabs in Israel: A Political Study* (Oxford University Press, London, 1969), pp. 108-55.

94. J. M. Landau, *Middle Eastern Themes: Papers in History and Politics* (Cass, London, 1973), pp. 189-97.

95. A. Mansur, 'Tzofim 'aliyya le Rakah veirida la Ma'arakh' (They predict that the new communist party will gain, and the alignment will lose, votes), *Haaretz*, 21 December 1973.

4. COMPARISONS

Jacob M. Landau

The comparison of electoral issues in various states is a difficult task. It is hardly surprising that very little of the rapidly growing psephologist literature has concentrated on this aspect of elections. This is in sharp contrast with the vast amount of material published on electoral issues in individual countries. On the British parliamentary elections, for example, there is an impressive set of nine volumes.[1] While most of these do devote some space to the issues, identification of those issues may still be risky and in some cases misleading, as the issues one reads and hears about most frequently may not necessarily be the major ones, and some may turn out to have been 'non-issues'. An intimate acquaintance with the politics of the state under discussion is indeed essential.

One reason for the scarcity of research in the area of comparison of electoral issues is that it is actually no more than a single aspect of comparing politics in different states. Students of comparative politics sometimes argue that there is little that warrants comparison in electoral issues. It is my contention that just the opposite is the case, as electoral issues could well reflect the core of both public consensus and internal discord. Moreover, the public is exposed to a great deal of campaigning; even if electoral propaganda does not always sway the vote, its issues are frequently remembered later and help in shaping public opinion and the political climate.

Another reason for the tendency of comparative psephologists to concentrate on comparing voting results or the attributes of those elected is that all these may be measured quantitatively, at least to a considerable degree. Needless to say, this is hardly the case in comparing electoral issues. Here one does not deal with figures and percentages, but rather with ideas—at least when electoral propaganda is stripped of its rhetoric. Nevertheless, any verdict on the results of an election may, in general, be as much or frequently more related to the nature of the issues presented and argued than to any other factor involved.

It is almost tautological to assert that the issues of parliamentary elections in democratic regimes are essentially those very political and socio-economic issues which are part and parcel of the political culture, as expressed in ideological arguments or pragmatic contests between elections. In any case, the issues emphasised in the heat of electoral strife are generally those which appear more pertinent to the general public on that occasion—or, at least, are so considered then by those party strategists who ought to know. That both academics and pollsters have been increasingly wondering whether electoral campaigning really influences the vote has had little impact on any party apparatus.

Most electoral campaigns in multiparty regimes are cases of in-fighting both over the government's record and policies and over the issues of the moment. Much of this is expressed in speeches, addresses over the media, handbills and newspaper articles. While the intensity of listening to or reading them is open to some doubt, their examination does give a fair idea of what the major and minor issues of a given election are and what themes are discussed with sufficient emphasis and frequency so as to render them issues. Not infrequently, public attention may shift during an electoral campaign from one issue to another, which makes overall analysis rather more complicated. The elections to the Knesset in Israel in December 1973 serve as an extreme example of this shift; much of the emphasis after the October 1973 war switched from socio-economic issues to foreign policy and external security. In general, however, most pronouncements by the same spokesmen repeat the same ideas, again and again, and it is not difficult to pinpoint the main issues in political elections, even though there are nuances in presentation by the various parties.

Differentiations in time, in one state, or in essence, among several, may then serve to better grasp the essence of political behaviour there. Each of the three states selected for examination in the current volume has exhibited a somewhat different pattern in its electoral issues. Before attempting to compare Lebanon, Turkey and Israel, by issue areas, I shall try to delineate the main trends of each pattern separately, considering them in the sequence in which the 1972-3 general elections were held in each of the three states and focusing on those major issues that warrant comparison. For clarity's sake, I shall group the main electoral issues into three categories: (i) foreign affairs and external security; (ii) socio-economic problems; (iii) ideological conflicts. All these are national issues, having a rather general bearing on the electoral campaign. At the local level, of course, the practical impact of elections is frequently non-political in nature.

The Lebanese political system is a precarious equilibrium between forces desirous of radical change and those which uphold Lebanon's continued existence. The delicate compromise between these forces survived surprisingly well during Lebanon's first thirty years as a state. Ralph Crow, in Chapter 2, doubts that the Lebanese case is based on an assumption 'that, although subject to change, there is a widespread agreement about the nature of the society, i.e. enough common ground to permit the political system, especially through elections, to provide the basis for the development of a common policy and to establish priorities for society'.

However, if one considers the first generation in the life of independent Lebanon, prior to the 1975-6 civil war, one cannot but be impressed at the large degree of national accommodation, one of whose characteristics was the following of the rules of the game punctiliously in parliamentary elections, by a people which Crow himself defines on the whole as broadly committed to constitutional government. The fact that the accommodation was between religious communities, rather than political parties, perhaps indicates a particular traditionalism/ modernisation relation, but does not materially alter a situation in which the major forces in state and society undertook to coexist on the basis of a 'gentleman's agreement'. It is no coincidence that the principal element which endangered and then shattered the shaky foundation of the Lebanese national consensus was largely an extraneous factor—the Palestinians in Lebanon, who comprise about a tenth of the entire population and have allied themselves with some of the Lebanese factions.

Some analysts have downgraded, rather exaggeratedly perhaps, the overall relevance of issues in Lebanese elections. For example, an entire book written about the 1968 elections has devoted a mere third of a page to this subject.[2] Actually, the matter is more complex. Since the results of parliamentary elections in Lebanon are predetermined, insofar as pertaining to religious communities is concerned, the national character of these elections is somewhat diluted and non-national issues predominate in the different constituencies—such as local, personal or factional ones. Nevertheless, since the 1960 elections,[3] national issues, chiefly of a political character, have had an increasingly prominent, although never dominant place in the electoral contests. It is hardly fortuitous that this trend began at that time, as a minor civil war had been fought in Lebanon some two years earlier.

Considering the electoral issues in our three-category model in order, one discovers that, in general, foreign affairs and external security have played a minor role in the public argument—except when Lebanon's future as a sovereign state was at stake; this, however, may be rather a matter of internal significance. The union of Egypt and Syria into the UAR—fifteen years after the gentleman's agreement of 1943, the National Pact, had become a basis for national accommodation—thrust the issue of Lebanon's foreign relations right into the centre of the Lebanese electoral campaign of 1960. Formerly, foreign relations with the world at large had been greatly ignored on the eve of elections, while relations with the other Arab states had been handled ritualistically ('co-operation with our sister states'), as had been the verbal attacks on Israel. However, since 1958, the pan-Arab presence of the UAR and then of the Baath Party in Syria, served as a constant reminder of the issue of Lebanon's future as a separate entity. The relevance of the problem—although not as a major electoral issue—was heightened by the activities of the Palestinian organisations in Lebanon. This, however, was more in the nature of an internal, rather than external, security matter. It was the ideological parties—more than the personal and local ones—which evidently focused on such issues as these; the Phalanges are a characteristic example.[4]

However, the main emphasis in Lebanese elections, with few exceptions, was hardly on national issues with a political content. When one disregards generally phrased slogans, more in the nature of pious wishes (such as 'love of country'), the remaining issues are usually expressed in socio-economic terms, in platforms of a largely local character, even in national elections. With the exception of such encompassing slogans as 'bolstering the economy', 'agriculture and industry' or 'stemming unemployment and inflation', much of the propaganda skilfully skirted national issues and centred on local economic ones, such as wages, prices, marketing, services and the like. Evidently the stressing of economic issues, with special emphasis on local interests, is fairly well known from other regimes which hold elections on a multi-constituency basis, including Turkey, and even from single-constituency ones such as Israel. What is especially relevant in Lebanon's case is that this emphasis is largely at the expense of issues of national significance.

In the context of issues relating to ideological conflict, that of the religious communities is of paramount importance. It is ever present in the electoral contests, but is usually underemphasised so as not to provoke hostile reactions or, in a more extreme case, violent disorder among the electorate. However, whether merely hinted at, or even not mentioned at all, the religious issue is well known to one and all in Lebanon and probably has an important share in determining how the vote goes. It is sufficient to remember that all voters, of whatever community, cast their ballots for candidates of pre-set religious affiliations. Above and beyond the formal mechanisms of parliamentary elections, the religious connection is significant enough (even for the secular-minded) to frequently draw a great deal of attention and, in many instances, to serve as the major issue leading to voting support. Of course, the personal character of the candidates and their attitudes to local issues also help in shaping the voter's decision. The varying possible combinations of those different sets of issues have made for increasing competitiveness[5] in both the electoral campaign and the voting that follows it.

The Turkish polity is very different, more homogeneous and well-established than the Lebanese. It is a consensual democracy that has survived the shock of passing from a single-party to a multiparty system after the Second World War, as well as the impact of the 1960 and 1971 military interventions. Parliamentary elections survived and increased in frequency and scope; they have indeed been more numerous (even if only the multiparty era is considered) than in either Lebanon or Israel. Between 1946 and 1957 they were held every three or four years, while since 1961—with the advent of a bicameral Grand National Assembly— they were held eight times in 14 years,[6] or about once every two years, on average. The Turks appear to have savoured each of these elections.

With such a long and active record, Turkish electoral contests have revolved around a fairly large number of issues. Again, these have reflected the issues facing Turkey as a whole. While many centred on the distinction between localism and centrism in their approach to government and society, the micro-issues were often as important as the macro-issues. This has perhaps been due not only to the greater number of electoral issues, but also to the marked variation in their character.

While, of course, emphases did shift from one election to the other, most Turkish parties referred, in the electoral context, to foreign policy issues, in one way or another—although hardly ever as their central theme—even though anti-Americanism (for example, as fostered by the Turkish Labour Party) or anti-Sovietism (as propounded by the Nationalist Action Party) were brought up with varying frequency.[7] This, however, although bearing on Turkey's foreign relations with the United States or the Soviet Union, was intimately related with internal politics, as was the stand of the National Salvation Party in 1973 for closer ties with the Muslim states.

In internal affairs, socio-economic issues appear to predominate in electoral propaganda. They were a major concern of the Republican

People's Party and the Democrat Party in the late 1940s and the 1950s; and later, other parties and groups joined the fray. Evidently the nature of these issues varied somewhat over the years, but in the 1960s they were very often related to the village-city dichotomy, housing conditions, rising prices and inflation, unemployment, speedy industrialisation, rural development and economic growth. Although the solutions proposed by electoral rivals differed, they all recognised the existence of such socio-economic issues and their far-reaching relevance, and promised some way to make income once more overtake prices, or, in other words, meet rising expectations.

Ideological issues appear increasingly important in Turkey's parliamentary elections as pointed out by Ergil (Chapter 1), and vie in overall significance with the socio-economic ones. Again, it should be stated that they vary in emphasis and content, according to the era and the party. On several points there appears to be an impressively large measure of public consensus, as on the need to return to civilian constitutional rule and to government by a parliamentary majority, following both brief military interventions and preceding the 1961 and the 1973 general elections. Otherwise, on many and possibly most political issues, a sharp ideological cleavage was in evidence,[8] transcending intellectual and bureaucratic circles and permeating the strata of business, workers and even the military establishment. Instead of the earlier precepts, be they etatist or liberal, various Marxist, socialist and 'Turkish socialist' solutions for Turkey's problems were regularly bandied about in the electoral campaigns of the 1960s and 1970s. Right-wing groups, with avowed pan-Turkish aspirations and militarist undertones, vied with the above in promising to solve political and other problems. Islamists, most recently active on an official level, have responded in turn by presenting their own panacea to all ills—a theocratic state and a society based on Islam.[9]

Not coincidentally, much of the discussion of political electoral issues in Turkey is linked to the socio-economic ones—more evidently so than in Lebanon. In the 1960s and 1970s particularly, nearly all groups have expressed their socio-economic views by relating them to their state's development and modernisation. This is perhaps less striking in the attitude of Turkey's two mass parties, for these could hardly afford to ignore socio-economics. It has also always been part and parcel of the platforms of left-of-centre groups. It is more remarkable in the case of the Nationalist Action Party, although it is true enough that contemporary right-wing parties do relate to the socio-economic needs of the population. However, it is quite unusual in the case of the

National Salvation Party, closely associating Islam and technology in its suggested treatment of all issues.

Electoral issues in Israel, despite similarities to those in Lebanon and Turkey, obviously reflect their country's special situation, particularly at the level of its armed conflict with its immediate neighbours—in which it differs greatly from both Lebanon and Turkey. Chapter 3 indicates that in all electoral contests a see-saw between external security and foreign affairs issues and socio-economic issues has been in evidence, with the 1973 parliamentary elections supplying the best example; the focus on the latter cluster of issues, before the October 1973 war, shifted to the former after that war.[10]

Israeli society is very politically alert, with the highest voting participation of the three countries under consideration. It is therefore not easy to grade sets of electoral issues by their relative importance, since this society's responses to political stimuli are more varied. Due to its fragmented, argumentative political character (resembling Lebanon to a degree and apparently more extreme than Turkey), Israel's numerous parties and groups have reacted to electoral issues in a bafflingly varied manner. Nevertheless, some conclusions may be reached even in this case by attempting to classify and discuss the issues within the context of the aforementioned three categories.

In all of Israel's electoral contests there has been a great deal of emphasis (although not always preponderantly so) on the issues relating to foreign affairs and external security. The very widely accepted connection (though not identification) between these two issues[11] is in itself suggestive of a general approach that the proper resolution of foreign relations issues would be a matter essential to Israel's security as a state. Even the Israeli communists, who have had few novel ideas concerning this argument, still have devoted a part of their electoral propaganda to this issue, repeatedly claiming that Israel's government was too concerned with external security![12] Foreign affairs indeed remained an absorbing electoral issue, reflecting much more than Israel's sensitivity about world opinion while its right to exist as a sovereign state was still contested by some. Actually, Israel's foreign relations were seen to have had implications in numerous other areas, perhaps more so than elsewhere. For example, relations with France for a decade or more meant an essential supply of military hardware and nuclear knowhow; the Reparations Agreement with the Federal Republic of Germany provided much-needed funds for the economic development of the new state and the absorption of immigrants, as did later agreements with the United States. The deepening rift with the

Soviet Union could not but affect Jewish emigration to Israel. Evidently, individuals and groups viewed such issues differently and interpreted them accordingly.

Israel's socio-economic issues resemble those of many other developing states. The fact that it has much of the know-how which others lack has only partially offset the drawback of its need for raw materials and of the urgency of investing in military preparedness. The increasing gap between the haves and the have-nots has compelled all participants in electoral campaigns to increasingly consider socio-economic issues. This applies to most parties, including the right-of-centre Herut (now the main component of the Likkud bloc). However, the religious parties appear to devote minimal attention to these issues in their electoral propaganda; in this they differ from Turkey's National Salvation Party. In Israel the following issues receive much attention: housing, wages and prices, inflation, taxes, red tape, economic growth and insufficient progress in the integration of the Oriental Jews into the fabric of Israeli society.

Within the set of issues bearing on internal ideological conflict, a rather complex situation may be perceived in the Israeli context. During the twenty-four years (1949-73) encompassing Israel's eight electoral campaigns, there has been a tapering off, not to say watering down, of the ideological fervour so evident in the pre-state and early state years. The achievement of statehood and day-to-day realities may have contributed to this process, as possibly have the hundreds of thousands of immigrants coming from other backgrounds and pressed by immediate material needs. Be that as it may, a pragmatic attitude increasingly pervaded the approach of many, perhaps most, parties to electoral campaigning; they must have sensed the general trend among the voters. Even though some marginal groups took their respective ideologies very seriously, a majority of the others brought up their own only perfunctorily, or at most as a poor second to realistic, pragmatic considerations.

A notable exception was Israel's religious parties. For them, the set of subjects revolving around the all-important issue of religion in the state predominated unequivocally. As they saw it,[13] religion ought to determine the nature of laws, education, labour relations and even the approach to external security and foreign affairs—more hawkish than not. The National Religious Party has been the only one with some real interest in social aspects; however, what has remained of primary importance to it and other religious parties and groups has been to contain the advance of secularism in the state; it was through this prism that they judged the merits of most other electoral issues.[14]

The following schematic models will illustrate some of the main points of resemblance and variance in the major electoral issues in the three states discussed. I shall begin with an attempt at an overview, to be followed by a more substantive comparison of major issues within the three categories selected.

The Relative Importance of Major Electoral Issues

	Foreign Affairs and External Security	Socio-economic Problems	Ideological Conflict
Lebanon	+	+ +	+ +
Turkey	+	+ +	+ +
Israel	+ +	+ +	+

+ Some importance
+ + Major importance

Foreign Affairs and External Security

Lebanon	Turkey	Israel
Hardly any attention to world affairs; only a sporadic interest in them, chiefly when they are liable to affect Lebanon's future and internal security. Not a real issue in Lebanese parliamentary elections. Some interest in pan-Arab affairs.	Some limited attention to world affairs, largely oriented to relations with Turkey's immediate neighbours, chiefly Greece and the Soviet Union, regarded by many as the traditional enemies. Contrariwise, anti-Americanism and opposition to Turkey's participation in NATO and CENTO. Increased co-operation with Muslim states has been raised more recently, as an electoral slogan, by the National Salvation Party.	Consistent attention to world and regional affairs. Topics of external security as an electoral issue recur in all of Israel's eight Knesset campaigns and, in several of them, hold a place of prime importance. Some groups (like Herut) have consistently considered this set of issues—chiefly security—as a national issue of life and death.

Socio-economic Problems

Lebanon	Turkey	Israel
A constant issue in electoral campaigns. While topics of national significance, such as aiding agriculture, encouraging tourism and transit commerce are mentioned, the emphasis is more on matters of immediate personal interest, such as unemployment or inflation.	A constant issue in electoral campaigns. Issues have included both topics of national significance, such as economic growth, speedy industrialisation or the development of agriculture, and of immediate personal interest, such as unemployment, inflation or housing.	A constant issue in electoral campaigns. Issues have included both topics of national significance, such as economic growth or the gap in the balance of payments, and of immediate personal interest, such as inflation or excessive taxation.

Ideological Conflict

Lebanon	Turkey	Israel
While ideological differences are not absent from electoral campaigns, many of them do not comprise real issues. When they do, they often focus on the argument of religion as a factor in Lebanese politics—practically always a major issue, whether mentioned expressly or covertly.	Ideological cleavages have always been real issues in electoral campaigns, even though their nature has changed over the years, from etatism versus private initiative in the late 1940s, to the merits of Turkish socialism and of extreme nationalism in the 1960s and, in addition, in the 1970s, to the place of religion in politics.	Ideological cleavages were real issues in the early days of the state—in the late 1940s and during the 1950s—for example, between 'left' and 'right'. In more recent years, pragmatism has somewhat eroded the status of ideology as a real electoral issue, although it is never absent from electoral platforms. Religion in politics probably remains the only major ideological issue in elections.

In comparing all three categories of electoral issues in Lebanon, Turkey and Israel, one notices both interesting similarities and relevant differences. There appear to be obvious variations of emphasis, with Lebanese elections less concerned than the Turkish, and the latter somewhat less involved than the Israeli, with national foreign relations and external security. In recent years Turkey seems much more attentive than either Lebanon or Israel in matters of ideology as a real election issue. The 1977 elections in Turkey witnessed a public debate, following a long sequence of violent incidents, about the tightening of law and order at the expense of individual freedoms. An exception is the controversy over religion in politics, which is still more of an issue in Lebanon and Israel (in this order) than in Turkey. Socio-economic subjects are very relevant as major electoral issues in all three states, but their nature varies. For example, both Lebanon and Israel have serious problems in integrating their various ethnic groups; in Turkey this has hardly been an electoral issue. Lebanon and Turkey suffer from unemployment—a real electoral issue in both—and both have had to export a part of their manpower; there is no joblessness in Israel, which has even been importing labour recently.

An analysis of the issues shows the best and the worst of a given electoral campaign—and much more besides. If there is any lesson to be learned from comparing electoral issues among states, it is that there are so many intangibles that the final conclusions are difficult and at best hazardous. This seems particularly apt in cases where there are covert issues clouding the overall perspective, for example (in our special case) the problem of self-identification or the personal rivalries between politicians in Lebanon, the centre-periphery cleavage or the role of the military in national decision-making in Turkey, and the intergeneration struggle within the political leadership in Israel. Briefly, the openly discussed campaign issues are not necessarily identical with the latent, frequently broader national issues. In the three states under discussion, the gap between these two sets of issues is deeper in Lebanon than in either Turkey or Israel.

Evidently the issues brought up in electoral contests tend to highlight divisiveness and conflict among rival parties and groups, rather than public consensus and national accommodation. Characteristically Lebanon, which has presented a mild form of dissension in the issues debated in its electoral campaigns, has disintegrated as a state unit, while Turkey and Israel, where electoral issues have been argued over much more heatedly and aggressively, have somehow got over the controversies after each voting day. This should not be taken to mean that the electoral issues and the in-fighting over them do not reflect national politics in these states. They do indeed, but they reflect mainly the then current climate and political culture, as well as the readiness to compromise in varying degrees. Clashing political ideologies and rival socio-economic interests, vociferously expressed in parliamentary elections in all three states, have dented public consensus, but not disrupted it permanently, except in Lebanon, of late. In Turkey and Israel, on the other hand, the spirit of compromise over national issues has survived, thanks to a feeling for the general community of interests, which has failed Lebanon.   In other words, the issue emphasis in Lebanese elections was largely artificial and the elections themselves solved nothing essential, while in Turkey and Israel they served as a safety-valve, giving hope of solving at least some of the more relevant issues.

Notes

1. The latest of which is D. Butler and D. Kavanagh, *The British General Election of February 1974* (Macmillan, London, 1974).

2. J. Zuwiyya, *The Parliamentary Elections of Lebanon, 1968* (Brill, Leiden, 1972).

3. J. M. Landau, 'Elections in Lebanon', *Western Political Quarterly*, vol. 14, no. 1 (1961), p. 135.

4. F. Stoakes, 'The Supervigilantes: The Lebanese Kataeb Party as a Builder, Surrogate and Defender of the State', *Middle Eastern Studies*, vol. 2, no. 3 (1975), pp. 215-36.

5. M. Hudson, *The Precarious Republic* (Random House, New York, 1968), pp. 225-31.

6. In 1961, 1973 and 1977 to the Grand National Assembly and the Senate; in 1965 and 1969 to the Grand National Assembly alone; in 1964, 1966, 1968 and 1975 to the Senate alone.

7. J. M. Landau, *Radical Politics in Modern Turkey* (Brill, Leiden, 1974), pp. 26ff, 229.

8. K. H. Karpat (ed.), *Political and Social Thought in the Contemporary Middle East* (Pall Mall Press, London, 1968), pp. 297ff.

9. J. M. Landau, 'The National Salvation Party in Turkey', *Asian and African Studies*, vol. 11, no. 1 (1976), pp. 1-57.

10. E. Torgovnik, 'The Election Campaign : Party Needs and Voter Concerns' in A. Arian (ed.), *The Elections in Israel—1973* (Jerusalem Academic Press, Jerusalem, 1975), pp. 59-93.

11. There is a single Knesset subcommittee for foreign relations and security, to deal jointly with both areas.

12. J. M. Landau, 'Israel' in R. F. Staar (ed.), *Yearbook on International Communist Affairs 1976* (The Hoover Institution for War, Revolution and Peace, Stanford, California, 1976), pp. 546-50.

13. S. N. Eisenstadt, *Israeli Society* (Weidenfeld and Nicolson, London, 1967), pp. 309-20.

14. E. Marmorstein, *Heaven at Bay: The Jewish Kulturkampf* (Oxford University Press, London, 1969).

PART II

Voting Behaviour

5. TURKEY

Ergun Özbudun

Introduction

As in most modernising societies, old and new live side by side in Turkey without being fully integrated. This is true for political as well as many other aspects of social behaviour. Thus, in what may be called the 'modern sector', we observe an essentially two-party competition, high levels of political institutionalisation, political information, political awareness and organisational involvement, as well as an autonomous, instrumental and increasingly class-based pattern of political participation. Conversely, in the 'traditional sector', political parties play a much less significant role, and an essentially personalistic style of politics predominates. Party loyalties are weaker and voting behaviour is characterised by sudden and erratic changes from one election to the next, owing to deep personal influences. Independent candidates and minor parties receive a much larger share of votes. Political participation, lacking a sufficient attitudinal and organisational base, tends to be mobilised, deferential and communally based. Furthermore, there seems to be a strong association between the level of socio-economic modernity and these different patterns of political behaviour. The aim of this chapter is to probe the relationships between socio-economic modernisation, political participation and political institutionalisation in Turkey.

The present analysis relies mainly, although not exclusively, on 1973 election data. Apart from being the most recent general elections in Turkey at the time of writing, these elections deserve to be carefully analysed for more substantive reasons: the 1973 Turkish elections bear many marks of a 'critical realignment', as defined by W. D. Burnham.[1] These elections marked the end of the long conservative domination (by the Democrat Party in the 1950s and the Justice Party (JP) in the 1960s) in Turkish politics, the JP dropping from the 46.5 per cent it had won in 1969 to 29.8 per cent, and from 256 seats to 149. The 'left-of-centre' Republican People's Party (RPP), by contrast, emerged as the strongest party, with 33.3 per cent of the votes and 185 of the 450 seats at stake, compared with 27.4 per cent and 143 seats in the 1969 election. The two newest parties, the Democratic Party (DP, a conservative offshoot from the JP) and the National Salvation Party (NSP, an Islamic-oriented party defending the interests of the small Anatolian business-men and merchants) each gained nearly 12 per cent of the vote and just under 50 seats apiece. The other minor parties, all conservative with the single exception of the Turkish Unity Party (TUP), won extremely small percentages of the vote and only a handful of seats (see Table 5.1).

Thus, while the total proportion of votes for all right-wing parties combined was still about two-thirds in 1973, it is noteworthy that the RPP registered a gain of nearly 6 per cent of the total votes cast, its first gain since 1957 and highest percentage of votes since 1961. Further-more, the party's upward trend continued after the 1973 elections. In the October 1975 elections for one-third of the Senate membership, the RPP received 43.4 per cent of the vote in the 25 provinces where such elections were held. A more detailed analysis of the changing electoral fortunes of the JP and the RPP suggests that such changes were not merely the result of the movements of the floating vote at the centre, but were associated with a major realignment in the mass coalitional bases of the major parties, a phenomenon most clearly visible in the big cities.

Other characteristics of eras of critical realignment were also present in Turkish politics in the early 1970s. The 1973 election campaign and its aftermath witnessed an increasing ideological polarisa-tion between the major parties, and the issue distances between them became 'exceptionally large by normal standards'. The major third-party revolts preceding the elections (especially that of the NSP) revealed the incapacity of 'politics as usual' to aggregate and integrate emergent political demands. Finally, there is little question that the present realignment is 'associated with abnormal stress in the socio-economic system'.[2]

Signs of such realignment had already been detected in the 1969 elections.[3] The 1973 elections, as well as the 1975 elections for one-third of the Senate, confirmed and magnified these trends. One can conclude, therefore, that the 1969 election was not an aberration, but rather marked the beginning of important new secular trends in the Turkish party system. Such political changes are closely associated with the rapid socio-economic modernisation that Turkish society is currently undergoing.

To test this hypothesis, we have employed methods of 'ecological

Table 5.1: *Voting Participation and Party Votes, 1965-75 (in Percentages)*

Year	Voting Participation	JP	RPP	RRP	DP	NP	NAP	NSP	TUP	TLP	NTP	Ind.
1965*	71.3	52.9	28.7	-	-	6.3	2.2	-	-	3.0	3.7	3.2
1969*	64.3	46.5	27.4	6.6	-	3.2	3.0	-	2.8	2.7	2.2	5.6
1973*	66.8	29.8	33.3	5.3	11.9	0.6	3.4	11.8	1.1	-	-	2.8
1975**	58.4	40.8	43.4	-	3.1	-	3.2	8.9	0.5	-	-	0.05

* Results of elections to the National Assembly (lower house).
** Results of the elections for one-third of the Senate membership held in 25 provinces.
Abbreviations: JP, Justice Party; RPP, Republican People's Party; RRP, Republican Reliance Party; DP, Democratic Party; NP, Nation Party; NAP, Nationalist Action Party; NSP, National Salvation Party; TUP, Turkish Unity Party; TLP, Turkish Labour Party (banned by the Constitutional Court in 1971); NTP, New Turkey Party (merged with the JP in 1973); Ind., Independents.

voting analysis', correlating voting data with socio-economic data pertaining to the 67 provinces of Turkey. Although results of a similar analysis for 1969 have been presented elsewhere,[4] they are reproduced here to enable the reader to compare them with the 1973 results. Admittedly, this type of analysis has certain disadvantages, as well as some advantages, compared to survey methods. First of all, it deals only with voting participation to the exclusion of other forms or modes of political participation, such as campaign activities, talking about politics, contacting local and national officials etc. Secondly, it does not allow us either to enquire into the motivations of the voters (except by way of inference) or to introduce other psychological 'intervening variables' between the information about the ecological characteristics and the recorded aggregate political behaviour. Finally, the much emphasised dangers of 'ecological fallacy' come readily to mind in this type of analysis. However, our focus in the present study is on political participation as a systemic property (i.e. the ways in which the nature and amount of participation in a political system affect the functioning of that system), rather than on the underlying psychological processes by which individuals become politically active. Hence, our reliance upon the ecological approach should not severely limit the scope of the present analysis.

Dependent Variables: Political Participation and Political Institutionalisation

In this study, our 'dependent' political variables are political participation and political institutionalisation.[5] The amount of political participation is measured mainly by the rates of voting turnout. However, voting data may also provide us with other, if less direct, measures of political participation. By observing the distribution of votes among parties, we can make certain inferences about the nature, motives and social bases of political participation. For example, strong support for the left parties in low-income areas may suggest a high degree of class-based and instrumental participation. Strong correlations between religion or ethnicity on the one hand, and preference for a certain political party on the other, may be indicative of communal-based and solidary participation. High levels of support for independent candidates can be taken as an indicator of mobilised and deferential participation.

Similarly, several indicators of political institutionalisation can be constructed from voting data. Here, following S. P. Huntington,[6] we define political institutionalisation as increasing adaptability, complexity, autonomy and coherence of political organisations and procedures. As Huntington argues, older organisations and procedures tend to be more adaptable and, consequently, more institutionalised than the newer ones: 'the longer an organisation or procedure has been in existence, the higher the level of institutionalisation'.[7] In the Turkish context, the oldest political parties are the RPP which dates back to 1923, and the Democrat Party which was founded in 1945 (the JP is nothing but its continuation). These two parties have shown their adaptability not only by their sheer 'chronological age', but also by the fact that they both have surmounted the problem of peaceful succession in leadership, and both have survived major functional changes: they both have shifted several times between government and opposition; the RPP has shifted from the status of an unchallenged single party to that of a competitive one; it experienced a major ideological reorientation in the late 1960s; the Democrat Party has survived (under the new name of the JP) a military coup staged against it and the execution or imprisonment of hundreds of its leaders. Conversely, all minor parties have a much shorter average life. Thus, the combined vote for the RPP and the JP can be taken as a measure of political institutionalisation in Turkey.

If political institutionalisation is conceived in terms of 'autonomy', again the RPP and the JP seem to be the most highly institutionalised Turkish parties. In fact, they are not only the oldest Turkish parties, but also the only *major* parties' far outranking all their competitors in terms of voting and parliamentary strength. As Huntington has already pointed out, 'Political institutionalisation, in the sense of autonomy, means the development of political organisations and procedures that are not simply expressions of the interests of particular social groups... A political party, for instance, that expresses the interests of only one group in society—whether labor, business, or farmers—is less autonomous than one that articulates and aggregates the interests of several social groups.'[8] Hence, by definition, major parties tend to be more autonomous and more highly institutionalised than minor parties.

Finally, if political institutionalisation is measured by the criterion of 'coherence', once more the RPP and the JP outrank their competitors. Our study of party cohesion in the National Assembly in the 1960s has shown that both parties attained a higher level of cohesion than the minor parties, among which only the Turkish Labour Party (TLP) had a degree of cohesion comparable to that of the major parties.[9]

If the combined major-party vote is taken as an indicator of political institutionalisation in Turkey, then the vote for minor parties and independents is associated with low levels of political institutionalisation. In other words, the more fractionalised the vote is, the lower the level of political institutionalisation.[10] Here, party system fractionalisation is measured by Douglas Rae's index of fractionalisation which is written as follows:[11]

$$F_e = 1 - (\sum_{i=1}^{n} T_i^2)$$

In this formula, derived from probability statistics, T_i is equal to any party's decimal share of the vote. Thus, in a perfect one-party system F_e equals zero; the more the vote is dispersed among competing parties, the more F_e approaches, but never reaches, one. Under a perfect two-party system (i.e. 50-50 split), F_e equals 0.5. The model is sensitive to both the number and the relative equality of the party shares. Consequently, 'two non-identical systems may, both conceptually and operationally, have the same level of fractionalisation. One might have more parties competing on rather unequal terms, while another equally fractionalised system might have fewer parties competing on more nearly equal terms'.[12]

Another 'negative' indicator of political institutionalisation is the level of support for independent candidates. Independents, by definition, lack an institutionalised base of electoral support, and independent representatives within legislative assemblies, again by definition, do not constitute an institutionalised political organisation. Furthermore, a high proportion of votes garnered by independents demonstrates the incapacity of the party system to articulate and/or aggregate interests.

Ideally, one more measure of political institutionalisation, or rather deinstitutionalisation, could have been constructed from voting data. It can be argued that where political institutionalisation is low, voting behaviour is characterised by sudden and erratic fluctuations in party votes. In other words, party loyalties tend to be weak, and voters tend to shift their allegiances from one party to another under the personal influence of local notables. This type of electoral behaviour is indeed characteristic of some of the least developed regions in Turkey. The magnitude of such shifts can be measured as one-half of the sum of the absolute differences between the shares (v_i) of all parties (K) at time $(t + 1)$ and time t, or by the formula:[13]

$$D(t) = 1/2 \sum_{i=1}^{K} | V_i(t + 1) - V_i(t) |$$
$$O \leq D(t) \leq 1.00$$

While this is a useful measure of deinstitutionalisation of the party system, it does not differentiate between two types of shifts in party votes. One, as described above, is conceptually and empirically associated with low political institutionalisation. But the second may reflect secular changes in the cleavage structure of a society and in its voter alignments. In that sense it may represent a movement toward higher levels of political institutionalisation in the long run. At the moment Turkey seems to be witnessing simultaneously the two types of shifts in different parts of the country. In the more modernised regions, and especially in the big cities, we observe a major voter realignment which results in substantial shifts in party votes. In the least modernised regions, on the other hand, party shifts are usually associated with local, personal and temporary factors. Thus, one single measure of 'deinstitutionalisation' would fail to give an accurate picture of the current situation in Turkey.

Independent Variables: Indicators of Socio-economic Modernisation

This study is concerned with the ways in which socio-economic modernisation affects political participation and political institutionalisation through voting behaviour. To this end, we have chosen 16 indicators of socio-economic modernisation on which province-level data are available.

Urbanisation (URB)

Since Turkish election statistics provide an urban-rural breakdown, it is possible to compare directly the voting behaviour in urban and rural areas. Here, 10,000 population is accepted as the cut-off point, as is commonly the case in most Turkish urban studies. In addition, voting data enable us to study the impact on electoral behaviour of 'city size' and of 'residential context' (i.e. the socio-economic status of the urban neighbourhood). The results of such an analysis will be presented later.[14] In the following multivariate analysis provincial urbanisation is defined as the percentage of provincial population living in communities with more than 10,000 inhabitants.[15] In both cases, two provincial capitals with less than 10,000 population have been included in the urban category.[16]

Males in Manufacturing Industry (MANIND)

This has been calculated as percentage of the active male population of 15 years old and over, on the basis of the 1965 Census. Due to the small number of females in manufacturing industry (a total of 77,419 in 1965) only males have been included.[17]

Location Quotient (LQ)
This index, used by the Turkish State Planning Organisation, measures the concentration of the manufacturing industry, based on the 1965 industrial survey.[18]

Total Population/Population under Social Security (SOCSEC)
The expansion of social security arrangements is an indication of the extent to which important social functions are taken over by secondary groups, and are no longer performed mainly within the context of primary social relations. Provincial scores are calculated by dividing the total provincial population by the number of people under social security. Thus, this indicator has taken an anti-developmental character. In other words, higher provincial scores mean lower levels of development.[19]

Value Added per Person (VALADD)
This indicator of industrialisation has been computed by dividing the total value added in manufacturing industry (in both public and private sectors) by total provincial population.[20]

Literacy (LIT)
This is the percentage of literate population of six years old and over.[21]

Total Population/Number of Radio Receivers (RADIOS)
As with social security, provincial scores have been calculated by dividing the total provincial population by the number of radio receivers in the province. Therefore, this indicator is also anti-developmental in character.[22]

Total Population/All Associations (ALLASS)
Multiplication and development of voluntary associations is an important aspect of the overall process of social modernisation. As has been empirically demonstrated, organisational involvement is one of the two principal channels, or intervening variables, through which socio-economic development affects political participation.[23] Ideally, this indicator should have measured the proportion of provincial population active in one or more voluntary associations. Unfortunately, membership figures are not available for most associations. We therefore had to substitute the present, and admittedly less satisfactory, one which is found by dividing total provincial population by the *number* of all voluntary associations active in that province. For reasons stated above, this indicator also has an anti-developmental character.[24]

Total Population/Religious Associations (RELASS)
This is calculated by dividing the total provincial population by the number of religious associations (i.e. those for building or repairing mosques, for promoting Koran education, and associations of religious functionaries etc.) active in that province. It is hoped that this indicator would measure, in addition to organisational involvement as stated above, the saliency of religion in a province.[25]

Total Population/Modern Associations (MODASS)
Here, the total provincial population is divided by the number of all associations excluding religious associations active in the province.[26]

Agricultural Product per Family (PROFAM)
This is calculated by dividing gross agricultural product by the number of agricultural families in each province, and provides a measure of the productivity of labour in the agricultural sector.[27]

Agricultural Product per Decare (PRODEC)
This is calculated by dividing gross agricultural product by the area cultivated (in decares) in each province, and provides a measure of the productivity of the land.[28]

Share of Cereals in Agricultural Product (CEREALS)
This is the percentage share of cereals in gross agricultural product. In the Turkish context, this can be taken as a negative indicator of agricultural development.[29]

GINI Concentration Ratio (GINI)
This ratio measures the concentration of agricultural holdings.[30]

Landless Families (LANDFAM)
This is the percentage of landless families in communities with less than 5,000 population. This category includes agricultural labourers and non-farming rural population, but excludes tenants and sharecroppers.[31]

Disappropriation Ratio (DISAPP)
This is the total of landless families, families engaged only in animal husbandry, families owning less than half of the land they cultivate, and families renting or sharecropping all of the land they cultivate, as percentage of all rural families.[32]

Urban-rural Differences in Electoral Behaviour

Table 5.2 demonstrates significant urban-rural differences in Turkish electoral behaviour. For one thing, the results of the 1973 elections

Table 5.2: Urban Residence, City Size and Electoral Behaviour, 1973

City Size*	Number of Registered Voters (Thousands)	Voting Participation (%)	JP (%)	RPP (%)	RRP (%)	DP (%)	NP (%)	NAP (%)	NSP (%)	TUP (%)	IND. (%)
Over 500,000 N = 3	2,695.8	62.8	29.2	49.1	2.7	6.4	0.4	1.9	8.1	1.5	0.7
100,000–500,000 N = 17	1,362.1	62.3	26.5	37.6	3.1	9.3	0.3	3.0	17.2	1.2	1.7
50,000–100,000 N = 20	652.4	62.1	36.5	37.7	2.3	9.6	0.5	3.5	9.2	0.7	0.3
25,000–50,000 N = 56	890.1	63.4	30.5	33.5	6.1	11.1	0.3	4.1	11.7	0.7	2.2
10,000–25,000 N = 140	939.1	63.4	32.6	35.8	4.0	10.6	0.4	3.4	10.0	0.5	2.6
All Urban	6,539.5	62.7 (+6.4)**	30.0 (−17.5)	41.6 (+8.8)	3.4 (−0.4)	8.6	0.4 (−2.3)	2.8 (0.0)	10.8	1.1 (−1.6)	1.4 (−1.7)
All Rural	10,258.7	69.4 (+1.3)**	29.7 (−16.4)	28.5 (+3.2)	6.3 (−1.3)	13.8	0.7 (−2.7)	3.7 (+0.6)	12.4	1.1 (−1.8)	3.7 (−2.9)

* City populations are based on the 1970 Census.
** Figures in parentheses refer to the percentage differences between the 1969 and the 1973 figures.

confirm our earlier observation[33] that the rates of voting turnout are higher in the rural areas than in the cities. This phenomenon requires an explanation, since Turkish urbanites seem to surpass their rural compatriots in terms of socio-economic (i.e. higher socio-economic status), organisational (i.e. greater organisational involvement) and attitudinal (i.e. higher levels of political information and awareness) concomitants of political participation. For example, a public opinion poll carried out in the province of Ankara just prior to the 1975 Senate elections established that, as opposed to 63.4 per cent of the old urbanites and 36.4 per cent of the *gecekondu*-dwellers (recent urban migrants), only 14.5 per cent of the villagers could recognise the emblems of all political parties. Similarly, the same poll revealed that 54.1 per cent of the city population of Ankara, as opposed to 14.5 per cent of the villagers, was exposed to all three types of mass media (newspapers, radio and TV). The percentage of respondents with no mass-media exposure was 0.6 in the city, and 11.8 in the villages etc.[34]

Why then do we have lower rates of voting participation in Turkish cities? One plausible answer to this question may lie in the distinction between 'autonomous' and 'mobilised' political participation.[35] In the urban centres, where voting is largely an autonomous act, some voters may simply lack the motivation to go to the polls. In certain under-developed rural areas, on the other hand, large numbers of peasants may be mobilised or induced to vote by their traditional leaders (tribal chiefs, clan heads, religious leaders or wealthy landlords). Abadan-Unat's 1975 survey lent further support to this hypothesis. Thus, 94.2 per cent of their urban Ankara respondents, as compared to 71.5 per cent of rural respondents, claimed that they made their voting decisions independently; of the latter, 15.8 per cent cited their husbands as the source of influence on such decisions, and another 8.1 per cent cited members of their families. Obviously, Ankara is not among the less developed Turkish provinces. One would therefore expect such mobilised voting patterns to be much more widespread in the rural parts of the least developed eastern regions. Actually, urban-rural differences in voting turnout are greatest in these regions.

The results of a region-level analysis which we have presented elsewhere[36] also support this exception. There we observed that both in the 1969 and the 1973 elections the three least developed eastern regions (south-eastern, north-eastern, and the east-central regions) had the highest rates of turnout, standing clearly above the national average.

The urban-rural difference in voting participation is 6.7 percentage points in 1973, as compared to 11.8 in 1969. In other words, the turnout gap seems to have narrowed. This may be due to the highly ideological and polarised nature of the 1973 election campaign, which plausibly aroused greater interest in the cities. Furthermore, if higher rural turnout rates in Turkey are indeed a function of socio-economic underdevelopment, then we would expect the gap to narrow, if not to disappear completely, with increasing modernisation. In fact, in most modernised nations, urban turnout rates tend to be higher than the rural ones.

With regard to party votes, we also observe some significant differences between urban and rural areas. In the 1960s the JP, despite its common image as a rural-based party, did better in the cities than in the countryside. However, between 1965 and 1969, as well as between 1969 and 1973, the JP lost proportionately more votes in urban areas, or held on better in rural regions. Thus, in 1973 there was almost no difference between the party's urban and rural percentages of votes.

As for the RPP, its urban strength exceeded its rural strength throughout the 1960s, but the difference became marked only in the 1969 elections, the RPP gaining some votes in the cities but losing further ground in the villages. In 1973, the urban-rural gap in the RPP votes widened to an impressive 13.1 percentage points. Between 1969 and 1973, the RPP increased both its urban and rural votes. But while its rural gains were rather small (3.2 per cent of the total valid votes cast), its urban gains were much more significant (8.8 per cent).

Of the two medium-sized parties, the DP performed distinctly better in rural areas, thereby lending some support to the argument which attributes the split of the DP to the discontent of the landowning elements within the JP. However, the rapid erosion of the DP strength since 1973 and the shift of most of the DP supporters back to the JP in the 1975 Senate elections suggest that not much sociological significance should be read into the DP split. The urban-rural difference in the NSP vote, on the other hand, was much smaller, indicating that religious conservatism in Turkey is not peculiar to rural areas. The other minor parties (with the single exception of the TUP) and the independents also garnered higher percentages of votes in rural areas.

Table 5.2 also provides information on the impact of the city size on electoral behaviour. It appears that turnout rates are not appreciably affected by city size. Smaller towns (10,000-50,000 population) have slightly higher turnout rates; but the difference between them and the larger cities is negligible. On the other hand, city size seems to be a source of variation in the distribution of party votes. The JP's strongest category is medium-sized cities (50,000-100,000 population). This is consistent with our findings for 1965 and our characterisation of the JP as the party of the modernising periphery.[37] The RPP, by contrast, is clearly ahead in the three major metropolitan centres with almost half of the total vote. In fact, one of the most interesting features of the 1973 elections, to which we shall return later, is that the RPP has clearly established its domination in such centres. The party was comparatively weaker in smaller towns; nevertheless, in all urban categories it received more votes than it did in the villages.

Among the minor parties, there seems to be a clear negative correlation between the DP vote and the size of the city. The DP vote shows an almost perfect progression from the large cities to small towns, with the exception of the 10,000-25,000 population category. The NAP and the independents display essentially the same pattern, while the TUP strength is positively associated with city size. The pattern for the NSP is much more complicated. The party performed rather poorly, compared to its national and urban average, in the three largest cities, but showed its best performance in the category immediately below (100,000-500,000 population) with an impressive 17.2 per cent of the total valid votes cast. One suspects, however, that what is involved here is a regional phenomenon, rather than the impact of community size. Thus, the NSP's particular strength in this category is due to its extraordinarily high percentage of votes in certain cities, most of which happen to be in one of the three eastern regions (Urfa, 43.5 per cent; Maraş, 41.1 per cent; Sivas, 38.2 per cent; Erzurum, 34.2 per cent; Malatya, 31.8 per cent; Elazığ, 26.6 per cent; Diyarbakır, 19.5 per cent). One may conclude, therefore, that the NSP vote does not show a clear association with community size.

Electoral Behaviour in Major Cities: Urban Migration, Class and Party

This section deals with the electoral behaviour of low-income groups in major Turkish cities. Since a substantial majority of the urban poor in Turkey are recent migrants to the cities, we shall thus be able to study the effects of urban migration on the electoral behaviour of the migrants. In fact, those rural-to-urban migrants are probably most profoundly exposed to the effects of social change and, therefore, pose some of the most intriguing problems for comparative research in developing countries, as attested by the fast-growing literature on the subject. Finally, focusing on urban migrants enables us to study the relationship between mobility and electoral behaviour, since urban migration in Turkey involves not only geographical mobility, but very often social mobility as well.

Recent rural-to-urban migrants in Turkey usually reside in neighbourhoods called *gecekondu*. The word *gecekondu* (literally meaning 'built overnight') has sometimes been used to denote those houses built on illegally invaded land and sometimes, as is done in this study, to include all low-standard, unsanitary houses which lack adequate urban services and were built recently in or around large cities. Keleş[38] estimates that the proportion of *gecekondu*-dwellers among the total city population in the five largest cities is 65 per cent in Ankara, 45 per cent in İstanbul, 35 per cent in İzmir, 45 per cent in Adana, and 25 per cent in Bursa.

Turkish election statistics since 1961 have provided breakdowns at the village level in rural areas and at the 'poll district' (*seçim sandığı*) level in the cities, the latter comprising approximately 300 registered voters and a relatively small geographical area. Thus, it is possible to delimit the *gecekondu* neighbourhoods, and to compare their rates of voting turnout and party preferences with those of the middle-income or high-income precincts. In the present study, I have carried out this analysis for the three largest metropolitan centres, namely İstanbul, Ankara and İzmir. In classifying the precincts (*mahalle*) of İzmir, I relied upon a recent study by Keleş[39] who applied a modified version of Shevky and Bell's social area analysis to İzmir.[40] Keleş distinguished four types of social areas in İzmir, roughly representing upper-middle-class, middle-class, lower-middle-class and lower-class (*gecekondu*) precincts. Based on such information, the present analysis was able to cover 80 per cent of all registered voters in the İzmir metropolitan area.

Our knowledge of the Ankara precincts is less complete, although the *gecekondu* areas and the predominantly lower-middle-class precincts of 'old Ankara'[41] have been carefully studied by Yasa and Keleş, respectively.[42] Regrettably, we do not have comparable data on the middle-class and upper-middle-class precincts. However, on the basis of somewhat more impressionistic classifications[43] we were able to select a number of such precincts and to maintain our fourfold breakdown. All told, some 50 per cent of all registered voters in Ankara are covered by our analysis. We are least fortunate with respect to İstanbul, since no comparable studies exist on the social ranks of İstanbul precincts. We therefore had to follow the less satisfactory procedure of selecting some known *gecekondu* neighbourhoods (in this case, they are Eyüp, Zeytinburnu, and Gazi Osman Paşa counties, all of which are predominantly *gecekondu* areas) and comparing their voting patterns with those of the city as a whole.

Tables 5.3, 5.4 and 5.5 clearly demonstrate that voting turnout rates were relatively uniform within the cities in all three national elections studied (those of 1965, 1969 and 1973). It seems that socio-economic status and the type of neighbourhood do not significantly affect voting participation of the Turkish urban-dwellers and that the *gecekondu* residents vote as often as the highest income groups. This finding is supported by the results of Karpat's[44] recent survey among the İstanbul *gecekondu*-dwellers: a large majority of his respondents (81 per cent of the men and 63 per cent of the women) said that they were regular voters in all elections, and similar percentages (85 and 66 respectively) stated their belief in the importance of voting. By all indications, they value 'democracy' highly and see political parties as useful instruments. A not very small proportion of them (14 per cent of the males) were registered as members in a political party. This party membership figure compares favourably with that found by Frey and Mardin[45] in their survey of electoral attitudes in the predominantly middle-class community of Yenimahalle, Ankara (9 per cent of the household heads).

Just as the rates of voting turnout were relatively uniform within the cities, so were the changes in turnout (the decline between 1965 and 1969, and the rise between 1969 and 1973). In both cases, the type of urban community did not appear to have a significant impact on

Table 5.3: Voting and the Type of Urban Community: Istanbul

Election	Type of Community	Number of Registered Voters (Thousands)	Voting Participation (%)	JP (%)	RPP (%)
1965	*Gecekondu*	144.0	64.6	62.4	19.1
	All Istanbul*	912.9	63.6	52.0	30.4
1969	*Gecekondu*	164.4	51.0	53.8	21.8
	All Istanbul*	1,085.8	51.5	46.3	34.9
	Municipality	896.0	51.7	45.4	36.6
1973	*Gecekondu*	247.5	61.8	26.7	47.5
	Municipality	1,291.4	60.3	28.0	50.3

* 'All Istanbul' figures include the population of those communities which are, from a sociological point of view, an integral part of the city even though some of them remain outside the municipal boundaries of Istanbul. The municipal figures, on the other hand, represent a somewhat better approximation of the non-*gecekondu* areas.

Table 5.4: Voting and the Type of Urban Community: Ankara

Election	Type of Community	Number of Registered Voters (Thousands)	Voting Participation (%)	JP (%)	RPP (%)
1965	*Gecekondu*	88.8	69.8	52.5	25.8
	Lower-middle class	27.1	68.5	48.7	31.8
	Middle class	33.7	67.8	27.4	53.1
	Upper-middle class	19.0	69.5	26.8	54.1
1969	*Gecekondu*	85.2	59.7	43.4	30.1
	Lower-middle class	23.5	55.7	47.1	32.5
	Middle class	59.8	59.8	24.8	60.4
	Upper-middle class	29.2	60.0	25.8	60.1
1973	*Gecekondu*	99.0	65.7	27.7	45.9
	Lower-middle class	18.9	62.2	32.4	41.9
	Middle class	55.3	67.8	21.8	62.6
	Upper-middle class	33.3	68.4	24.9	57.2

changes in voting turnout. To put it differently, the major Turkish cities, both within and among themselves, seem to display a rather uniform electoral behaviour with respect to voting turnout. Our analysis does not support an earlier observation by Abadan-Unat and Yücekök[46] on the 1961-5 period that depoliticisation (decline in participation) was most marked among the urban middle classes.

Our data also present clear evidence for an ongoing realignment in the Turkish party system. Students of *gecekondu* politics in Turkey have often observed that the JP received disproportionately more votes from the *gecekondu* areas.[47] Our figures for the 1965 and the 1969 elections clearly supported this observation. Such predominant lower-class support for a conservative party may, at first glance, seem paradoxical. Yet, in view of the substantial social mobility displayed by the urban migrants, it is hardly surprising that they give their support to a party which they perceive as instrumental in bringing about this change. Furthermore, the JP's domination of the national and most of the municipal governments may also have helped the party in the *gecekondu*

Table 5.5: *Voting and the Type of Urban Community: Izmir*

Election	Type of Community	Number of Registered Voters (Thousands)	Voting Participation (%)	JP (%)	RPP (%)
1965	*Gecekondu*	38.6	69.4	72.1	17.0
	Lower-middle class	57.6	72.0	73.4	17.4
	Middle class	70.8	71.2	65.9	25.6
	Upper-middle class	66.7	70.6	54.1	36.5
1969	*Gecekondu*	50.2	58.7	60.7	22.6
	Lower-middle class	75.8	61.2	61.3	25.7
	Middle class	58.6	59.3	58.9	32.3
	Upper-middle class	88.5	59.1	46.8	43.9
1973	*Gecekondu*	49.9	66.1	36.5	44.2
	Lower-middle class	92.7	68.7	41.9	44.1
	Middle class	80.5	64.0	42.7	44.4
	Upper-middle class	119.0	65.4	37.8	50.4

areas, which are particularly vulnerable to government reprisals and highly dependent upon its favours.

However, this picture changed completely in the 1973 elections. In fact, one of the most noteworthy characteristics of the 1973 elections is the shift in big-city votes. Although the JP lost votes across the country between 1969 and 1973, it seems that it lost most heavily in the large cities. The RPP, by contrast, has substantially increased its urban strength in this period, and a major part of this gain seems to have come from the urban lower classes.

In contrast to the JP, the RPP had performed very poorly in the *gecekondu* areas prior to 1973. This should have been rather disappointing for a party which has, for some years, been making a determined effort to win the support of urban and rural lower classes by its new 'left-of-centre' approach. As of 1969, it appeared that this strategy could not yet overcome the party's old image as the party of the rich, educated, cosmopolitan urban groups. In fact, the RPP did much better in the middle-class and upper-middle-class precincts than in the *gecekondu* areas in the 1965 and 1969 elections. However, the 1969 elections gave some indications of the beginnings of a realignment in the party system: the JP losses in the *gecekondu* neighbourhoods between 1965 and 1969 far exceeded those in the other urban neighbourhoods. On the other hand, relatively few of such lower-class JP defectors had switched to the RPP, as can be seen in the very modest RPP gains in such precincts. It appears that some of the urban poor who were disenchanted with the conservative socio-economic policies of the JP governments either voted for one of the minor parties or did not vote at all in 1969. This also explains the decline in voting participation between 1965 and 1969.

The pattern in 1973 is much more pronounced than in 1969. Not only was the JP base of support among urban lower classes substantially eroded, but also this time there was a far greater amount of direct switching from the JP to the RPP. While the RPP retained and increased its former middle-class and upper-middle-class support in the cities, its most spectacular gains came from the urban poor. In the three *gecekondu* communities in İstanbul, for example, the RPP more than doubled its votes while the JP lost half of its own (Table 5.3). Thus, the 1973 elections continued and accelerated the process of realignment which had already started in 1969.

It may be hypothesised that socio-economic modernisation tends to increase class-based political participation and to decrease communal-based political participation. Since the relative importance of functional (i.e. class) cleavages increases with modernisation, we would expect to find greater class voting (a majority of lower-class voters voting for the left parties as opposed to a majority of upper-class and middle-class voters voting for the right parties) in more modern societies. Secondly, with increasing modernisation, deferential motives for participation tend to be replaced by instrumental and civic motives. Deferential patterns weaken in periods of rapid socio-economic change, and political loyalties can be maintained only through a relationship of greater reciprocity involving the widespread use of concrete, short-run, material inducements.[48] The urban party machines and rural patron-client relationships, both characteristic of transitional societies, depend on such reciprocity. Further socio-economic modernisation encourages both civic participation and instrumental participation based on sectoral, rather than individual and communal, inducements.

Motives for political participation among the Turkish urban poor seem to have followed this sequence.[49] In Turkey, deferential motives for participation play an important role in the more traditional rural areas. These motives tend to be largely replaced by instrumental motives in the cities. At first, recent urban migrants seem to be motivated chiefly by individual and communal inducements. Special developmental needs and problems of the *gecekondus* reinforce this attitude. The illegal status of their dwellings, inconsistencies in the implementation of the *gecekondu* laws, the practice of preferential treatment in municipal services, and the willingness of party organisations to offer material inducements make urban migrants particularly vulnerable to reprisals by governmental authorities and heavily dependent upon their short-term favours. This period corresponds to the domination of conservative majority parties (the Democrat Party in the 1950s and the JP in the 1960s) among the Turkish urban poor. Finally, with further socio-economic modernisation and the increased political awareness that goes with it, the bases of political participation shift from local community or urban neighbourhood to social class, and individual-communal inducements tend to be replaced by 'sectoral' inducements. The results of the 1973 elections clearly support this hypothesis.

Socio-economic Modernisation and Electoral Behaviour

It has been hypothesised at the outset that, in Turkey, the level of political institutionalisation, as well as the nature, motives and social bases of political participation, are associated with socio-economic modernisation. Thus, in terms of the operational measures of political institutionalisation and political participation employed in this study, we would expect to find positive correlations between indicators of socio-economic modernisation, and (i) major-party support; (ii) autonomous and instrumental political participation. Conversely, we would expect to observe negative associations between socio-economic modernisation and (iii) minor-party support; (iv) independent votes; (v) party system fractionalisation; (vi) mobilised and deferential political participation.

Table 5.6 gives simple correlation coefficients (Pearson r) between our independent (socio-economic) and dependent (political) variables. Almost all the correlations are in the expected direction. Major-party support (JP and RPP) both in 1969 and 1973 correlates positively with developmental indicators (or negatively with anti-developmental indicators). Correlations with the JP vote in 1973 are weaker than in 1969, but still generally significant. This confirms the trend we observed in the 1965 and 1969 elections,[50] and suggests that the JP's differential appeal to the more modernised sections of the country has

Table 5.6: Correlation Coefficients between Socio-economic and Political Variables

Soc.-econ. Variables	(1) Particip. 1969	(2) JP 1969	(3) RPP 1969	(4) RRP 1969	(5) NP 1969	(6) NAP 1969	(7) TUP 1969	(8) TLP 1969	(9) NTP 1969	(10) Ind. 1969	(11) Particip. 1973	(12) JP 1973	(13) RPP 1973
1. URB	−.267	.188	.290	−.154	−.124	.018	.065	−.001	−.135	−.210	−.097	.102	.272
2. MANIND	−.449	.416	.409	−.228	−.079	.058	−.027	−.047	−.375	−.365	−.290	.259	.321
3. LQ	−.411	.358	.374	−.214	−.099	.016	−.027	.016	−.300	−.317	−.239	.244	.328
4. SOCSEC	.425	−.459	−.332	.248	.244	−.156	−.054	.072	.227	.405	.210	−.399	−.260
5. VALADD	−.129	.139	.265	−.117	−.041	−.018	−.004	−.055	−.076	−.190	.010	.057	.188
6. LIT	−.541	.631	.367	−.302	.049	.106	−.002	.077	−.594	−.543	−.390	.477	.380
7. RADIOS	.617	−.632	−.317	.412	−.110	−.262	−.144	−.065	.672	.528	.539	−.463	−.377
8. ALLASS	.550	−.667	−.292	.325	−.175	−.217	.001	−.007	.549	.627	.444	−.431	−.206
9. RELASS	.283	−.428	−.204	.173	−.194	−.224	−.051	.022	.410	.482	.224	−.271	−.030
10. MODASS	.591	−.725	−.323	.287	−.098	−.178	.030	−.001	.567	.665	.469	−.515	−.295
11. PROFAM	−.284	.305	.135	−.187	.068	.170	−.022	−.020	−.263	−.249	−.230	.142	.166
12. PRODEC	−.188	.315	.296	−.167	−.066	.008	−.112	−.147	−.254	−.214	−.078	.209	.221
13. CEREALS	.186	−.302	−.241	.200	.236	−.010	.163	.047	.167	.098	.153	−.269	−.260
14. GINI	.248	−.328	−.232	.178	−.209	−.205	.001	−.001	.475	.323	.266	−.227	−.158
15. LANDFAM	−.101	.160	.043	.009	−.290	−.047	.015	−.069	.008	−.054	−.050	.106	.068
16. DISAPP	.037	−.098	−.052	−.002	−.308	−.117	.096	.044	.187	.188	.059	−.048	.078

Table 5.6. (contd.)

Soc.-econ. Variables	(14) RRP 1973	(15) DP 1973	(16) NP 1973	(17) NAP 1973	(18) NSP 1973	(19) TUP 1973	(20) Ind. 1973	(21) Fraction. 1969	(22) Fraction. 1973	(23) JP+RPP 1969	(24) JP+RPP 1973	(25) JP Change 1969-73	(26) RPP Change 1969-73
1. URB	−.079	−.072	−.160	.032	−.158	.117	−.193	−.164	−.135	.292	.275	−.165	.084
2. MANIND	−.189	−.001	−.085	.028	−.170	.029	−.400	−.392	−.209	.540	.429	−.323	.047
3. LQ	−.172	−.041	−.096	−.026	−.204	.029	−.328	−.360	−.255	.475	.422	−.250	.082
4. SOCSEC	.061	.065	.127	.071	.248	−.128	.454	.406	.348	−.541	−.490	.209	−.036
5. VALADD	−.062	−.090	−.073	−.087	−.031	.056	−.121	−.131	−.074	.240	.180	−.148	.007
6. LIT	−.286	−.024	.043	.110	−.342	.028	−.559	−.559	−.396	.703	.636	−.381	.147
7. RADIOS	.313	.018	−.143	−.227	.205	−.144	.712	.474	.339	−.681	−.624	.400	−.183
8. ALLASS	.282	.047	−.140	−.277	.138	.000	.514	.517	.256	−.699	−.475	.498	−.006
9. RELASS	.182	.089	−.169	−.265	−.042	−.028	.314	.342	.125	−.456	−.227	.326	.126
10. MODASS	.290	−.001	−.070	−.230	.260	.030	.618	.569	.346	−.762	−.603	.479	−.084
11. PROFAM	−.155	.232	−.032	.298	−.200	.001	−.334	−.193	−.005	.320	.227	−.300	.084
12. PRODEC	−.244	.200	−.073	−.060	−.193	−.074	−.262	−.295	−.132	.403	.318	−.229	.020
13. CEREALS	.170	−.186	.243	.101	.316	.121	.276	.281	.199	−.367	−.392	.129	−.109
14. GINI	.133	.122	−.306	−.078	.065	−.014	.319	.241	.162	−.385	−.286	.225	.001
15. LANDFAM	.010	.136	−.280	−.126	−.145	.010	−.119	−.159	−.103	.155	.130	−.115	.045
16. DISAPP	.039	.064	−.348	−.073	−.077	.030	.042	.042	−.048	−.107	.020	.094	.130

Political Variables

N = 67   d.f. = 65

further weakened in the 1969-73 period. The RPP correlations for 1973, on the other hand, are sometimes stronger and sometimes weaker than the 1969 correlations. It is clear, however, that in recent years the RPP has become a party with disproportionately greater support in the more modern regions, which certainly was not the case until the 1969 elections. Predictably, the combined JP-RPP support also correlates positively with socio-economic modernisation both in 1969 and 1973. If major-party support is indeed a measure of political institutionalisation in Turkey, as was argued above, then these findings clearly suggest a positive association between socio-economic modernisation and political institutionalisation.

Of our 16 socio-economic variables, only two (percentage of landless families; disappropriation ratio; and also, to some extent, value added per person) did not show significant associations with either individual or combined major-party support. This is hardly surprising, since these two variables are not really indicators of socio-economic modernisation. As we have shown elsewhere,[51] inequalities in land tenure are observed both in some of the least developed regions (like the south-east) and in some of the highly developed ones (like the Mediterranean and the Aegean). As for the value added per person variable, it did not show strong associations either with the other socio-economic variables. This may be due partly to some problems in data collection, and partly to the fact that a small province with a few technologically advanced industrial establishments may score high on this index even though its overall level of industrial development may be low.

Table 5.6 also displays generally negative correlations between socio-economic modernisation and support for minor parties. Such correlations are particularly strong for the NTP, and moderately strong for the NSP and the RRP. The NAP vote correlates positively, but weakly, with socio-economic modernisation, while almost no such association is observed for the TUP, the NP, the DP and the TLP.

Interestingly, in both 1969 and 1973 we observe a strong negative association between the independent vote and socio-economic modernisation. In the Turkish context, the independent vote is an indicator of both a low level of political institutionalisation (see above) and a substantial amount of 'mobilised' political participation. In the latter sense, a large independent vote suggests the existence of strong traditional influences upon voters and the prevalence of voting out of deferential motives. When powerful local notables fail to get a good spot on a party ticket, they may choose to run as independents and often succeed in their ventures. As our data demonstrate, such a pattern is likely to be found in the less developed parts of the country.

Another indication of mobilised voting in less developed areas is the negative association between provincial modernity and voting participation in both the 1969 and the 1973 elections. High rates of turnout without the socio-economic and attitudinal concomitants of political participation are likely to be the result of mobilisation of voters by traditional local notables. However, the negative correlations for 1973 are consistently weaker than those for 1969. This is consistent with our earlier observation on the narrowing of the urban-rural participation gap.

Party system fractionalisation also correlates negatively with provincial modernity. If we measure political institutionalisation in Turkey by major-party support, as was explained above, then such fractionalisation indicates a low level of institutionalisation. This again supports our hypothesis that the higher the level of socio-economic modernisation, the higher the level of political institutionalisation. It will be noticed from Table 5.6 that the negative correlations for 1973 are weaker than the 1969 correlations. This may be due to the split of the DP which increased fractionalisation in the provinces where the JP is strongest (i.e. generally more modernised provinces). With the erosion of the DP support, we would expect such correlations to go back to their pre-1973 level in future elections.

Finally, an interesting pattern emerges with respect to the changes in JP support between 1969 and 1973. Positive changes in the JP vote are negatively correlated with the indices of modernisation, suggesting that the JP lost proportionately greater support in the more modernised provinces. An explanation for this phenomenon will be provided below. No such clear pattern is observed with respect to the changes in the RPP vote between 1969 and 1973. This can be attributed to the fact that the RPP increased its votes in different parts of the country for different reasons. Thus, while the RPP gains in the more modernised provinces can be explained as part of a long-term process of realignment, its gains in the less developed east-central region, for example, may well mark the return to the RPP of Shiite voters who had swung to the TUP in 1969.[52]

Socio-economic modernisation is a complex and multidimensional process. To identify its principal components, we ran a factor analysis of our original 16 socio-economic variables, using a varimax orthogonal rotation technique which does not allow the factors to be intercorrelated.

The results of such analysis are presented in Table 5.7. It can be seen from the table that the first factor (F1) explains 27.6 per cent of total variance and has particularly high factor loadings (i.e. correlation between the individual variable and the factor) on the first five individual variables: literacy; population/radios; population/all associations; population/religious associations; and population/modern associations. As such, this factor can perhaps be termed 'cultural and organisational development'. While it thus provides a measure of overall social development of a province, one should note that it can also be interpreted as an indicator of 'rural' social development, since a moderately urbanised average Turkish province can score high on this factor only if its rural sector has a fairly high rate of literacy, a good number of radios and fairly intense associational activities.

Factor 2 explains 19.1 per cent of total variance and has high positive factor loadings on urbanisation, males in manufacturing industry, and location quotient in manufacturing industry. Consequently, this factor has been termed 'urbanisation and industrialisation'. Factor 3, which we have called 'agricultural development', has high loadings on two individual variables: agricultural product per decare, and the share of cereals in agricultural product. Finally, Factor 4 has high loadings on the three variables describing the distribution of land holdings: GINI concentration ratio, percentage of landless families and the disappropriation ratio. Cumulatively, all four factors explain 73.4 per cent of total variance with respect to socio-economic characteristics of the provinces. Three of our individual variables do not have high loadings on any of the four factors, as also indicated by their low commonalities (i.e. the amount of total variance in each of the individual variables which is accounted for by all the factors; this equals the sum of the squared loadings in each row). These are: total population/population under social security, value added per person and agricultural product per family.

After we had identified four components of socio-economic modernisation, we computed the 'factor scores' of all provinces for each factor. Such scores are given in Table 5.8. We then ran a multiple regression analysis, utilising factor scores as independent variables (X1 = cultural and organisational development; X2 = urbanisation and industrialisation; X3 = agricultural development; X4 = equality of land holdings) and our political variables (Y1-Y26 = turnout rates, party votes, party system fractionalisation, combined JP-RPP votes and changes in the JP and the RPP votes between 1969 and 1973) as dependent variables.

Table 5.7: Varimax Orthogonal Rotated Factor Matrix of Sixteen Socio-economic Variables

Variable	F1 Cultural and Organisational Development	F2 Urbanisation and Industria-lisation	F3 Agricultu-ral Deve-lopment	F4 Equality of Land	Commu-nalities
LIT	.777	.404	.070	− .072	.777
RADIOS	− .831	− .267	− .121	− .055	.779
ALLASS	− .958	− .146	− .070	− .162	.970
RELASS	− .793	.189	.045	− .316	.766
MODASS	− .937	− .218	− .145	− .060	.950
URB	.050	.836	− .069	− .307	.800
MANIND	.299	.862	.204	− .137	.893
LQ	.230	.903	.150	− .207	.934
SOCSEC	− .338	− .324	− .251	.077	.288
VALADD	.076	.373	.117	− .104	.169
PROFAM	.191	.208	.150	− .280	.181
PRODEC	.148	.101	.890	.205	.866
CEREALS	− .066	− .110	− .929	.093	.888
GINI	− .565	.041	− .095	− .586	.673
LANDFAM	− .063	.328	.002	− .891	.905
DISAPP	− .222	.189	− .069	− .902	.903
% of Total Variance	.276	.191	.118	.149	
Cumulative % of Total Variance	.276	.467	.585	.734	

The results are presented in Table 5.9. The coefficients are standardised beta weights displaying the direct explanatory contribution of each factor. We shall thus be able to tell how much of the total variance accounted for by all the factors (R^2) is contributed by each factor.[53]

Table 5.9 shows that factors of agricultural development (X3) and of land equality (X4) do not have much explanatory power with respect to most of the dependent political variables. There are, however, weak positive relationships between agricultural development on the one hand, and the JP vote, the RPP vote, the DP vote and the combined JP-RPP vote, on the other. The NSP vote correlates negatively with agricultural development. The factor of 'cultural and organisational development' (X1) seems to have the greatest explanatory power on voting behaviour. This factor correlates positively with the JP vote, the

Table 5.8: Factor Scores by Province Factor

Province	F1	F2	F3	F4
Adana	−0.1088	0.9898	0.3904	−0.4910
Adıyaman	−2.4684	−0.4900	0.7937	−0.3953
Afyon	0.7190	−0.5511	−0.8769	−0.7491
Ağrı	−0.2883	−0.0605	−0.9171	−0.2643
Amasya	0.3718	−0.4549	−0.1984	−0.6468
Ankara	0.5149	1.7121	−1.8717	0.7083
Antalya	0.5647	−0.8820	1.1067	−1.6501
Artvın	0.6140	−0.9007	2.0475	0.7139
Aydın	0.9760	−0.4143	2.3594	−2.2388
Balıkesir	0.9253	−0.1119	0.5316	−0.1950
Bilecik	1.1172	−0.7024	−0.2027	−0.2615
Bingöl	−1.0982	−0.5390	−0.2533	−0.0458
Bitlis	−0.5897	−0.2683	−0.7918	0.3968
Bolu	0.5685	−0.4043	−0.3687	0.4661
Burdur	0.8437	−0.2888	−0.5568	−0.4319
Bursa	0.3508	1.9143	0.8292	0.6135
Çanakkale	1.1558	−1.0204	0.2992	−1.3170
Çankırı	1.0661	−0.7715	−0.4894	0.5341
Çorum	−0.0777	−0.4161	−1.1649	−0.2983
Denizli	1.0202	0.1199	0.2745	−0.1446
Diyarbakır	−1.0003	−0.3535	−0.1362	−0.6216
Edirne	0.7230	−0.3118	−0.2927	0.9393
Elazığ	−0.1951	−0.3977	−0.0537	1.5208
Erzincan	0.4439	−0.4599	−0.8741	−0.1773
Erzurum	−0.1262	−0.3340	−0.3742	0.5826
Eskişehir	0.3800	1.5296	−0.0104	0.7467
Gaziantep	−0.5705	1.9591	−0.0940	−0.7299
Giresun	−0.3559	−0.3358	1.5795	1.6576
Gümüşhane	0.4421	−0.5136	−0.6764	0.0056
Hakkâri	−2.7171	−0.7941	0.1876	−0.5015
Hatay	0.0336	−0.0882	1.0454	−1.3942
İçel	0.0445	−0.6298	0.9740	−0.8737
Isparta	1.0196	0.3974	−0.3087	−0.2567
İstanbul	−0.2762	5.5041	0.0679	−1.3498
İzmir	0.2332	2.4158	1.7568	−0.8145
Kars	−0.4797	−0.3741	−0.3391	1.3413
Kastamonu	0.5148	−0.3929	−0.4268	1.3099
Kayseri	0.3571	0.7212	−0.9389	−0.0921
Kırklareli	1.0566	−0.2374	−0.0789	−0.2143
Kırşehir	0.2200	−0.0870	−1.0456	1.1568
Kocaeli	0.9107	0.3908	−0.4810	−0.5218
Konya	0.6966	−0.0426	−1.5798	−0.0362
Kütahya	0.9390	−0.6401	−0.7611	−1.1140
Malatya	0.1178	−0.0417	−0.6403	−0.8228

Table 5.8. (contd.)

Province	F1	F2	F3	F4
Manisa	0.4648	−0.0803	1.1481	−0.1905
Maraş	−0.4389	−0.0460	−0.0915	−0.1992
Mardin	−3.8375	0.0060	0.1620	−0.6006
Muğla	0.8984	−1.1680	1.5941	−1.9671
Muş	−2.0658	−0.3635	−0.9034	0.5029
Nevşehir	0.8335	−0.7285	−0.2505	0.8851
Niğde	0.6768	−0.8191	0.2577	−0.6093
Ordu	−0.5370	−0.1121	0.9078	1.2948
Rize	−0.2385	0.3804	3.4197	2.5679
Sakarya	0.2352	1.0135	0.3847	1.3630
Samsun	−0.3063	0.1154	0.3967	1.5196
Siirt	−2.4847	−0.7649	0.4595	−0.6642
Sinop	−0.1209	−0.2903	−1.0412	1.8306
Sıvas	−0.4768	−0.0154	−1.4411	0.8933
Tekirdağ	0.3158	0.0204	−0.4706	1.5182
Tokat	−0.3295	0.0490	0.1712	1.2287
Trabzon	0.0964	0.2760	2.4966	1.7299
Tunceli	0.7108	−1.2305	−0.2580	−0.1507
Urfa	−1.6866	−0.0951	−0.7467	−1.7172
Uşak	0.5644	0.6469	−0.5425	0.5561
Van	−1.5483	−0.4636	−0.9262	−0.0336
Yozgat	0.3185	−0.5427	−0.5390	0.1106
Zonguldak	0.3676	0.9178	−0.7192	0.6227

RPP vote and the combined JP-RPP vote; it correlates negatively with the rate of turnout, the NTP vote, the RRP vote, the independent vote and party system fractionalisation. Correlations with the votes of the other minor parties are not significant. These findings support our earlier observation that the level of political institutionalisation in Turkey is positively associated with socio-economic modernisation. Also, the significant negative correlations between the turnout rates and the level of cultural and organisational development again suggest the existence of a considerable amount of mobilised voting participation in the less developed parts of the country.

The direction of the relationships between Factor 2 (urbanisation and industrialisation) and the dependent variables is essentially the same as for Factor 1. Only here the statistical associations are much weaker, with the exception of those with the RPP vote (both in 1969 and 1973). In other words, the urbanisation and industrialisation factor appears to have greater explanatory power with regard to the RPP's voting strength.

The data presented in Table 5.9, especially when compared to our findings on earlier elections,[54] also provide us with information on the

Table 5.9: Results of Multiple Regression Analysis of Factor Scores and Dependent Political Variables

	X1 Beta Weights	X2 Beta Weights	X3 Beta Weights	X4 Beta Weights	Multiple R	R^2	F Ratio
Y1(Part.-69)	−.523	−.267	−.086	.015	.593	.352	8.421
Y2(JP-69)	.659	.144	.223	−.080	.715	.511	16.177
Y3(RPP-69)	.220	.315	.202	.063	.439	.193	3.699
Y4(RRP-69)	−.288	−.112	−.133	−.010	.337	.113	1.984
Y5(NP-69)	.149	−.045	−.192	.338	.418	.175	3.284
Y6(NAP-69)	.183	−.017	−.046	.090	.210	.044	.714
Y7(TUP-69)	.032	−.023	−.163	−.075	.184	.034	.543
Y8(TLP-69)	.044	.010	−.095	.011	.106	.011	.175
Y9(NTP-69)	−.551	−.190	−.128	−.086	.604	.364	8.881
Y10(Ind.-69)	−.591	−.166	−.041	−.062	.618	.382	9.601
Y11(Part.-73)	−.455	−.134	−.057	.014	.478	.229	4.598
Y12(JP-73)	.460	−.069	.188	−.088	.509	.259	5.421
Y13(RPP-73)	.213	.237	.197	.035	.376	.142	2.559
Y14(RRP-73)	−.286	−.095	−.191	−.008	.357	.127	2.258
Y15(DP-73)	−.025	−.086	.230	−.114	.272	.074	1.238
Y16(NP-73)	.112	−.048	−.209	.340	.417	.174	3.263
Y17(NAP-73)	.263	−.016	−.127	.120	.316	.100	1.717
Y18(NSP-73)	−.166	−.089	−.242	.107	.324	.105	1.824
Y19(TUP-73)	−.004	.039	−.140	.003	.146	.021	.337
Y20(Ind.-73)	−.543	−.142	−.176	.055	.591	.349	8.301
Y21(Frac.-69)	−.508	−.180	−.227	.102	.593	.352	8.401
Y22(Frac.-73)	−.298	−.113	−.131	.122	.365	.133	2.386
Y23(JP+RPP-69)	.659	.266	.282	−.039	.765	.585	21.916
Y24(JP+RPP-73)	.502	.225	.285	−.092	.626	.392	9.989
Y25(JP 73-69)	−.447	−.138	−.109	.012	.481	.231	4.658
Y26(RPP 73-69)	.071	.024	.066	−.090	.135	.018	.286

N = 67
d.f. for F-test (4,62)

nature of the ongoing voter realignment in Turkey. We have observed elsewhere that the strong positive associations between the JP vote and the indicators of socio-economic modernisation weakened in the 1969 elections. Table 5.9 shows that this trend has continued in the 1973 elections, and such correlations have further weakened. More particularly, the correlation between the JP vote and the urbanisation and industrialisation factor turned negative in 1973. Further evidence for this process lies in the negative correlations between changes in the JP vote in the period 1969-73, and Factors 1 and 2. It appears that the JP has steadily been losing its differential appeal in the more modernised sections of the country.

The trend for the RPP has been just the opposite. Until the 1969 elections, there was no significant association between the RPP vote and socio-economic modernisation. Such a positive association appeared for the first time in 1969, and it was also observed in 1973.

These divergent trends in the two major parties' electoral bases of support can be explained by the change in the nature of the dominant social cleavage in Turkey. As we have argued earlier, with increasing socio-economic modernisation the once dominant centre-periphery cleavage has tended to be replaced by a functional (i.e. class) cleavage. In the 1950s and the early 1960s, the Democrat Party and the JP, respectively, had been identified as parties of the periphery against the RPP which was popularly perceived as the party of the urban, intellectual, bureaucratic and elitist centre. There was practically no class-voting in the party system, as evidenced by the fact that urban business-men and industrial workers, big landlords, small farmers and landless peasants joined forces in the DP and JP coalition. However, one would expect that with increasing social modernisation and differentiation, such concepts as centre and periphery would lose their meaning and new divisions would emerge both within the centre and within the periphery. Changes in popular attitudes toward parties were made easier by the RPP's repudiation of its old elitist posture and its acceptance of a more populist left-of-centre approach. Consequently, voters of low socio-economic status have recently swung, by and large, from the conservative JP to the left-of-centre RPP. This is most clearly evident in the major cities, as we demonstrated above. On the other hand, the RPP's opening to the left has deprived the party of the votes of some influential local notables and their mobilised followers in the less developed regions, who had supported the RPP until the mid-1960s. Thus, the RPP increased its vote in the more modern regions while losing some ground in the less developed provinces.

Patterns of Party Competition: Perspectives in Political Institutionalisation

Table 5.10 presents the correlation matrix for our 'political' variables (i.e. provincial turnout rates and provincial voting percentages of all parties for 1969 and 1973, percentage change in the votes of the JP and the RPP between 1969 and 1973). It is hoped that several important clues regarding political institutionalisation can be obtained from such

Table 5.10: Correlation Matrix for Political Variables: Voting Participation and Party Votes 1969-73

	(1) Part.1969	(2) JP 1969	(3) RPP 1969	(4) RRP 1969	(5) NP 1969	(6) NAP 1969	(7) TUP 1969	(8) TLP 1969	(9) NTP 1969	(10) Ind. 1969	(11) Part.1973
(1) Part. 1969	1.000										
(2) JP 1969	−.455	1.000									
(3) RPP 1969	−.240	.093	1.000								
(4) RRP 1969	.199	−.182	−.094	1.000							
(5) NP 1969	−.214	−.045	−.140	−.162	1.000						
(6) NAP 1969	−.232	.047	.102	.032	.007	1.000					
(7) TUP 1969	.036	−.212	.001	−.207	−.098	.158	1.000				
(8) TLP 1969	.015	−.258	.081	−.244	−.038	−.119	.146	1.000			
(9) NTP 1969	.460	−.489	−.474	−.032	−.126	−.307	−.147	.112	1.000		
(10) Ind. 1969	.469	−.714	−.401	−.083	−.181	−.218	.008	.109	.518	.1000	
(11) Part.1973	.816	.437	−.101	.118	−.229	−.211	.095	.066	.486	.354	1.000
(12) JP 1973	−.205	.780	.138	−.124	−.167	−.149	−.302	−.220	−.297	−.485	−.230
(13) RPP 1973	−.246	−.086	.518	−.273	−.068	−.074	.235	.618	−.228	−.125	−.066
(14) RRP 1973	.254	−.200	−.337	.551	−.073	.241	−.105	−.104	.208	.069	.142
(15) DP 1973	−.256	.150	−.043	.146	.066	.173	−.138	−.290	−.190	−.080	−.252
(16) NP 1973	−.246	.004	−.047	−.094	.709	.045	−.121	.042	−.137	−.192	−.272
(17) NAP 1973	−.316	.041	−.027	−.078	.336	.600	.124	−.153	−.380	−.193	−.350
(18) NSP 1973	.089	−.252	−.248	−.156	.156	.009	.282	−.183	.139	.310	.032
(19) TUP 1973	.001	−.143	.043	−.184	−.096	.226	.823	.040	−.160	−.022	.033
(20) Ind 1973	.604	−.603	−.262	.069	−.068	−.294	−.126	.023	.683	.615	.578
(21) JP Change 1969-73	.456	−.572	.032	.127	−.148	−.269	−.059	.123	.390	.501	.395
(22) RPP Change 1969-73	−.093	−.172	−.193	−.238	.033	−.165	.269	.644	.111	.172	.004

Table 5.10. (contd.)

	(12) JP 1973	(13) RPP 1973	(14) RRP 1973	(15) DP 1973	(16) NP 1973	(17) NAP 1973	(18) NSP 1973	(19) TUP 1973	(20) Ind. 1973	(21) JP Change 1969-73	(22) RPP Change 1969-73
(1) Part.1969											
(2) JP 1969											
(3) RPP 1969											
(4) RRP 1969											
(5) NP 1969											
(6) NAP 1969											
(7) TUP 1969											
(8) TLP 1969											
(9) NTP 1969											
(10) Ind. 1969											
(11) Part.1973											
(12) JP 1973	1.000										
(13) RPP 1973	−.089	1.000									
(14) RRP 1973	−.197	−.433	1.000								
(15) DP 1973	−.158	−.140	−.176	1.000							
(16) NP 1973	−.037	−.059	−.040	.039	1.000						
(17) NAP 1973	−.209	−.108	.017	.209	.207	1.000					
(18) NSP 1973	−.343	−.353	−.073	−.159	−.027	.117	1.000				
(19) TUP 1973	−.239	.158	−.134	−.128	−.130	.170	.283	1.000			
(20) Ind. 1973	−.450	−.314	.147	−.180	−.112	−.217	.115	−.137	1.000		
(21) JP Change 1969-73	.068	.020	.060	−.446	−.055	−.341	−.049	−.085	.372	1.000	
(22) RPP Change 1969-73	−.211	.739	−.231	−.127	−.030	−.102	−.210	.147	−.154	.002	1.000

N = 67   d.f. = 65

an analysis. First, correlations between the provincial voting percentages of a certain party in two consecutive general elections (1969 and 1973) provide a measure of the stability of that party's social base. High correlation coefficients indicate greater stability. Second, correlations between the percentage changes in one party's level of support and those of other parties may provide us with clues (but certainly not with conclusive evidence) as to the direction of change in party preferences. For example, a high correlation between Party A's electoral gains and Party B's electoral losses may indicate a considerable amount of direct switching from B to A, although in a multiparty situation many other possibilities exist. Third, correlations between two parties' provincial voting percentages inform us about the nature of party competition.[55] Thus, a positive correlation between two parties' provincial voting percentages indicates that they both appeal to the same regions of the country, and that they are in greater competition in a 'symbiotic' sense. This does not necessarily show, however, that the two parties are competing for the *same* electorate. A similarity between the provincial voting profiles of the JP and the RPP, for example, may result from the fact that their different blocs of supporters tend to live in the same provinces (such as modern peasants for the JP and urbanites for the RPP). A negative correlation, on the other hand, means that one party's areas of strength tend to coincide with the other's areas of weakness, which may indicate greater 'zero-sum' competition.[56] For example, if the JP and the NTP captured higher percentages of the anti-RPP (or the former DP) votes in different regions of the country (as actually happened in the 1961 elections), their provincial voting profiles would correlate negatively, and this would mean greater competition in a zero-sum fashion, since the higher the percentage of votes in a province one party secures, the less the percentage obtained by the other.

It appears from Table 5.10 that provinces with relatively high (or low) rates of turnout were fairly constant during the period under study. The correlation coefficient between provincial rates of turnout in 1969 and 1973 is .816. Among the major parties, the JP's provincial voting patterns are considerably more stable than those of the RPP. The correlation between the JP vote in 1969 and the JP vote in 1973 is quite strong (.780), while the corresponding correlation for the RPP is much weaker (.518). This supports our findings for the earlier elections[57] and provides further evidence for the rapidly changing social base of the RPP. Of the minor parties that contested both elections, the TUP seems to have the most stable electoral base of support (.823), followed by the NP (.709). A high correlation here does not, of course, necessarily mean that a party's absolute voting percentages remained constant; it only indicates that the relative distribution of its votes across Turkey's provinces remained fairly stable.

With respect to interparty correlations, we observe almost no relationship between the provincial voting profiles of the two major parties, the JP and the RPP (.093 in 1969 and .089 in 1973). In 1969, both the JP and the RPP vote correlated negatively with the NTP and the independent vote, indicating that both parties were comparatively weaker in regions (namely the eastern regions) where the NTP and the independents did particularly well. In other words, the NTP and the independents were in direct competition with (i.e. garnered votes at the expense of) both major parties. Similarly, in 1973, both major parties' provincial voting percentages correlated negatively with those of the independents and of the NSP. In a sense, the NSP in 1973 played the former role of the NTP, gaining votes at the expense of both major parties in certain provinces. We should note, however, that the NSP support was not as clearly localised as that of the NTP. Although the NSP, like the NTP, received proportionately more votes in the eastern regions, its base of support was much more diversified as indicated by the rather weak correlation (.139) between the NSP vote in 1973 and the NTP vote in 1969. Finally, both major parties' provincial voting percentages correlate negatively with provincial turnout rates, while such rates show strong positive correlations with the NTP and the independent votes. This may provide further support for our argument that high rates of voting turnout in the less developed parts of the country are an indication of mobilised participation.

Of the minor parties, the TLP (in 1969) and the RRP (in 1973) seem to have been in greater direct competition with the RPP. The TLP vote in 1969 correlates positively with the RPP vote in 1973 (.618) and with the positive changes in the RPP vote between 1969 and 1973 (.644). This means that in 1973 the RPP increased its strength and became relatively stronger in provinces where the TLP was relatively stronger in 1969. In other words, a good proportion of the former TLP voters must have swung to the RPP in 1973. On the other hand, the RRP vote in 1973 correlates negatively (−.433) with the RPP vote in 1973. This may be owing to the fact that the RRP captured a certain portion of the anti-JP vote in some provinces.

By the same token, the TUP can be said to be in greater direct competition with the JP than with the RPP. The TUP vote is negatively correlated with the JP vote both in 1969 and 1973, while it shows no association with the RPP vote in 1969 and a weak positive association in 1973. But the greatest direct competition to the JP in 1973 seems to have come from the DP, as could be expected. The DP vote in 1973 correlates negatively with the changes in the JP vote between 1969 and 1973 ($-.446$), suggesting that a great many of the DP voters were the JP defectors. To put it differently, the DP garnered comparatively higher percentages of the vote in provinces where the JP lost comparatively more votes. No such association is observed, however, between the NSP vote and the change in the JP vote. This can be taken as evidence for our earlier argument[58] that the NSP drew its voting strength, not only from the former JP voters, but from a variety of sources. Finally, one should note that between 1969 and 1973 the JP lost proportionately more votes in provinces where it was comparatively stronger in 1969 (the correlation coefficient between the JP vote in 1969 and the JP change in 1969-73 is $-.572$). It appears that the split of the DP hit the JP especially hard in the latter's former strongholds.

Conclusion

To recapitulate our major points, we observe a clear positive correlation between socio-economic modernisation and the level of political institutionalisation in Turkey. With respect to political participation, on the other hand, we should make a distinction between voting and the other aspects of political participation. Both in 1969 and 1973, voting has been negatively correlated with provincial socio-economic modernity. However, available survey data and other more impressionistic evidence suggest that other forms of political participation, as well as its attitudinal concomitants, are positively associated with modernisation. We have argued that the anomaly with respect to voting can be explained by the substantial amount of 'mobilised' participation in the less developed regions of the country.

Our analysis has also provided information on the nature of the current voter realignment in Turkey. We have observed that the 'old' Turkish party system based primarily on a centre-periphery cleavage is giving way to a 'new' party system in which class cleavages play an increasingly significant role. This is understood from the recent changes in the social bases of support of the two major parties.

Notes

1. W. D. Burnham, *Critical Elections and the Mainsprings of American Politics* (Norton, New York, 1970), p. 10.

2. Ibid., p. 10; E. Özbudun and F. Tachau, 'Social Change and Electoral Behaviour in Turkey', *International Journal of Middle East Studies*, 6 (October 1975), pp. 478-9.

3. E. Ozbudun, *Social Change and Political Participation in Turkey* (Princeton University Press, Princeton, New Jersey, 1976); F. Tachau, 'The Anatomy of Political and Social Change: Turkish Parties, Parliaments and Elections', *Comparative Politics*, 5 (July 1973), pp. 551-73.

4. Özbudun, *Social Change in Turkey*.

5. For a similar research design see R. W. Benjamin, 'Modernization and Political Change: A Comparative Aggregate Data Analysis of Indian Political Behaviour' in R. W. Benjamin *et al.*, *Patterns of Political Development: Japan, India, Israel* (McKay, New York, 1972), pp. 30-80.

6. S. P. Huntington, *Political Order in Changing Societies* (Yale University Press, New Haven, Conn., 1968), pp. 12-24.

7. Ibid., p. 13.

8. Ibid., p. 20.

9. E. Özbudun, *Batı demokrasilerinde ve Türkiye' de parti disiplini* (Party discipline in Western democracies and Turkey) (Hukuk Fakültesi Yayınları, Ankara, 1968), pp. 185-97.

10. Benjamin *et al.*, *Patterns of Development*, have also used the degree of fractionalisation as one measure of political institutionalisation. It is not entirely clear, however, whether they associate high or low fractionalisation with high political institutionalisation. Benjamin seems to have a curvilinear view of this relationship. Arian, on the other hand (in *Patterns of Development*, pp. 81-132), argues that 'as modernisation increases, so do political participation and political institutionalisation... The vote is less concentrated as modernity advances and fractionalisation increases', thereby implying that political institutionalisation involves increasing fractionalisation. This ambiguity may be due to a confusion over the concepts of competitiveness and fractionalisation. For example, a two-party system is perfectly competitive, but only moderately fractionalised. Increasing competition in the party system and decreasing one-party dominance may well be aspects of political institutionalisation. But further and extreme fractionalisation can hardly be accepted as part of the institutionalisation syndrome, since under such a system each party would be less autonomous than those in a two- or three-party system. In Turkey, one-party dominance at provincial level is extremely rare. Therefore, what the fractionalisation index really measures in the Turkish context is the degree to which party competition is a two-party or multiparty affair. Hence, my identification of low fractionalisation with high political institutionalisation.

11. D. W. Rae, *The Political Consequences of Electoral Laws* (Yale University Press, New Haven, London, 1967), p. 56.

12. Ibid., p. 54, note 7.

13. A. Przeworski, 'Institutionalization of Voting Patterns, or is Mobilization the Source of Decay?', *American Political Science Review*, 69 (March 1975), p. 53.

14. Devlet Istatistik Enstitüsü (DIE), *14 Ekim 1973 Milletvekili Seçimi Sonuçları* (Results of the 14 October 1973 elections for the National Assembly) (Pub. No. 702, Ankara, 1974); DIE, *Genel Nüfus Sayımı: İdarî bölünüş, 25.10.1970* (Census of population by administrative division) (Pub. No. 672, Ankara, 1973).

15. Devlet Planlama Teşkilâtı (DPT), *Kalkınmada öncelikli yörelerin tesbiti ve bu yörelerdeki tesvik tedbirleri* (The determination of localities with developmental priority) (Pub. No. DPT 1304-KÖYD 4, Ankara 1973), pp. 132-3.

16. In calculating the 'city population' of İstanbul and İzmir a special procedure has been adopted, since many communities within the greater İstanbul and İzmir areas are

totally integrated with the city both in the physical and sociological sense, even though legally they remain outside the respective municipal boundaries and are considered villages or 'sub-district seats' *(bucak merkezi)* in election statistics. Thus, in the present study, İstanbul's city population includes the entire population of the province except those of the Çatalca, Silivri, Şile and Yalova counties, and İzmir includes the total population of the Merkez, Karşıyaka and Bornova counties.

17. DIE, *Genel nüfus sayımı: nüfusun sosyal ve ekonomik nitelikleri, 24.10.1965* (Census of population: social and economic characteristics of the population) (Pub. No. 568, Ankara, 1969), pp. 570-3.

18. DPT, *1970 yılına girerken bölgelere genel bir bakış* (An overview of the regions in 1970) (Pub. No. 821-188, Ankara, 1969), p. 202.

19. DPT, *Kalkınmada öncelikli*, pp. 27, 126-7.

20. Based on unpublished data obtained from the DPT.

21. DPT, *Kalkınmada öncelikli*, pp.31, 130-1.

22. Ibid., pp. 27, 126-7.

23. N. H. Nie *et al.*, 'Social Structure and Political Participation: Developmental Relationships', *American Political Science Review*, 63 (June 1969), pp. 361-78 and (September 1969) 808-32.

24. A. N. Yücekök, *Türkiye' de dernek gelişmeleri, 1946-1968* (Associational developments in Turkey, 1946-1968) (Siyasal Bilgiler Fakültesi Yayınları, Ankara, 1972), pp. 16-149.

25. Ibid.

26. Ibid.

27. K. Boratav, 'Türkiye tarımının 1960'lardaki yapısı ile ilgili bazı gözlemler' (Some observations on the structure of Turkish agriculture during the 1960s), *Siyasal Bilgiler Fakültesi Dergisi*, 27 (September 1972), pp. 794a, 802-4.

28. Ibid., pp. 794a, 804-7.

29. Ibid., p. 794a.

30. Ibid.

31. Ibid., pp. 794a, 799.

32. Ibid., pp. 794a, 799-801.

33. Özbudun, *Social Change in Turkey,* Ch. 5; Özbudun and Tachau, 'Social Change and Electoral Behaviour', pp. 470-3.

34. N. Abadan-Unat *et al.*, 'Kim kime niçin oy veriyor?' (Who votes for whom and why), *Milliyet*, 29 September-10 October 1975.

35. S. P. Huntington and J. Nelson, *No Easy Choice: Political Participation in Developing Countries* (Harvard University Press, Cambridge, Mass., 1976), Ch. 1; Özbudun, *Social Change in Turkey*, Ch. 1.

36. Özbudun and Tachau, 'Social Change and Electoral Behaviour', pp. 461-70.

37. Özbudun, *Social Change in Turkey*, Ch. 5.

38. R. Keleş, *100 Soruda Türkiye' de şehirleşme, konut ve gecekondu* (Urbanisation, housing and squatter settlements in Turkey) (Gerçek Yayınevi, Istanbul, 1972), pp. 176-7, 184-6.

39. R. Keleş, *İzmir mahalleleri: bir tipleştirme örneği* (Izmir's urban neighbourhoods) (Sosyal Bilimler Derneği Yayınları, Ankara, 1972).

40. Shevky and Bell used the indices of social rank, urbanisation, and segregation in their analysis, while Keleş used only the first two. In the present study, I classified İzmir precincts solely on the basis of their 'social rank' scores, since my main concern was the effects of socio-economic status upon electoral behaviour. Furthermore, the urbanisation index, as it is applied to Turkey, seemed neither very reliable nor sociologically significant, and it correlated very weakly with the social rank index (.096). The latter is a composite index which includes such variables as occupation, income, education, and type of dwelling. See Ibid., pp. 3-15.

41. 'Old Ankara' is a typically lower-middle-class community with considerable

socio-economic homogeneity. About two-thirds of the residents are small merchants, low government officials and skilled workers. Relatively few of them are recent migrants; half of them have lived in Ankara for at least twenty years, and over 80 percent for at least five years. A large majority are in the income bracket of 400-1,500 TL per month, and half have primary school education. Such socio-economic characteristics clearly differentiate 'old Ankara' from the *gecekondu* communities. See R. Keleş, *Eski Ankara' da bir şehir tipolojisi* (An urban typology in Old Ankara) (Siyasal Bilgiler Fakültesi Yayınları, Ankara, 1971), pp. 24-48, 149-63.

42. İ. Yasa, *Ankara'da gecekondu aileleri* (Squatter families in Ankara) (Sağlık ve Sosyal Yardım Bakanlığı Sosyal Hizmetler Genel Müdürlügü Yayınları, Ankara, 1966); Keleş, *Ankara.*

43. Keleş, *Eski Ankara,* pp. 64-7; Keleş, *Şehirleşme,* pp. 131-2.

44. K. H. Karpat, 'The Politics of Transition: Political Attitudes and Party Affiliation in the Turkish Gecekondu' in E. D. Akarli and G. Ben-Dor (eds.), *Political Participation in Turkey: Historical Background and Present Problems* (Boğaziçi University Press, Istanbul, 1975), pp. 89-119.

45. F. W. Frey and Ş. Mardin, 'Electoral Attitudes in an Ankara Community: Yenimahalle', mimeo, n.d., p. 6.

46. N. Abadan-Unat and A. N. Yücekök, '1961-1965 seçimlerinde büyük şehirlerin oy verme davranışlarıyla ilgili bazı yorumlar' (Some comments on the voting behaviour of the large cities in the 1961 and the 1965 elections), *Siyasal Bilgiler Fakültesi Dergisi,* 21 (December 1967), pp. 103-19.

47. Ibid., pp. 108-9; Keleş, *Şehirleşme,* p. 193; D. Makofsky, 'Shantytowns, Workers and Strikes: Evidence from Turkey', paper presented at the Annual Meeting of the Middle East Studies Association, Binghamton, New York, 1972, pp. 3-6; Karpat, 'Politics of Transition', pp. 105-7.

48. J. C. Scott, 'Corruption, Machine Politics and Political Change', *American Political Science Review,* 63 (December 1969), pp. 1146.

49. Özbudun, *Social Change in Turkey,* Ch. 8.

50. Ibid., Ch. 6.

51. Ibid., Chs. 3 and 7.

52. Özbudun and Tachau, 'Social Change and Electoral Behaviour', p. 463.

53. For a similarly designed analysis and parallel results, see Ü. Ergüder, 'Türkiye'de siyasal katılma, parti desteği ve tarım fiyat destek siyasası: ekolojik bir yaklaşım' (Political participation, party support and agricultural price support policy: an ecological approach), unpublished manuscript, Istanbul, 1975, pp. 72-110.

54. Özbudun, *Social Change in Turkey,* Ch. 6.

55. It should be noted that we are here measuring 'only the degree of concomitant variation in voting percentages by province, not the absolute magnitude of those percentages' (F. W. Frey, 'Themes in Contemporary Turkish Politics: General and Empirical Views', mimeo, 1970, p. 22).

56. Ibid., pp. 21-2.

57. Özbudun, *Social Change in Turkey,* Ch. 6.

58. Özbudun and Tachau, 'Social Change and Electoral Behaviour', p. 475.

6. LEBANON

Iliya Harik*

Voting studies in Western democracies are concerned with subjects such as attitudes, the stability of the party vote, the relations of socio-economic standards to voting participation and accountability of representatives. In this chapter, however, focus will be on participation trends, the institutionalisation of voting behaviour, the adaptability of the electoral system to changing political conditions and the voters' attitudes in two electoral districts in the Greater Beirut area. The political party vote in Lebanon does not have the same significance as it does in other countries, simply because the Lebanese send only about one-third of their representatives to Parliament with party labels; the rest are independent. As for socio-economic standards, one has to be considerably more modest than if one were studying other countries. Statistical data on socio-economic conditions are lacking and one may have to resort to rough measures such as the general conditions of various regions.

The formal constitutional rules that govern political life in Lebanon have endured for half a century, but not without changes along the way. The Lebanese Constitution was promulgated in 1926 and amended several times, only three of which were extensive and significant—1927, 1929 and 1943. Not only is Lebanon the first republic to be instituted in the Arab world and the second in the Middle East (Turkey was the first), but it also continued to abide by its Constitution longer than any other country in the area.[1] If institutionalisation is to be judged by the single criterion of longevity, the fundamental laws of Lebanese politics can be said to have become institutionalised. Yet instead of celebrating the fiftieth anniversary of constitutional life, the Lebanese have been engaged in one of the worst wars they have ever known, seriously disrupting constitutional government. The war is a subject that intrudes into any discussion of Lebanese society and it will be dealt with in another context in this chapter. Here, it is necessary to refer to the fact that none of the Lebanese fighting factions demanded change of the republican democratic system; indeed those who demanded changes in the system claimed to seek its reform rather than its demise. Although the question of reform can be argued, it is important to remember that the struggle centres around the assimilation of new groups such as the Palestinians and the redistribution of power among various groups. This is in one sense a step in the right direction, namely making the system more responsive to demographic and power shifts in society. The fact remains, however, that in 1975 the system failed to adjust to major political developments through peaceful and constitutional means, a fact that will be discussed later.

In discussing the institutionalisation of electoral politics in Lebanon, it will be hypothesised that freedom of political activity leads to self-corrective and self-induced reforms. By reforms we mean changes that have the effect of producing greater involvement of the populace in the electoral process, more accurate representation and better opportunities for exercising freedom of political choice. Social reforms are excluded, not because they are irrelevant to the hypothesis, but because they fall outside the limits of this chapter.

Regardless of recent events, it may be reasonably stated that the Lebanese have become increasingly committed to the representative system and to the electoral process. The fact that warring factions in the recent civil war have not sought to overthrow the system is perhaps due to their investment of fifty years of experience in their representative institutions. To a considerable extent they have adjusted them to their changing needs. Moreover, most groups and individuals have come to appreciate the advantages and virtues of a free representative system. Studies of Lebanese politics have already demonstrated an increasing involvement of citizens in the electoral process based on an increase in the voting turnout since independence in 1943. Writing in 1965, Michael Hudson observed that:

> Three important trends show that the system is capable of limited, self-induced, structural modernization. First, there is substantial increase in voter participation. Second, there is a gradual broadening of the recruitment process, as indicated by the changing occupational backgrounds of deputies. The third and most complex trend is a growing competitiveness in parliamentary election contests.[2]

In the ten years after this statement was made, two additional electoral contests took place, and trends identified by Hudson have persisted. Elite background has continued to change to the extent that professionals, lawyers and businessmen now occupy about 88 per cent of parliamentary seats in comparison to 77 per cent in 1964. Turnover of deputies from one election to another averaged 42 per cent between 1943 and 1960 and rose to 44.6 per cent between 1960 and 1972. While no significant change in the turnout rate of voters was registered in the 1968 and 1972 elections, elite competitiveness became more keen. For instance, while the national mean score by which a deputy was elected was 61 per cent of the votes cast in 1964, it dropped to 51 per cent in 1968.

This is not the context for a discussion of structural changes in the system as a whole. Instead, we shall limit our discussion to structural changes in the electoral process as an indication of institutionalisation of electoral politics. Institutionalisation is to be understood here in two of the meanings in which Huntington uses the term: continued commitment to a practice over a reasonably long time and adaptability of the practice to changing conditions. Electoral politics have persisted in Lebanon since 1922[3] and corrective measures to achieve a greater degree of representativeness by means of structural changes have been taken over the years.

Changes in the Electoral System

The first major development in the electoral rules occurred in 1934 when direct elections of deputies replaced the indirect system (*le suffrage à deux degrés*) which the French found in practice upon their arrival. The second major change occurred before the elections of 1943 when the system of appointing some representatives (usually around one-third of the Chamber) was abolished. Nationalist pressure forced the French to give up the exercise of this prerogative and a new law stipulated that all members of parliament were to be chosen by direct election. In the 1952 election law, eight years after independence, further steps were taken to improve the electoral process: (i) the vote was given to literate women, then extended to all women in 1957; (ii) the secret ballot was introduced; (iii) the run-off election practice (*ballotage*) was abolished and victory was determined by a plurality of votes on the first count; and finally (iv) a small-size constituency was established. In 1969 voters were given a greater opportunity to exercise freedom of choice by the introduction of the isolating booth where voters could cast their ballots in complete secrecy.

Modifications of constituency size occurred in stages and made the system more responsive to constituents' concerns. From the beginning of the modern electoral system in 1922, multiple-member constituencies prevailed. Between 1922 and 1952 the whole country was divided into five constituencies, with voters in some cases entitled to vote for as many as 15 deputies at once. The multiple-member constituency survived into the 1970s but instead of five there were now 26 constituencies each with the right of sending more than one deputy to parliament. The number of seats varied from two to eight,[4] an average of four deputies per constituency compared to eleven for the previous period. In the large constituencies of earlier times, it used to be difficult for the voter to know all the candidates, and in a non-party parliamentary system such as Lebanon, this constituted a major defect. It also used to be difficult to determine which of the numerous deputies was accountable to the voter, who was to receive credit and who was to bear the blame. Moreover, the large constituency system gave considerable advantage to a few notable leaders who enjoyed a stable political base. Two strong leaders could bind together and form a slate according to their wishes, thus practically hand-picking a very large number of the deputies in parliament. The smaller constituency, by contrast, encourages more direct relations and better knowledge of the candidates.

The preceding are some of the major structural reforms in the electoral system, but there are other changes of a qualitative nature. A qualitative improvement in the conduct of elections has been noticeable in the last twenty-five years. During the mandatory period, flagrant government interference in the elections and fraudulent practices were quite common. The disrespect for democratic institutions which the French mandatory authorities showed was not limited to suspension of the Constitution for a good many years but toward the electoral process as well. This attitude reappeared during the early part of the independence period and reached its peak during the elections of 1947 when flagrant irregularities were committed by the authorities. Since 1953 governments have shown greater self-restraint and fairness in conducting national elections. During crisis periods, such as the elections of 1957, the government in charge of conducting the elections was caught in a tense struggle with the opposition and used the full advantage of office to influence voters, but it did not commit any fraud. However, both the government and the opposition were actively engaged in buying votes. In the 1968 elections, insidious pressures from the Intelligence Department of the military forces (the *Deuxième Bureau*) were strongly resisted by the civilian government with considerable success. One of the banes of Lebanese elections has been the practice on the part of a number of candidates, mostly in urban centres, of buying votes. No one knows exactly the extent to which this practice existed, but its presence is acknowledged by all observers. There are signs, however, that buying votes declined in recent years. In short, the tendency for the government to conduct fair electoral contests has been on the ascendant since 1953 and reached its highest point in the 1972 elections.

A second trend in the electoral process of Lebanon is the increasing tendency of political parties to contest elections with a larger number of candidates, even the anti-system parties, among them the communists, the Syrian Social Nationalist Party and the Baath. Consequently, political parties increased their representation to one-third of the total number of seats in parliament. Some of the radical parties gained seats in the Chamber, though quite negligibly.

On the basis of the preceding brief account of some characteristics of Lebanese elections, a number of generalisations may be put forth as commonsense conclusions rather than statistical inferences. First, it may be observed that the longer a free representative system lasts, the greater its self-corrective tendencies will be. Continuous adherence to the principle of free elections brought about structural reforms in a gradual manner. As a corollary, it may be added that the tendency toward self-correction has not been the result of an ideological commitment to political ideals, but rather as a natural product of the competitive system. Irregularities were fought not by reformers but by men of the same mind as those who were violating the rules, but since the freedom allowed by the rules gave those who suffered most from malpractices the right to fight back, excesses were contained and malpractices removed. It was free competition, rather than reformist ideology, that brought about improvements in the electoral practices.

The second generalisation to which we wish to draw attention is that electoral contests over a period of half a century indicate that elections are an expression of a force that steers the system toward moderation. Practically every new regime came into being as a result of a struggle against the excesses of a previous one.

Social Changes and State Institutions

The political institutions of representative government have met rising challenges and adapted to new situations for half a century now. Whether they have made sufficient adjustment is a debatable question in view of the recent eruptions of violence. The major cleavages in Lebanese society run along sectarian lines,[5] and the political institutions of the republic were engineered in such a way as to create a mechanism which enabled the diverse communities to participate in the system freely while preserving their political rights and their special social identities. In other words, the political formula sought to generate unity within diversity. It is this question of social cleavages and political integration to which we shall turn now. In more specific terms, the question is what role has the electoral system played in maintaining unity within diversity?

Lebanon is a segmentary society insofar as it is composed of diverse communities which, although they share a common language and cultural attributes, are still characterised by a distinct sense of identity. The communities are neither so different as to constitute separate nations, nor so similar as to fuse into a single uniform community. The segmentary nature of Lebanese society is a historical heritage, not the product of Lebanon's political system (see Chapter 2). There are some, however, who feel that the political institutions of Lebanon which acknowledge communal identity have given communalism legitimacy, made it difficult to overcome, and have even stimulated sectarianism. That the political institutions have bestowed legitimacy on communalism, there can be no doubt; that they made it difficult to overcome is possible; but that they stimulated sectarianism is contrary to the facts that will be presented here.[6] Scholars, as well as Lebanese intellectuals, cannot seem to stop being exercised over communalism, as if Lebanon is the only segmentary society in the world. Moreover, they give the impression that social cleavages can either be wished away or resolved by issuing formal secular decrees. Just as it is possible for Lebanese political attitudes to develop beyond sectarianism, it is also possible that the Lebanese will continue to behave according to communal biases under a system that does not legally acknowledge sectarian divisions.

Whatever their other effects may have been, social cleavages, which happen to be sectarian in this case, have made a significant contribution to the institutionalisation and survival of democracy in Lebanon. Although this is not the place to discuss this thesis, it is necessary to say by way of explanation that, in the absence of strong political and labour organizations, communalism proved to be the only major stable force which checked the powers of the executive. It has contributed toward preventing a small section of the elite from imposing its hegemony over the country by that very element of disunity that always mitigated against elite cohesion and absolute power.

The Lebanese Constitution invests enormous powers in the office of President. As most political actors seek to maximise their influence, the

Lebanese President was in a position to use his constitutional privileges to become practically unopposed. Every single President tried to take advantage of these constitutional privileges, yet in over thirty years of independence the presidency has suffered a loss of power without any constitutional changes. Presidential powers have gradually eroded in response to actual shifts in the power balance of competing communities. Appointment of ministers, for instance, has for long become the shared responsibility of the Prime Minister designate and the President. The veto power, which the Premier informally enjoyed as a representative of the Muslim community in government, has become formalised in the practice of counter-signature, which was constitutionally the privilege of ministers only.

Why has this unusual development of power-sharing occurred peacefully in a Third World country? One of the main reasons, but not the only one, is the countervailing influence of Muslim groups. As the political weight of Muslim groups increased, the gain was registered in the office of Premier; as the Christian groups' power waned the change was reflected in the declining powers of the presidency. Every Lebanese President without exception sought to increase his power and every one of them ended up enjoying less than he had received at the time he assumed the office. The tendency of the President to exercise arbitrary power was often opposed by Christian and Muslim leaders alike, but it was Muslim opposition that was the most effective and the determining factor, especially from the 1950s onwards. The reason was that an increase in the power of the President could only occur at the expense of Muslim political privileges, a factor which united diverse Muslim leaders and the community in opposition. Christian Presidents always found themselves checked by Muslim leaders and could not push their powers too far without producing civil strife, as some indeed did, but to no avail. However, cleavages did not lead to the dissolution of the system because of cross-cutting ties which unite the Lebanese such as language, culture and common interests in the survival of the democratic system.

Another major reason why communal cleavages did not lead to the dissolution of the system is political engineering by which I mean mainly the quota system in elections. The quota system is the arrangement by which partners in an undertaking are assigned shares that are judged by each as acceptable under the circumstances. The Lebanese political system is based on such an arrangement: to prevent intense competition for political prizes from arousing communal feelings, each community is assigned a fixed share of parliamentary seats relative to its population ratio. Of course, this is also the principle which makes the President a Maronite Christian, the Premier a Sunnite Muslim and the Speaker of the House a Shiite Muslim. Although presumably this is based on population ratio, it is actually a political heritage which goes back to the mandate period and reflects the political ascendancy and strength of the Christians. The quota system also prevails in the civil and military bureaucracies.

The quota system is most likely to reduce tension and have its greatest integrative value in the elections to parliament. Election to parliament is the only point in the recruitment process to national office at which the public is directly involved. (The President is elected by members of parliament). Should candidates from one community be allowed to run against candidates from another community, communal strife is likely to flare up every time an election takes place. The quota system forces candidates to compete against contenders from their own sects because the number of seats to which a sect is entitled in a constituency is defined by law. Take for instance al-Zahrānī, which is a two-seat constituency. By law this constituency is entitled to one Shiite representative and one Catholic.[7] Voters, regardless of their own religious affiliations, choose which Shiite and which Catholic candidates they want, but they cannot vote for two candidates of the same sect or from any other sects than Shiite and Catholic. Under these legal constraints, Shiite candidates compete against each other and so do the Catholics. This makes the contest intrasectarian not intersectarian, and reduces the chances of sectarian clashes during the elections.

Excluding the possibility of communal strife is not the only way the electoral system contributes to coexistence and communal integration. The multimember, multisect constituency tends to build cross-cutting linkages between members of various communities, affecting both candidates and voters. The major contributing factor is that a voter is entitled to choose a number of candidates equal to the number of seats assigned to the constituency, regardless of whether he is Shiite or Catholic. Thus, while positions are sorted out on a religious basis, the voters are not. Of 26 constituencies, 16 are entitled to representatives from more than one sect, 13 of which are of Muslim-Christian mix.

Since in a multiseat, multisect constituency, no candidate can hope to get elected without support from voters of other religious groups, candidates try to appeal to and to build electoral ties with individuals and local leaders of all sects. Having to appeal to voters from other religious communities, a candidate often moderates his views on issues that divide the communities. Quite often, one finds in such constituencies strong political ties between a candidate and supporters from religious communities other than his own.

On the elite level, one notices similar cross-cutting linkages inspired by the mixed multiseat constituency. Hardly ever does a candidate get elected unless he joins with other candidates to run on a joint slate. This compels candidates of different communities to unite and face the voters as one team. Such electoral alliances often change from one election to the next, but in many cases they endure over several elections and build lasting ties between team-mates on a slate. While running on the same slate does not necessarily compel team-mates to co-operate in parliament, they often do, if only for electoral considerations. In effect, electorally and in parliament, members of the elite establish links cutting across sectarian lines.

The multimember multiseat constituency has in some respects confounded the quota system designers, particularly because of the cross-cutting ties that developed among the elite. In some constituencies, a strong political leader co-opts candidates from other communities than his own, and these will owe their success at the polls to his electoral pull. The tendency of a political leader to co-opt candidates from other communities and be the major factor in their success is not limited to the mixed constituencies. It could cut across constituency lines in case a leader or party has a strong following beyond the constituency limits. Most often the influence of an independent leader is limited to his constituency but some may have a marginal influence on other constituencies, whereas political parties often have a following in several constituencies.

The fact that political linkages occur among elites of different communities modifies the official distribution of shares among the communities. For instance, in the 1972 elections 12 Christian deputies were elected under the sponsorship of Muslim parliamentary leaders and five Muslim deputies under Christian sponsorship. This amounts to a loss of seven seats to the Christians, insofar as those elected on a slate dominated by a Muslim or a Christian leader are constrained to act according to his wishes. This fact modifies the sectarian shares in parliament based on the formal arrangement of 54 Christians to 45 Muslim seats and makes it more like 47 'Christian' to 52 'Muslim' deputies, defined politically. The alignments and linkages established among members of parliament once in the chamber are, however, another question and cut deeply across sectarian lines.

It is interesting to note in this respect that the Druze community's six-seat share in parliament makes it the greatest beneficiary of the informal realignments, while the Christian Orthodox community, whose quota is eleven, is the greatest loser. Druze leaders brought with them to parliament in 1972 seven deputies from other communities, mostly Christian, and gave away one Druze seat only, bringing their total strength to twelve seats in parliament. The Orthodox, on the other hand, show the least independent strength; they lost seven seats to influentials from other sects, gained none, and could claim only four deputies on their own electoral strength.

The Druze have traditionally had strong leaders and benefited from the fact that the two constituencies in which their population is concentrated are large. This enables Druze leaders to influence the choice of candidates from other communities in those districts. One of the traditional Druze leaders, Kamāl Junblāṭ, had also cast his influence beyond his constituency and sect, and his example gives credit to the political prowess of the Druze in Lebanon. It is of interest to note here that, during the drafting of the Lebanese Constitution in 1926, the Druze representatives made the strongest plea for the communal distribution of parliamentary seats. They saw in the quota system the means to protect their minority status from incursions by larger and more powerful communities. Being traditionally active in politics and endowed with strong leaders who enjoyed the loyalty of their community, the Druze benefited from the quota system, preserving their minimum share, and also from the flexibility of the free competitive system, extending their influence beyond their communal confines. Now, however, the quota system seems to be the victim of its success, as illustrated by the Druze who have recently turned against it. Encouraged perhaps by his political strength and his ability to influence the election of deputies from other communities, the late Kamāl Junblāṭ could no longer see any advantage in the quota system and became one of its most vehement opponents. For the quota system extends also to other public offices and there it works against an influential man who aspires to the presidency.

The example of the Druze of Lebanon serves to show that the electoral system has safeguarded the interests of minority groups to the extent that they now feel sufficiently confident to do without a quota guarantee.

To conclude, it may be pointed out that political engineering in Lebanon consisted of measures taken to alleviate fears and minimise the possibility of clashes between vertically divided communities over the question of elite recruitment. The political engineering instrument adopted has been the quota system which allocates political and administrative offices to the various communities in accordance with their population ratio, yet without segregating voters or prohibiting intersectarian alignments. It has been proposed in this chapter that political engineering, especially in the electoral process, has contributed to the development of cross-cutting ties among the vertically divided communities and reduced the occurrence and intensity of communal strife. Further evidence in support of this proposition will be presented in the discussion of voters' attitudes in the capital city of Beirut.

Naturally the quota system contributes to national integration to the extent that each community is satisfied that its share of political responsibility is a fair representation of its political population ratio. In Lebanon, adjustments of the quotas to changes in population and political weight have occurred in the civil bureaucracy and the military and to a certain extent in various parts of the executive branch, but not in the parliamentary seats. Muslim communities in Lebanon have therefore shown dissatisfaction with the distribution of the shares. The inability of the system to move toward a readjustment or new political alignment has contributed seriously to the civil war of 1975. At the end of this chapter we shall briefly discuss the reasons why the system failed to make this crucial adjustment at the right time.

Electoral Organisation and Participation

One of the curious features of the Lebanese political system is the proliferation of small political parties and the continuing predominance of constituency-centred electoral contests among independents.[8] Independents, however, are not a different breed from political party candidates nor are their supporters any different socially or economically from supporters of political party candidates. A great deal of error has been perpetrated by ill-informed accounts of independents as feudal lords or political bosses. Voters' support is based on diverse grounds which include kinship ties, patronage, partisanship, political orientation and personal likes and dislikes of candidates. Almost all these factors enter into the consideration of those who vote for party candidates too. Voters for political party candidates are in a minority and have not been able to elect more than one-third the number of representatives in parliament. Moreover, it took nine parties to achieve this result, an average of 3.5 seats per party.

It is not easy to explain the weakness of political parties in the Lebanese political system. In Turkey, Özbudun[9] has observed that where independents predominate, political modernisation lags behind.

Moreover, he has observed that the fractionalisation of party support is also indicative of a less politically advanced population. The comparative strength of these propositions obviously cannot be tested in the Lebanese case unless one considers the whole political system as backward. Such a conclusion would be hard to sustain in view of Lebanon's old tradition of constitutionalism, high rate of voting participation and political awareness of voters. It may well be that Lebanon does not conform to the generalisation derived from the Turkish case due to the fact that regional diversity is not as significant in Lebanon, which is a much smaller country. In many respects, Lebanon is one big suburb of Beirut where most voters visit and/or work. (Voters in Lebanon retain their voting registration in their natal towns, not where they actually live.)

It may be less difficult to explain the fragmentation of political groups than the failure of the electorate to organise along party lines. Fragmentation of political groups is obviously a function of the vertically divided communities and in certain cases traditional regional differences. However, in other societies that are divided politically along vertical communal lines, such as the Netherlands, political parties do prevail, though along segmentary lines. It may be suggested that perhaps the large number of communal groups, their geographic distribution, the traditionally strong local base of leadership and the voter's independence have discouraged and frustrated the growth of political parties. The last point is supported by responses of voters in Beirut who show a strong sense of independence and reluctance to give in to political parties. Another possibility may be the plethora of political currents and forces that pull the Lebanese internally and from the outside, all of which make for dispersion of votes over a large number of groups. It is, however, a curious phenomenon that voters in Lebanon feel that parties deprive them of the freedom of choice and consider them a lower form of political life.

The weakness of party organisation does not seem to have had ill effects on voting participation. The First and Third Districts of Beirut are the only two constituencies where one can make a comparison in this respect. The First District is almost completely party oriented, whereas in the Third District independents are in control, yet voting participation is higher in the Third District and the contest is more competitive.

Voting Participation
Voting participation in Lebanon has been comparatively high and it has more than kept pace with the population. While the population

doubled betweeen 1943 and 1970, the voting population increased five times. Most of the increase, however, has resulted from reforms in the electoral laws, especially female suffrage in 1953. However, the increase in voters' participation has lagged behind the growth of the voting population. Since 1959, the population increased by 39.3 per cent while the increase in the rate of voting participation has been 29.2 per cent.

The voting participation trend since independence has been stable, rising slightly from 56 per cent of registered voters in the 1940s to 57.5 per cent in the 1950s, then declining to 52.5 per cent where it remained in the election of 1972. There is reason to believe, however, that this rate, which is based on official figures, is a gross underestimate. Official figures for registered voters are highly inflated and include a high proportion of Lebanese emigrants who have been physically absent for such a long time that their participation in the political life of the country can be virtually excluded. I am not aware of any study which has sought to determine the size of the gap in the number of officially registered voters and the actual number of resident voters in the country.

A reasonable but by no means definitive estimate of the gap between officially registered voters and the actual voting population can be obtained from two sets of data. The first was provided for us by a former high-ranking official in the *Securité Générale* as an estimate rather than as documentary evidence. According to this source, the number of officially registered voters exceeds the actual voting population by more than 20 per cent. This seems consistent with results obtained from the 1970 Census taken by the Ministry of Planning and adjusted by the demographers Courbage and Fargues.[10] On the basis of this census, we have found the number of Lebanese citizens of voting age, 21 years old and over, to be less than the number of officially registered voters by 20 per cent.

It may, therefore, be reasonably assumed that official figures of registered voters should be readjusted downward by 20 per cent. On this basis the voter turnout should be 65.45 per cent in the 1960s rather than 52.5 per cent (see table 6.1). Adjusted further to account for registration errors, and other incidentals, it would seem that a rough estimate of actual voters should be around 70 per cent.

Another problem with the assessment of voter participation in Lebanon is the comparison between urban and rural turnouts. Writers who have based their conclusions on official figures for Beirut, have pointed out that rural voting participation is higher than urban participation. This observation indeed conforms to returns from Turkey and India as well. In Lebanon, however, this attributed discrepancy is not as serious as has been maintained. First, the low participation rate in Beirut (Table 6.2) is not matched by a similarly low voter turnout in other cities such as Tripoli, Sidon and Zahla. In all these major cities, voter turnout is comparable to voting rates in the countryside. An examination of the voting districts in Beirut shows that the low figure is mainly due to the large number of Armenians who abstain from voting. More than half the First District constituency is made up of Armenians who are refugees of recent origin and have not yet demonstrated a strong integrative tendency.

Table 6.1: Official Figures of Voters Turnout Compared With Corrected Estimate Based on Population, 1960-1972 (in Percentages)

	1960	1964	1968	1972
Official Figures	50.00	53.30	53.80	52.50
Adjusted Figures	62.25	66.60	67.25	-

Table 6.2: Voting Participation According to Province (Not Adjusted)

Beirut	Northern Lebanon	Biqa'	Mount Lebanon	South Lebanon
35	53	55	59	60

Despite variations in socio-economic standards of different provinces, voting participation has not varied significantly from one region to another, leaving Beirut aside. In the 1972 elections, for instance, voting rates (in percentages) in the five provinces were as follows:[11]
The South and the North, which are two of the least advanced provinces socially and economically, show the highest and the lowest participation rates (leaving Beirut aside). Similarly, the advanced provinces of Beirut and Mount Lebanon show extremes of low and high voting participation. Annual increase in voting participation has been greater in socially and economically less advanced provinces.[12] At the beginning of independence, voting rates in these provinces were lower and the rapid increase in voting participation is indicative of greater involvement and commitment to the system.

If it is comparatively established that less educated and lower-income people show less participation in politics, why then do not urban voters in Lebanon show greater voting participation rates than voters of southern districts and districts in the Biqaʻ where the population's educational and economic standards are lower than the national average? Indeed, why do rural voters in Turkey turn out in larger numbers than urban voters? Many suggestions have been made in this regard. The most common is that in the less advanced rural areas, political notables and chiefs drive villagers to vote. This observation cannot be discounted lightly and it was certainly true in many Egyptian villages during the constitutional period (1923-52). Yet the strength of the hypothesis for the contemporary period requires more careful examination and documentation than has been provided thus far. We may advance a modified version of this hypothesis which explains high voting turnout among rural people in terms of the close political and personal ties between leaders and ordinary villagers.[13] It is not so much compulsion as social ties such as kinship, partisanship and patronage that define the linkages between leaders and voters in rural society. Such links are sustained by mutual benefits and exchange of services, between leaders and followers.

Other related hypotheses may be advanced to explain the high rates of voter participation in rural societies. Villagers, especially in the Middle East and North Africa, are often divided into factions that vie for status and seek to assert themselves over other groups in a variety of ways. Elections provide them with an opportunity to draw attention to themselves, demonstrate their strength and establish links with leaders or parties on the national scene. A detailed example of this case can be observed from a study of Saruhanlı in south-western Turkey.[14]

It can be observed, moreover, that when political competition for leadership becomes more intense in rural areas, voting participation increases. An example is the Baalbek-Hermel district in north-east Lebanon, most of which is poor, rural and clan-dominated. Clan organisation and alliances, however, have shown signs of erosion in recent years and professionals have made a strong showing in the last two elections. Competition has increased from two candidates per seat to nearly four candidates, a higher ratio than the national average. In line with this, voting participation increased at a higher rate than the national average. As clans which used to support notable families like the Ḥammādas and Ḥaydars started to run their own members for office, proliferation of contenders and competition increased. Political parties also entered the arena and further diversified the choices facing the voters.

A corollary to this hypothesis is that voting is an index of self-respect and assertion of an individual's own position or the position of his group and party in the community. Face-to-face relationship and the visibility of each individual in small communities bring about subtle social pressures on an individual to conform and to show his face in public affairs. Villagers tend to appreciate the vote as a privilege more than urban voters, who enjoy other forms of social advantages.

Finally, it may be pointed out also that villagers often draw favours from elections in their capacities as individuals or as a community. In Lebanon, villagers often bargain with candidates for a public project which benefits the village before they promise to vote. Sometimes a candidate finds it necessary to 'pay' in advance, i.e. to provide the money for building a school, a mosque, a church, or donate to clubs and charities. Often he makes promises to introduce a school, drinking water etc. when elected, and will be called to account in the second round if he does not deliver.[15]

It may therefore be concluded that the modern sector in Lebanon does not differ from the provinces with respect to political participation, organisation along political party lines or in political involvement in general. As Hudson observed in the 1960s, the growth in numbers of voters indicates that representative institutions have taken firm root in Lebanese society.

Attitudes of Urban Voters

In 1972 I conducted a survey in collaboration with Professor Halim Barakat to elicit voters' attitudes in Beirut. The survey was taken before the last week of the election and included the Third and First Districts of Beirut and a suburban community south of the city. The voters in the First District elect eight deputies to parliament, four of whom are Armenians. The heavily Armenian precincts were left out of the survey because of practical problems. Voters in the Third District elect five deputies to parliament, four Sunnite Muslims and one Orthodox Christian. In order to elicit voters' attitudes among the Shiites it was decided to survey a Shiite community, Burj al-Barājina, which is situated on the southern borders of Beirut and can be considered residentially part of the city, although it votes in the Baabda District. This Baabda District elects one Shiite deputy, one Druze and three Maronites, but most of the Shiite population of the district live in this town. The survey findings presented here are suggestive, but more surveys need to be conducted before we reach conclusive results.

Voters' intentions and attitudes regarding participation confirm the point made earlier that not less than 70 per cent of Lebanese voters go to the polls. A large majority (71 per cent) reported voting in the previous elections; of the remaining group, 16 per cent were then under age. Similarly, a very large group, 90 per cent, said they intended to vote in the coming elections. Because of financial limitations, no follow-up was conducted to determine how many actually voted. However, it can be safely maintained that less than 90 per cent of registered voters went to the polls, for the following reasons. The sample was biased in favour of males, who are believed to vote in larger numbers than females. Second, the sample was determined on the basis of residential blocks, and only those who were physically present in the country were actually interviewed.

Data were collected relevant to a hypothesis generally accepted among observers of Lebanese politics, namely that in making up his mind the voter is strongly affected by personal pressure. Corollaries of this hypothesis were also examined: (i) that personal pressure on the voter is exercised strongly by the candidates and election-brokers (election 'keys', in Lebanese parlance), and (ii) pressure from kinsmen or kinship solidarity. In all three districts, survey returns show that the majority, 65 per cent, obtained information on the elections and the candidates through the mass media, which mostly means in this case the printed press. Only a group of 15 per cent said that they obtained their information from personal sources.

If, as we have found, electoral information is not communicated mainly through oral channels, what about influence? Survey returns show that 22 per cent only of those interviewed had been personally contacted regarding the elections. Variations according to district are noticeable here: 32 per cent in the Third District and 13 per cent in each one of the two other districts reported personal contact.

With respect to corollary (i), it was found that pressure to which voters are exposed comes directly from candidates and local influentials in this order of importance. However, only a small group of those interviewed, 15 per cent of the sample, were actually contacted, and the hypothesis is not confirmed. On the basis of results from this survey, the hypothesis should read: a small number of voters are directly contacted by the candidate, his representatives and local influentials. It is interesting here to observe another related finding, namely that as many if not more voters (25 per cent) take the initiative to contact the candidate personally. The majority of those said that they call on the candidates to pay their respects. Others mentioned specifically political reasons and matters of a personal business nature. To make a social call on the candidate usually means to draw attention to one's political presence, especially the attention of the candidate. In another related question, 26 per cent of the respondents stated that they contact deputies for personal business matters. It may be inferred here that about one-fourth of the electorate is strongly involved in politics to the extent that they help in the campaign, seek personal favours and assert their political presence.

Corollary (ii): relatives constitute a pressure on each other to vote in a particular way. According to the survey, relatives constitute a small proportion of those who make personal contacts with voters, running behind candidates and local influentials. A group of 13 per cent only indicated that they consult relatives; this can hardly be said to confirm the hypothesis. Many, however, expressed their willingness in principle to conform to family pressure, should that be exercised.

In short, the failure of the data to confirm the hypothesis indicates that factors related to personal contact are not dominant in determining the attitudes of voters. If the Beirut voter is not subject or does not respond to personal pressures, then how does he form his opinion during the election?

In contrast to widespread belief, the voter in Beirut is strongly individualistic and decides on his own how to vote. A group of 76 per cent reported that they do not consult anyone and decide individually. Moreover, a fairly large number (42 per cent) believe that no one can be considered influential in their community and that no one enjoys any special influence over anyone else. In view of the finding stated earlier that a negligible number of voters were actually contacted by local influentials, such an opinion should be taken seriously.

The voter in Beirut who has to make up his mind independently as to how to vote is not helped by political parties since very few candidates run with party labels. In general, Lebanese avoid membership of political parties; even in the First District, only 11 per cent stated that they belonged to a political party, 8 per cent more than the Third District. However, the voter in the First District votes for party candidates and shows more interest in political parties than his counterpart in the Third District. Asked if they prefer their deputies to belong to political parties, voters answered differently according to district.

Those who dislike partisan candidates express a very low opinion of existing political parties and very little liking for political parties in

Table 6.3: Attitudes Toward Political Parties (in Percentages)

	First District (Christian)	Third District (Muslim)
Prefers candidate to belong to a party	58	39
Prefers candidate not to be a member of a party	35	55

principle. Many think political parties are self-serving and discriminate against non-party members, while others resent giving away their freedom of choice to impersonal political party organisations.

As can be expected in a segmentary society like Lebanon, communal differences explain more than class differences. Voters in Beirut and Burj al-Barājina seem to have a diffuse sense of class identity. When asked what social class they thought they belonged to, the majority of those interviewed (72 per cent) said that they belonged to the middle class.

It is obvious from the data that voters at both ends of the scale, the poor and the rich, viewed themselves as belonging to a middle level socially, and although it is difficult to see what they had in mind regarding the idea of class, it is clear that they had no strong sense of class identity. Many were baffled by the question, while some took it quite naturally and indicated casually that they viewed themselves in the middle, neither high nor low. This attitude of social levelling which characterises the Beirut voter, however, is not a symptom of economic equality but rather a reflection of a sense of social equality. Indeed, the Lebanese are not separated by strong social barriers and mix quite easily. The voter's attitudes on a variety of issues did not positively correlate with his self-assessment of class position nor with his income. The most important factor next to confessionalism in explaining differences in voters' political attitudes is education followed by exposure to the mass media. In view of this, we shall discuss how attitudes are affected by communal identity according to the various issues used in the interviews.

The Lebanese system is marked by partially overlapping zones of agreement and differences. A tolerance point can be observed in the relations of religious communities and constitutes a threshold the crossing of which leads to conflict. There are certain issues which are particularly sensitive to the communal stimuli, such as excessive presidential power, the Palestinian presence in Lebanon, alignment in foreign policy and shares of influence of each community. On all these issues one detects an acceptable minimum which makes it possible for the diverse communities to coexist and which most people respect. Some of these issues like the presidency and the communal arrangement were touched upon in the survey. If survey results in Beirut are any indication, it can be concluded that the zones of agreement have grown bigger, and vertical lines of division are no longer as deep as they used to be before independence. The attitude tests which we have run do not conceal the communal differences which in some cases are quite distinct and statistically significant, but they confirm that in addition to the vertical divisions there is sufficient similarity in attitudes to make the system of coexistence viable.

Some differences in Christian and Muslim attitudes are related to social and political issues that are connected with religious dogma. One example is attitudes towards civil marriage which is accepted by a majority of Christians and rejected by a majority of Muslims (Table 6.4).

Another point of difference between the two communities reflects diffuse class bias. When asked if they would favour the election of peasants and labourers to parliament, fewer Christians (65 per cent) expressed acceptance of the idea than Muslims (85 per cent). Another significant difference is over the question of lowering the voting age to 18, a proposal which received greater support from Muslims (76 per cent) than Christians (61 per cent).

It will be noticed that on all these issues, except civil marriage, a majority of Muslims and of Christians line up on the same side, with the difference being limited to the range of support. Greater agreement is noticeable in the attitudes of members of the two communities regarding support of the free economic system in the country: Christians by 88 per cent and Muslims by 80 per cent. Interestingly enough, there is little difference in the attitudes of the two groups regarding the

Table 6.4: Christian and Muslim Attitudes Towards Civil Marriage

	Support (%)	Oppose (%)
Christians	66	34
Muslims	39	61

freedom of a woman to vote contrary to the wishes of her husband: Muslims approve by 74 per cent and Christians by 82 per cent.

The exploration of attitudes regarding political communalism as an institution reveals unexpected results. In the first place, it seems that a majority in both camps approve the organisation of parliamentary elections according to the communal quota system. However, support of the quota system by Muslims is noticeably greater than that of the Christians, 62 compared to 51 per cent (Chi-square significant at the .04 level). This may seem curious in view of the fact that it is the Muslims who have been more vocal in demanding abrogation of the quota system. Thus, it should be explained in this context that the Muslim demand for a secular system is actually a matter of tactics in their struggle to gain political ascendancy. For them, the presidency is locked, in the sense that it is confined to members of the Maronite community. Muslims would naturally like to open up the office of the presidency for all or exchange places with the Maronites. However, an outright demand of this nature would create turmoil and communal strife. In contrast, demands to secularise the system would satisfy their objectives and appeal to a larger number of people from both sects. So the secularisation demand is a veiled move to acquire Muslim political ascendancy; it is not necessarily an ideological commitment to secularism.

When the reasons respondents gave for opposing the quota system are examined, this issue becomes clearer. Out of the total sample, 57 per cent expressed satisfaction with the quota system and 42 per cent were against it. However, only 14 per cent said that they were opposed to the principle of sectarianism and wanted to see a free secular system take its place. On the other hand, 10 per cent explicitly stated that they were opposed to the limited share of their community not to the quota system itself. A group of 7 per cent stated their preference for another electoral system such as proportional representation or the single-seat constituency, which does not necessarily exclude opposition to the communal quotas.

Another significant difference in attitudes between the two communities is the presidency. A very strong majority of Muslim respondents (86 per cent) were in favour of removing the religious limitation on the selection of the President, i.e. that the office should not be reserved to members of one community. Among the Christians, 61 per cent were in favour and 34 per cent opposed. What is remarkable here is not so much the difference, but rather the fact that an impressive majority of

Christian respondents were in favour of freeing the office and making it accessible to all Lebanese regardless of their religious denomination.

A considerable agreement prevails among members of the two camps regarding communal unity. When asked if they would prefer to see an electoral system in which Muslims would vote for Muslim candidates only and Christians for their own, the same ratio of Muslims as of Christians was opposed: 80 per cent opposed, 17 per cent approving. Such a step, argued those who were opposed, would consecrate and intensify sectarianism. A similarly large majority in both camps expressed readiness to vote for a candidate from another community running against a candidate from their own. Only 10 per cent expressed categorical refusal to do so.

The narrowing of the attitudinal gap between the Muslims and Christians of Lebanon was also noted on a nationwide scale by David and Audrey Smock in 1972.[16] Younger and more educated Christians, the Smocks' survey shows, tend to move closer in attitude toward the Muslims on questions of Arab identity and unity. Similarly, the more educated Muslims were found to be more committed to the Lebanese system than the less educated Muslims.[17]

In sum, examination of voters' attitudes suggests a strong commitment to representative institutions and a narrowing of the attitudinal gap between the two communities. While some differences in attitudes continue to exist, they are not diametrically opposed and by no means constitute vertical divisions in political positions of the communities. Even on the most critical question, that of opening up the presidency to all, a favourable majority obtains in both camps. All this suggests a growing tendency toward accommodation and moderation of community attitudes among voters.

The Threats to Stability

The moderation in sectarian feeling demonstrated in our survey and that of the Smocks may seem quite surprising in view of the bitter war which pitted Christians and Muslims against one another in 1975-6. This is the more surprising when one considers that this civil war was fought more sharply along community lines than the conflict of 1958. What can the explanation be?

The answer to this question is too complex to be fairly treated in as brief a manner as is permitted by this chapter. However, it should be noted that the coincidence of several political challenges which started to take a sharp turn by 1973 led to a reversal in the integration gains made in the past. Most of these factors happen to act on the areas where the two communities disagree most. External and internal challenges coincided in time and converged to rock the Lebanese system which is quite vulnerable to external strains.

One of the serious factors impinging on the system is the Palestinian challenge. After the expulsion of the Palestinian guerrillas from Jordan in 1970, they moved to Lebanon with their political organisations and top leadership. In addition, large numbers of Palestinians had been entering Lebanon illicitly since 1967 and acquiring residential cards to the extent that by 1975 the number of Palestinians living in Lebanon was estimated at 400,000 instead of 200,000. The Lebanese Christians and Muslims have diametrically opposed attitudes and interests regarding the Palestinian presence in Lebanon. The Palestinians are a challenge to the Christian political power position as well as to their ideology of putting Lebanese interests above all other interests. In contrast, they constitute a base of political strength for Muslims in so far as Palestinians are overwhelmingly Sunnite Muslim, and better organised politically and militarily. Moreover, after the 1967 war and 'Abd al-Nāṣir's death in 1970, the Palestinian resistance became the conscience of Arab nationalism and drew a great deal of support among Arab masses, especially in Lebanon where the movement could freely recruit, indoctrinate and train Lebanese devotees, who happen to be mostly Muslim and/or leftists. Stunned by the isolation they had experienced in Jordan and the ability of the Jordanian authorities to crush them, the Palestinians sought political allies in Lebanon as a precaution against possible government action to control or expel them. Naturally, such alliances were drawn up with Muslim groups and only marginally with Christians who belonged to leftist organisations. The Palestine Liberation Organisation is also composed of ideologically revolutionary groups who are obviously ill suited to serve a pluralist and moderate system of conservative economic and political orientation. The Christians were the most adversely affected in this case, being the stronger economic group.

The Palestine Liberation Organisation put another serious strain on the Lebanese political system when, as an autonomous body, it acted as a government over all Palestinians in the country. As a quasi-state within a state, it also became involved in relations with Lebanese people who had relations with the Palestinians and spread influence over them. Acting freely as a body and as individuals, often not respecting Lebanese sovereignty, the Palestinians undermined the authority of the government which wanted to, but could not, contain them.

In short, the injection of the Palestinian resistance into internal
Lebanese affairs threatened to upset the traditional communal balance,
contribute to the instigation of sectarian feelings, and undermine
national authority.

The second challenge and one that is related to the former is the
Israeli challenge. With the rising importance of the Palestinian resistance movement in Lebanon, the Israelis markedly stepped up their
attacks on Lebanon in the late spring of 1972. Israeli strategy was
apparently to pressure Lebanon to get rid of the Palestinian guerrilla
movement by attacking Lebanese villages and towns in addition to
Palestinian camps. About 30,000 Lebanese from the southern parts of
Lebanon became refugees in and around Beirut as a result of Israeli
attacks. Depending for its security on international goodwill, the
Lebanese government failed to stand up to Israeli attacks and thus did
not fulfil its basic responsibility of protecting peaceful citizens. The
legitimacy of the government and the system was thus undermined,
and political unrest became widespread. In effect, Lebanon was
subjected to a revolutionary situation, for revolution sticks out its horns
most where governmental authority is least felt.

The Israeli challenge, just like the Palestinian one, contributed to
inflaming sectarian feelings and differences. Those who were hit
hardest by Israeli attacks were Muslims, whereas the foreign policy of
Lebanon and its timidity *vis-à-vis* Israel is attributable to the Christians
who through the control of the presidency and the Ministry of Foreign
Affairs also control Lebanese foreign policy. Muslims were therefore
upset about the failure of the government to protect their people, just as
Christians were upset by Muslim support for Palestinians who were
threatening the independence and integrity of Lebanese territory by
provoking Israeli attacks.

On the domestic scene, the major issue that was seriously preoccupy-
ing the political elite by 1973 was the power balance prevalent since
1943. This issue has been with the Lebanese for a long time, but in
1973 it was brought more forcefully into the open, stimulated by the
growing strength of the Palestinian presence on Lebanese soil. It took
the form of the traditional struggle between the Sunnite Muslim
Premier and the Maronite President. Their differences over the issue
of how to meet the Israeli-Palestinian challenge led the Maronite
President to violate the traditional balance by ignoring the standing of
the Premier as representative of the Muslim community. Instead of
nominating a strong Premier, he resorted to choosing weak political
leaders among the Sunnites for the job, which infuriated the Muslims

who became more insistent on their political demands and wanted to make constitutional changes. Evidently, by 1973 the various Maronite groups and parties, with the exception of the al-Kutla al-Waṭaniyya of Raymond Edde, reached the conclusion that a confrontation with the Palestinians, the largest armed political group in Lebanon, was inevitable. Apparently, having become convinced that the Palestinians had won over the Lebanese Muslim masses and undermined the positions of the Sunnite Muslim leaders, the Maronites reconciled themselves to the bitter fact of having to confront a united Muslim-Palestinian alliance. Thus Christian militias emerged and engaged Palestinian guerrillas, while the Lebanese Muslims relied heavily on Palestinian arms.

The Lebanese paradox may be summarised as follows: two parties in the field each of which wanted from the other what the other party did not have the power to give. The Christians felt threatened by the Palestinians and wanted the Muslims to break up the political alliance with them, while the Muslims wanted more power in the system at the expense of the Christians. The Muslims could not sever their ties with the Palestinians without losing political ground, while the Christians could not give away some of their power privileges at exactly the time when they felt threatened by an ascending Palestinian-Muslim alliance. Neither political nor military measures seemed enough to break up the vicious circle. Elite rivalry and opportunism contributed in no small measure to the stimulation of communal fears and suspicions at the mass level.

The intensity of sectarian feelings demonstrated during the war is not consistent with the moderation shown by voters in Beirut. This obviously calls for an explanation. In the first place, the fighting was ignited by small but organised extremists on both sides. These showed a strong sectarian bias in their conduct of the war, and outrageous acts under such circumstances become easily attributed to the opposite community as a whole. It is part of the tactics of extremists to arouse primordial feelings of the public in order to rally as many of the members of their community as possible in the service of their extremist goals.

Second, once conflict breaks out, its course follows an expansionist logic of its own. One such course is that conflict generates partisans as it spreads from a select group at the centre of the confrontation to others who initially were not involved in it. Conflict draws the lines and compels members of the affected groups to take sides. The longer it lasts, the less of a chance it leaves for moderates and the non-involved to stay out of it. Then, as conflict spreads and claims more partisans, it creates new groups, not originally in the arena. In Lebanon, entirely new organisations fighting in the war emerged and others that were of marginal political standing rose in importance and occupied the centre of the stage.

Third, communal conflict tends to increase the intensity of hostile feelings among members of the opposite community in direct relation to the expansion and duration of the conflict. Every new day of war creates more victims whose loss is suffered by members of their community. The more victims fall, the greater the hostility grows and the more it encompasses indiscriminately all members of the other camp. Fourth, the importance of individual opinion and attitudes fades as a basis for determining friends and foes, while communal identity becomes the separating line. Many innocent people in Lebanon became victims of the war by the sheer coincidence of falling into the hands of members of the opposite camp. Indiscriminate assault on members and quarters of the opponent community became the rule, regardless of the political attitudes of the victims. Individuals were condemned by their collective identity, and, as is the case with original sin, a Lebanese individual could not free himself from his birthright. The unexpected severity and harshness of the Lebanese civil war confirms what has already been observed of other civil wars in history.

If there is any consolation from all this bloodshed it is the fact that no group or leader during this long struggle has demanded the overthrow of the democratic system. Those who claimed to be challenging the system, not the communal power of another group, wanted to change the power balance, not to create another political system.

It is true that political integration produced by political engineering during almost half a century has been seriously undermined by the civil war, but the hope of a restoration lingers on. Moreover, what is certain is that the conflict of 1975-6 was in no way due to a failure of the political mechanisms created to accommodate pluralism. Changing the balance of power could have occurred without such a war, as in the past, had it not been for the extraordinary load placed on the system by the Palestinian-Israeli conflict. For those who see in the communal civil war a proof that the formula was deficient, we may ask how many systems in the world could take as much external strain as the Lebanese system has taken since 1967, without being shaken up or broken down.

Notes

*   A slightly different version of this chapter has been published in *Middle Eastern Studies,* January 1980.

1. The Iranian Constitution which dates back to 1906 has not been respected in practice. In Turkey a new Constitution was promulgated in 1961.

2. M. Hudson, 'The Electoral Process and Political Development in Lebanon', *Middle East Journal,* vol. 20, no. 2 (1966), p. 174.

3. Indirect elections and limited suffrage were known in Mount Lebanon since 1861. See A. I. Baaklini, *Legislative and Political Development : Lebanon, 1842-1972* (Duke University Press, Durham, N. Carolina, 1976).

4. The town of Sidon is the only single-member constituency.

5. I. Harik, 'The Ethnic Revolution and Political Integration in the Middle East', *International Journal of Middle East Studies,* vol. 3, no. 3 (1972); S. Khalaf, 'Primordial Ties and Politics in Lebanon', *Middle Eastern Studies,* vol. 4, no. 3 (1968); F. Khuri, 'Sectarian Loyalty Among Rural Migrants in Two Lebanese Suburbs' in R. Antoun and I. Harik (eds.), *Rural Politics and Social Change in the Middle East* (Indiana University Press, Bloomington, 1974); F. Khuri, *From Village to Suburb: Order and Change in Greater Beirut* (University of Chicago Press, Chicago, 1975).

6. I. Harik, *Man yaḥkum Lubnān ?* (Who governs Lebanon ?) (Dar al-Nahār, Beirut, 1972).

7. Voters from other sects are entitled to the same rights of choosing one Shiite and one Catholic candidate of their liking.

8. Harik, *Man yaḥkum Lubnān ?;* I. Harik, 'Political Elites of Lebanon' in G. Lenczowski (ed.), *Political Elites in the Middle East* (American Enterprise Institute, Washington, DC, 1975); E. Salem, *Modernization Without Revolution* (Indiana University Press, Bloomington, 1973); Baaklini, *Legislative Development.*

9. E. Özbudun, *Social Change and Political Participation in Turkey* (Princeton University Press, Princeton, New Jersey, 1976).

10. Y. Courbage and P. Fargues, *La Situation Démographique du Liban* (Oriental Press, Beirut, 1973).

11. Percentages computed on the basis of officially registered voters and not adjusted, since the ratio from one province to another would not be affected.

12. M. Hudson, *The Precarious Republic* (Random House, New York, 1968).

13. I. Harik, *The Political Mobilization of Peasants: A Study of an Egyptian Community* (Indiana University Press, Bloomington, 1964); Harik, *Man yaḥkum Lubnān ?*

14. A. Leder, 'Kemalist Rule and Party Competition in Rural Turkey: Politics and Change in an Anatolian Community', unpublished Ph D dissertation, Indiana University, 1974; A. Leder, *Catalysts of Change: Marxist vs. Muslim in a Turkish Community* (University of Texas Press, Austin, 1976).

15. Harik, *Man yaḥkum Lubnān ?,* Chs. 7-8.

16. D. Smock and A. Smock, *The Politics of Pluralism: A Comparative Study of Lebanon and Ghana* (American Elsevier Press, New York, 1975), pp. 155-60.

17. Ibid., pp. 158 and 161.

7. ISREAL

Asher Arian

Despite marked social and economic change, the political system of Israel seemed remarkably stable with one party (Mapai, later Labour) consistently receiving a plurality of the votes. But the Israeli political system was hardly static. The anomaly of the Israeli case stemmed from the very large change in voting publics (primarily due to immigration) from election to election and the apparent stability of the voting results. Part of the effect was illusory: votes changed but the government did not.

The floating vote in Israel—some 25 to 30 per cent—was no less extensive than in other Western democracies. The impact of the floating vote on the Israeli political system, however, was negligible.

The tendencies associated with Israel's proportional representation list system of elections were clear: many parties and electoral lists competed (21 in the 1973 elections), encouraged by the possibility of representation in the Knesset, which was assured if more than one per cent of the vote was won. The resulting array was a hotchpotch of organised parties, personality cults, specialised interest groups and one-issue enthusiasts. The results had always affirmed and perpetuated the dominant party system which was the hallmark of the Israeli political system until 1977: one party (Labour) always won a plurality of the vote and had always been at the arithmetic centre of any coalition calculation. The dominance of Mapai-Labour provided the system with the aura of stability even though change occurred constantly.

The results of the 1973 vote allowed the Labour Alignment to retain power. Its power was curtailed from 57 seats in the outgoing 120 seat Knesset to 51 seats in the new one. The second-largest parliamentary bloc, the Likud, increased its seats from 31 to 39. But the election results emphasised the consistent voting behaviour of a large segment of the population in election after election. While the election results had important political consequences, on the whole the behaviour of individual voters remained consistent with past behaviour. The Alignment received 6 per cent less than it did in 1969 but the Likud received only 4 per cent more. Part of Likkud's gain was clearly at the expense of the Alignment. But the significant fact was that a substantial part of the "punishment" vote was not won by the Likkud but went to the smaller parties—especially the Independent Liberals and Shulamit Aloni's Movement for Citizen's Rights—and other lists which barely missed achieving the minimum one per cent of the vote required by law for Knesset representation.

The proportional representation system and the emergence of a dominant party system in Israel prevented the translation of voting change into government change. Changes in the vote, however, were very accurately reflected in the size of the delegations which represented parties in the Knesset. The results of the 1973 elections found the two largest parties more evenly balanced than they ever had been as a result of the previous seven elections.[1] At its high point as a result of the 1959 elections, Mapai found itself with 2.8 seats for every one won by Herut, the second biggest winner. After the 1973 elections, the ratio was 1.3 to one. The previous low point was in 1965, the year in which Rafi split off from Mapai and the Mapai-Ahdut Haavoda Alignment bettered the second-place Gahal by a ratio of 1.7 to one. In 1951, Mapai won 2.2 seats for every one won by the General Zionists.

As seen in Table 7.1, election results over time have been fairly stable. Moreover, the political groupings which presented themselves to the electorate changed little over the years. While formal party names often changed because of splits and mergers, there was more continuity to the system than appeared on the surface. The rule of thumb was that, for all the apparent surface motion, fundamental change in Israeli political life was very slow to occur. For all the changes in name, personnel and ideologies in Israeli politics had tremendous staying power. The system was institutionalised early in the national history and the parties comprising it largely resisted fundamental change.

When examined in terms of the factional groupings a stable picture was provided. Parties of the left (including the communists) never won fewer than 64 nor more than 69 seats in the 120-seat Knesset in the seven elections through 1969. In 1973, they won 59 seats.[2] The centre parties ranged between 27 and 34 seats (43 in 1973) and the religious parties between 15 and 18 (in 1973, 15 seats). Smith[3] divided the parties into six such groupings and calculated the average deviation for each grouping over the 1949 through 1969 period. The average deviation from the 1949-69 average vote for the parties which are in the Labour grouping (excluding the communists) was only one per cent.

Table 7.1: Knesset Election Results (120 Seats in the Parliament)

Year of Election	1949	1951	1955	1959	1961	1965	1969	1973
Knesset	1st	2nd	3rd	4th	5th	6th	7th	8th
Left of Centre								
Communist[a]	4	5	6	3	5	4	4	5
Mapam	19	15	9	9	9	8 ⎫		
Ahdut Haavoda[b]	-	-	10	7	8 ⎱		⎫	
Mapai	46	45	40	47	42 ⎰	45 ⎬	56	51
Rafi						10 ⎭		
Movement for Citizen's Rights								3
State List							4 ⎫	
Centre and Right								
Free Centre							2 ⎬ (Likkud) 39	
Herut	14	8	15	17	17 ⎱ (Gahal)		⎭	
Liberal[c]	7	20	13	8 ⎱	17 ⎰	26	26	
Independent Liberal[d]	5	4	5	6 ⎰		5	4	4
Religious								
National Religious Party	16 ⎫	10	11	12	12	11	12	10
Agudat Israel and Poalei Agudat Israel[e]	⎬	5	6	6	6	6	6	5
Arab and Other	9	8	5	5	4	5	6	3

[a]—In the 1965, 1969 and 1973 elections, the Israel Communist Party won one seat, the New Communist List the rest.
[b]—Ahdut Haavoda included in Mapam for the first two elections.
[c]—'General Zionist' until after the 1959 election.
[d]—'Progressives' until after the 1959 election.
[e]—In the 1965 and 1969 elections, Agudat Israel won four seats of the six.

The average deviation for the centre and religious groupings was even lower: 0.8 and 0.6 respectively. The overall strength of factional groups was relatively stable. Changes which occurred were occasioned by the mergers and splits, alignments and divisions which characterised the relationships among the parties within factional groupings. But these swings should not obfuscate the basic fact that the parties of the Labour grouping—and especially Mapai—dominated the voting results and the politics of the entire period.

In 1973, after the postponement of the elections as a result of the Yom Kippur War, the rate of vote stability remained remarkably high[4] (see Table 7.2). To be sure, the Alignment was weakened and the Likkud strengthened. The Likkud won 8 per cent of the 1969 Alignment vote while it lost only one per cent of its own 1969 vote to the Alignment. But when the overall rate of stability is calculated by dividing the number of stable votes in the two elections by the number of voters who reported a 1969 vote, the stability rate was 68 per cent.

The religious parties' voters were most loyal, with 79 per cent reporting identical votes in 1969 and 1973. Only two-thirds of the 1969 Alignment voters reported that they voted for the Alignment in 1973, with 17 per cent reporting a vote for the Likkud and 4 per cent for the Citizen's Rights' List.

The 1969 lists which formed the 1973 Likkud were not uniformly successful in delivering their 1969 votes to the joint 1973 list. Gahal's success was greatest, with 84 per cent continuity. Only about a third of the Free Centre and State List voters went Likkud in 1973, with many Free Centre respondents not answering the 1973 question, and many State List voters voting Alignment in 1973. The Independent Liberals had trouble in keeping the faithful, with 37 per cent voting Independent Liberal again, but an equal number voting for the Alignment. This was particularly interesting since the Independent Liberals managed to retain their 1969 strength, indicating that they attracted votes but lacked a hard core of loyal voters who habitually supported the party.

For the 1965 to 1969 period, a stability rate of 74 per cent was reported. This result is similar to the Butler and Stokes[5] findings in England. V. O. Key Jr[6] reviewed United States election surveys

Table 7.2: The Stable and Floating Vote, 1969-73. (Stable Votes are Boxed)

	1973						T
	Alignment	Likkud*	Religious†	Other	No Answer	No Vote	
Alignment	[29]	8	1	3	2	1	4
Likkud*	1	[15]	-	1	1	1	
Religious†	-	1	[4]	-	-	-	
1969							
Other	1	1	-	[3]	1	-	
No Answer	11	-	-	-	[8]	-	
No Vote	5	5	1	2	2	[2]	
Total	37	30	6	9	14	4	1

* Including Gahal, the Free Centre and the State List
† Including the National Religious Party, Agudat Israel and Poalei Agudat Israel.
N = 1,066

between 1936 and 1960 in which questions were asked about two elections. He found that the stability rate for these elections ranged between 80 and 87 per cent of the respondents using as the base for the calculation only those who reported a party vote for both elections. Between the elections of 1956 and 1960, using the same measure, Converse *et al.*[7] found that the swing was 23 per cent. This is evidently very high in the American experience and was occasioned by the popularity of Eisenhower in the 1956 campaign and the closeness of the Kennedy-Nixon campaign of 1960.

If the rates of stability and floating vote were not all that different in 1973 from what had occurred before, what was different was the unbalanced nature of the trade-off. Usually the floating vote is a multi-sided affair with the losses of one party being made up for by the gains it wins from another. Many of the losses sustained by the Alignment then were net gains for the Likud. Perhaps this was the uniqueness of the 1973 results—not in the scope of the shift but in the relatively uniform movement of its direction.

This can be demonstrated by concentrating on the responses of those who reported that they would vote for either the Alignment or the Likud. Of this group, 44 per cent said that they were Alignment supporters and had not changed their vote as a result of the war, 8 per cent said that their support for the Alignment was a decision taken after the war, 32 per cent said that their decision to support the Likud was pre-war, and 16 per cent said that they made their decision as a result of the war. These figures show that while the Alignment began from a larger base, the flow to the Likud as a result of the war was twice as big as was the flow to the Alignment. The changes in the 1973 vote were not compensatory and did not balance each other out.

These data provide us with the background for assessing the role of the war in determining the 1973 election results (see Table 7.3). Twenty-three per cent reported that they changed their vote decision as a result of the war, whereas only 2 per cent reported that they voted differently in 1973 from their previous vote. Regarding the period after 1973, the situation was obviously more volatile, with 55 per cent uncertain whether they would again vote the way they had in the past.

Those who voted the same in 1973 as they did in 1969 and reported that they would vote the same again in the future were least affected in their voting decision by the war. The floaters who changed from their 1969 vote and were uncertain about their future vote were most affected. Much of the Likud's added strength came from this group but it was hardly a stable group of Likud support. This group could

*Table 7.3: Vote Change Due to War by 1969 Vote, 1973 Vote and Future Vote**

1969 Vote	1973 Vote	Future Vote	N	Vote Change Due to War Yes(%)	No(%)
	Alignment	Same	127	4	96
		Uncertain	175	8	92
Same	Likkud	Same	93	11	89
		Uncertain	62	13	87
	Religious	Same	45	4	96
		Uncertain	17	24	76
	Alignment	Same	6	33	67
		Uncertain	33	73	27
Different	Likkud	Same	22	77	23
		Uncertain	71	85	15
	Religious	Same	1	100	-
		Uncertain	7	57	43
		Total	659	23	77

* The other variable distributions are:

1969 Vote	*1973 Vote*	*Future Vote*
Same—79%	Alignment—52%	Same—45%
Different—21%	Likkud—38%	Uncertain—55%
	Religious—10%	

have been wooed back to more traditional voting patterns or it could have comprised the nucleus of a floating independent vote.

Voting behaviour in Israel until 1977 was most easily understood in terms of Israel's dominant party system. The dominant party—Mapai, now Labour—was identified with the epoch of independence and had been in virtual control of the major decisions and key personnel appointments for a half-century. No less important, the labour movement was successful in having its values dominate the society as a whole. In the process of having party and movement values permeate the society, the distinction between party and state was often blurred. Achievements of state accrued to the benefit of the party.

As a whole, support for the dominant party came from the more conservative elements in society. These included the old more than the young, women more than men, and the middle ranges of education and income categories. Labour was strongest in the category that contained the median respondent, that is, the one that has 50 per cent of the sample with less education/income and 50 per cent with more.

Israel's dominant party found support among all groups, but especially among those who identified with the epoch in which the party rose to its peak and to that epoch's dominant values. The highlight of Mapai's (Labour's) epoch was the achieving of independence. Jews who immigrated to Israel before independence and immediately thereafter support the Alignment heavily. The rate falls off for those who arrived after 1955, and for Israeli-born.

The opposition Likkud, of which the right-wing, nationalistic Herut (Freedom) movement and the bourgeois Liberal Party are the major components, gave the appearance of being broadly based in its electoral support (as was the Labour Alignment). But much of this spread was an artifact of the differences between the Liberals and Herut. The Liberals are a bourgeois party that receives most of its support from middle and upper-middle-class merchants and businessmen. Herut, on the other hand, is a party that appeals disproportionately to lower and lower-middle-class workers and to Israelis born in Asia and Africa. Since the followers of the Liberal Party have higher levels of education than supporters of Herut, the spread evident for the Likkud is a balancing of two counter tendencies; thus it is misleading to read into the data that the Likkud is beginning to generate the appeal characteristic of a mass party.

The support of the Likkud came heavily from the young, from Israeli-born, from Israelis of Afro-Asian background, and from those with lower education and income levels. Undeniably, many of these social and economic cleavages overlapped with the differences in political opinion. To give but one example, the same groups which tended to support the Likkud also tended to have more hawkish opinions on foreign and defence policy. Those who were older, from a European background and had more education tended to hold more flexible views.

The National Religious Party received about 10 per cent of the vote and had been the consistent coalition partner of the Labour Party. Its support was composed of many different types: traditional Jews from Afro-Asian backgrounds with low income and low education levels, highly educated intellectuals from European origins, and Israeli-born and educated youth imbued with religious ideals through formal

Table 7.4: Party Vote in 1969 and 1973 by Education and Place of Birth

		1969 Vote					1973 Vote			
		N	Alignment	Gahal	Religious	Other	N	Alignment	Likkud	Religious	Other
Elementary or Less	As-Afr	179	55%	27%	16%	2%	56	32%	50%	14%	4%
	Eur-Am	182	69	10	18	3	85	55	24	18	3
	Israel	63	53	32	5	11	51	27	59	14	-
Through High School	As-Afr	121	56	27	7	10	74	38	32	4	26
	Eur-Am	364	65	16	11	8	153	65	24	5	6
	Israel	136	46	28	14	13	176	43	42	4	11
More than High School	As-Afr	12	58	-	25	17	7	43	29	-	29
	Eur-Am	148	58	17	8	18	131	44	31	10	15
	Israel	80	49	18	15	19	126	37	37	7	19
Total		1,285	59	20	12	9	859	45	35	9	11

schooling in state-supported religious schools, a vigorous youth movement connected with the party and in their own homes. But on the
whole, the religious parties were relatively more successful among those
with lower levels of education. The picture becomes more complex
when support for the religious parties is studied by both education and
place of origin (see Table 7.4).

The European-American-born support for the religious parties
tended to decrease with educational attainment. The Israeli-born,
however, provided the opposite picture, with religious parties' support
increasing with additional education. The pattern for Afro-Asian-born
was harder to ascertain since so few of the respondents in this category
had more than a high-school education. What was clear, though, was
that between the first two categories of educational achievement, there
was an extreme decrease of support for religious parties among Afro-
Asian-born as education increased.

The 1973 elections did not refute these generalisations. On the
contrary, what seemed to have happened was that processes already in
progress were accelerated as a result of the war. The 1973 elections
were not critical in Key's sense that 'more or less profound readjust-
ments occur in the relations of power within the community, and in
which new and durable election groupings are formed'.[8] Evidence of
the lack of the basic change can be seen in Figure 7.1. It reveals that the
competition gap—the difference between the Alignment and Likkud
support levels—decreased between 1969 and 1973. However, the
Alignment lost more than the Likkud gained in each category. Thus,
the curve of the Alignment fell at a greater rate than the curve of the
Likkud rose; moreover, both 1973 curves remained similar to the
respective 1969 curves. The effect of the war seemed to have been felt
in a consistent manner in all types of settlement. In the kibbutzim,
where Alignment support was greatest, the vote loss was smallest
between 1969 and 1973 and the Likkud did not benefit at all by it.

It was clear by 1973 that if these trends were to persist, the Likkud
was likely to win an ever larger share of the vote. Two crucial variables—
age and ethnicity—pointed this up very well. Support for Likkud was
inversely related to age. This was in keeping with the trends observed
in the 1969 elections, with the difference that in 1969 even the youngest
groups supported the Alignment more heavily.[9]

The same was true for ethnicity. Familiar patterns were again
discovered but their intensity seemed to have been accelerated in the
1973 elections. In other words, the relative success of the Likkud was
not gained by drawing off votes from all social strata. It increased its

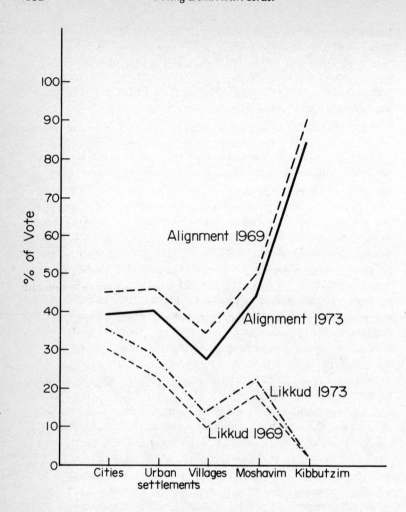

Figure 7.1: Alignment and Likkud Percentage of Total Vote, 1969 and 1973, by Type of Settlement

share of the vote disproportionately in those strata in which it was already relatively successful. Conversely, Alignment strongholds (in demographic terms) were much less susceptible to Likkud gains. Both the oldest age group and the Europe-American-born group continued to give more than half of their votes to the Alignment.

The young and the Afro-Asian groups were to increasingly represent a larger share of the total vote. The question whether the young would retain their relatively high support rate for the Likkud or would, with age, revert to the pro-Alignment voting patterns of their elders may have been at the heart of the matter. The ethnic distribution[10] presented a clue concerning the unfolding trends of the future. In 1972, 42 per cent of the Jewish population were of European-American origin, 36 per cent came from Asian-African countries and 22 per cent were born in Israel. But adding the younger part of the population changed the picture. Considering the ethnic origins of the Jewish population as a whole with the Israeli-born classified by their fathers' continent of birth, 47.5 per cent were Asian-African, 43.7 per cent European-American and 8.8 per cent were children of native Israelis. Whereas in 1972 half of those who were born in Europe were over 51.4 years of age, the median age of Asian-Africans was 35.1. In addition to the difference in median age, which in itself would indicate more children being born to the latter group than to the former, the gross reproduction rate of Asian-African mothers was 1.85 as compared with 1.33 for European-American mothers. It should be noted that the gross reproduction rate for both groups had declined since 1951, from 3.06 and 1.54 respectively. Of all Jewish children born in 1972, 44.6 per cent were to mothers born in Africa or Asia.

Projecting the trends of 1973, the Likkud would be strengthened by the coming of age of individuals from groups which had historically been more supportive of the Likkud. As more of the electorate was made up of Israeli-born voters of Asian-African-born fathers, the Likkud's strength was likely to increase. But a countervailing tendency must also be noted. Increased education had been shown to moderate this tendency in both the 1969 and 1973 surveys (see Table 7.4). The tendency of the Israeli-born of Asian-African background to support the Likkud decreased as education increased. This same moderating effect was also in evidence for the Alignment supporters of European birth. Increased education tended to lessen the support of both the Alignment and the Likkud in their respective ethnic strongholds; increased education tended to be associated with voting for the small 'other' parties.

Electoral change had always characterised the Israeli system, although vote change had not been translated into change of governmental power. The floating vote had been as large as a third of the electorate; in 1973, much of this shift was one-sided, prospering the Likkud at the expense of the Alignment. The parameters of change in the Israeli political system were widely set and a transference of power to the opposition was possible.

The 1977 election saw this likelihood take place. The past few elections had witnessed an incremental change in the Likkud's favour and we have seen how demographic changes also worked in its favour. The Alignment's dominant position and the social and economic resources at its command could counteract some of the Likkud's advantages. The images which the parties projected and the party which was more 'in tune with the times', the leaders each offered, and such factors as the international and economic situation all influenced the destinies of the parties.

In and of itself, the 1973 war and the elections which followed it were not the political blow to the Alignment which many had foreseen. All things considered, the Alignment rebounded well in a very difficult situation. But it was clearly on the decline. The fascinating question of the second generation of Israeli politics was whether the traditionally dominant party could renew itself for a second generation of rule, whether a new dominant party would emerge, or whether Israel would enter an era of rotation of parties in power.

Notes

1. All election statistics are from the official publications of the Central Bureau of Statistics.

2. Including Shulamit Aloni's Movement for Citizen's Rights. The three seats won by the list may be attributed to the left since Mrs Aloni herself was a former Labour Party Knesset member and made overtures to the party to run on their list in the 1973 elections as well.

3. H. Smith, 'Analysis of Voting' in A. Arian (ed.), *The Elections in Israel—1969* (Jerusalem Academic Press, Jerusalem, 1972), pp. 63-80.

4. The data for the 1973 elections are from a sample of 1,066 respondents of the adult population conducted in January 1974. The 1969 election data were collected in the summer and autumn both before and after the October election. Three independent representative samples of the adult urban Jewish population were drawn, with a total of 3,519 respondents. Details are to be found in A. Arian, *The Choosing People: Voting Behavior in Israel* (Case Western Reserve University Press, Cleveland, 1973). All the surveys were conducted by the Israel Institute of Applied Social Research.

5. D. Butler and D. Stokes, *Political Change in Britain* (Macmillan, London, 1969).

6. V. O. Key Jr, *The Responsible Electorate* (Harvard University Press, Cambridge, Mass., 1966).

7. P. Converse *et al.*, 'Stability and Change in 1960: A Reinstating Election', *American Political Science Review,* 55 (1961), pp. 269-80.

8. V. O. Key Jr, 'A Theory of Critical Elections', *Journal of Politics,* vol. 17, no. 1 (February 1955), p. 4.

9. Arian, *The Choosing People,* p. 42.

10. *Statistical Abstract of Israel 1972,* (Central Bureau of Statistics, Jerusalem, 1972) Tables 2.20-2.30 and 3.21; A. Antonovsky, 'Social Structure of Israel' in R. Patai (ed.), *Encyclopedia of Zionism and Israel* (McGraw-Hill, New York, 1971), pp. 1,049-52.

8. COMPARISONS

Ergun Özbudun

Introduction

Electoral behaviour is assumed to be particularly amenable to comparative analysis because it produces large amounts of quantitative data. Yet
obstacles to such analysis remain quite formidable, since elections are,
obviously, multivariate phenomena. Richard Rose,[1] for example,
includes nearly a dozen basic variables in his model depicting how an
election result is determined: eligibility to vote rules, turnout rules,
turnout factors, party system, party actions, political events, social
characteristics, standing party identification, issue predispositions and
conversion rules (i.e. those determining the conversion of votes into
parliamentary seats). Furthermore, each of these variables is flexible
enough to accommodate a host of subvariables.

Clearly, it is not the purpose of this chapter to cover such a wide area
of electoral research. Some variables cited above (electoral rules,
political events and issue predispositions) have been dealt with in the
first part of the book. For some others (party identification and all other
attitudinal variables) comparable data do not exist. To compound the
problem of comparability, we do not have the same type of data for all
three countries. While Arian's chapter is based largely on nationwide
survey data (more precisely, on surveys of the adult urban Jewish
population), Harik's contribution (Chapter 6) depended on more
limited use of survey information (his survey included only the First
and Third Districts of Beirut and the suburban Burj al-Barājina
community south of the city). For Turkey, in the absence of pertinent
survey data, we had to rely almost exclusively upon ecological voting
analysis.

To overcome, at least partly, such difficulties, we have chosen to
stress those variables that are related to social cleavages, socio-economic
modernisation and the party system, since they have been dealt with,
in varying degrees, by all three authors. Furthermore, the variables
chosen have the advantage of being amenable to both ecological and

survey analysis. For example, a survey-based correlation between literacy and voting participation can be compared to, although it is by no means identical with, an ecological correlation between the rates of literacy and voting participation. Even so, in view of the limitations pointed out above, the reader should be well aware of the tentative and suggestive, rather than rigorous and conclusive, nature of the comparisons attempted in this chapter.

Electoral behaviour is closely related to two central concepts of comparative politics, as well as of the present book: political participation and political institutionalisation. Thus, voting is one of the principal, and perhaps the most effective, modes of democratic political participation. On the other hand, the fact that political leadership changes hands and at least some political issues are resolved through regular elections is a main property of an institutionalised democratic polity. It is tempting, therefore, to compare electoral behaviour in three countries within the framework of the broader concepts of political participation and political institutionalisation.

In this chapter, direct cross-national comparisons are consciously avoided. For example, a proposition attributing the higher rates of voting turnout in Israel to higher levels of urbanisation or education in that country would be impossible to prove or disprove, since in such cross-national comparisons 'all things' are never equal. Rather, an attempt has been made to establish whether the same relationships hold true, separately, *within* each of the three nations; and, when they do not, to suggest some possible causes for such discrepancy.

Social Cleavages and Electoral Behaviour

In none of the three countries does social class loom large as the most important social cleavage upon which political alignments are based. In Turkey, using Lipset and Rokkan's[2] suggestive typology, a centre-periphery cleavage dominated much of the political life until the late 1960s. This was a cleavage in the socio-cultural, rather than the territorial, sense of the term, i.e. one between the political ins and outs, between those who wielded state authority and those who remained outside it.[3] Only recently has there been a tendency toward a political alignment based more distinctly on class cleavages, and this has been limited mostly to urban areas.

Interestingly, in Israel too, which is more heavily industrialised and urbanised than Turkey, party alignments are hardly based on class cleavages, and this is so despite the political and ideological domination of the Labour Party (the Alignment). Arian argues that the left-of-centre Labour Party receives its greatest support from the middle ranges of education and income categories, while the right-wing Herut (one of the major components of the Likkud) appeals disproportionately to lower and lower-middle-class workers. The religious parties also have an occupationally heterogeneous clientele.

Political alignments in Israel thus seem to be based less on occupational or class ties than system-specific political and historical factors. The earlier immigrants and those born in Europe and America are more likely to support the Alignment, while the Likkud appeals more to the native-born and to those born in Asia and Africa. To put it differently, those who were involved in the founding of the state, who lived through the independence epoch in Israel are more likely to identify with the Alignment. This suggests the influence of a centre-periphery cleavage in Israeli politics. As in Turkey, this cleavage exists in a socio-cultural, rather than an ecological, sense: those who founded and dominated the state (and also happened to be mostly of European origin) tended to support the Alignment heavily, much as those strata active in the Turkish war of independence and in the founding of the republic were natural supporters of the RPP. On the contrary, those who remained on the periphery of this power structure (the native-born, the more recent immigrants and the Asian-African-born in Israel; the commercial middle class, the urban poor and a major part of the peasantry in Turkey) were more likely to support the opposition (the Democrat Party in Turkey and the Likkud in Israel) against the dominant party. Both the Democrat Party's and the Likkud's support distinctly cut across class lines and combined, for example, the urban bourgeoisie on the one hand, and the lower classes on the other. This is one of the distinguishing marks of centre-periphery cleavages.

Class ties are not prominent as a basis of voter alignments in Lebanon either. As Harik's survey evidence shows, a majority of the Beirut voters perceive themselves as members of the middle class, irrespective of their objective socio-economic status. This may be partly attributed to the fact that the Lebanese economy, although a highly complex and differentiated one, does not depend primarily on large scale industry. The major cleavages in Lebanese society run along sectarian lines, and to the extent that modernisation affects the cleavage structure of the society and the bases of political loyalties, this represents a movement from family to sectarian allegiances. Khuri[4] observes, for example, that in contrast to traditional village politics where family connections are the major determinants, sectarian political loyalties become much more salient among recent urban migrants. This accords with Huntington's[5] view that 'modernisation induces not just class consciousness but new group consciousness of all kinds: in tribe, region, clan, religion, and caste, as well as in class, occupation, and association. Modernisation means that all groups, old as well as new, traditional as well as modern, become increasingly aware of themselves as groups and of their interests and claims in relation to other groups.'

Modernisation and Electoral Behaviour

While all three countries can be included in the broad and somewhat abstract category of 'modernising societies', modernisation-related variables do not have the same influence upon electoral behaviour in all of them. Socio-economic modernisation seems to have the greatest explanatory power for Turkish electoral behaviour. In Turkey, both the rate of voting turnout and party preferences correlate significantly with the level of socio-economic modernity. But such relationships are hardly observed in the same strength in Israel and Lebanon. In Israel, Arian[6] found no connection between voting participation and modernisation as measured by percent of the population aged 20 to 29 enrolled in universities.

In Lebanon, Harik observes, despite variations in socio-economic standards of different provinces, voting participation has not varied significantly from one region to another. However, somewhat similarly to the Turkish case, the rate of increase in voting participation has been higher in the less developed North, South and the Biqa' regions than in Beirut and Mount Lebanon.[7]

The difference between Turkey and the other two countries may be a function of much greater regional diversity in Turkey[8] than is found either in Israel or Lebanon. Both of the latter are much smaller countries in size and population. Israel is the most highly modernised among the three, and Lebanon (also relatively highly modernised) is dominated by Beirut to such an extent that the whole country can be considered 'one big suburb of Beirut where most voters visit and/or work', thus rendering regional and urban-rural variations much less significant than is the case for Turkey. To this general observation one may add the fact that in Israel the primacy of party politics (to be dealt with in greater detail below) has altered the direction of causal flow between modernisation and political behaviour: the level of modernisation (especially industrialisation) of a particular settlement is often influenced by political decisions of the government, instead of that community's political behaviour being influenced by a more spontaneous process of socio-economic modernisation.

If we turn now to some of the more specific aspects of modernisation (urbanisation and industrialisation) we see essentially the same pattern. In Turkey, such modernisation-related variables account for a much larger portion of the variance in voting behaviour than in Israel and Lebanon. In Turkey, urban residence is correlated with lower rates of voting turnout and a greater propensity to vote for left parties. In Israel, the urban-rural difference is much less important, since the country, as a whole, is heavily urbanised (in 1969 71.7 per cent of the country's population and 78.5 per cent of its voters were living in urban settlements). Nevertheless, in Israel, too, size of community seems to be a source of variation in party support: Likkud support is greatest and the competition between it and the Alignment is closest in the cities, while both are comparatively weaker in the villages; Alignment support reaches its highest level in the moshavim and especially in the kibbutzim. One can argue, however, that such differences are less a function of the size of settlement than of more specific factors unrelated to urbanisation. For example, the relative weakness of both the Alignment and the Likkud in the villages can be attributed to the fact that this category includes many Arab settlements where the New Communist Party (Rakah) ran particularly well. Similarly, the Alignment domination of the kibbutzim can be explained by a political socialisation process to be mentioned below. With respect to greater Likkud support in the cities, one wonders whether this is a spurious correlation resulting from the fact that Likkud supporters (the young, the Afro-Asian-born, and lower-class voters) are more likely to reside in the cities.

In Lebanon, too, the urban-rural discrepancy in voting turnout is not great, if we leave Beirut aside (Beirut had a turnout rate of 35 per cent in 1972). Harik attributes the low turnout in Beirut to Armenian abstention from voting in large numbers, and observes that in the other major cities voting turnout is comparable to that in the countryside. Hudson adds, to explain the low turnout rate in Beirut, that 'impressions and interviews suggest that in many parts of the urban core area there is disdain and even contempt for the electoral process. In Beirut, the "new men" ... cannot come to power via traditional family means because urban political success depends on money and traditional organisation outside the family. At the same time communal particularism still hampers the development of nontraditional machines.'[9]

The low turnout in Beirut and in the major Turkish cities raises an interesting question that requires an explanation. Why, contrary to the expectations of social modernisation theory, are urban turnout rates not higher in Lebanon (even if we leave Beirut aside) and, still more interestingly, distinctly lower in Turkey than the rural turnout rates? On this question, the explanation offered for Turkey stressed the distinction between autonomous and mobilised participation, while the one offered for Lebanon emphasises more specific factors such as closer personal and social ties, greater exchange of benefits and stronger feelings of self-respect in rural areas.

One may argue that the apparent differences in such explanations stem less from substantive disagreement than from different levels of abstraction pursued in the two chapters. Autonomous participation, as defined by Huntington and Nelson[10] is 'activity which is designed by the actor himself to influence governmental decision-making', while mobilised participation refers to 'activity which is designed by someone other than the actor to influence governmental decision-making'. As such, mobilised participation does not necessarily denote the idea of compulsion. Although overt or covert compulsion may be one of the means for mobilising voters, the likelihood of its occurrence is admittedly very small in a competitive polity. Rather, voter mobilisation may be found in a variety of contexts. Thus, a voter voting out of deference to his tribal, communal or village leader, or one casting his vote in exchange for cash or some other material reward provided by his urban boss or rural patron, is, according to the definition given above, a mobilised actor, since he is involved in a political activity designed by someone other than himself.

In this broader sense, many factors cited by Harik in Chapter 6 to explain high voting turnout in Lebanese villages (such as kinship solidarity, clan competition, patronage benefits and social pressures) do not refute the mobilised participation hypothesis. On the contrary, they are among the principal factors which lead to higher rates of turnout in Turkish villages. However, there remain some differences between Turkish and Lebanese rural political behaviour that make the mobilisation hypothesis somewhat more convincing for Turkey. Thus, while in Lebanon political competition tends to increase voting turnout, in Turkey high turnout is more likely to be found in one-party or predominantly one-party villages (both high rural turnout and one-party domination are, in turn, associated with low levels of rural development). Also, while the feeling of self-respect and the sense of community voting are stronger in the more advanced Lebanese villages, their approximate equivalent (sense of political efficacy) is stronger in the less developed Turkish villages.[11] Harik's survey findings demonstrating the weakness of personal influence upon Beirut voters also support the hypothesis that the urban voters are more likely to be autonomous participants. However, the absence of comparable attitudinal data for Lebanese villagers does not allow us to make direct comparisons here.

It may appear tempting, at first sight, to compare the tendency toward bloc voting in the less developed Turkish villages with the one-party domination in the Israeli kibbutzim. Such a comparison would be misleading, since the latter is not a function of socio-economic under-development, but of the original affiliation between the party and the settlement, of ideological self-selection and of powerful political socialisation processes.

The effect of industrialisation upon voting behaviour is broadly similar to that of urbanisation. In Turkey, industrialisation is nega-tively correlated with voting participation and positively correlated with major party votes. In Israel, for reasons stated above, no clear pattern of relationships can be discerned between industrialisation and voting behaviour.

Party System and Electoral Behaviour

Turkey, Israel and Lebanon differ significantly in terms of the func-tional salience of parties in their political systems. Such salience is very high in Turkey and Israel, and very low in Lebanon. Turkish politics and, even more so, Israeli politics are primarily party politics, while Lebanon is closer to a no-party model. Although parties have recently shown some growth in Lebanon, too, still only one-third of the representatives (the highest such percentage so far) elected in 1972 bear party labels.

It is not easy to explain the weakness of parties in Lebanon. Sectarian cleavages are not incompatible with a highly institutionalised party system, as is clear from the Dutch experience. Similarly, the negative association we found in Turkey between the level of socio-economic development and the institutionalisation of the party system does not help us here, for Lebanon has a highly complex economy, high levels of literacy, education, urbanisation and per capita income (especially by Middle Eastern standards), and a relatively long experience with constitutional government. Hence, we cannot attribute the weakness of political parties in Lebanon to socio-economic underdevelopment. Finally, the individualism of the Lebanese voter and his general preference for non-party candidates, documented by Harik in Chapter 6, are more the immediate reasons, rather than the underlying causes, of the phenomenon under study, since the question then becomes, why does the Lebanese voter, despite his relatively high levels of objective and attitudinal modernisation, show so little inclination to organise in political parties? In the following pages, we shall offer a tentative, and no doubt partial, answer to this question, utilising the machine politics model.

In contrast to Lebanon, both in Turkey and Israel, political development preceded socio-economic modernisation. In Israel, a major phase in political institutionalisation was reached as early as the 1920s, long before independence and even before the mass migrations of the 1930s and the 1940s. The founders of the state were primarily immigrants from Europe. Consequently, the later immigrants from Asian and African countries—many of them traditionals—were placed in a political system which was essentially modern, indeed. Comparably, in Turkey, due partly to the strong Ottoman-Turkish tradition of 'statehood' and partly to the success of the Atatürk revolution in institutionalising political power, major political institutions took root before the rapid socio-economic modernisation of the 1950s and the 1960s.

Thus, interestingly, in none of the three countries did the expected sequence between socio-economic modernisation and political institutionalisation take place. Instead of socio-economic modernisation gradually leading to more modern forms of politics, in Turkey and Israel such forms were established largely independently of, and prior to, socio-economic modernisation. In Lebanon, on the other hand, socio-economic modernisation did not lead to high levels of political institutionalisation.[12] However, this should not be taken as a direct negation of the presumed relationship. Israel, obviously, is a 'special', if not a deviant, case. Besides, one cannot deny that the modern nature of the Israeli political system is largely a function of the modern socio-economic attributes of the early immigrants who founded the state. In Turkey, even though political institutionalisation preceded large-scale modernisation when the whole country is taken as a unit, within-country variations in political institutionalisation show a strong association with the level of modernity. Even in Lebanon, which displays the least clear pattern in this respect, caucus and organised party representation in parliamentary elections is overwhelmingly concentrated in the most highly developed Beirut/Mount Lebanon area.[13]

With regard to party system fractionalisation, Turkey and Israel

display different, even opposite, patterns. In Turkey, such fractionalisation is negatively correlated with socio-economic modernisation,
while this relationship presents a U-curve in Israel, settlements with
highest and lowest levels of. industrialisation having higher rates of
fractionalisation than the others. The Turkish pattern appears to be
more in accord with Benjamin *et al.*'s[14] theorising on the basis of Indian
data. They maintain that one-party dominance (little or no fractionalisation) 'may reflect high normative consensus typical of traditional
societies'. At intermediate levels of modernisation, especially in cases
where 'interest associational activity is low in relation to increased
participation', one would expect 'an increase in the support for
fractionalised particularistic parties of local colouration. Finally, as one
moves into higher stages of modernisation, one would expect a decrease
in the number of political organisations [and] a decline in support for
breakaway and maverick groups.' In Turkey, one-party dominance at
the provincial level is extremely rare, chiefly because no single traditional group can dominate the relatively large Turkish provinces.
However, the incidence of such dominance at village level is indeed
negatively associated with rural development.[15] Fractionalisation at
province level is higher in the less developed areas of Turkey (which,
compared to Indian constituencies, may represent an intermediate stage
of modernisation in the Benjamin hypothesis) and lower in the more
modern provinces where an essentially two-party competition prevails.

Thus, the Turkish pattern (low development-low fractionalisation;
intermediate development-high fractionalisation; high development-low
fractionalisation), although consistent with Benjamin's findings, is the
exact opposite of the Israeli pattern (low development-high fractionalisation; intermediate development-low fractionalisation; high development-high fractionalisation). Part of the discrepancy here may be due
to the technical limitations of the fractionalisation index discussed
above (Chapter 5). For example, a system which has more parties
competing on rather unequal terms may have the same level of fractionalisation as one which has fewer parties competing on more nearly equal
terms. In the Israeli case, the measurement of fractionalisation is
complicated by the phenomenon of domination, for the precincts that
score high with respect to dominance score low with respect to fractionalisation. Indeed, the U-curve for dominance observed in the Jewish
urban sector is almost the reverse of the one for fractionalisation.[16] In
Turkey, on the other hand, a low score on fractionalisation indicates
two-party competition, rather than one-party dominance. Thus, while

in Israel fractionalisation scores are heavily influenced by such domination, in Turkey the same index measures the degree to which party competition is a two-party or multiparty affair. Indeed, decreasing one-party dominance in Israel and decreasing fractionalisation in Turkey, both of which may be different aspects of political institutionalisation, are associated with high levels of modernisation.

Finally, we should consider whether the machine politics model has relevance for the three countries under study. Political machines are more likely to be found in transitional, rather than traditional or modern, societies. The impact of machine inducements (patronage, pork-barrel, bribes) 'is minimised, on the one hand, when a great many voters are still closely tied to traditional patron-landowners who control their means of subsistence and hence their votes. Their impact is minimised, on the other hand, when the growth of ideological or class loyalties and concerns ... fosters an orientation to broad policy goals as distinct from short-run material gains. If correct, this analysis implies that it is especially among new electorates for whom traditional vertical ties have weakened, but have not yet been replaced by new ideological or class ties, that machine politics is most likely to flourish'.[17] More specifically, favourable conditions for machine politics include rapid social change, early introduction of competitive elections, fragmentation of political power, widespread ethnic cleavage and/or social disorganisation, and widespread poverty.[18]

While most of these conditions are absent in Israel, and only some of them are present in Turkey, Lebanon seems to be an ideal case for development of political machines. To rapid social change and competitive elections are added, in this country, a highly fragmented power structure based on fragile balancing mechanisms, deep sectarian cleavages, social disorganisation in urban areas and poverty for about half of the population.[19] Predictably, it is in Lebanon that we have the closest approximation of the machine politics model. Characteristic machine inducements (patronage, pork barrel, bribes) play an important role in determining the voter's choice. 'Villagers,' Harik observes, 'often bargain with candidates for a public project which benefits the village before they promise to vote. Sometimes a candidate finds it necessary to "pay" in advance, that is to provide the money for building a school, a mosque or church, or donate to clubs and charities. Often he makes promises to introduce a school, drinking water etc. when elected, and will be called to account in the second round if he does not deliver.'[20] Even the practice of buying votes, although seemingly on the decline in recent years, is acknowledged by all observers. As a corollary to all this, a majority of deputies show strong local orientation, that is, greater concern for their constituencies than for national issues.[21]

What distinguishes Lebanon from a number of other countries where machine characteristics are also observed (for example the nineteenth-century and the early-twentieth-century United States and present-day India) is the personal, rather than party-oriented, nature of its machines. That party machines can be quite effective and disciplined has been demonstrated by some American examples. Consequently, what needs to be explained in Lebanon is not so much the incidence of machines as the absence of all kinds of effective political parties, with such few exceptions as the Phalanges Party[22] and the Armenian Tashnaq Party.[23] Indeed, most of the political machines in Lebanon are personal organisations which rely heavily upon relatives and friends. This also explains the hereditary phenomenon (the tendency to succeed one's relatives in parliament) often observed in Lebanese politics.[24] This is not surprising in view of Lebanon's small size, sectarian fragmentation, the strength of primordial sentiments, and especially its *de facto* decentralisation.[25] Since the effectiveness of machines depends on their capacity to deliver short-run particularistic material benefits, a nationwide machine party can be maintained only where political control over the material resources of politics is sufficiently centralised. Clearly, social and political conditions in Lebanon do not allow such centralisation, and consequently, the Lebanese political machines are local, rather than national, phenomena. Within the rather narrow limits of Lebanese electoral districts, personal machines are often sufficient to do the job; hence, little need to organise in political parties.

Turkey, having much greater regional variation than Lebanon and Israel, presents all three patterns of loyalty ties and party inducements aptly described by Scott.[26] In some of the less developed rural areas where traditional patterns of deference are still strong, there is little need for machine inducements to mobilise voters. In major cities, on the other hand, class and occupational ties have recently gained importance, with the result that most voters are not likely to respond to particularistic rewards to be distributed by party machines. However, in the more developed rural areas and, to some extent, in the *gecekondu* (squatter) neighbourhoods of major cities, machine-type inducements (especially such pork barrel inducements as roads, water wells, schools, mosques, agricultural credits etc.) are known to have been widely employed. The analysis of changing voting patterns in the *gecekondus*,

presented in Chapter 5, implies that the effectiveness of such inducements among the urban poor has sharply declined in recent years. At
any rate, we should not forget that Turkish parties have always had a
centralisation of power and national orientation which cannot be
explained by the machine model. The tradition of strong central
government and the absence of deep ethnic or sectarian cleavages have
made Turkish national parties much more than a loose conglomeration
of local, constituency-bound political machines.

Predictably, the machine model is still less relevant to Israel. Even
there, parties do perform some functions usually associated with
machine politics. For example, parties have become major agents of
absorbing and socialising the immigrants to the new country. Taking
the immigrant to a co-operative village organised by the party or its
affiliate, providing the immigrant with lodging, medical aid, a job,
schooling, a newspaper—all of these may have been done by individuals
explicitly identified with a certain political party. Yet the socialising
aspects of such party activities in Israel seem to weigh much more
heavily than the particularistic rewards distributed by parties. This
three-way comparison thus generally supports the hypotheses concerning the incidence of machine politics.

The 1977 Turkish and Israeli Elections: Continuation of Earlier Trends?

After completion of final drafts of all the chapters of this book, new
elections took place in two of the countries studied, in Israel on 17 May
1977, and in Turkey on 5 June 1977. Although no attempt will be
made here to fully integrate the results of the 1977 elections in our
analysis, we were gratified to observe that hardly any of our observations regarding the 1973 elections seemed to be in need of modification.
If anything, the 1977 elections confirmed and magnified the trends we
observed in the 1973 elections.

In Turkey, the rise of the RPP continued at an accelerated rate
(Table 8.1). The party increased its national percentage of votes from
33.3 in 1973 to 41.4 in 1977 (more than 8 per cent), and came quite
close to gaining an absolute majority of seats in the National Assembly
(213 out of 450 seats, or 47.3 per cent). The RPP made very respect-
able gains in most of the populous and heavily urbanised provinces. But
it failed to make a significant breakthrough in rural areas, and remained
particularly weak in the eastern and south-eastern regions.

The JP recovered in 1977 some of its losses, increasing its percentage of votes from 29.8 in 1973 to 36.9 in 1977, thereby gaining 42 per cent of the Assembly seats. The JP's recovery was due, to a large extent, to the erosion of the Democratic Party strength, as was predicted in our analysis. But the JP is still far from its dominant position in the 1960s, and its chances for substantial further recovery seem slim, since two of its competitors for conservative votes (the NSP and the NAP) appear to be more safely anchored in their own distinctive ideological and social bases.

Actually, the NSP lost exactly half of its seats in 1977, but only a quarter of its votes (a decline from 11.8 per cent to 8.6 per cent). The weakening of the NSP suggests that the 'revival of Islam' argument should be treated with great caution in the Turkish case. The NSP's losses were mainly in western and central Turkey, and half of its 24 seats were gained in the eastern and south-eastern provinces: Adıyaman, Bitlis, Diyarbakır, Erzurum, Kars, Malatya, Mardin (2), Muş, Siirt, Urfa and Van. In other words, the 1977 elections gave the NSP a much more distinctively regional character.

One of the most interesting and surprising aspects of the 1977 elections was the sudden growth of the NAP. The NAP almost doubled its percentage of votes (from 3.4 to 6.4) and increased its number of Assembly seats from three to 16. A preliminary analysis of the 1977 results suggests that most of the NAP gains were made at the expense of the NSP. Similarly to the NSP, the NAP displays some regional characteristics. Ten out of 16 seats won by the NAP were in central Turkey: Ankara (2), Çorum, Kayseri, Konya (2), Niğde, Sivas, Tokat and Yozgat.

The 1977 elections almost eliminated, as predicted, two parties with sizeable representation in the 1973 Assembly but with no clear-cut social base, the Democratic Party and the Republican Reliance Party. They each received 1.9 per cent of the vote, and won one and three seats, respectively. Thus, the pattern emerging out of the 1977 elections was an essentially four-party system, where the two major parties obtained almost 80 per cent of the votes and nearly 90 per cent of the Assembly seats. As in earlier elections, independent candidates were successful only in some of the least developed eastern and south-eastern provinces.

As in the case of Turkey, the 1977 elections in Israel supported our observations. The 1977 elections ended the half-century domination of Israeli politics by the Labour Party (Table 8.2). Labour's popular vote dropped from 39.6 per cent in 1973 to an all-time low of 24.6 per cent in 1977, and its number of Knesset seats fell from 51 to 32. By contrast,

Table 8.1: Results of the Election to the Turkish National Assembly, 5 June 1977

Party	Votes	Percentage	Seats
Total eligible	21,207,303		
Total voting	15,358,210	72.4	
Valid ballots	14,827,712		
Republican People's Party	6,136,171	41.4	213
Justice Party	5,468,202	36.9	189
National Salvation Party	1,269,918	8.6	24
Nationalist Action Party	951,544	6.4	16
Republican Reliance Party	277,713	1.9	3
Democratic Party	274,484	1.9	1
Turkish Unity Party	58,540	0.4	-
Turkish Labour Party	20,565	0.1	-
Independents	370,035	2.5	4
Total seats			450

Source: *Milletvekili Genel ve Cumhuriyet Senatosu Üyeleri Üçtebir Yenileme Seçimi Sonuçları* (Başbakanlık Devlet İstatistik Enstitüsü, Ankara, 1977).

the Likkud increased its popular vote from 30.2 to 33.4 per cent and the number of its Knesset seats from 39 to 43, thereby coming to head the first Israeli cabinet since statehood that is not led by Labour. Another interesting feature of the 1977 elections was the emergence and strong showing of the Democratic Movement for Change (DMC) led by Yigael Yadin. The DMC finished the race as the third largest party with 11.6 per cent of the vote and 15 Knesset seats. Many analysts observed that most of the DMC votes came from former Labour supporters.

No doubt many factors contributed to the defeat of the Labour Alignment: financial scandals involving some Labour leaders, the effects of the Yom Kippur War, the continuing drift to the right of Israeli public opinion on matters of foreign and defence policy and the Labour leadership's growing unresponsiveness to public concerns and to its own rank and file.[27] But at least equally important were the long-term trends caused by demographic changes in Israeli society. While Labour is strongest among the older age groups and among the European and American-born immigrants, the Likkud appeals more to the native-born than to any of the immigrant groups, and more to those born in Asia and Africa. As the latter groups became increasingly dominant, this has been a major factor in the decline of Labour and the rise of the Likkud.

Arian,[28] in his analysis of the 1977 elections, observes 'a tendency toward class politics in Israel. In the past, the dominance of the Labour party had precluded this possibility ... In the 1977 elections the Alignment's historical dominance was shattered and in its wake a major realignment of forces occurred.' Thus, he found that 'low income was related to Likkud voting ... middle income to Alignment support, and high income to DMC preference'. However, the Likkud also received substantial support from high-income voters because of the presence of the Liberal Party in the Likkud, and it succeeded in the 1977 elections 'in adding substantial numbers of middle-class voters to its high-low class coalition in order to win the election'.[29] This observation suggests that the element of class politics in Israeli elections is still of somewhat secondary importance. The closest parallel to the Israeli election of 1977 is perhaps the Turkish election of 1950. In both cases, a dominant party identified with the establishment of the state was defeated by a coalition of 'outs' representing different social classes.

Table 8.2: Results of the Election to the 9th Knesset, 17 May 1977

Party	Votes	Percentage	Seats
Total eligible	2,236,293		
Total voting	1,771,726	79.2	
Invalid ballots	23,906	1.3	
Valid ballots	1,747,820		
Likkud	583,075	33.4	43
Alignment (Labour)	430,023	24.6	32
Democratic Movement for Change	202,265	11.6	15
National Religious	160,787	9.2	12
Agudat Israel	58,652	3.4	4
Poalei Agudat Israel	23,956	1.4	1
Democratic Front	79,733	4.6	5
Shelli	27,281	1.6	2
Flatto-Sharon	35,049	2.0	1
Shlomzion (Sharon)	33,947	1.9	2
United Arab list	24,185	1.4	1
Independent Liberal	21,277	1.2	1
Citizen's Rights	20,621	1.2	1
Others	46,969	2.7	-
Total seats			120

Source: Final official returns as released 26 May 1977.

Notes

1. R. Rose (ed.), *Electoral Behavior: A Comparative Handbook* (The Free Press, New York, 1974), pp. 8-13.

2. S. M. Lipset and S. Rokkan (eds.), *Party Systems and Voter Alignments : Cross-National Perspectives* (The Free Press, New York, 1967), pp. 1-64.

3. For details see E. Özbudun, *Social Change and Political Participation in Turkey* (Princeton University Press, Princeton, New Jersey, 1976), Ch. 2.

4. F. Khuri, 'Sectarian Loyalty Among Rural Migrants in Two Lebanese Suburbs' in R. Antoun and I. Harik (eds.), *Rural Politics and Social Change in the Middle East* (Indiana University Press, Bloomington, 1974), pp. 198-213.

5. S. P. Huntington, *Political Order in Changing Societies* (Yale University Press, New Haven, 1968), p. 37.

6. A. Arian, 'Modernization and Political Change: The Special Case of Israel' in R. W. Benjamin *et al., Patterns of Political Development: Japan, India, Israel* (McKay, New York, 1972), pp. 96-7.

7. M. Hudson, *The Precarious Republic* (Random House, New York, 1968), pp. 223-5.

8. Özbudun, *Social Change in Turkey,* Ch. 4.

9. Hudson, *Precarious Republic,* pp. 224-5.

10. S. P. Huntington and J. Nelson, *No Easy Choice : Political Participation in Developing Countries* (Harvard University Press, Cambridge, Mass., 1976); see also Özbudun, *Social Change in Turkey,* p. 5.

11. For details see Özbudun, *Social Change in Turkey,* Ch. 7.

12. One may argue, of course, that the absence of effective political parties does not necessarily indicate a low level of political institutionalisation. However, in a modern political system, parties are the chief agencies for aggregating interests and structuring the vote, not to mention their many other functions. In the absence of parties, the interest-aggregation function falls necessarily upon the output institutions, such as parliaments, executives and bureaucracies which, by their nature, are not as well suited to this task as are political parties. Also, in their absence, structuring the vote becomes very difficult. The voter tends to vote on the basis of the personal attributes of candidates and/or their stand on local issues. Thus, the link between voter preferences and the conduct of government on national issues becomes very tenuous. (For this theme, see also the Conclusion below.)

13. Hudson, *Precarious Republic,* pp. 235-6.

14. Benjamin *et al., Patterns of Development,* pp. 35-6.

15. Özbudun, *Social Change in Turkey,* Ch. 7.

16. Arian, 'Modernization and Change', pp. 106-12, 130.

17. J. C. Scott, *Comparative Political Corruption* (Prentice-Hall, Englewood Cliffs, New Jersey, 1972), p. 104.

18. Ibid., pp. 106, 114-18.

19. Hudson, *Precarious Republic,* p. 65, cites a study by the French Institut de Recherches et de Formation en Vue de Développement in 1959, which classifies 40 per cent of the population as poor and another 9 per cent as destitute.

20. See Chapter 6 of the present volume. Also see I. Harik, 'Political Elites of Lebanon' in G. Lenczowski (ed.), *Political Elites in the Middle East* (American Enterprise Institute, Washington, DC, 1975), p. 213; Hudson, *Precarious Republic,* p. 221.

21. Harik, 'Elites of Lebanon', pp. 214-15.

22. J. Entelis, *Pluralism and Party Transformation in Lebanon: al-Kata'ib, 1936-1970* (Brill, Leiden, 1974).

23. Hudson, *Precarious Republic,* pp. 126, 140, 236.

24. Harik, 'Elites of Lebanon', pp. 215-16; see also Chapter 10 of the present volume. There seems to be some association, as one would expect, between the

'hereditary phenomenon' and socio-economic underdevelopment. Harik, ibid., p. 210, observes that seven out of eight parliamentary heirs in the elections to the 1964 Chamber came from less developed South Lebanon 'where entrenched families have succeeded in restricting access to Parliament'.

25. Although Lebanon is formally a unitary state, 'central government control is a tenuous thing, depending on the agreement of powerful local leaders who themselves command sizeable deterrent forces and who can take advantage of certain geographical, cultural and historical conditions to assert their autonomy if their interests are threatened' (Hudson, *Precarious Republic,* p. 6).

26. Scott, *Political Corruption,* pp. 104-6. For details on Turkey see Özbudun, *Social Change in Turkey,* pp. 209-13.

27. H. R. Penniman (ed.), *Israel at the Polls: The Knesset Elections of 1977* (American Enterprise Institute, Washington, DC, 1979), Chs. 5 and 10.

28. A. Arian, 'The Electorate: Israel 1977' in ibid., pp. 85-9.

29. Ibid., p. 88.

PART III

Parliamentary Elites

9. TURKEY

Frank Tachau

This chapter analyses the membership of the Turkish parliament primarily as it emerged from the 1973 elections. We shall see that the composition of this political elite, particularly by contrast with earlier years, suggests that the Turkish social and political system has become more open and more fragmented.[1] We shall first present an overview, tracing changes in the composition of the Turkish parliament since the establishment of the republic in the early 1920s. Then, we shall examine the relationships between socio-economic characteristics of constituencies and the social and political backgrounds of members of the most recent parliaments. Although, as has been pointed out elsewhere, social background data cannot be directly correlated with political values or behaviour patterns, yet the data we propose to analyse do provide useful insights into the political system.

An Overview

It is useful to provide some background before we begin our analysis. Specifically, let us note changes in the character of the Turkish parliamentary elite over the years.

Among the most indicative of social background data, particularly over time, are the occupations from which members of the parliamentary elite are drawn. This is particularly the case in a developing or modernising system. In the case of Turkey, the Grand National Assembly was dominated in its early days by government officials, both civilian and military. It has been suggested that this group was available and sympathetic to Atatürk's goals, capable of managing the institutions needed to implement them and subject to his control and influence. In addition, it should be noted that official occupations undoubtedly accounted for a larger proportion of the Muslim Turkish population in the late Ottoman Empire than perhaps any other non-agricultural occupational grouping. In any event, they accounted for roughly half of the membership of the parliament for every session from 1923 to 1943.[2] From 1943 to 1950 there was a precipitous drop in the

Table 9.1: Occupations of Deputies (in Percentages)

	1920	1927	1931	1946	1950	1954	1957	1961	1965	1969	1973	1977
Official	43[a]	54[a]	45[a]	36[a]	22[a]	21[a]	27	22[d]	29[e]	24[a]	23[d]	15
Professional	18[b]	22[b]	22[b]	35[b]	45[b]	44[b]	35	44	42	41	44	45
Economic[g]	18	15	20	22	29	27	34	29	21	27	23	23
Religious	17	4	3	1	1	1	0.3	0.4	0.6	2	5	4
Other[f]	4	5	7	3	4	5	5	4	8	6	5	1ω

Sources: For 1920-54: F. W. Frey, *The Turkish Political Elite* (MIT Press, Cambridge, Mass., 1965). For 1957-73: albums of the relevant sessions and 50th Year Album (Ankara: TGNA, various dates and 1973, respectively). There are slight differences in classification between the 1920-54 sessions and the 1957-73 sessions as explicated in the text.

[a]—Not including judges and prosecutors.
[b]—Including government-employed lawyers. Note that this accounts for about half of the lawyers among these deputies (Frey, *Turkish Elite*, pp. 111-12).
[c]—Including 4 per cent judges and prosecutors
[d]—Including 2 per cent judges and prosecutors
[e]—Including 1 per cent judges and prosecutors
[f]—Including journalists and, from 1957 on, workers and labour union officials.
[g]—Including agriculture.

proportion of former officials in the parliament to a level slightly above 20 per cent. This was the period which saw the introduction of competitive party politics. The regime was shifting from an authoritarian bias to a more consensual, pluralist or participant one. The proportion of officials has never again risen above 30 per cent.

An examination of the breakdown of types of officials over time reveals some additional interesting trends. Civil servants,[3] in the beginning the largest single occupational group in the Assembly, consistently declined from 1931 to 1961, and their proportion has changed only marginally since then. Former military officers similarly declined from a high of 20 per cent in 1923 to a low of 4 per cent in 1954. In the 1960s this group rose to a new peak of 8.5 per cent, but by 1973 their numbers had again dwindled to less than 4 per cent. Educators, on the other hand, almost tripled from 5 per cent in 1920 to 14 per cent in 1943, then declined again to between 5 and 10 per cent. Their numbers have remained in that range since 1961. It should be noted that teachers were singled out by Atatürk as major advocates of his reform programme. Education was one of the prime instruments through which he sought to bring about basic cultural and social change. With the advent of multiparty politics, however, the pace and direction of the reform programme became the subject of partisan controversy. Correspondingly, the proportion of teachers declined rather rapidly back to the level of the early 1920s. In the 1960s the identification of a large number of teachers with the RPP became increasingly clear. By 1973, they emerged as a significant element within the party, and specifically in its parliamentary delegation (see below). It is also notable that from 1965 on, the number of educators in the parliament exceeded the number of civil servants.

A second major occupational grouping in the Turkish parliament consists of free professionals (lawyers, medical and health practitioners—doctors, dentists, pharmacists and veterinarians—and engineers and architects). Their representation over the years has followed a trend basically in contrast with that of the officials. That is to say, beginning from relatively modest numbers (18 per cent) in 1920, they increased consistently until they accounted for nearly half of the membership in the 1950s and 1960s. The sharpest rise in their numbers occurred during the 1940s, that is, just prior to the advent of the multiparty regime. Among professionals, lawyers have consistently dominated; they have, in fact, constituted the most numerous single occupational grouping since 1946 (with the exception of the 1957 session). Medical practitioners recorded a peak of 15 per cent in 1950, levelling off at approximately 7 per cent from 1965 on. Engineers and architects, on the other hand, constituted an insignificant proportion of the membership in the years prior to 1950, and only a modest 4 per cent during the 1950s. After 1961, their numbers rose; by 1973, they accounted for over 9 per cent of the parliamentarians.

Following Lasswell, Frey has suggested 'that stages of political development, if not actual distributions of power, may be marked by regularities in the differential participation in formal politics of distinctive social groups'.[4]   The predominance of professionals, particularly lawyers, in the Turkish parliament since the advent of multiparty politics thus symbolises the end of the tutelary hold over Turkish society and politics exercised by the previously dominant official elite. It is further notable that the emergence of lawyers as the single largest occupational group in the parliament brings Turkey in line with older Western democratic regimes. Whether this tendency is due to the fact that lawyers are better able to 'slip in and out of a hazardous political career without serious professional damage',[5] or whether it has to do with the fact that the legal profession is inherently more directly concerned with government and politics than any other career line is less clear. While it is true that other professionals may not be as free to move in and out of their practice as lawyers, the same cannot be said for such non-professional occupations as commerce and agriculture, particularly in Turkish society where family enterprise and close-knit partnerships are quite common. Yet these occupations have never been as well represented in the parliament as have lawyers.

A third major occupational grouping consists of those engaged in business, trade, banking and related 'economic' activities. Their numbers have also tended to increase over the years, though not as dramatically as those of the professionals. In 1957, they peaked at just over 26 per cent of the membership; since 1961, their numbers have fluctuated between 16 and 21 per cent.

Agriculture, as is well known, continues to account for the livelihood of the bulk of the Turkish population. Since agriculturalists have never constituted more than 10 per cent of the membership of parliament at any time, this occupational category has consistently been the most underrepresented. Several reasons may be cited for this. First, as Frey has amply demonstrated, criteria other than occupational activity have figured more prominently in the recruitment process, particularly education and local influence. Since most Turkish agriculturalists are small-scale peasant farmers, they lack the wherewithal and the influence to gain election to the parliament. Second, largely for these reasons, the vast bulk of agriculturalists who have been members of parliament have been relatively large-scale landowners. Since large-scale landowners constitute only a very small proportion of the Turkish population, they have, in fact, probably been grossly overrepresented in the parliament. By the same token, peasant farmers have been virtually unrepresented. Finally, it should be noted that the published statistics on parliamentary membership understate agriculture as an occupational activity. Many members of large landowning families have undergone professional training or higher education of one sort or another. Many of these parliamentarians list both agriculture and another occupational activity in the biographical sketches published in the parliamentary album (the primary source of our data). The two most frequent combinations are agriculture and trade and agriculture and law. We have followed Frey's example in counting such individuals as non-agriculturalists, because 'such a man would probably have rather different perspectives from one who was strictly a farmer and without mercantile [or legal] experience'.[6] Had we counted as agriculturalists all those who listed agriculture as an occupational activity, the figures for the Assemblies elected from 1957 on would tend to follow the same trend as the professionals, although in a less dramatic fashion.

We should also note the proportions of Turkish parliamentarians who have been religious functionaries. In the First Assembly of 1920, they constituted the second-largest occupation, after government officials. In no single subsequent session did they again approach such prominence. In fact, by the late 1930s they virtually disappeared. This development was obviously a reflection of the decisiveness with which Atatürk moved to make secularism a basic plank in his platform. Moreover, Frey's data show that between 1931 and 1946 'not one new deputy with religion as his occupation was elected to the Grand National Assembly'.[7] The proportion of clerics remained constant throughout the 1950s. However, as we approach the present, the picture changes markedly again. There is a slight upturn in the proportion of clerics in 1969, and by 1973 we again have a significant percentage of parliamentarians who are either clerics outright, or involved in religious activities of one sort or another. The political significance of this resurgence is clear: it is an overt sign of opposition to the secularist modernising reforms of Atatürk, opposition which from the 1920s until the 1960s was essentially latent in terms of political expression. We shall have more to say about the ramifications of this development and the polarisation of which it is an indication.[8]

Finally, we might note that 'other' occupations have tended to remain stable between 3 and 8 per cent of the deputies. For sessions prior to 1957, the bulk of these deputies were journalists. Since 1961, however, the number of journalists has steadly declined. In 1973, for example, the journalists were outnumbered by union officials.[9]

Other characteristics of parliamentary deputies may be succinctly summarized. In terms of education, the members of the Grand National Assembly have consistently represented a very select elite. Two-thirds or more of them have undergone university-level education in every session from 1920 to 1973. While the general educational level of the population as a whole has risen during those years, the literacy rate has only recently (1970) crossed the threshold of 50 per cent. There are also indications that the deputies are generally better educated than civil servants.[10] The general expansion of the educational system is, however, reflected in higher proportions of members educated at the secondary level.

Localism (defined as birth in constituency or province represented) shows a curvilinear trend which reflects changes in regime, though less clearly than occupation. Starting from a level of approximately 60 per cent locally born deputies in 1920, the proportion dropped to a low of less than 40 per cent in 1935. From that Assembly to the one of 1961, there was a steady rise in the proportion of locally rooted deputies, particularly between 1943 and 1946 (again, with the coming of multi-party politics). The 1965 Assembly recorded a dip, followed by new highs in the 1969 and 1973 sessions. In short, under the strict tutelage of the Atatürk regime, politics was clearly controlled from the national centre. As tutelism gave way to more competitive politics, local influence rose steadily.

Over the years, the Turkish parliament has been a relatively youthful body, especially by comparison with legislatures in the West. The curve of average age began at precisely 43 years in 1920, rose steadily to a peak of 54 in 1943, and then declined precipitously in the 1940s, more gradually in the 1950s. Again, this is a reflection of changes in regime: when Atatürk first came to power, he brought into office with him a relatively youthful group of politicians. This group remained fairly stable (as reflected in other data), with the result that the parliament aged over the years of single-party rule. With the advent of multiparty politics, a new generation of younger individuals gained access, and the age curve fell.

Overwhelming majorities of the deputies have been married men from the beginnings of the Turkish Republic. There was a slight increase in the proportion of married members in 1950, with the inauguration of the Democrat regime. This has been attributed to rising local influence which accompanied the advent of multiparty politics. Although Turkish society in general puts a high premium on marriage as an institution and lifestyle, this tendency seems more pronounced in the more traditional sectors. Thus, we see no reason to doubt the continuing validity of Frey's assumption that married men evince 'the sobermindedness that local [i.e. more traditional] opinion ascribes to those who have assumed marital responsibilities'.[11]

Family size, as indicated by average number of children per married member, may be more indicative of social and cultural conditions than marital status. At any rate, the data are more suggestive. Beginning at a level of 2.8 in the 1920s, this figure declined until it reached a low of 2.3 in 1957. From 1961 on, it has risen steadily until by 1973 it was back to the peak of 2.8. In 1977 the average number of children per married member was 2.7. Here, too, the multiparty period seems to differ from the preceding regime. The largest family prior to 1950 consisted of nine children. In 1950, three deputies appeared with larger families, and there was at least one such deputy in each of the sessions from 1961 on. In 1977 one member reported 17 children. It would appear that this trend towards larger families is part of a more general pattern bringing the social characteristics of members of parliament into somewhat closer alignment with the characteristics of Turkish society at large.

In terms of social backgrounds, then, it can be said in general that the advent of multiparty politics in Turkey produced several significant changes in the Turkish parliament. The occupational structure of the legislature changed from dominance by officials to dominance by professionals. Locally rooted politicians have become increasingly numerous. Although the proportion of university-educated members does not seem to have been affected by the change in the regime, there was an increase in the number of members with high school backgrounds probably reflecting rising levels of education in the society at large. Average age and family size also show the effects of the change of regime.

Finally, we should take note of a more political indicator, the turnover rate of parliamentarians. Once again, we find a clear impact of changes in regime. The sessions of 1920, 1950 and 1961, marking the inauguration of new regimes, invariably were characterised by the election of exceptionally large numbers of deputies with no previous parliamentary experience. The single-party regime of Atatürk, by contrast, recorded very low rates of turnover, with the session of 1931

Table 9.2: Turkish Provinces Ranked by Level of Socio-economic Development (Highest to Lowest)

Rank	Province	Rank	Province
Group I		*Group* III	
1.	Istanbul	27.	Amasya
2.	Ankara	28.	Malatya
3.	Izmir	29.	Kırklareli
4.	Adana	30.	Nevşehir
5.	Kocacli	31.	Muğla
6.	İçel	32.	Erzurum
7.	Bursa	33.	Burdur
8.	Eskişehir	34.	Erzincan
9.	Konya	35.	Çanakkale
10.	Kayseri	36.	Kırşehir
11.	Balıkesir	37.	Giresun
12.	Rize	38.	Denizli
13.	Zonguldak	39.	Bolu
		40.	Artvın
Group II		*Group* IV	
14.	Hatay	41.	Uşak
15.	Sakarya	42.	Siirt
16.	Gaziantep	43.	Niğde
17.	Aydın	44.	Afyon
18.	Trabzon	45.	Çorum
19.	Antalya	46.	Kars
20.	Samsun	47.	Çankırı
21.	Manisa	48.	Sıvas
22.	Isparta	49.	Kahramanmaraş
23.	Tekirdağ	50.	Diyarbakır
24.	Edirne	51.	Bitlis
25.	Kütahya	52.	Bilecik
26.	Elazığ	53.	Urfa
		54.	Tokat
Group V			
55.	Kastamonu		
56.	Gümüşhane		
57.	Van		
58.	Ordu		
59.	Tunceli		
60.	Sinop		
61.	Ağrı		
62.	Yozgat		

Table 9.2. (contd.)

Rank	Province
63.	Mardin
64.	Adıyaman
65.	Muş
66.	Hakkâri
67.	Bingöl

Source: Devlet İstatistik Enstitüsü, *Census of Population by Administrative Division* (Pub. No. 672, Ankara, 1973), Table I, p. 104.

marking the nadir of 29 per cent.[12] Since 1950, less than 50 per cent of each session have been experienced parliamentarians. In this respect, the Turkish parliament differs markedly from most Western legislatures (with the single exception of Finland).[13]

Such, in brief, are the leading characteristics of Turkish parliamentarians over the first fifty years of the Turkish Republic. We turn now to a more detailed examination of recent trends with specific attention to the apparent effects of socio-economic factors and interparty differences.

Socio-economic Development and Background Characteristics of Parliamentarians

Numerous analyses of Turkish socio-economic data have been undertaken in recent years by both Turkish and Western scholars.[14] Since we are specifically interested in discovering what, if any, relationships exist between the level of socio-economic development of constituencies and the parliamentary elites which represent them, we shall utilise the State Planning Organisation's general index of socio-economic development. Although this index was developed without reference to geographical or spatial factors (unlike the Albaum-Davies system), thus minimising cultural and territorial variables, it is impossible to separate the two types of data altogether, for they are to some extent interrelated. Thus, if we project the provinces as ranked in Table 9.2 onto a map of Turkey, we find that six of the top 13 are located in the Marmara, Aegean and Mediterranean regions, and another two along the Black Sea coast, while only five are interior provinces. At the opposite extreme, eight of the bottom 13 are located in eastern Turkey. Moreover, eight of the top 13 provinces include the largest cities of the country; none of the last 13 include cities of any significant size.

The SPO index is a composite of the following variables: industriali-sation; commerce and finance; agricultural development; social and cultural development; health; education; demography; and communica-tions and transport. The data base covers the years between 1963 and 1970.[15] For the sake of clarity in projecting trends and patterns, we have divided the 67 provincial constituencies into five roughly equal groupings, or quintiles, ranked from most developed (I) to least developed (V).

Occupations

Looking first at the distribution of gross occupational categories across the five developmental groupings of provinces as given in Table 9.3, we find that professionals predominated in virtually all provincial groupings in 1973 as well as in each of the three preceding sessions. If we examine the rank ordering of each occupational category, it seems that association between level of development and representation of occupations was higher in 1973 than in previous sessions. Thus, in 1961, the rank order of the provincial groupings in terms of representa-tion of professionals does not follow any clear line of progression. In 1973, by contrast, the three least developed provincial groupings had the highest representation of professionals. Among officials, too, the relationship between occupation and level of development appears to be stronger in 1973 than was the case earlier, with the three most highly developed provincial groupings recording the highest proportions of officials. Economic activities, by contrast, show some indications of negative association with development. In all sessions save that of 1969, the highest proportion of deputies engaged in these occupations appears in the least developed provincial grouping; rank ordering, however, does not assume real shape until the 1973 session, in which the two least developed provincial groupings record the highest proportions of deputies engaged in economic activities. In short, in the 1973 Turkish parliament professional and official occupations tend to be positively associated with socio-economic level of constituency, while economic occupations tend to show a negative relationship. It may be inferred that this pattern reflects differences in the occupational structures of the constituencies. Occupational structures of constituen-cies, in turn, are at least in part reflective of levels of socio-economic development.

Of the remaining occupational categories, religious activities appeared in visible proportions for the first time in 1973, as noted earlier. In that session, the highest proportions are in the fourth and second provincial groups, respectively, while the lowest is in the fifth group. On the face of it, this suggests no clear association. Finally, 'other' occupations, consisting primarily of journalists and labour union officials, generally appear in substantially higher proportions in the more highly developed provincial groupings. In view of the clear association between these occupations and more highly organised and developed industry and commerce, this is what one would expect to find.[16]

Turning to the more specific occupational categories, lawyers lead the way, not only for professionals in general, but for the parliament as a whole. Health practitioners (primarily doctors) are far less numerous than lawyers in all provincial groupings. They also tend to be more evenly distributed across provincial groupings prior to 1973, with some shifts in rank ordering from one session to another. There seems to be no clear relationship to level of development, however. Engineers and architects, by contrast, increase in numbers from 1961 to 1973. Moreover, while in 1961 the rank order of the provincial groupings in terms of proportions of engineers and architects is identical with their rank order in terms of level of development, this association tends to break down increasingly with the passage of time.

Among the official occupations, only one shows clear signs of association with levels of development in 1973. Rank ordering of provincial groupings in terms of representation of educators is identical with rank order in terms of level of development. This is undoubtedly a reflection of the greater politicisation of the profession, as well as greater group or social autonomy in more developed constituencies.

Although the relation of the figures for businessmen and merchants to level of development is not altogether clear, it may be significant that in three of the four sessions the least developed provincial group V had the highest proportion of these deputies. Finally, representation of agriculturalists tends to be negatively related to levels of development, with the lowest proportions appearing in provincial groups I and III, and the highest in group V.

If we examine the occupational structures of the provincial groupings, the familiar pattern emerges of the dominance of the professionals. Interestingly, more often than not the economic occupations outrank the official category. The gap between officials and the economic occupations appears to widen in 1973: in groups IV and V, the latter outnumber the former by a factor of two to one and more. In no case do officials outnumber those engaged in economic activities by such a wide margin. At this point we cannot determine whether this foreshadows a new trend in the characteristics of parliamentary representatives in

Table 9.3: Occupations of Deputies by Level of Development of Provinces

Provincial Group	1961						1965					
	I	II	III	IV	V	Whole House	I	II	III	IV	V	Whole House
No. of deputies	158	89	69	80	51	447[a]	160	86	66	81	52	445[b]
	%	%	%	%	%	%	%	%	%	%	%	%
Professions	42.4	40.5	49.2	53.8	35.3	44.3	40.1	34.8	39.3	53.1	42.2	41.5
Official	22.8	19.0	27.5	15.2	25.5	21.7	29.4	27.9	33.3	27.1	26.9	28.9
Economic	26.6	32.6	21.7	30.1	39.3	28.9	16.9	27.9	19.7	16.0	28.9	20.7
Religious	0.6	1.1	0	0	0	0.4	1.3	0	0	1.2	0	0.6
Other	7.6	6.7	1.4	1.3	0	4.4	12.5	9.3	7.6	2.5	1.9	8.1

Table 9.3. (contd.)

Provincial Group	1969						1973					
	I	II	III	IV	V	Whole House	I	II	III	IV	V	Whole House
No. of deputies	163	85	66	78	52	444[c]	168	85	64	77	52	446[d]
	%	%	%	%	%	%	%	%	%	%	%	%
Professions	35.1	34.2	48.4	47.4	48.1	40.6	43.5	36.5	51.5	46.8	48.5	44.3
Official	27.6	22.4	24.1	21.8	19.2	23.7	26.2	24.7	28.1	14.3	13.4	22.6
Economic	23.9	34.1	22.7	26.9	28.8	26.9	19.1	27.1	15.7	27.3	30.8	23.0
Religious	2.5	2.4	3.0	2.6	0	2.3	3.6	7.1	3.1	9.1	1.9	4.9
Other	11.0	7.1	1.5	1.3	3.8	6.4	7.7	4.7	1.6	2.6	5.8	5.0

[a]—There are three missing observations.
[b]—There are five missing observations.
[c]—There are six missing observations.
[d]—There are four missing observations.

Turkey, or whether the poor performance of the officials in these less developed provinces is the product of an aberration in the 1973 election, possibly associated with differences among the political parties.

There appears to be a general tendency for occupational distribution to be more highly skewed in the less developed provincial groupings. This is reflected both in the range between the most and least numerous occupations, and also in the frequency with which cells appear in our tables with no entries whatsoever. For the sessions of 1961, 1965 and 1969, provincial group V consistently has a larger number of occupations with no entries than any other group. Moreover, the range between highest and lowest tends to be greater in the less developed provincial groups IV and V than in groups I-III in all sessions; indeed, in the 1969 session, the rank order from most developed to least developed is perfectly correlated in this respect. This finding is in conformity with the hypothesis that development tends to be associated with a more complex occupational structure.

Education

Although the proportion of Turkish parliamentary deputies who have undergone university training has remained fairly constant throughout the half-century of the republic, further analysis indicates some interesting variations and trends in educational backgrounds of the parliamentarians. These are almost certainly associated with the increasing openness and mobility which has come to characterise Turkish society over the last twenty-five to thirty years. Indeed, the expansion of the educational system at all levels has been one of the chief means of achieving such mobility. Among the many changes brought about by this expansion is that the impact of specific secondary schools as socialising agencies of elite aspirants may have been considerably diluted. Here we will confine ourselves to aggregate data regarding the parliamentary deputies only, leaving more refined analysis of specific educational factors for future research.[17]

Table 9.4 shows educational level attained by parliamentary deputies in the four sessions since 1961 arranged, again, by developmental provincial groupings. It is notable, first, that there appears to be increasing association of level of development of constituency with education of deputies over time. In 1961 the highest proportions of deputies with both intermediate or less (eight years or less) and with secondary education (eleven or twelve years) are to be found among the least developed provinces, but the highest proportion of university graduates appears in the intermediate provincial group III. In 1973, by

Table 9.4: Education of Deputies, by Socio-economic Development of Provinces (in Percentages)

	Provincial Group	I	II	III	IV	V	Whole House
1961	Intermediate or less						
	(0 to 8 years)	11.4	10.1	8.7	17.3	17.3	12.5
	Secondary	18.4	22.5	14.5	13.4	23.1	18.3
	Post-secondary	70.2	67.4	77.0	69.3	59.6	69.3
1965	Intermediate or less	7.5	10.3	6.0	6.2	17.0	8.6
	Secondary	16.0	23.0	20.9	12.3	18.9	18.1
	Post-secondary	75.6	66.7	73.1	81.5	64.0	73.0
1969	Intermediate or less	13.5	13.6	9.0	15.0	22.6	14.0
	Secondary	20.9	20.5	19.4	16.7	18.9	19.6
	Post-secondary	65.6	65.9	71.6	69.2	58.8	66.4
1973	Intermediate or less	7.6	11.8	7.8	24.4	26.4	13.6
	Secondary	19.4	25.9	20.3	14.1	15.1	19.3
	Post-secondary	72.9	62.4	71.9	61.5	58.9	67.1

contrast, the proportions of university-educated deputies correspond almost precisely to the relative level of development of the various provincial groups, while for the first time the group with intermediate or less education shows precisely the reverse trend. Secondary-educated deputies in this session show a more mixed pattern. Nevertheless, even this group shows up most strongly in the three relatively more developed provincial groupings.

Table 9.5 presents this tableau in more graphic form, showing the extent and direction of deviations from the educational backgrounds of the whole house for each of the four sessions. Here the least developed provincial group V stands out even more clearly: it consistently exceeds the whole house in the proportion of deputies with intermediate or less education more widely than any other group of provinces. Conversely, group V falls below the whole house in the proportions of university-educated deputies by the widest margins. Moreover, the differences among provincial groups in terms of deputies with intermediate or less education tends to become sharper over time. The range between the greatest positive deviation and the greatest negative deviation more than doubles from 1961 to 1973 (from +4.8 to −3.8 (8.6) to +12.8 to −6.0 (18.8)). Deputies representing the least developed provinces were by 1973 clearly considerably less well educated than deputies from more developed constituencies.[18]

It follows that in 1973 the deputies were more representative of their

Table 9.5: Education: Deviations of Developmental Groupings from Whole House*

	Provincial Group	I	II	III	IV	V	Range
1961	Intermediate or less	−1.1	−2.4	−3.8	+4.8	+4.8	8.6
	Secondary	+0.1	+4.2	−3.8	−4.9	+4.8	9.7
	Post-secondary	+0.9	−1.9	+7.7	0	−9.7	17.4
1965	Intermediate or less	−1.1	+1.7	−2.6	−2.4	+8.4	11.0
	Secondary	−2.1	+4.9	+2.8	−5.8	+0.8	10.7
	Post-secondary	+2.6	−6.3	+0.1	+8.5	−9.0	17.5
1969	Intermediate or less	−0.5	−0.4	−5.0	+1.0	+8.6	13.6
	Secondary	+1.3	+0.9	−0.2	−2.9	−0.7	4.2
	Post-secondary	−0.8	−0.5	+5.2	+2.8	−7.6	12.8
1973	Intermediate or less	−6.0	−1.8	−5.8	+10.8	+12.8	18.6
	Secondary	+0.1	+6.6	+1.0	−5.2	−4.2	11.8
	Post-secondary	+5.8	−4.7	+4.8	−5.6	−8.2	14.0

* Arithmetic difference between percentage figure for each grouping in each educational category for each session and percentage for that educational category and session for the whole house.

constituencies, at least in terms of education. One might surmise from these data that the deputies are also becoming more locally rooted. An examination of the data pertaining to localism will enable us to determine whether this conjecture is accurate.

Localism

Table 9.6 presents the relevant data. The association between localism, as defined by birth in constituency represented,[19] and relative level of development is manifest. Provincial group I consistently falls well below the whole house, while group V equally consistently is well above it. The intermediate groupings also fall almost perfectly into line in terms of rank ordering. It seems safe to conclude, therefore, that prior to 1973 education had less to do with localism than was the case in that session. This might conceivably reflect a pattern of young men returning to their communities upon completion of higher education or professional training, thus manifesting both a relatively high degree of education and high levels of localism. None the less, the conclusion stated at the end of the previous section still stands: deputies have tended to become more characteristic of their constituencies. This conclusion applies to both education and localism, for the levels of

Table 9.6: Localism: Percentage of Deputies Born in Province Represented, by Socio-economic Development of Provinces

Provincial Group		I	II	III	IV	V	Whole House	Range
1961	%	57.6	69.7	71.0	80.2	84.6	69.3	
Deviation from House		− 11.7	+ 0.4	+ 1.7	+ 11.4	+ 15.3		27.0
1965	%	46.3	67.0	64.2	69.1	72.2	60.2	
Deviation from House		− 13.9	+ 6.8	+ 4.0	+ 8.9	+ 12.0		25.9
1969	%	61.3	79.5	77.9	88.5	88.7	75.3	
Deviation from House		− 14.0	+ 4.2	+ 2.6	+ 13.2	+ 13.4		27.4
1973	%	57.6	80.0	82.8	85.9	92.5	74.4	
Deviation from House		− 16.8	+ 5.6	+ 8.4	+ 11.5	+ 18.1		34.9

localism tended to rise over time as well, particularly in the least developed provinces.

Age

Average age does not appear to differ much among the provincial groupings. As with education, deviations from the house as a whole give a clearer indication of the differences that do exist. Thus, the deputies representing the most highly developed provinces consistently were slightly older than the norm for the parliament. In a sense, this runs counter to what assumptions about the relation between development and politics would lead one to expect. In other words, if we assume that less developed communities are likely to be more tradition-oriented, and if we assume further that traditional communities tend to attribute greater status to age than modern communities, then we would expect to find older political leaders emerging from less developed (more traditional) constituencies. The fact that our data do not confirm these assumptions suggests that other factors are operative. In the absence of detailed data pertaining to individual constituencies, we are left to speculate what these might be. One possibility is that in the more urbanised, more heavily populated, more complex constituencies included in provincial group I, competition for elective office is sharper than elsewhere, with the result that older candidates with correspondingly greater professional achievement, visibility, political connections and general prestige are available in larger numbers and block access for younger politicians. In the simpler, less crowded,

Table 9.7: Average Age of Deputies, by Level of Development of Provinces

Provincial Group	I	II	III	IV	V	Whole House
1961	44.0	44.3	41.7	42.9	41.7	43.4
Deviation from Whole House	+0.6	+0.9	−1.7	−0.5	−1.7	
1965	46.1	43.9	43.6	44.0	44.7	44.7
Deviation	+1.4	−0.8	−1.1	−0.7	0	
1969	46.3	44.5	44.1	45.1	45.3	45.3
Deviation	+1.0	−0.8	−1.2	−0.2	0	
1973	46.4	44.8	44.5	44.0	46.1	45.4
Deviation	+1.0	−0.6	−0.9	−1.4	+0.7	

more remote constituencies included in the other provincial groupings, factors such as educational attainment, professional status and family connections may open the way to elective office for relatively younger men. This might also explain the appearance of a larger proportion of university-educated deputies in the less developed provinces in several of the sessions, as noted above.

None the less, it is also notable that after 1961 the least developed grouping of provinces produced older deputies than most of the other groupings. Here, perhaps, the traditional prestige associated with age did play a greater role after all.

Marital Status and Size of Family
Marital status does not show sufficient variations over time or among provincial groupings to warrant analysis.

Table 9.8: Average Number of Children per Married Deputy, by Level of Development of Provinces

Provincial Group	I	II	III	IV	V	Whole House
1961	2.34	2.39	2.19	2.55	2.70	2.4
1965	2.27	2.39	2.20	2.82	2.53	2.5
1969	2.40	2.62	2.28	3.08	3.34	2.7
1973	2.29	2.79	2.57	3.35	3.92	2.8

Family size is a different matter. Two trends appear in Table 9.8. First, there is a clear demarcation between provincial groups I, II and III on the one hand, and groups IV and V on the other. The former consistently elected deputies with smaller families than the latter. What is more, the disparity between the two grows greater over time: in 1961 and 1965 all groupings elected deputies with average family sizes of less than three children. In 1969 and 1973, on the other hand, the two least developed groupings exceeded the average of three children per family by increasing margins. It is also notable that average number of children increased over time for all provincial groupings with the single exception of group I, and the amount of increase was substantially greater for groups IV and V than for groups II and III. Lacking hard data, we can nevertheless say impressionistically that average family size for Turkey as a nation has probably not increased during the time period in question. It follows that the deputies, in this respect at least, are becoming more representative of their constituents; and this appears to be true both of the parliament as a whole and of deputies grouped according to level of development of constituencies.

Turnover

Turnover of parliamentarians, as shown in Table 9.9, does not show any clear relationship with level of development of constituencies. The 1961 session may be discounted because of the unsettled state of the electorate and the parties in the wake of the 1960 military coup. In the remaining three sessions, both rank order and deviation of the various provincial groupings change abruptly from session to session with no apparent pattern. For example, group V records the lowest turnover in 1969 and the highest in 1973. If there is a pattern here at all, it lies perhaps in the fact that groups I and II tended to show less fluctuation in turnover rates, adhering fairly closely to the norm for the parliament as a whole over time. Group V, by contrast, fluctuates widely from one session to another, as noted. This could reflect the less settled condition of institutionalised party voting that one would expect of less developed constituencies, based on our assumptions regarding the relationship between institutionalised parties and relative level of socio-economic development. But that assumption does not explain why provincial group IV follows a more stable pattern from session to session than does group III which, in this respect at least, behaves more like group V. Our tentative conclusion must be that factors other than relative level of socio-economic development determine the tenure of individual members of parliament.

Table 9.9: Proportion of Deputies with No Previous Parliamentary Experience, by Level of Development of Provinces (in percentages)

Provincial Group	I	II	III	IV	V	Whole House
1961	83.5	83.1	85.5	75.3	84.6	82.4
1965	45.1	53.4	46.3	58.0	57.4	50.9
1969	50.9	51.1	58.8	59.0	43.4	52.7
1973	57.6	57.6	42.4	55.1	69.2	57.3

Political Parties

We turn now to an analysis of parliamentary deputies grouped according to their political party affiliations. As with the provincial groupings which have been our concern above, we wish to determine what, if any, differences exist among the parties in terms of the social backgrounds of the deputies, and what trends or patterns are evident particularly in the most recent elections.

Tables 9.10, 9.11 and 9.12 show the proportions and numbers of seats won by the parties in the various provincial groupings in three of the most recent elections (the 1961 election has been omitted because massive shifts in partisan affiliation of deputies after the election make it virtually impossible to correlate party strength with socio-economic level of development of constituencies in any reliable manner). The data in Tables 9.10, 9.11 and 9.12 in some measure confirm the hypothesis that larger, more institutionalised parties manifest greater electoral strength in more highly developed constituencies. Thus, the JP consistently has gained proportionately fewer seats in the least developed provinces than elsewhere in the country; moreover, in 1965 and 1973 its performance in group IV provinces tended in the same direction. The RPP, by contrast, showed a remarkably even spread of strength (or weakness) across the developmental spectrum in 1965 and 1969. In the 1973 election, the RPP profile began to show some differentiation; in particular, the least developed provinces (group V) returned the lowest proportion of deputies. By contrast, in all three elections the smaller parties and independent candidates garnered substantially larger proportions of parliamentary seats in less developed constituencies.

Table 9.10: Election Results, by Provincial Grouping, 1965

Provincial Group	I		II		III		IV		V		Whole House	
	No. MPs	%	No. MPs	%	No. MPs	%	No. MPs	%	No. MPs	%	No. MPs	%
JP	94	58.8	52	59.8	37	55.2	37	45.7	20	37	240	53.5
RPP	47	29.4	26	29.9	20	29.9	26	32.1	16	29.6	135	30.1
Small Parties: NP, NTP, RP, RPNP, TLP, Ind.	19	11.9	9	10.3	10	14.9	18	22.2	18	33.3	74	16.5
Total	160	100.1	87	100.0	67	100.0	81	100.0	54	99.9	449	100.1

Table 9.11: Election Results, by Provincial Grouping, 1969

Provincial Group	I		II		III		IV		V		Whole House	
	No. MPs	%	No. MPs	%	No. MPs	%	No. MPs	%	No. MPs	%	No. MPs	%
JP	93	57.1	54	61.4	44	64.7	45	57.7	28	52.8	264	58.7
RPP	55	33.7	28	31.8	20	29.4	22	28.2	17	32.1	142	31.6
Small Parties: NP, NTP, NAP, RRP, TLP, TUP, Ind.	15	9.2	6	6.8	4	5.9	11	14.1	8	15.1	44	9.8
Total	163	100.0	88	100.0	68	100.0	78	100.0	53	100.0	450	100.0

Table 9.12: *Election Results, by Provincial Grouping, 1973*

Provincial Group	I		II		III		IV		V		Whole House	
	No. MPs	%	No. MPs	%	No. MPs	%	No. MPs	%	No. MPs	%	No. Mps	%
JP	58	34.1	35	41.2	21	32.8	23	29.5	13	24.5	150	33.3
RPP	75	44.1	33	38.8	29	45.3	30	38.5	19	35.8	186	41.3
DP	16	9.4	9	10.6	5	7.8	9	11.5	4	7.5	43	9.6
NSP	15	8.8	7	8.2	7	10.9	13	16.7	7	13.2	49	10.9
Small Parties: NAP, RRP, TUP, Ind.	6	3.5	1	1.2	2	3.1	3	3.8	10	18.9	22	4.9
Total	170	99.0	85	100.0	64	99.0	78	100.0	53	99.9	450	100.0

Abbreviations for Tables 9.10, 9.11 and 9.12:

DP = Democratic Party
Ind. = Independents
JP = Justice Party
NAP = Nationalist Action Party
NP = Nation Party
NSP = National Salvation Party
NTP = New Turkey Party

RP = Reliance Party
RPNP = Republican Peasant Nation Party
RPP = Republican People's Party
RRP = Republican Reliance Party
TLP = Turkish Labour Party
TUP = Turkish Unity Party

Table 9.13: Occupations, by Party (in Percentages except for N)

Party	Law	Health	Engr	All Profs	Civil Sv.	Mil.	Education	Judge and Pros.	All officials	Business Commerce	Agriculture	All Econ.	Religion	Other	N
1961															
JP	31.3	7.8	4.8	43.9	6.6	6.6	4.2	0.6	18.0	22.2	7.8	30.0	0.6	7.2	166
RPP	28.0	15.3	3.3	46.6	6.0	7.1	5.5	2.2	20.8	18.3	10.4	28.7	0.5	3.3	182
Small Parties and Ind.	32.3	6.1	2.0	40.4	8.1	8.1	10.1	3.0	29.3	22.2	6.1	28.3	0	2.0	99
Whole House	30.2	10.5	3.6	44.3	6.7	7.2	6.0	1.8	21.7	20.4	8.5	28.9	0.4	4.4	447[a]
1965															
JP	30.3	4.6	4.6	39.5	10.1	5.9	9.3	0.4	25.7	19.3	5.0	24.3	1.2	5.0	238
RPP	31.1	8.8	5.1	45.0	8.1	13.3	11.8	1.5	34.7	11.1	3.0	14.1	0	5.8	135
Small Parties and Ind.	26.4	11.1	4.2	41.7	6.9	8.3	12.5	1.4	29.1	16.7	4.2	20.9	0	8.3	72
Whole House	29.9	6.9	4.7	41.5	9.0	8.5	10.5	0.9	28.9	16.4	4.3	20.7	0.6	8.1	445[b]

Table 9.13. (contd.)

								1969							
JP	25.4	5.7	6.5	37.6	8.0	3.8	9.1	1.9	22.8	25.1	4.9	30.0	3.5	6.1	263
RPP	33.3	10.0	5.8	49.1	5.8	8.7	7.9	0.7	23.1	12.9	7.2	20.1	0	7.2	138
Small Parties and Ind.	20.9	4.7	4.7	30.3	14.3	7.0	14.0	0	35.3	18.6	9.3	27.9	2.3	4.7	43
Whole House	27.5	7.0	6.1	40.6	7.9	5.6	9.2	1.4	24.1	20.8	6.1	26.9	2.3	6.4	444[c]
								1973							
JP	23.6	5.5	9.5	38.6	9.5	5.4	6.8	2.7	24.4	20.0	9.3	29.3	4.1	3.0	150
RPP	32.9	7.0	8.6	48.5	8.6	3.2	13.0	1.6	26.4	11.8	5.4	17.2	0.5	8.5	186
DP	28.6	11.9	9.6	50.1	4.8	0	7.1	0	11.9	14.3	11.9	26.2	7.1	4.8	43
NSP	22.4	8.2	14.3	44.9	4.1	2.0	2.0	4.1	12.2	18.3	0	18.3	24.4	0	49
Small Parties and Ind.	31.8	4.5	4.5	40.8	9.1	9.1	4.5	0	22.7	22.7	9.1	31.8	0	4.5	22
Whole House	28.3	6.9	9.3	44.5	8.1	3.8	8.7	2.0	22.6	15.8	7.0	22.9	4.9	5.2	450

[a]—There are three missing observations.
[b]—There are five missing observations.
[c]—There are six missing observations.

Socio-economic Characteristics of Party Groups
Occupations

As for the characteristics of individual deputies, Table 9.13 indicates the occupational backgrounds of members of parties in four sessions.

The first point worthy of note is that the distribution among gross categories was within generally similar ranges for all parties in all sessions: between 40 and 50 per cent professionals, and 20 and 30 per cent each for officials and economic activities. There were, however, exceptions: in 1965 RPP businessmen and farmers dropped to 14 per cent and officials rose to 35 per cent; in 1969 the small parties had only 30 per cent professionals while their proportion of officials rose to 35 per cent; and again in 1973 RPP businessmen and farmers fell below 20 per cent.

A second noteworthy point is that lawyers predominate in all party groups in all sessions with the sole exception of the NSP in 1973, whose contingent of religious functionaries outnumbered the lawyers by a small margin. Businessmen, merchants and industrialists constituted the second-largest occupational grouping, with the exception of the RPP in 1965 and 1973 and the NSP in 1973.

Looking at change in the composition of the parties over time, we note that the proportion of JP deputies who have been professionals declined from 44 per cent in 1961 to about 38 per cent in 1969 and 1973. This was clearly due to a consistent decrease in the proportion of JP lawyers (from 31 per cent in 1961 to 24 per cent in 1973), compensated for to some extent by a rise in the proportion of engineers and architects, particularly in 1973. JP officials remained generally stable in the 23 to 26 per cent range after 1961. Similarly, the proportion of JP deputies engaged in economic activities remained at about 30 per cent throughout the four sessions, with the exception of 1965. Finally, JP deputies engaged in religious activities increased consistently, if only minimally, during the time period in question, while those engaged in other occupations (primarily journalism) declined.[20]

The proportion of RPP deputies engaged in the professions increased somewhat from about 45 per cent in 1961 and 1965 to almost 50 per cent in 1969 and 1973. This marginal increase was due to a slight rise in the proportion of lawyers (from 28 to 33 per cent) as well as engineers. Notably, there were proportionately more lawyers in the RPP in each session than in any other partisan grouping shown in Table 9.13 in all sessions save that of 1961. Among RPP officials, there was a relatively high proportion of military men in 1965 and of educators in 1965 and 1973. By contrast, the proportion of RPP businessmen has been relatively low since 1961, as have farmers.[21] Religious activities have been virtually unrepresented in the RPP, as one might expect, given the party's past heavy emphasis on secularism as a basic principle of ideology and policy. Finally, 'other' occupations, primarily journalism but also an increasing delegation of union officials, have grown marginally within the RPP from 1961 to 1973.[22]

Contrasting the JP and RPP across these four sessions, we may note that while their proportions of officials generally remained similar, they showed distinct differences in the proportions of members engaged in the professions and economic activities. Specifically, the RPP delegation has been dominated by professionals to a greater degree than the JP, while economic activities have been better represented among JP parliamentarians than among those of the RPP. This contrasting profile clearly reflects the dominant and contrasting popular image of these two parties.

The small parties are too varied to justify extended comment here. We should, however, note the composition of two medium-sized parties which made their electoral debut in 1973. The Democratic Party, a splinter from the Justice Party, was relatively strong in the professions, especially medicine, remarkably weak in official occupations, notably the military, and relatively strong in economic pursuits, particularly agriculture, and in religious activities.[23] In terms of occupational backgrounds, then, the DP is not simply a carbon-copy of the party from which it split off.

The NSP has perhaps the most unusual occupational profile of all the parties of any size in any parliamentary session from 1961 on. Although it has proportionately fewer lawyers than any other party, its professional cadre is among the larger ones. The difference is caused by the unusually large proportion of engineers.[24] This is a politically significant group, centring around the party leader, Necmettin Erbakan, formerly a faculty member at Istanbul Technical University. The group consists essentially of his students and professional protégés. None the less, it is important to recall that the NSP is not unique in this respect. Engineers have appeared with increasing frequency among the other parties, and their representation in the parliament as a whole has also consistently risen over the years, particularly since 1961, as we noted earlier.

Clearly, the most unusual feature of the NSP is the extraordinarily high proportion of its deputies who report involvement in religious activities for their occupations.[25] They alone account for more than half the religiously occupied deputies in the 1973 session, and are thus primarily responsible for the sudden upsurge of this category in this parliamentary session. Here we have one of the clearest single indicators of the polarisation and dissensus which is now bubbling to the surface of Turkish politics. In the interest of accuracy it should be pointed out that half the NSP religious deputies were, in fact, religious educators (that is, teachers in religious schools or teachers of religious subjects in general schools). Considerations of political attitudes and commitments indicate that they are more appropriately classified with clerics than with other teachers. Most of the other teachers elected to parliament are in the RPP delegation, and their values and ideology are decidedly secular.

Education

Table 9.14 shows educational backgrounds of members of the various political parties. The RPP appears here with a consistently higher proportion of university-educated members than any other party or group of parties. The same pattern seems to have prevailed between 1946 and 1960.[26] On the other hand, the JP and other parties—except for the DP and smaller parties in 1973—outrank the RPP in terms of the proportion of members with high-school training or the equivalent.

Table 9.14: Education of Deputies, by Party (in Percentages)

	Party	JP	RPP	DP	NSP	Small Parties and Independents	Whole House
1961	Intermediate or less						
	(0 to 8 years)	12.6	12.6			12.1	12.5
	Secondary	21.6	13.7			21.2	18.3
	Post-secondary	65.9	73.8			66.7	69.3
1965	Intermediate or less	10.0	4.4			12.3	8.6
	Secondary	19.6	11.9			24.7	18.1
	Post-secondary	70.0	83.7			63.0	73.0
1969	Intermediate or less	13.6	12.7			20.9	14.0
	Secondary	20.8	18.3			16.3	19.6
	Post-secondary	65.5	69.0			62.8	66.4
1973	Intermediate or less	16.0	10.2	16.3	12.2	22.7	13.6
	Secondary	20.0	19.4	14.0	22.4	18.2	19.3
	Post-secondary	64.0	70.4	69.7	65.2	59.1	67.1

Given the greater representation of professionals in the RPP, this conforms to what one would expect.

Localism

In terms of localism, the relative positions of the parties have changed several times. The advent of the multiparty regime had an obvious effect here, for the RPP's proportion of locally born deputies rose from 45 per cent in 1943 to 56 per cent in 1946. In the latter session, the small DP delegation (36 members) had 69 per cent locally born members. During the 1950s the RPP's locally born deputies were proportionately more numerous than those of the DP. From 1961 to 1969 the RPP again had proportionately more locally born representatives than the JP, while in 1973 the JP outdistanced the RPP by a small margin. Some of these changes are easier to explain than others. Clearly, the initial upsurge of locally rooted deputies in the RPP between 1943 and 1946 was a response to the advent of political opposition. But the tremendous increase in localism in the RPP in 1954 (to 91 per cent!), accompanied by the near obliteration of the party from the parliament (it retained only 32 seats in that session) is not what one would expect, nor is it confirmed by the experience of smaller parties, who have apparently tended to slate nationally prominent candidates in 'safe' constituencies regardless of local ties. The only consistent relationship which is suggested by these figures is that the governing party seems to lag in terms of localism behind the major opposition party. This was certainly the case throughout the 1950s. The 1961 and 1965 elections would have to be discounted, since neither the RPP nor the JP was in full control of the government prior to the election (although the JP clearly dominated the election government in 1965 and was favoured to win the election).

The 1969 and 1973 data show very little difference between the major parties, and also mark new peaks of localism for the parliament as a whole. It is thus conceivable that partisan differences in terms of localism have effectively disappeared or become insignificant.

Age

Generally speaking, RPP deputies have been older than those of the major opposition parties. There are important exceptions, however. Here again, the RPP parliamentarians' decline in age began with the appearance of the Democrat Party in 1946. In that session the Republicans averaged 53 years of age as against 49 for the Democrats. With the Democrat landslide in 1950, there was only marginal change in the age relationship, the Republicans dropping to 52, the Democrats

Table 9.15: Localism: Percentage of Deputies Born in Province Represented, by Party

	1957	1961	Session 1965	1969	1973
Democrat Party	60.4				
Justice Party		64.7	60.8	76.1	78.0
Republican People's Party	75.1	74.9	64.4	78.2	76.3
Democratic Party					67.4
National Salvation Party					63.3
Small Parties and Independents		66.7	50.7	61.4	72.7
Whole House	64.9	69.3	60.2	75.3	74.4

Table 9.16: Average Age at Election, by Party

	1957	1961	Session 1965	1969	1973
Democrat Party	46.5				
Justice Party		41.3	43.7	45.2	47.7
Republican People's Party	44.4	45.0	46.8	45.0	43.8
Democratic Party					46.7
National Salvation Party					42.1
Small Parties and Independents		44.1	44.3	47.0	47.0
Whole House	45.8	43.4	44.7	45.3	45.4

to 47. Given the vast increase in the size of the Democrats' delegation (from 36 to 394) and a corresponding decline among Republicans (from 435 to 71), the decline in the Democrats' average age is not surprising. The parallel trend among the Republicans is notable, however. Moreover, average age of Republicans declined precipitously in the face of the near obliteration of the party from the parliament in 1954, while the Democrats remained at an average age of 47. This suggests that the surviving remnant of the RPP in 1954 was not made up of old-guard stalwarts; and this indication is strongly confirmed by data on previous parliamentary experience, as we shall see below. In 1957 the average age of the Republicans dropped again to 44.4, clearly signifying a large influx of younger deputies. The Democrats again remained at an average age of about 47.

With the restructuring of the party system in 1961, the Republicans came into the new National Assembly approximately at the same average age at which they bowed out in 1957 (i.e. 45). There was an increase to nearly 47 in 1965 followed by a rejuvenation of the party in terms of age in 1969 and 1973. Once again, we shall see below that trends in the age curve conform to developments in data on parliamentary experience. In short, there was a high rate of turnover in Republican ranks in the late 1960s and early 1970s bringing in a sizeable contingent of new and more youthful figures.

The Justice Party, by contrast, has consistently aged since its first emergence on the political scene in 1961. In that year, its parliamentary delegation was the youngest in Turkish history. By 1973, the average age of the reduced JP contingent was greater than that of any Democrat delegation of the 1950s. This trend is again confirmed by the data on previous parliamentary experience, as we shall see.

Family Size

In terms of family size, there are some interesting differences among the parties. While the two largest parties do not differ very much (except in 1965), the small parties and Independents consistently have had larger families. Moreover, this tendency is also manifested by the two medium-sized parties in 1973.[27] In the case of the Democratic Party, this may reflect a combination of somewhat greater traditionalism and higher average age. But in view of the younger average age of the NSP and the distinctly greater family size for that party, we may take that datum as a clear sign of greater traditionalism.

Table 9.17: Average Number of Children per Married Deputy, by Party

	1957	1961	Session 1965	1969	1973
Democrat Party	2.1				
Justice Party		2.3	2.6	2.6	2.7
Republican People's Party	2.7	2.4	2.2	2.6	2.6
Democratic Party					3.0
National Salvation Party					3.5
Small Parties and Independents		2.5	2.7	2.9	3.0
Whole House	2.3	2.4	2.5	2.7	2.8

Turnover

The rate of turnover, or infusion of new blood into the partisan delegations in the parliament, provides perhaps the clearest indication of the prevailing tendencies in social backgrounds over time. Thus, in Table 9.18 we see extremely high rates of turnover for the Democrat Party in 1946 and 1950, when the party scored its first successes at the ballot box. In 1954 and 1957 there were far smaller infusions of new blood, though still half or more of the party's parliamentary faces were new. The 1961 JP delegation had the highest proportion of new faces, signifying the wholly new character of this party at that time. Like its predecessor, it too settled down to a turnover rate of approximately 50 per cent after this first appearance.

The RPP, by contrast, elected a relatively experienced delegation in 1946, although the turnover rate that year was already somewhat higher than the 30 per cent which had prevailed in 1943. Interestingly, in 1950, with the dramatic decline in RPP numbers, almost half of the surviving RPP delegation had never before served in parliament. And in 1954, with the further sharp decline in RPP fortunes, almost three-fourths of the survivors had had no previous parliamentary experience! Thus, while one might have expected old-guard party stalwarts to survive the electoral deluge with younger political warriors falling by the way, instead we find the RPP remnant consisting overwhelmingly of new faces! The high rate of turnover in 1957 is less surprising, for the RPP delegation increased more than fivefold from the previous session. The result is that from 1950 to 1957, the RPP parliamentary delegation, while it did not change appreciably in terms of other indicators of social background, was entirely transformed in terms of the individuals involved.

Nor did the winds of change stop blowing through the ranks of the RPP after the bruising blows of the 1950s. Although its turnover rate was the lowest of all those indicated for the 1961 session, once again

Table 9.18: Turnover Rates, by Party (in Percentages)

	Session							
	1946	1950	1954	1957	1961	1965	1969	1973
Democrat Party								
& JP	83	83	51	41.5	92.2	52.1	48.5	46.7
RPP	35	44	72	74	73.8	39.3	64.1	68.3
DP								34.9
NSP								87.8
Small Parties								
and Independents					81.8	67.6	40.9	27.3
Whole House				51.0	82.4	50.9	52.7	57.3

nearly three-fourths of its parliamentarians had had no previous experience in that body, signifying another massive infusion of new blood. The low rate of turnover in 1965 turned out to be merely a temporary respite. The subsequent rise in turnover rates in 1969 and 1973, combined with the drop in average age, is unquestionably the result of the struggle for control within the party which culminated with the ousting of the aged leader İsmet İnönü in 1972, and had been clearly foreshadowed by the 'left of centre' slogan adopted in 1965. By 1973 we have not only a whole new phalanx of RPP parliamentarians, but, as we have noted in the discussion of individual indicators above, signs of change in social background patterns as well. If we relate these harbingers of change within the RPP to the dramatic changes in electoral behaviour manifested between 1969 and 1973, as analysed by Özbudun,[28] we have a double measure of some basic changes in Turkish politics. We will return to this point in our summary below.

Among the smaller parties, the Democratic Party once again demonstrates its basic character as an offshoot of the well-established JP. Indeed, this party brought proportionately fewer new faces into the parliament in 1973 than even its parent party. Thus, it stands revealed as a dissident segment of the old guard of the JP rather than as a new force in Turkish politics.

The NSP, by contrast, is in every respect a new force. Only six of its 49 deputies had served in parliament prior to 1973. Indeed, the only occasion on which any party elected a higher proportion of inexperienced deputies was the JP in 1961, when office-holders of the defunct Democrat Party of the 1950s were legally barred from running. As we have seen, and as we shall reiterate in our summary below, this is but another indicator of wholly new developments in the Turkish political elite and in Turkish politics.

Finally, we need only note that small parties and independents have not been very instrumental in bringing new blood into the parliament. As their numbers declined from 1961 to 1973, so did the proportion of new, inexperienced deputies among them. In effect, by 1973 these parties had become vestiges of older and apparently less representative political forces. This was particularly true of the Reliance Party, the largest grouping among them.

Conclusion

One general conclusion emerges from our analysis: over time, and particularly during the 1960s and early 1970s, the Turkish parliamentary elite has tended to become more representative of the society at large. This is especially evident in the data on education (particularly secondary education), localism and family size. There have been parallel changes in other indicators, particularly in occupational distribution. Moreover, when indicators of social and political background were correlated with levels of socio-economic development of constituencies, a similar trend toward greater representativeness was found. To take just two examples, deputies representing less developed constituencies reported lower levels of education and larger family size.

A number of more specific conclusions may also be stated. First, characteristics of the Turkish political elite manifested distinct changes with changes in regime, particularly in 1950 and 1961. As with changes in electoral behaviour, these shifts were in both cases foreshadowed in sessions preceding the 'critical' election. Thus, the 1946 parliamentary session manifested changes in terms of localism, average age, occupational backgrounds, family size and turnover rates, all of which were strongly confirmed in the election of 1950. The 1957 session does not clearly fit this pattern, perhaps because of the extra-constitutional and abrupt manner of the change of the regime which occurred in 1960. However, the 1973 election and parliamentary session in many respects resembles the change-of-regime election and session of 1961, and in this case, the shifts are indeed foreshadowed by the 1969 data, both for electoral behaviour in general[29] and some social background indicators, such as localism, education and family size, for example. In this respect, changes in the indicators analysed here may resemble the build-up of pressure of a rain-swollen river system behind a dam. At a certain critical point, the pressure becomes so great that either the dam bursts, or the water spills over the top— unless, of course, the rain stops.

A second conclusion suggested by these data is that the 1973 parliament saw the introduction of new elements into the political elite. One of these elements is represented by the NSP with its openly anti-Kemalist ideology, and its relatively large contingent of religious functionaries and educators. Another is the rejuvenated RPP, with its relatively large delegation of teachers. The two parties are alike in the relatively young age of their deputies, their relative lack of previous parliamentary experience, and their tendency towards the professions rather than official or economic activities. For the RPP, the latter is a major departure from its earlier character and image.

Third, our data suggest that there is greater polarisation and dissensus in the Turkish political elite than perhaps at any time since the early days of the republic. This is manifested in the differences that emerge particularly in the late 1960s and in 1973 between more developed and less developed constituencies. Thus, not only is the parliamentary elite becoming more representative, but apparently it also now reflects cleavages within Turkish society far more clearly than ever before.

Another manifestation of this point lies in the differences among the political parties, particularly in the 1973 session, and especially between the two parties which have brought the greatest numbers of new faces into the political elite. If we compare the values and policy preferences of the reformist teachers and lawyers who predominate in the RPP with the religionists and pious engineers who lead the NSP, we have a measure of the ideological and value dissensus which has now been injected into the Turkish political elite. Alongside these elements, we have the survival of a sizeable segment of more conservative, business-oriented deputies in the form of the JP and DP delegations.

In short, there is little question that Turkish society has over the years become more pluralistic, and that this greater pluralism is now reflected in the character of the political elite. Greater pluralism carries with it, however, the seeds of greater social and political instability.

Notes

1. Although the Turkish parliament has been bicameral since 1961, only data from the lower house, or National Assembly, are analysed here. This has the advantage of simplicity: Senate membership has been complicated by the fact that members' terms overlap (one-third of the seats are subject to election every two years). Furthermore, the Senate is constitutionally very much the weaker body, and is clearly so perceived in political terms as well, both by political leaders and by the politically attentive public.

2. F. W. Frey, *The Turkish Political Elite* (MIT Press, Cambridge, Mass., 1965), Figure 7.3, p. 184.

3. Parliamentarians are classified on the basis of self-reported occupations as published in the parliamentary album for each session. Occupational groupings are somewhat flexibly defined. Type of activity, function, and/or training serve as major criteria. Thus, the category 'civil servant' includes civilian officials of government ministries and agencies, but does not include publicly owned corporations or economic enterprises. The activities of these enterprises seem more akin to activities characteristic of the private sector of the economy. Educators, judges and prosecutors, and religious functionaries are distinguished from civil servants because their training, function and

activities are sufficiently specialised to warrant such a distinction. Judges and prosecutors are similarly distinguished from lawyers because these occupations constitute distinct careers for those graduates of law faculties who choose to pursue them. Parliamentarians who list themselves as *avukat* ('lawyer') have been counted as such. Lawyers and legal functionaries other than *avukat*, judges or prosecutors have been classified according to place of employment. This system of classification is based on the assumption that place of employment has a major socialising impact on individuals. Moreover, only those who have been admitted to the bar are entitled to call themselves *avukat*. Others may have law degrees and may be legal experts, but they are not practicing lawyers and therefore not truly free professionals. By the same token, all those who claim the title *avukat* have been listed as lawyers, regardless of other occupational activities which they may also have reported. On the other hand, following Frey's practice, engineers and medical and health practitioners have been listed as professionals, even if they are government employees, as many of them are. The assumption here is that the nature of the training and activity involved has a greater socialising impact than mode or place of employment.

I have not followed the practice adopted by Harik and Khalaf in Chapters 6 and 10 of this volume of listing secondary occupations. Given the size of the Turkish Parliament and the scope of Turkish society (particularly as compared to Lebanon), the limited research resources available made it virtually impossible to arrive at individual judgements regarding primary as opposed to secondary occupations. Calculations based on multiple responses are likely to produce more misleading conclusions than the method used here. It is in any event difficult to settle on a completely satisfactory method for assessing the occupational backgrounds of a group as large as this. See further below and Frey, *Turkish Elite*, p. 78.

Also unlike Khalaf, I have not created an occupational category labelled 'intellectuals'. Although intellectuals clearly play important roles in Turkey and Lebanon, as a group they are not as clearly defined as professionals, officials etc. Journalists and educators are perhaps most closely identified with intellectuals among our categories. There have been too few of the former, however, to warrant a separate category. Some parliamentarians list journalism as a second occupation. Most of these are apparently individuals who have started up or bought out a local newspaper, or who write political and social commentary as an avocation.

4. Frey, *Turkish Elite*, pp. 180-2.

5. Ibid., p. 64.

6. Ibid., p. 78.

7. Ibid., p. 126.

8. Unlike the clerics of the early 1920s religious functionaries in contemporary Turkey are assigned and salaried by the Directorate of Religious Affairs, an agency of the central government. Religious educators, on the other hand, are under the jurisdiction of the Ministry of Education. None the less, because of the political significance of this occupational group, we have listed religion as a distinct occupation rather than including these individuals among either civil servants or educators.

9. Frey included labourers among the economic occupations (Ibid., p. 78). Since their numbers were probably very small, it is doubtful that his data are seriously affected. Industrialisation in Turkey did not seriously get underway until the 1930s. Organised labour began showing signs of life only in the 1950s. The right to strike was not enacted into law until 1963. This may explain the marginal increase in union officials in the Assembly from 1965 on. The specific data are as follows:

	Union Officials in Parliament					
	1957	1961	1965	1969	1973	1977
Number	6	2	7	10	8	10
Percentage	1.0	0.4	1.6	2.3	1.7	2.2

10. L. Roos and N. Roos, *Managers of Modernization* (Harvard University Press, Cambridge, Mass., 1971), Table 5.7, p. 83.

11. Frey, *Turkish Elite,* p. 175.

12. Curiously, this was the session which was marked by response to and recognition of oppositionist trends revealed by the abortive Free Party experiment in 1930. Apparently, the very small cohort of new members differed considerably from the main body of holdovers. See Ibid.

13. J. Blondel, *Comparative Legislatures* (Prentice-Hall, Englewood Cliffs, New Jersey, 1973), Appendix C.

14. Devlet Planlama Teşkilâtı (DPT), *Kalkınmada öncelikli yörelerin tesbiti ve bu yörelerdeki teşvik tedbirleri* (The determination of localities with developmental priority) (Pub. No. 1304-KOYD 4, Ankara, 1973); M. Albaum and C. S. Davies, 'The Spatial Structure of Socio-Economic Attributes of Turkish Provinces', *International Journal of Middle East Studies,* 4 (1973), pp. 288-310.

15. DPT, *Kalkınmada öncelikli,* p. 44; the DPT does not indicate what specific statistics have been used to construct the various composite indices. Technical details relating to their construction are given on pp. 42-3.

16. The only pronounced departure from this pattern occurs in the fifth provincial grouping in 1973. This cell contains three deputies, only one of whom is a journalist. The other two are listed as engaged in 'other' occupations, meaning there was either insufficient information to justify placing them in one of the more specific occupational categories in our coding system, or their occupations simply did not fit any of these categories.

17. Frey emphasises the impact of specific secondary schools (*Turkish Elite,* Ch. 3) see also R. E. Ward and D. A. Rustow (eds.), *Political Modernization in Japan and Turkey* (Princeton University Press, Princeton, New Jersey, 1964), Ch. 5B). Frey's data are derived from a time when educational institutions and opportunities were quite limited. With the expansion of the system, the homogenising effect on elite aspirants has weakened. (For a comment on this development as a general phenomenon in modernising societies, see J. S. Coleman, *Education and Political Development* (Princeton University Press, Princeton, New Jersey, 1965), reprinted in F. Tachau, *The Developing Nations : What Path to Modernization?* (Dodd, Mead and Co., New York, 1972), pp. 98-105.) Another effect of the expansion of the educational system and the concomitant opening of new and more varied career opportunities in the Turkish social and economic system may well be the relative denigration of the status of parliamentarians, with consequent rippling effects on the recruitment process. For data on similar trends among bureaucrats, see Roos and Roos, *Managers.*

18. It is also notable that provincial group I ranks first in post-secondary education only in 1973. This could conceivably be due to the greater availability of intermediate and secondary schools in these provinces. It may also reflect the fact that parliamentarians tend to emerge from local and regional elite strata, and that differences among these elites in terms of access to higher education are only significant at the lower levels of socio-economic development. See further the discussion of localism immediately below.

19. This is only an imperfect measure. It fails to take into account such factors as length of residence in the community, family roots and ties, and birth in a neighbouring province which might serve as a regional centre. Because of the difficulties involved in gathering such data and/or devising usable measures for them, birth in constituency remains a convenient indicator.

20. In terms of raw numbers, JP deputies engaged in religious activities tripled from one to three between 1961 and 1965, and tripled again to nine in 1969; in 1973, there were six, but in the reduced JP delegation their proportionate weight was greater.

21. Notably, prior to 1973, JP farmers were also among the smallest occupation for that party. The actual size of the JP agricultural group has been almost constant at

between 12 and 14 per cent suggesting that this group may have survived consecutive elections quite well as individuals. The actual survival of the individual deputies would have to be checked to confirm this indication.

22. The relevant figures for the two large parties are as follows:

		Journalism	Union Officials
	1957	2	1
	1961	6	0
RPP	1965	6	0
	1969	5	5
	1973	4	5
DP	1957	13	5
JP	1961	9	2
	1965	16	4
	1969	9	4
	1973	0	3

23. There were actually only three DP deputies engaged in religious activities. Interestingly, the total of DP and JP religious deputies remained the same from 1969 to 1973, while their combined proportion increased somewhat (from 3.5 per cent of 263 to 4.7 per cent of the combined JP-DP delegation of 193). Since there were also some switches from the JP to the NSP, including some religious deputies, individual checks are required to determine the specific political background of the 1973 members involved—if such data are available for them (unlikely if they are new to the parliament).

24. In terms of raw numbers, the NSP does not stand out here; there were seven NSP engineers elected in 1973 as opposed to 16 in the RPP and 13 in the JP. As second occupations, two JP deputies reported engineering as against one each for the RPP and the NSP. By contrast, there were only four engineers in the DP.

25. Nor does any NSP deputy report agriculture as a second occupation.

26. In 1946 Frey reports 74 per cent of the RPP membership with university-level education as contrasted with 69 per cent for the DP. He does not report the data for the 1950 and 1954 sessions; my own data file for those sessions is not yet complete at the time of writing. In 1957 the two parties were remarkably close, with 60.4 per cent of the RPP being university-educated as against 58.6 per cent of the DP. There may be some minor variations in the coding between Frey's data and ours because of uncertainty about the level of some of the institutions. At any rate, the data are internally comparable—i.e. the RPP seems to have a higher proportion of university-educated members both by Frey's calculations and by ours. See Frey, *Turkish Elite*, Table 12.1, p. 353.

27. One possible explanation of the rather large difference in 1957 might lie in the nature of the constituencies represented. Testing of this hypothesis requires analysis of the 1957 election results in the developmentally grouped provinces. The 1977 data show an average of 4.3 children for NSP members, 3.0 for Independents and 2.3 to 2.7 for the other parties.

28. E. Özbudun, *Social Change and Political Participation in Turkey* (Princeton University Press, Princeton, New Jersey, 1976); see also Chapter 5 of the present volume.

29. See Özbudun, *Social Change in Turkey*.

10. LEBANON

Samir G. Khalaf

Studies of the Lebanese parliamentary elite reveal inconsistent and paradoxical tendencies. One such striking feature is the wide discrepancy between the changing backgrounds of the deputies and the continuities in their political behaviour and orientations. The rapid socio-economic transformations Lebanon has witnessed, particularly during the past few decades, have broadened processes of elite recruitment and circulation. They have drawn a more literate, professional and skilled elite into the body politic and politicised a growing segment of the population. Such changes, however, have not been accompanied by any perceptible change in political attitudes and behaviour of the elite. Nor have they rendered parliament more effective as a legislative body.

From one perspective, the changing social composition of parliament attests to the decline of descendants of feudal aristocratic and notable families and the gradual ascendancy of deputies with more plebeian and bourgeois social origins.[1] Occupational background also reveals a sharp shift from landed proprietors to lawyers, professionals and businessmen. This trend, among others, bespeaks a shift away 'from the traditional and parochial and toward the achievement oriented and sophisticated'.[2] The high educational level of the deputies is equally impressive. The proportion of deputies with university degrees has been persistently increasing. While 51 per cent of the 1943 Chamber held university degrees, the proportion rose to 73 per cent for the 1972 Chamber.[3]

The electoral process, particularly on indices such as voter participation, competitiveness in parliamentary elections and turnover rates, also reveals some interesting manifestations. The persistent increase in the number of people voting since 1943 suggests a broadened suffrage, increasing popular involvement and greater civic consciousness among a growing segment of the adult population.[4] Electoral contests have also become steadily more competitive. The number of candidates competing for a given seat has been increasing; consequently they have been winning by smaller margins. This, among other things, suggests that deputies do not have overwhelmingly popular backing and hence cannot afford to be indifferent to their political constituencies. More important, a competitive electoral process is seen by Hudson as a sign of 'a healthy pluralistic system because it indicates flexibility and responsiveness ... and that a process of institutionalised change is developing'.[5]

Studies of elite circulation clearly indicate a comparatively high rate of turnover of Lebanese deputies.[6] With an average turnover rate of 40 per cent for the nine parliaments since independence, it is evident that political recruitment has been significantly broadened. This incessant change in the parliamentary elite is, once again, seen as a symptom of the system's fluidity.[7] It has prompted at least one observer to deny the often-made charge regarding the oligarchic character of Lebanon's political elite.[8]

Finally, other observers point to the growing role of political parties and organised caucuses in both parliamentary representation and election campaigns. The proportion of deputies representing various organised political parties, as opposed to loosely organised cliques and coalitions, has been persistently increasing. This, too, is seen as a reflection of greater organisational development and politicisation as prerequisites for political modernisation.[9]

Altogether, changes in the socio-economic composition of the parliamentary elite along with other trends in the direction of increasing voter participation, competitiveness in elections and the broadening of the recruitment process are taken to mean that the 'system is capable of limited, self-induced, structural modernisation'.[10]

From another perspective, however, particularly if one makes inferences regarding the political behaviour and attitudes of the elite, one emerges with an entirely different impression. The image of the deputies as political actors and the general impact of the legislature on the political system from this perspective are far from favourable. In fact, both invite considerable derision and scorn from the popular and more serious literature on the subject. Regardless of their background and professional skills, deputies emerge more as political brokers concerned with the parochial and often petty interests of their local constituencies than with formulating and articulating broad policy issues of national and civic significance.[11] Although the proportion of deputies with what Hudson terms 'sophisticated and modern' political orientations has been increasing, 'the great majority of Lebanon's parliamentary deputies have no political orientation beyond the list or clique that got them elected'.[12]

The fragmentation, ineffectiveness, hesitation and impotence of parliament has been repeatedly decried by various observers. Much like its individual members, parliament is notorious for its subservience to the executive. It is often reduced to the role of a 'puppet' manipulated and managed by a skilful President.[13] It avoids critical and controversial issues,[14] and makes only a minimum contribution to the policy-formation and rule-making functions. Nor is it effective as a check on the executive and bureaucracy.[15]

The foregoing should be sufficient to caution us against drawing inferences about the elite's attitudes and political behaviour from its social background. An analysis of the background and changing composition of deputies, in and of itself, is clearly not a meaningful gauge of their political behaviour. Fruitful as such analysis is in identifying changing trends in political representation, it does not tell us much about the power structure of society. Nor does it explain why there is such a discrepancy between the seemingly changing background characteristics of the elite on the one hand and the rigidities in elite behaviour and political orientations on the other. If we are to understand the discrepancy between background and political behaviour of the parliamentary elite, we must look beyond a mere documentation of the changing patterns of elite composition. An exploration into the nature of patronage and political clientelism offers, I think, a more meaningful context for such an analysis. Accordingly, this chapter has a threefold objective: first, to re-examine some of the changing trends in elite composition and circulation; second, to identify a few of the continuities in patterns of political behaviour, particularly with regard to political orientations and the ineffectiveness of parliament as an innovative legislative body; third, to attempt, through a brief analysis of the nature of patronage, to account for the persisting disjunction between changing composition of the elite and continuities in its behaviour.

Composition and Circulation of the Elite
Age

The average age of the Lebanese deputy has been gradually increasing since 1943. On the whole the deputy in the 1972 chamber was almost six years older than his earlier colleague in 1943. As shown in Table 10.1, the average age rose from 45.6 in 1943 to 51.1 in 1972. Some observers see this as a sign that electoral and political processes are producing a more mature and stable elite,[16] a feature which compares favourably with the age profile of US Senators and British MPs, though it is considerably older than elites in revolutionary and unstable political regimes such as those of Syria and Libya.[17]

In the light of such evidence it is rather surprising to find occasional reference being made to the 'youthful character' of the Lebanese Chamber.[18]   One writer in particular, after comparing the age composition of the 1964 and 1968 chambers, concludes: 'clearly, the elections of 1968 marked a turning point in what appears to be a quickening shift of power, from the traditional older elites to a more youthful leadership by modern politicians'.[19] No such quickening shift of power has taken place. In fact the trend is unmistakably in the opposite direction.

The progressive maturity or ageing of Lebanon's parliamentarians becomes more apparent when one examines changing trends in three major age groups. While 31 per cent of the 1943 deputies belonged to a younger generation (i.e. between 25 and 40), the proportion declined to 17 per cent in 1972. Conversely, the proportion of older deputies (over age 51) increased from 38 to 51 per cent over the same 30-year period. It is instructive to observe that the most appreciable increase occurred among those over 60 years old. Their share of seats in parliament increased from 5 to 18 per cent (see Tables 10.1 and 10.2).

What might have given this misleading impression regarding the alleged youthfulness of the parliamentarians is the tendency of the average deputy to begin his parliamentary career at the relatively early age of 40. As shown in Table 10.3, nearly one-third of the deputies in the 1972 chamber first entered parliament when they were less than 35

Table 10.1: Age Distribution of Deputies in Nine Lebanese Parliaments (as Percentage of all Deputies)

Age Group	Parliament								
	1943	1947	1951	1953	1957	1960	1964	1968	1972
25-30	7	7	5	5	1	1	-	1	3
31-35	11	6	10	6	6	6	8	6	5
36-40	13	16	13	18	14	14	12	11	9
41-50	31	38	48	43	52	49	30	30	32
51-60	33	27	17	14	15	26	39	38	33
Over 60	5	6	7	14	12	4	11	14	18
Total	100	100	100	100	100	100	100	100	100
Average Age	45.6	46	45.1	46	47	48.4	49.3	50.5	51.1

Table 10.2: Trend in Age Groups of Lebanese Deputies (as Percentage of all Deputies)

	1943	1947	1951	1953	1957	1960	1964	1968	1972
Young (25-40)	31	29	28	29	21	21	20	18	17
Middle (41-50)	31	38	48	43	52	49	30	30	32
Old (Over 50)	38	33	24	28	27	30	50	52	51
Total	100	100	100	100	100	100	100	100	100

Table 10.3: Age at Which 1972 Deputies Began Their Parliamentary Careers

Age Groups	25-30	31-35	36-40	41-50	51-60	Over 60	Total
Number of Deputies	14	17	20	31	14	3	99

years old. In a political culture which venerates old age and pays deference to elders, this may seem at first glance surprising. A closer look, however, at the type of younger deputies and the manner in which they seek entry into parliament prompts us to attach less significance to this phenomenon.

Virtually all 14 deputies who had an early initiation into politics—Ṣabrī Ḥammāda (23), Kāmil al-Asʿad (24), Joseph Skāf (25), Kamāl Junblāṭ (26), Ṭalāl Mirʿabī (27), Ẓāhir al-Khaṭīb (28), Salīm Dāʾūd (28), Sulaymān al-ʿAlī (28), Rashīd Karāma (30), Antoine Franjiyya (30), Amīn Jumayyil (30)—are descendants of feudal or notable families or those who 'inherited' their parliamentary seat from a close relative. They also represent traditional political communities in which primordial ties and personal allegiances sustain the political loyalties and motivations of the electorate. The only notable exception is Najāḥ Wākīm (26), who, as we shall see, won one of the Greek Orthodox seats in Beirut by receiving the votes of a religious community other than the one he represents. Given such evidence, we certainly cannot interpret this 'youthfulness'[20] as a 'clear sign of systemic evolution away from traditionalism and towards modernity'. Likewise, the fact that 84 per cent of the deputies were born in post-Ottoman times[21] in and of itself is not very significant given the traditional loyalties which continue to underlie much of their behaviour and political orientations. Even the few who are products of post-mandate times seem intensely bound by such traditional commitments.

Finally, the advanced age or maturity of the deputies becomes more pronounced given the relative youthfulness of the Lebanese population in general. Since 53.7 per cent of the population is under 19 years of age,[22] the generational gap between the elite and the masses they are supposed to represent is quite striking and has considerable implications for the political alienation of the youth.

Level of Education

The exclusive character of the parliamentary elite is quite visible in its relatively high educational accomplishments. In comparative terms, particularly if one considers the trend in the direction of increasing university and professional education, the general educational profile of the Lebanese deputy is quite impressive. With 73 per cent of the 1972 deputies[23] holding university degrees, their educational level is considerably higher than the average adult Lebanese citizen. This is expected since political elites are normally better educated than the people they represent. But the Lebanese deputy is also better educated than other modernising elites in Lebanese society, such as entrepreneurs, industrialists and labour union leaders.[24] Even a highly educated university community like Ras Beirut, perhaps one of the most literate communities in Lebanon and the Arab world, where 47.5 per cent of household heads are university graduates, is still below the educational level of the deputies.[25]

Table 10.4: Type and Place of Education

Type of Education*		University Attended [†]	
Law	41	Saint Joseph University	33
Medicine	10	American University of Beirut	11
Engineering	4	Other foreign universities	18
Pharmacy	1	European 9	
Social Sciences	5	Arab 4	
Liberal Arts	3	United States 1	
Secondary	35	Other 4	
Total	99	Secondary	37
		Total	99

Source: A. Messarra, 'La Structure Sociale du Parlement Libanais', unpublished doctoral thesis, University of Strasbourg, 1974, pp. 260-4.
* Based on averages of past three chambers.
[†] For 1972 chamber only.

The high educational level of the deputies, as an earned and achieved attribute, becomes more pronounced when it is considered that many of them are 'heirs' of political families and could have relied instead on some other ascribed traditional quality to reinforce their political career. The proportion of university graduates in parliament has been persistently increasing. While only 17 per cent of the deputies in the First Representative Council of 1922 had higher education, the number increased to 50 per cent for the parliaments of the 1940s, 55 per cent for those of the 1950s and 60 per cent for the 1960s. Estimates for the 1972 chamber range from 68 to 73 per cent.[26]

The type of education, both in terms of professional training and the universities or schools the deputies attended, continues to reflect the well-entrenched bias in favour of legal and French education. More than 40 per cent of the deputies are graduates of law schools and a significantly larger proportion, if one considers those who received their education in Europe or French-oriented secondary schools, are French-educated. One-third of the deputies alone are alumni of Saint Joseph University. This is perhaps the one homogeneous and persistent feature in the deputies' backgrounds. Possibly in the future, graduates of less elitist universities—such as the Lebanese National or Arab universities—might begin to have more access to Lebanon's exclusive political club. For the time being, no trend in that direction is visible.

Occupational Background

The occupational composition of the Parliament continues to reflect the intimate association between legal training and the political career of the deputies. There is more than just historical accident in this association. The social and political disturbances between 1840 and 1861 had eroded the political supremacy of feudal chieftains and began gradually to introduce a new administrative aristocracy into the political life of the country. With the declining influence of feudal families, lawyers, magistrates and government officials emerged as the closest groups to the loci of power in society, and consequently many of them were drawn into the movements of reform, independence and Arabism which had consumed the intellectual resources of the emerging elite at the time.

The abolition of feudalism by the *Règlement Organique* of 1861 undermined the security and social standing of feudal families and threatened to make a disgruntled class out of them. The Ottomans, accordingly, pursued the policy of absorbing such families into the new administration. A civil-service appointment became the surest and most prestigious source of livelihood. And legal education, with its concomitant bureaucratic and administrative skills, was naturally the most relevant for such career mobility. The late President Bishāra al-Khūrī (1943-52) poignantly expressed this association between the declining feudal aristocracy and competition for government positions:

> High government positions virtually became the exclusive preserve, a *waqf*, for the leading families of the country. This came as a consequence of the continuing influence of feudalism though officially abolished by the *Règlement Organique*. Office in those days was everything. It was the object of ambition and the source of all influence and prestige. Members of the same house and close friends would fight for it; they could risk peril to secure a coveted government job. It became a cause for hostility and heavy expenditure. Many an aristocratic house has been shaken, even ruined by it. This competition for office helped the Mutesarrif perpetuate his influence over the Lebanese families and dispense with Lebanese affairs according to his own whims and without any restraints.[27]

Considerations of this kind, plus of course the relative accessibility of legal education, no doubt account for the continuing popularity of the legal profession. It is still largely considered, by many political aspirants, as a natural stepping-stone to a political career. It is the one traditional source of political recruitment which continues to attract a disproportionate number of deputies.

It is quite apparent from Table 10.5 that occupationally the parliamentary elite is far from stable and is characterised by significant shifts in its occupational composition.

Table 10.5: Occupational Composition, 1943-72 (as Percentage of all Deputies)

				Parliament					
Occupation	1943	1947	1951	1953	1957	1960	1964	1968	1972*
Landlords	46.5	48.2	42.5	40.9	33.3	23.0	23.2	10	10
Lawyers	33.9	27.3	25.0	34.1	36.3	29.0	27.3	44	45
Businessmen	10.2	10.9	12.5	6.8	11.1	14.0	17.2	17	21
Professional	10.2	12.7	20.0	18.2	19.0	34.0	32.3	28	24
Total	100.0	100.0	100.0	100.0	99.7	100.0	100.0	99	100

Source: I. Harik, 'Political Elites of Lebanon' in G. Lenczowski (ed.), *Political Elites in the Middle East* (American Enterprise Institute, Washington, DC, 1975), p. 203.
* Updated by the present author.

Table 10.6: Distribution of Basic and Secondary Occupation,
1968 Parliament

	As a Basic Occupation	As a Secondary Occupation	Total	Percentage Of Total
Landowning	10	18	28	17
Legal Professions	44	-	44	27
Business	17	28	45	27
Other Professions	28	20	48	29
Total	99	66	165	100

Source: Harik, 'Elites of Lebanon', p. 205.

Consistent with the broader socio-economic changes in Lebanon, the proportion of landlords has sharply declined from 46 per cent in 1943 to 10 per cent of the 1972 chamber. Conversely, the number of professionals has increased from 10 to 24 per cent over the same period. Professionals—particularly doctors, engineers and, to a lesser extent, intellectuals, journalists and teachers—account for almost 30 per cent of the four successive chambers after 1960. The number of businessmen and entrepreneurs has also exhibited a moderate increase, particularly in the last three chambers.

Since many of the deputies hold multiple occupations, it is instructive to distinguish between basic and secondary occupation on the basis of a deputy's primary economic pursuit as Harik has done.[28] For example, several of the deputies are the heirs of large estates but are also practicing lawyers. Others are entrepreneurs and urban professionals who have acquired small or extensive areas of agricultural land.[29] Such a compounded computation of occupations is a more realistic measure of the diversity and trend in occupational composition. It also reveals a slightly different profile than the simple occupational distribution. For example, if multiple occupations are considered, lawyers, businessmen and professionals are almost equally represented in parliament. In fact, the professional character of the deputies becomes more pronounced. Altogether, law, business and professions are the chief occupational bases from which deputies are recruited in Lebanon.

Michael Hudson[30] noted some regional and religious differentiation in the occupational composition of parliament. Interestingly, Beirut and Mount Lebanon appear to exhibit a greater degree of consistency in occupational distribution, while the predominantly rural regions have been characterised by more striking occupational changes. For example, the increase in the number of professionals has been greater in the hinterland. The same is true of the decline in landlords. There are also notable occupational differences between Christian and non-Christian deputies. While the rate of increase of professional deputies is roughly the same, the proportion of non-Christian landlords has been declining faster. Conversely, the percentage of non-Christian deputies recruited from legal professions has been increasing faster.[31]

Significantly, the crisis of 1958 marks a sort of watershed in the changing occupational composition of parliament. The shift in the direction of greater professionalisation of the political elite was most apparent then. The incidence of professionals leaped from 19 per cent in 1957 to 34 per cent in 1960. It is interesting to speculate whether the protracted crisis of 1975-6 might not produce yet another shift, however slight, in the direction of the 'proletarianisation' of the elite. It is quite possible that this gradual process of broadening the occupational base from which deputies have been recruited may create more access for labourers, peasants, small businessmen, schoolteachers and other such groups who have thus far been excluded from the political elite.

Elite Circulation

How exclusive or stable is Lebanon's parliamentary elite? If we perceive the 'circulation of elites' statistically, i.e. in terms of the growing incidence of new entrants and the changing socio-economic composition of the deputies, then the parliamentary elite appears to be neither stable nor exclusive. Pareto's concept, after all, draws attention to the fact that this process of replacement—by virtue of the natural process of human attrition and replenishment—is bound to occur. Furthermore, Lebanon, particularly after the Second World War, has experienced sufficient socio-economic mobility to allow individuals with relatively modest social origins to join the ranks of the powerful and influential. In this sense the process of elite recruitment is fairly open and has been significantly broadened. But if one probes into the nature of this process, and also asks who the new entrants are and how they are recruited, and explores further certain dimensions of their political behaviour, then the extent of this circulation and its impact on the orientations, commitments and political styles of the new recruits must be qualified.

The turnover of deputies in the nine successive parliaments since independence, by almost any comparative standard, is very high. If one adopts a specific measure of elite circulation—i.e. in terms of the incidence of new entrants appearing in parliament for the first time— parliament is certainly characterised by an impressive degree of change

Table 10.7: Elite Circulation in Nine Lebanese Parliaments (in Percentages)

	1943	1947	1951	1953	1957	1960	1964	1968	1972
Newcomers	54.5	45.4	54.5	27.3	36.4	51.5	28.3	28.3	39.4
Total Deputies	55	55	77	44	66	99	99	99	99

and fluctuation in its personnel. Such a new-entry rate of 41.7 per cent for all nine parliaments is considerably higher than comparable rates observed in some Western democracies.[32]

Such deceptively high rates of elite circulation may, it could be argued, reflect changes in electoral laws which have on several occasions increased the number of seats in parliament. For example, the highest turnover rates in newcomers occurred in the chambers of 1951 and 1960, each of which was considerably enlarged over preceding chambers. The 1951 chamber was increased by 22 seats, and the 1960 by 33. A more realistic measure would be the last four chambers (1960-72) when the number of deputies was stabilised at 99. The new-entry rate over this period is 37 per cent compared to 45 per cent for the preceding five chambers (1943-57). Thus, the high turnover tendency is confirmed regardless of the fluctuating size of parliament.

Such numerical measures of elite circulation, impressive as they may be, become meaningful only if one probes into the background of the new entrants, particularly their kinship ties, and the process by which they are co-opted or recruited by other political veterans. As shown in Table 10.8, 45 per cent of all new entrants are, in fact, descendants of families with a history of parliamentary representation.

The incidence of such family succession is even higher—56 per cent— for the last three chambers. It is only the chambers of 1957 and 1960 which experienced a relatively lower degree of family succession. It is instructive to find out what happens to such deputies, particularly to

Table 10.8: New Entrants with Family History of Parliamentary Representation

	1943	1947	1951	1953	1957	1960	1964	1968	1972	Total
Number	14	10	22	9	7	10	18	14	22	126
Percentage	46.6	40.0	52.4	75.0	29.6	19.6	64.3	50.0	56.4	45.2

newcomers to the 1960 chamber which, as we have seen, was also marked by the highest incidence of turnover rates. Thirteen deputies (56 per cent) among the new entrants to the 1957 and 15 (30 per cent) of the 1960 chamber served only one term. This is a relatively high casualty figure and does demonstrate, as we shall see, the continuing relevance of kinship ties in political succession. A closer examination of the type of new deputy who demonstrates staying power beyond one or two terms confirms this tendency. A considerable number of these new entrants are either heirs of notable political families or candidates with little personal political support but who secure a seat on the coat-tails, so to speak, of a traditional *za'īm* or one of the *aqṭāb*. The patrons, in short, both the *aqṭāb* and lesser *zu'amā'* rarely change. It is the clients that experience the turnover.

Kinship Ties and Political Succession

The socio-economic transformation Lebanon has been undergoing, as we have seen, has broadened political recruitment and hastened the process of elite circulation. Political power and influence, which was once the exclusive preserve of the traditional feudal aristocracy and landed gentry, is being gradually transferred to a more literate, economically active and occupationally mobile group. Wider political participation, party slogans and popular ideological movements have also politicised a growing segment of the population and have, on occasion, introduced individuals with more plebeian social origins into the political system. The political dominance of notable and privileged families has not, however, been seriously challenged. Family ties and kinship networks continue to be viable sources of political socialisation and tutelage. More important, they continue to be—all other evidence to the contrary notwithstanding—effective avenues to political power and perpetuation of leadership.[33]

I have elsewhere[34] suggested (perhaps in an exaggerated manner) that the whole political history of Lebanon may be viewed as the history of a handful of leading families competing to reaffirm their name, power and prestige in their respective communities. An analysis of the extent of kinship ties among parliamentarians and the persistent impact of the family in political succession and recruitment clearly confirms such an inference. One is, in fact, prompted to argue that a comparatively small number of prominent families continues to exert almost monopolistic control over the political process in the country.

Over the entire span of roughly fifty years of parliamentary life, 425 deputies belonging to 245 families have occupied a total of 965 seats in

16 assemblies. Deputies are considered to belong to the same family if they are characterised by close kinship ties and carry the same name. Not all families bearing the same name are related. For example, deputies with the surname of al-Khūrī—one of the most numerous families in parliament—are not all descendants of the same lineage. Khalīl of Aley, Ilyās of Baabda, Shahīd of Jbeyl and Rashīd of Zahrānī are all unrelated Khūris who occupied seats in the 1964 Chamber. The same is true of the Baydūn, al-Husaynī and Shihāb families, to mention a few. Care was taken to keep such distinctions in mind in identifying family units. If distant relatives and those related through intermarriage were included then the estimate would certainly not exceed 200 families.[35]

It is revealing that only 129 deputies (30 per cent) of all parliamentary representatives are unrelated to other parliamentarians. The remainder, with the exception of approximately 10 per cent of the earlier pre-independence cases whose family ties could not be ascertained, bear some close or distant relation to other deputies. As shown in Table 10.9, 45 per cent of all parliamentarians can be considered closely related, through direct kinship, descent or marriage, to other colleagues in the chamber. Another 17 per cent might be considered distant relatives. Altogether, in other words, roughly 60 per cent of the entire universe of deputies have had some kinship attachments to other parliamentary families.

Table 10.9: Kinship Ties Among 425 Parliamentarians

Kinship Ties	Number	Percentage
Fathers*	36	8
Sons†	41	10
Brothers	33	8
Cousins	37	9
Nephews	12	3
Uncles	19	4
Brothers-in-law	16	4
Distant relatives	76	18
Unrelated	129	30
Not determined	44	10
Total	443	100

Source: A. Messarra, 'La Structure Sociale du Parlement Libanais', unpublished doctoral thesis, University of Strasbourg, 1974, p. 201.
* Includes two grandparents: Qabalān Franjiyya and Ahmad al-Khatīb.
† Includes two grandchildren: Antoine Franjiyya and Zāhir al-Khatīb.

That there are oligarchic or dynastic tendencies is also apparent in the disproportionate share of parliamentary seats a few of the prominent families have enjoyed. Table 10.10 identifies the year each of those families was initiated into politics, the number of assemblies in which they served and the parliamentary seats they occupied. Altogether, not more than 26 families have held 35 per cent of all parliamentary seats since 1920. What this means in more concrete terms is that 10 per cent of the parliamentary families produced nearly one-fourth of the deputies and occupied more than one-third of all available seats. In some instances, it is one man (Şabrī Ḥammāda), or fathers and sons (Arslān, Edde, Karāma, Ghuṣn, Khāzin, al-Asʿad, Skāf, al-Khūrī, al-Zayn, Zuwayn, Jumayyil), brothers (al-Zayn, Edde, Shāhīn, Skāf),

Table 10.10: Longevity of Selected Parliamentary Families, 1920-72

Family	Year of Initiation	No. of Deputies	No. of Seats	No. of Chambers
Arslān	1922	4	19	15
al-Zayn	1920	5	18	13
al-Faḍl	1922	4	17	10
al-Ḥusaynī	1922	4	17	14
al-Khāzin	1920	6	16	15
al-Asʿad	1925	4	16	12
ʿUsayrān	1922	3	15	13
Ḥaydar	1920	3	15	13
Edde	1922	3	15	13
Ḥammāda	1925	1	14	14
Junblāṭ	1920	3	14	13
al-Şulḥ	1943	5	14	7
al-Khūrī	1925	5	13	12
Skāf	1925	4	13	11
Franjiyya	1929	4	13	12
Ghuṣn	1920	2	12	12
Sālim	1925	3	11	10
Qazʿūn	1922	3	11	11
Laḥḥūd	1943	5	11	8
al-Khaṭīb	1937	5	10	8
Baydūn	1937	7	10	7
Zuwayn	1925	2	9	9
Karāma	1937	3	9	9
Jumayyil	1960	3	9	4
Harāwi	1943	5	9	8
Shamʿūn	1934	2	9	8
Total		98	339	

cousins (the five al-Ṣulḥs, four Khāzins, two Jumayyils, two Sihnāwis and two Kayrūzes) or brothers-in-law (Ḥammāda-Asʿad, Salām-Karāma, Arslān-Junblāṭ, Ṣafi al-Dīn-ʿArab) who perpetuate family succession. In two particular instances—Franjiyya and al-Khaṭīb—three successive generations of grandfathers, fathers and sons have already insured the continuity of their family mandate in parliament. This is rather remarkable given the comparative recency of Lebanon's experience with parliamentary life.

The staying power of the family is particularly demonstrated during by-elections. In several elections when a parliamentary seat is vacated in mid-term, the deputy is succeeded by a son, if he has an apparent successor, or a relative. Majīd Arslān, Kāmil al-Asʿad, Antoine Franjiyya, Ẓāhir al-Khaṭīb, Bahīj al-Faḍl, Maurice Zuwayn, Myrna Bustāni, ʿAbd al-Laṭīf al-Zayn, Amīn Jumayyil, Philip Taqlā—to mention a few—have all inherited their seats from a father, brother or uncle. A recent such incident illustrates the process of family succession. When Ṣabri Ḥammāda, the veteran politican who was reelected to all 14 successive chambers since 1925, passed away in January 1976, his followers in Hermel al-Baalbek, in a traditional but dramatic gesture, vowed allegiance to his 30-year-old son.

Nearly all the *aqṭāb*, with an eye on their imminent retirement, make strenuous efforts to bequeath their political capital and influence to their children. Camille Shamʿun, Ṣāʿib Salām, Sulaymān Franjiyya, Majīd Arslān, Pierre Jummayyil have been lately encouraging their sons to assume more visible public roles and delegating to them some of their official and non-official responsibilities. Dāni Shamʿūn, Bashīr Jumayyil, and Antoine Franjiyya headed their fathers' private militias and took charge of the military operations in the fighting of 1976. Tammām and Fayṣal Salām accompany their father's parliamentary bloc on goodwill visits to Arab countries, participate in secret talks and occasionally issue press releases on behalf of their father. Fayṣal Arslān attends to many of his father's traditional and social obligations.

The above evidence should be sufficient to confirm the continuity of kinship ties in political succession. In terms of both the number of seats they occupied and the successive assemblies in which they served, it is clear that a disproportionately small number of families have been able to retain and extend their power positions. Expressed differently, at least a significantly larger number of families have demonstrated staying power in comparison to those whose political fortunes have suffered setbacks. The political casualty rate among prominent families, in other words, is remarkably low. What is even more striking

Table 10.11: Family Succession in Nine Lebanese Parliaments:
Sons of Deputies

	Parliaments								
	1943	1947	1951	1953	1957	1960	1964	1968	1972
Sons of Deputies	6	4	13	11	12	12	23	21	13
Percentage of Membership	10.9	7.3	16.9	25.0	18.2	12.1	23.2	21.2	13.1
No. of Seats	55	55	77	44	66	99	99	99	99

Table 10.12: Family Succession in Nine Lebanese Parliaments:
Descendants of Parliamentary Families

	Parliaments								
	1943	1947	1951	1953	1957	1960	1964	1968	1972
Deputies from Parliamentary Families	23	27	40	26	33	35	50	48	44
Percentage of Membership	41.8	49.1	51.9	59.1	50.0	35.3	50.5	48.5	44.4
No. of Seats	55	55	77	44	66	99	99	99	99

is that this trend in kinship succession does not at all, contrary to what
Harik[36] suggests, evince any decline. If the nine successive parliaments
since independence are any measure, both the incidence of sons of
deputies and descendants of parliamentary families have definitely
persisted. In fact, over the last three parliaments, the proportion of sons
who have 'inherited' their seats from their fathers is 19.2 per cent
compared to 10.9 per cent in 1943. Nearly the same magnitude of
change occurred among the deputies who are descendants of families
with a history of parliamentary representation.

Patterns of Political Behaviour

Given the survival of such kinship and communal loyalties, the
disjunction between the changing social backgrounds of the deputies
and the persistence of traditional political behaviour becomes clearer.
This is not meant as a categorical denial of the impact such factors as

education, occupation and age might have on the ideas and outlook of the parliamentary elite. Such background characteristics, under normal circumstances, certainly help determine what skills and experience a deputy is likely to bring to the decision-making process. They also might determine the interests he represents, and is prone to promote once in office. The impact of such factors in Lebanon, however, is mitigated by other considerations which quite often override and dilute the presumably secular and rational interests of profession or occupation. Primordial loyalties and personal allegiances are clearly more significant in determining a deputy's stand or outlook with regard to a particular issue or event.[37]

Deputies in general, irrespective of their political affiliations or ideological commitments, continue to show greater concern for their constituencies than for national issues. In an opinion survey of 70 deputies, more than half of the respondents showed strong local orientations and only one-third were nationally oriented.[38] Such localism is inevitable given the strong communal ties which link the deputy to his client groups in his political constituency. With rare exceptions, the deputies are born in the constituencies they represent. They are compelled to devote much of their time and attention to the petty and private interests of their clients. Manifestations of this form of political localism are legion: the non-programmatic nature of electoral campaigns, the almost total absence of ideological platforms in national elections, the political styles, public fronts and demeanours deputies have to assume. It is also visible in the ritualistic concern politicians display for the ceremonial and social obligations of their communities. Even the veterans among them cannot afford not to be seen in funeral processions, weddings, receptions or other such religious and social functions. The electoral system sustains such localism and accounts, in part, for the survival of the *aqṭāb* and political patrons. It also accounts for the political subservience of the newer deputies to such *aqṭāb*. Much of the clientelistic character of the political process in general is a reflection of the peculiarities of this system. A brief elaboration of this point is in order.

The electoral system, which was promulgated by the constitution of 1926, is based on a combination of a single electorate with proportional representation of the various religious communities. The system was conceived to enable each community to be represented in parliament in proportion to its size.[39] To accomplish this, the electoral system induces each candidate to depend on votes outside his own religious community. In fact, in mixed electoral districts (and of the 26 districts only nine are confessionally homogeneous communities) a candidate cannot be elected unless he is reasonably well accepted by other confessional groups in his constituency. In some instances it is the religious communities other than that of the candidate which guarantee his success or failure. In the national elections of 1972, Najāḥ Wakīm, a virtually unknown candidate—supported by the so-called Progressive Nasserist Coalition popular among the urban Sunnite Muslims—won one of the Greek Orthodox seats in Beirut while in fact receiving few of the votes of his own religious sect.

These safeguards or constitutional peculiarities of the Lebanese electoral system, reinforced by the National Pact of 1943, may have done much to promote harmony, justice and balance among the various communities but they accomplished little in curtailing the power of the *zuʿamā'*. If anything, the division of the country into small electoral units gives the *zuʿamā'* a freer hand to assert their influence and perpetuate their power over local communities. Each of the *aqṭāb* reigns supreme in his own district and runs virtually unchallenged electoral contests. They exercise complete authority in selecting the candidates on their lists, set the going or market price for each candidate (i.e. the sum they owe the *zaʿīm*) and dictate the strategy or policy which the list as a collectivity is to follow. The candidates are usually more than happy to oblige. In addition to paying the set tribute, they defray the full financial burdens of the campaign, act on behalf of their *zaʿīm* in dispensing favours and services and, in some instances, declare their total and unrelenting obedience to him. In short, they are no longer partners in a joint venture but 'clients' in a reciprocal though asymmetrical exchange. A poignant manifestation of this rather extreme form of patronage appears in a pledge signed by those on the list headed by Sulaymān al-ʿAlī in the elections of 1953. The text reads as follows:

We swear by God Almighty, by our honour, and by all that is dear to us, that—having agreed to participate in the battle of legislative elections on the same list—we pledge ourselves, in the case of victory by the grace of God, to follow in the Lebanese Parliament the directives and the policy that will be dictated to us by His Excellency our companion in the struggle, Sulaymān Bey al-ʿAlī al-Maraʿbī, and to act in a manner to carry out all that he wills. We pledge ourselves to back him in all that he desires, in the Ministry or outside of it, and not to swerve one bit from the attitude he intends to adopt with regard to the authorities as a partisan or as an opponent. If we do not keep our promise and fail to fulfil this oath we recognize ourselves to be unworthy of the human species, and deprived of honour and gratitude.[40]

All other such instances notwithstanding, the relationship between the *zaʿīm* and his clients remains fundamentally one of reciprocity. The *zaʿīm* throws in his political weight, influence and social prestige, and his clients reciprocate by providing other resources he (the *zaʿīm*) may lack, such as money, youthfulness, advanced education, a 'progressive' outlook and, most signficantly, a kinship, regional or communal affiliation which might weaken an opposing list. Kamāl Junblāṭ, for example, persistently and skilfully relied on the latter—i.e. incorporating some of the Maronite notable families of the Shuf—to erode the strength of his arch-rival in the area, Camille Shamʿūn. In other instances, two or three of the *aqṭāb* may resort to a coalition, mostly in the form of an *ad hoc* alliance, to extend the scope of their patronage and to ward off possible defeat at the polls. The Triple Alliance (*al-Ḥilf al-Thulāthī*) between Shamʿūn, Edde and Jumayyil in the wake of the 1967 Arab-Israeli war was one such effective though short-lived coalition.[41] Given the divergent personalities and perspectives of the three *aqṭāb*, the alliance was bound to be transient. It did, however, pose a positive challenge to the political system and struck a responsive chord among the electorate. Its share of the 1968 elections was 23 deputies, nearly one-fourth of the chamber.

Very few of the coalitions among the *aqṭāb* are prompted by ideological or national interests. In most cases purely Hobbesian motives of self-interest and political survival underlie such coalitions. During the national elections of 1972, Kamāl Junblāṭ and Majīd Arslān, heirs of the two feudal rivals for Druze supremacy for over two centuries, found it politically expedient in the face of emergent political threats to ignore their traditional enmity and assist each other in their respective districts. This alliance guaranteed the return of both traditional leaders along with their clients and safeguarded Druze hegemony against possible sources of new challenge.

The survival of primordial allegiances (particularly in the form of kinship, fealty and confessional sentiments), the peculiarities of the electoral law along with the adaptability of the traditional politician have enabled some of the *aqṭāb* and lesser *zuʿamā'* to enjoy a measure of power that is sometimes not commensurate with their personal electoral strength. The consequences of such survival for political change are many and grievous. First, it has doubtlessly meant the persistent failure of truly secular and ideological parties or candidates to make any significant headway in undermining the power of the *aqṭāb*. The only notable exceptions are the election of Baathists 'Alī al-Khalīl in Tyre and 'Abd al-Majīd al-Rāfi'ī in Tripoli and the Nasserite Najāḥ Wākim in Beirut during the 1972 elections. This is why it is misleading to interpret the increasing strength of political parties in parliamentary representation, as some observers have done,[42] as manifestations of non-traditional political affiliations or symptoms of the gradual transformation of Lebanon's political institutions and leadership towards modernity.

Second, and more important, the survival and extension of this form of political clientelism has crippled the role of the legislature as a forum for national debate and eroded the powers of the state. Like other highly personalised political cultures, political processes in Lebanon take place largely in informal cliques and through the pervasive networks of kinship and personal ties. Formal institutions are not the settings for political decision-making and bargaining. The chamber is no exception. As the legislative body, it is a forum for public debate and the airing of views. It acts as a buffer for balancing power and mitigating tension. In this sense, it is more of a 'deliberative' than a legislative assembly.[43] Most cardinal decisions, however, are taken elsewhere. For example, while constitutionally parliament is designated as having sole legislative powers, on repeated major occasions it has granted such powers to the executive. And cabinets, once empowered, do in fact promulgate decrees of a fundamental nature (reorganisation of the bureaucracy, new tax laws, a purge of the civil service etc.) which are too controversial to be handled by an open forum such as parliament.[44]

Much of the behaviour of the deputies within parliament—particularly voting on bills, casting of ballots in the election of the President of the Republic, Speaker of the House or parliamentary committees—is conducted in such a manner as to confirm promises and concessions made outside parliament. In casting their votes, for example, deputies resort to the ingenious but devious practice known as 'election keys' by which they enter the name of their candidate in a specific prearranged manner to confirm their predetermined commitments. The implications of such a practice for limiting the deputies' freedom and deepening their political subservience are self-evident.

The regular sessions of parliament, though frequent, are so plagued by formalistic and ritualised behaviour, a high degree of absenteeism and exchange of personal invectives, that the time during which the chamber is truly active in the course of a year is rather limited.[45] The most serious indictment against parliament is its impotence in times of crisis. During every major crisis the country has faced so far, parliament has been virtually crippled.[46] Political initiative reverts back to the real actors in the political system: clerics, communal leaders, a handful of *aqṭāb*, prominent bankers and businessmen and, of late, the various spokesmen of Palestinian resistance groups, private militias and some of the newly politicised 'counter-elite' who are excluded from participation in the formal political system. Even the deputies among them cease to act as parliamentarians and become defenders of the particular interests and privileges of their client groups or local communities.

The behaviour of parliament during Lebanon's protracted civil war of 1975-6 was no exception. While the country was besieged and beleaguered by endless rounds of violence, civil disorders, bitter sectarian rivalry, sedition and total anarchy, parliament could not even muster enough collective will, let alone a quorum, to convene and take appropriate measures to contain the crisis.[47] Of the few occasions parliament was able to meet during the prolonged crisis, three sessions stand out: the first was after the dramatic putsch of 11 March 1976 staged by Brigadier-General al-Aḥdab, in which he proclaimed the 'Corrective Movement' and, among other things, demanded the resignation of the government and the President of the Republic, and called on parliament to elect a new President within seven days. Frantically, parliament did produce a petition with 70 signatures requesting the resignation of the President. The second was on 11 April 1976, when a majority of 90 deputies made it to makeshift premises[48] and voted a constitutional amendment permitting the President to resign six months prior to the expiration of his term. The third was in May 1976, at which Eliyās Sarkīs was elected President.

The impotence of parliament and the clientelistic behaviour of the deputies has rendered the executive powers fairly independent of the collective will of the deputies. Indeed, no government since Lebanon's independence in 1943 has had to resign because of a vote of no confidence. The so-called 'parliamentary game'—often invoked during the frequent cabinet crises—is no more than a game of musical chairs among its *aqṭāb* jockeying to extend their share of clients in the government. In this sense, 'politics exists only in Lasswell's limited sense of "who gets what, when, and how," as a competition for the honours and spoils of office'.[49] The abiding concern of politicians, once in power, is to enlarge the scope of their patronage. Accordingly, politics, like practically everything else in a society sustained by the reciprocal exchange of favours, becomes a delicate act of distributing and managing patronage. Squabbles over civil service appointments, jurisdictional competition, allocation of public funds—all essentially patronage squabbles—assume more prominence (if judged by the time and attention devoted to them) than questions involving substantial issues of national and public policy.[50]

Political Patronage

It should be clear by now that the survival of primordial allegiances and the nature of patronage account for much of the persistent discrepancy between the 'progressive' social backgrounds of the parliamentary elite and its more traditional clientelistic behaviour. On nearly all the attributes underlying the socio-economic characteristics of the deputies, they are clearly distinguished from the rest of the society: they do stand out as an elite. They are highly educated and enjoy elevated social origins and the acquired professional skills that go with high-status positions. While they might not be true descendants of Lebanon's feudal aristocracy, they certainly belong to notable and prominent families. More important, they are economically very active and occupationally mobile. In terms of their loyalties, however, and their supporting orientations and patterns of behaviour, the deputies do not depart much from the prevailing norms and expectations of the rest of the society.

Because of the survival of primordial loyalties, kinship, communal and sectarian commitments supersede secular and ideological groups as agencies of political socialisation or as avenues for political power and leadership. This is far from unusual in a pluralistic society marked by persistent disparities in status and opportunity and sustained by highly personalised networks of reciprocal obligations. Within such a context, the middleman, the *wasīt* and the broker—who provides 'crucial linkages between the centre and the periphery',[51] and promises greater access to opportunity, needed services and protection—emerges as the most prized and viable political actor. Likewise, the patron-client tie becomes one of the most fundamental of the social bonds that hold the society together. In their most rudimentary form, all such ties involve the 'reciprocal exchange of extrinsic benefits'.[52] Both parties, in other words, the patron and the client, have a vested interest in maintaining this kind of mutually beneficial transaction. Despite their asymmetrical nature—and all patron-client ties bring together people with marked disparities in wealth, status and power[53]—they remain essentially an exchange partnership. What this has meant in more concrete terms is that clients in Lebanon have no accessible avenue to secure personal services, favoured treatment and protection other than through their allegiance to a patron (particularly in the form of gratitude and compliance which in some instances borders on filial loyalty), and patrons can only maintain their power by extending the size of their clientage support. Herein lies the ubiquity and survival of political patronage in Lebanon.

The ubiquity of patronage reveals another feature of the political elite which cannot be understood solely in terms of the qualitative superiority of its socio-economic composition. More important, in other words, than elevated social origins are the patronage and manipulative skills to which the politicians have access for securing protection and privilege on behalf of their clients. In this sense the parliamentary elite, despite its varying backgrounds or political orientations, is fundamentally homogeneous. Its power and influence rarely extend beyond closely circumscribed communities.[54] Likewise, its political assets are those typical of most patron-client ties—namely reciprocal loyalties and obligations.

From this perspective the seemingly more liberal and emancipated political leaders have much in common with the *aqṭāb* they frequently admonish and deride. These younger aspirants for public leadership, with rare exceptions, seek to establish their political base not by articulating a programme or identifying critical issues or specific problems requiring reform, but by building up a personal entourage of clients and followers. Much like the *aqṭāb*, the bulk of their time and efforts is devoted to interceding with public officials on behalf of their clients. Both the private interests of clients and the political careers of patrons are served by such a system of patronage. Clients, who normally lack the power, wealth and connections to obtain favoured treatment, are more than willing to pledge their allegiance in return for the benefits and private gains the patron can secure on their behalf. To the patron, such a devoted following is a priceless asset and, in most instances, the only political capital which can guarantee his tenure in office.

This, more than any other feature, accounts for the relatively small part played by Lebanese politicians in formulating broad policy issues of national and civic significance. To launch and sustain one's political career on the basis of a clearly defined ideological programme or platform of reform requires, among other things, continuous critical study and devotion to public issues and nagging societal problems.

Such civic-minded concerns, if they are to be more than *ad hoc* and arbitrary pronouncements, necessitate some disregard of the personal demands and favours of the clients. But politicians in Lebanon rise or fall on the basis of the size of their clientage and competence at dispensing personal favours, rather than on their merit in articulating and coping with public issues and problems. To refuse favours is to risk losing votes, and ultimately diminishes one's client support. Instances of this kind of failure are legion in Lebanon. Resourceful and spirited young intellectuals, sparked by a genuine concern for public service and civic reform, have consistently failed in national elections. The few that succeeded are invariably ones who have been adopted or sponsored by a traditional *zaʿīm*. Efforts directed at undermining the political power and economic base of the traditional *zuʿamāʾ* have so far accomplished very little in eroding the extensive support such leaders continue to enjoy among their clients. Despite far-reaching institutional and infrastructural changes introduced during the nineteenth century, the basic social ties that have traditionally held the society together—kinship and confessional loyalty, village solidarity, ties of patronage, the power and autonomy of feudal chiefs—remained almost untouched.

More recent efforts have scarcely been more successful. The two attempts of the Syrian Social National Party in 1949 and 1962—the only organised revolutionary attempts to bring about political change in Lebanon—have both been abortive. The impact of other progressive parties has been no more decisive. In fact, the distinction between a political party and a client group is not always very clear in Lebanon. The fact that a party has an internal structure, formal by-laws, elected officers and specific aims does not mean, as Arnold Hottinger has suggested, that it no longer serves as a locus for patron-client networks. A sizeable number of the *aqṭāb* and lesser *zuʿamā* have formed their own blocs and parties. The basis of support in most such collectivities remains essentially confessional or personal, rather than ideological.

Even the more gradualist efforts directed at undermining the power of the traditional *zuʿamāʾ* have not been very successful. For example, the so-called 'Shihābist' doctrine associated with President Shihāb (1958-64) and his followers was, if anything, an effort to discredit or bypass the traditional *zuʿamāʾ* as the exclusive intermediaries or spokesmen of underprivileged groups and communities. Measures were taken to modernise the state bureaucracy to gain more effective and direct access for individuals in remote communities. State planning was encouraged to curtail or moderate the adverse effects of free enterprise. Specific administrative reforms—geared mainly toward rescuing the bureaucracy from the direct and personal pressure of *zu'amā'*—were also undertaken. Finally, national social security and other state agencies emerged to provide citizens with needed welfare and services. None of these measures, however, as Shihāb himself painfully admitted after his retirement from politics, accomplished their intended objectives. Like the religious communities, patronage has almost become institutionalised in Lebanon's body politic.

The protracted civil war of 1975-6, by far the most violent and devastating Lebanon has ever experienced, has done little by way of preparing for any fundamental changes in the social and political structure of society. It remains yet to be seen, for example, whether the urgent appeals made during the crisis for secularisation, deconfession-alisation, changes in the electoral law, democratic reforms of political institutions, more equitable distribution of power and privilege are more than just rhetorical and catchy slogans. In the meantime, more than five years of bitter confessional rivalry, diffuse hatred, fear, widespread disorder, chaos and anarchy only polarised the various factions, deepened the fragmentation of society and retrenched the position of traditional leadership. Moreover, threats of partition, foreign intervention and concern for Lebanon's sovereignty only resuscitated, as they did at similar instances in the past, the old slogans of 'No Victor and No Vanquished', and the soothing rhetoric and vague appeals for confessional unity and harmony and an almost myopic concern with the immediate problems of law and order. Once again, the deeper social and historical sources of the crisis were ignored and politicians seemed more concerned with squabbles over the honour and spoils of office. The established elite, in short, was reluctant to introduce any changes which might destroy the very system which sustains and reinforces its patronage.

Continuities of this kind prompt us to argue that patronage is not, as some writers have suggested, a transient phenomenon, one which is bound to disappear as other, more secular, agencies and institutions emerge to offer alternative avenues for gaining access to privilege and opportunity. In assessing the nature of political change in Lebanon, Leonard Binder, to cite one such instance, has suggested that the extension of roads, health, electrification and other amenities to more remote parts of Lebanon; the emergence of a modern middle class capable of exerting its influence among rural communities; and the recruitment of younger political aspirants are bound to 'open a gulf between traditional political leaders and the increasingly educated and politically alert population'.[55] It is doubtful, in the light of evidence supplied earlier, that this 'gulf' has appeared. If it has, it certainly has not weakened the traditional patron-client ties; nor has it eroded much of the political legitimacy of patrons.

More important perhaps, patrons have been able, by skilful manoeuvring and adaptability, to forestall and circumvent their own possible obsolescence. All the *aqṭāb*, at one point in their political careers, sought to extend the scope of their patronage by incorporating secular and ideological elements. By forming political coalitions, parties and blocs, sponsoring labour organisations and other voluntary and benevolent associations, and by invoking liberal and progressive rhetoric, they have been able to retain and extend their clientage support which could have, under other circumstances, sought alternative sources of patronage. Expressed differently, the persistent influence of patrons stems from their ability to provide services, goods and values that no other group has so far been able to provide as effectively. These services and benefits are so desired by others as to induce them to reciprocate these gratifications in the form of gratitude and compliance.

Indeed, the power veteran politicans continue to enjoy in Lebanon is partly due to their monopoly of such vital benefits. Two simple but effective strategies are often pursued to retain this form of monopoly. First, access to alternative suppliers of these or substitute services is blocked. In instances where more than one *zaʿīm* happens to be vying for supporters within one electoral district or region, direct efforts are sought to prevent or block a service to an individual unless he turns to a particular patron for support.[56] Second, the traditional scope of patronage is extended to meet or incorporate a variety of new demands and services. By establishing benevolent or welfare societies, political parties and militia groups, and co-opting—as they appear to be doing in the wake of the current civil crisis—some of the emergent counter-elite, many of the political leaders have been able to extend and secularise the scope of their patronage without eroding their traditional basis of political support.

Notes

1. I. Harik, *Man yaḥkum Lubnān ?* (Who governs Lebanon ?) (al-Nahār, Beirut, 1972), pp. 15-27; I. Harik, 'Political Elites of Lebanon' in G. Lenczowski (ed.), *Political Elites in the Middle East* (American Enterprise Institute, Washington, DC, 1975), pp. 201-2.

2. M. Hudson, *The Precarious Republic* (Random House, New York, 1968), p. 241.

3. A. Messarra, 'La Structure Sociale du Parlement Libanais', unpublished doctoral

thesis, University of Strasbourg, 1974, pp. 257-64. The estimates of Harik and Messarra differ slightly, but both, none the less, point in the same direction.

4. Hudson, *Precarious Republic,* pp. 219-25; Messarra, 'Structure Sociale', p. 30; Harik, *Man yaḥkum Lubnān ?,* pp. 79-82.

5. Hudson, *Precarious Republic,* p. 225.

6. Ibid., p. 239; Messarra, 'Structure Sociale', p. 39; Harik, *Man yaḥkum Lubnān ?,* pp. 47-52.

7. Hudson, *Precarious Republic,* p. 239.

8. Harik, *Man yaḥkum Lubnān ?,* pp. 49-52.

9. J. Zuwiyya, *The Parliamentary Elections of Lebanon, 1968* (Brill, Leiden, 1972); Hudson, *Precarious Republic,* pp. 231f.

10. Hudson, *Precarious Republic,* p. 174.

11. Harik, 'Elites of Lebanon', pp. 214-15.

12. Hudson, *Precarious Republic,* p. 246. See also M. Suleiman, *Political Parties in Lebanon* (Cornell University Press, Ithaca, 1967), p. 265.

13. M. Kerr, 'Political Decision Making in a Confessional Democracy' in L. Binder, *Politics in Lebanon* (Wiley, New York, 1966), p. 202; L. Binder, 'Political Change in Lebanon' in Binder, *Politics in Lebanon,* p. 287.

14. P. Rondot, 'The Political Institutions of Lebanese Democracy' in Binder, *Politics in Lebanon,* p. 133.

15. R. Crow, 'Parliament in the Lebanese Political System' in A. Kornberg and L. Musolf (eds.), *Legislatures in Developmental Perspective* (Duke University Press, Durham, N. Carolina, 1970), pp. 296-7.

16. Hudson, *Precarious Republic,* p. 240; Messarra, 'Structure Sociale', p. 247.

17. B. Winder, 'Syrian Deputies and Cabinet Ministers, 1919-1959', *Middle East Journal,* vol. 16, no. 4 (1962), pp. 407-29.

18. J. M. Landau, 'Elections in Lebanon', *Western Political Quarterly,* vol. 14, no. 1 (1961), p. 131; Zuwiyya, *Elections of Lebanon,* p. 95.

19. Zuwiyya, *Elections of Lebanon,* p. 95.

20. Ibid.

21. Hudson, *Precarious Republic,* p. 240, has arbitrarily chosen the birth date of 1910 as a dividing line between deputies raised in a traditional as opposed to a post-Ottoman or modern era.

22. Y. Courbage and P. Fargue, *La Situation démographique du Liban* (Oriental Press, Beirut, 1973), p. 52.

23. Messarra, 'Structure Sociale', p. 261; Harik, *Man yaḥkum Lubnān ?,* p. 28.

24. Y. Sayigh, *Entrepreneurs of Lebanon* (Harvard University Press, Cambridge, Mass., 1962); S. Khalaf, 'Managerial Ideology and Industrial Conflict in Lebanon', unpublished Ph D dissertation, Princeton University, 1963; S. Khalaf, 'The Lebanese Labour Leaders: A Comparative Profile', mimeo, American University of Beirut, 1967.

25. S. Khalaf and P. Kongstad, *Hamra of Beirut* (Brill, Leiden, 1973), pp. 74-6.

26. Messarra, 'Structure Sociale, p. 261; Harik, *Man yaḥkum Lubnān ?,* p. 28.

27. B. al-Khūrī, *Lebanese Truths* (Lebanese Documents Publications, Harissa, 1960), p. 30.

28. Harik, 'Elites of Lebanon', pp. 203-6.

29. In instances of multiple or dual occupations, the one the deputy lists in his biographical sketch is considered by Harik as his basic occupation. See ibid., p. 209.

30. Hudson, *Precarious Republic,* p. 244.

31. Ibid., pp. 244-5.

32. See L. Froman, *The Congressional Process: Strategies, Rules and Procedures* (Little, Brown, Boston, 1967), p. 170; J. Ross, *Parliamentary Representation* (Yale University Press, New Haven, 1948), p. 107; D. Matthews, *U.S. Senators and Their World* (University of North Carolina Press, Chapel Hill, 1960), p. 240.

33. In two of his recent publications, Harik, *Man yaḥkum Lubnān?*, pp. 15-29; 'Elites of Lebanon', pp. 210-11, has questioned the importance of kinship ties in the recruitment of the parliamentary elite.

34. S. Khalaf, 'Changing Forms of Political Patronage in Lebanon' in E. Gellner and J. Waterbery (eds.), *Patrons and Clients in Mediterranean Societies* (Duckworth, London, 1977).

35. The incidence of close kinship ties among parliamentarians is both complex and numerous and deserves fuller treatment. One instance of such interrelationship among five prominent political families (al-Khūrī, Shīha, Firʿawn, al-Saʿd and ʿĪsā al-Khūrī) is sufficient to illustrate the intensity and pervasiveness of family networks in Lebanese politics : Bishāra al-Khūrī is the brother-in-law of Michael Shīha, who in turn is the paternal cousin of Henry Firʿawn. Ḥabīb Pasha al-Saʿd is the maternal cousin of Bishāra al-Khūrī's father, who in turn is a distant relative of Nadra ʿĪsā al-Khūrī.

36. Harik, 'Elites of Lebanon', pp. 210-11.

37. It was my intention to document such an inference by a systematic analysis of how various parliamentarians voted on particular issues and bills. Because of the protracted civil crisis it was impossible to gain access to the files or archives of the Parliament to undertake such an exploration.

38. Harik, 'Elites of Lebanon', pp. 214-15.

39. For further details of the electoral system see Chapter 6 of the present volume.

40. *al-Jarīda,* 7 September 1953.

41. Initially conceived as a loosely organised alliance to defend the national integrity of Lebanon against the emergent socialist and revolutionary trends sweeping Arab countries at the time, the Triple Alliance evolved into a rather cohesive political coalition with a unifying ideological base and a concern for national priorities. For further details see J. Entelis, *Pluralism and Party Transformation in Lebanon, al-Katā'ib, 1936-1970* (Brill, Leiden, 1974).

42. Zuwiyya, *Elections of Lebanon,* pp. 92-4; Hudson, *Precarious Republic,* pp. 246-7.

43. Landau, 'Elections in Lebanon', p. 147.

44. Crow, 'Parliament', pp. 296-7.

45. Ibid., p. 288.

46. Mr Kāmil al-Asʿad, Speaker of the 1972 Chamber, has spoken of the total absence of the parliament during the crises of 1958 and 1969. See *al-Nahār* (a Beirut daily), 20 December 1975.

47. A parliamentary 'Initiative Committee' composed of eleven deputies was formed in December 1975 and submitted a set of socio-economic, political and administrative proposals for reform. Sensible as some of the proposals were, they were neither presented before the parliament nor were they expressed in the form of specific legislative bills. For a full text, see *al-Nahār,* throughout December 1975.

48. The official Parliament House is in the centre—an unsafe district of the city. It had been ransacked and partially destroyed.

49. Kerr, 'Confessional Democracy', p. 190.

50. For documentation see ibid., pp. 193-6.

51. R. Lemarchand and K. Legg, 'Political Clientelism and Development: A Preliminary Analysis', *Comparative Politics,* vol. 4, no. 2 (January 1972), p. 158.

52. P. Blau, *Exchange and Power in Social Life* (Wiley, New York, 1964), p. 314; R. Lemarchand, 'Political Clientelism and Ethnicity in Tropical Africa: Competing Solidarities in Nation-Building', *American Political Science Review*, vol. 66, no. 1 (March 1972), pp. 75-6.

53. J. Scott, 'Patron-Client Politics and Political Change in Southeast Asia', *American Political Science Review*, vol. 66, no. 1 (March 1972), p. 93.

54. For further details, see A. Hottinger, 'Zu'amā' in Historical Perspective' in Binder, *Politics in Lebanon*, pp. 85-105; S. Khalaf, 'Primordial Ties and Politics in Lebanon', *Middle Eastern Studies*, vol. 4, no. 3 (1968), pp. 243-69; P. Gubser, 'The Zu'amā' of Zahlah: The Current Situation in a Lebanese Town', *Middle East Journal*, 27 (Spring 1973), pp. 181-2.

55. Binder, 'Change in Lebanon', p. 301.

56. Gubser, 'Zuamā' of Zahla', pp. 181-2.

11. ISRAEL

Emanuel Gutmann

The elections to the 8th Knesset were held under extraordinary circumstances. Originally scheduled for 31 October 1973, the candidate lists had actually been submitted by the end of September, but the elections were postponed for two months owing to the October war. Thus the electorate voted for lists of candidates which hardly reflected the changing mood caused by the war and its aftermath. In other words, the war had hardly any impact on the personal composition of the Knesset, or only a very indirect one. The electors, of course, had the option to switch their vote to another list, and some did, but in all lists the old names predominated. In retrospect it seems more than likely that if the option of making changes in the party lists and of submitting new lists had been available, the results of the elections would have been quite different.

As things were, a paradoxical situation arose. Although a third (40 of 120) of the MKs (Members of Knesset) elected in 1973 were new members, the composite profile of the new Knesset was not markedly different from the previous one, and that in spite of the considerable shift in the party composition of the Knesset. On the other hand, although the same parties continued to form the government coalition (with one small exception, for a few months), almost one-half of the Cabinet members in office were changed within six months of the election, and all major Cabinet posts, including the Prime Minister, changed hands in a constitutionally orderly and politically smooth manner. This change was to be of considerable importance, although even keen observers missed it for what it was, namely the first instalment of a volte-face in Israeli politics. What is more, such a turnover was no mean feat at the time, given a country known until then for the perennialism and resilience of its leadership. However, during twenty-five years, with eight general elections and almost a score of cabinets in office, gradual changes were often imperceptible to contemporaries, although they significantly altered the personal composition of Knesset and Cabinet, even if for no other reason than that 'each year removes many old men, makes all others older, brings in many new'.[1]

The Old Leaders and the New

The accession of the Cabinet formed by Itzhak Rabin in June 1974 after Golda Meir's resignation denoted at the time the final political demise of the first generation of the Founding Fathers, i.e. that of David Ben-Gurion, Itzhak Ben-Zvi and Moshe Sharett, and not only in a purely symbolic sense. Furthermore, it also meant the displacement of most of those who constituted the second, or intermediary political generation[2] in Israeli politics, namely that of Levi Eshkol, Golda Meir, Pinhas Sapir and their contemporaries. Most of the first group were men of the second *aliya* ('wave of immigration') who came into the country in the early years of the twentieth century; the second group mostly belonged to the third *aliya* of the years immediately after the First World War. Begin, head of the government after the 1977 election, is also one of the Founding Fathers, but he came into the country much later, and his Cabinet, with one or possibly two exceptions, is of a different generation altogether.

True to the oft-quoted words of Montesquieu, whereas the first generation of the leaders of the commonwealth had created the institutions at the inception of the society—and in this particular case much ahead and in anticipation of sovereign status—the new set of leaders now taking over have been moulded by the institutions already functioning. The Founding Fathers had established their rule even before independence by creating a system of self-government, political parties and other quasi-political organisations. By their political acumen they realised the primacy of the political element and the importance of the early establishment of suitable organisational machinery. They thereby reversed the usual developmental pattern and created a modern type of political system by a process of political institutionalisation which actually preceded or ran parallel to economic development and societal modernisation. In any event, these latter processes were clearly subordinated to political decisions.[3] In this way these nation-cum-state-builders moulded the political system, institutions, processes and culture in their own image.

Most of these leaders had come from Eastern Europe in the first quarter of the twentieth century. They had brought with them a mixture of contradictory traditions, of quasi-democratic and oligarchic self-rule, of East European autocracy with socialist-revolutionary *élan* and elements of collectivism. These were curious combinations of ideological dogmatism with political pragmatism, of selfless devotion to the cause and the group with traits of personal idiosyncracies.[4]

Within the various political parties the differences between the first and second generations have been blurred over the years; the second generation was gradually integrated into major leadership positions before and after independence. The third generation of top leaders was prepared and nurtured for elite positions by their elders and predecessors. Frequently they were actually co-opted by the founders into senior positions so that the turnover in leadership positions should have been primarily a problem of timing. Nevertheless, for over a decade (roughly, the 1960s and early 1970s) this anticipated turnover created acrimonious conflicts between the generational groups and among them in almost all parties, but particularly so in the ruling Labour Party. These conflicts left rather severe scars which were not fully healed when the third generation took over the reigns of office.[5] What did occur with the accession to power of this new generation of top leaders, symbolised by Rabin, the first locally born Prime Minister, was the closing of the gap between chronological age and generational age,[6] a gap which had been a prominent feature of Israeli public life for the previous decade or longer. This situation was at times ridiculed by comments about the young country with an old leadership. These comments returned in 1977 with Begin in power, but are less justified now, both for the country and the man.

Continuity and Change: The Nature of Succession

At the time, the transfer of top leadership positions to the new generation of Rabin and his colleagues was viewed as an indication of the adaptability of the political system, and as an indication of its dynamic stability. Seen from the vantage point of the 1977 elections this evaluation may still stand, but the element of vitality has become much more prominent.

Although of considerable symbolic significance and accompanied by the abandonment of the outward manifestations of the outgoing ruling group, the 1974 change was no 'circulation of elites', certainly not in the usual sense of the displacement of the established elite by a counter-elite, whether abruptly or in a gradual manner, nor in the more restricted meaning of a turnover among different groups within the governing elite itself.[7] Indeed, what took place was primarily a transition in terms of personalities and of political generations, and even then only partially so. It included a group dimension only insofar as the leading elements of the new elite constituted a sort of generational network with little more in common than ambiguous sentiments towards their elders. Despite the continuity of the political culture and the basic value system, the leadership style, patterns of elite political behaviour and the policy-making processes gradually took on new shape, although more in intention than in actual practice. A dynamic conservatism, in the sense of meeting the challenges of new needs by adapting existing machinery, was attributed to the old guard,[8] perhaps primarily during the years of what has here been termed its second generation. Rabin's government made the effort to create what one might call a conservative dynamism, i.e. meeting challenges by a display of innovative vigour tamed by a hesitancy to upset the prevailing patterns of policy and behaviour. But, except for the diplomatic achievements of the disengagement agreements with Egypt, the government achieved very little in its foreshortened term in office before it was defeated in the 1977 elections. The Rabin government did not bring to power any new socio-economic group or class, and no other structural change occurred upon its accession. Indeed, this continuation of the ruling elite was to become a major contributing factor to its loss of power three years later.

What changed was the quality of the leadership itself. The best indication of this was the leadership duel between Rabin and Shimon Peres, an unknown occurrence before, and the marginal victory of the former in this contest. The passage from prominently charismatic rule (Ben-Gurion) or that of a strong personality (Golda Meir) to one in which the personal element was minimal, was crucial. This kind of change of leadership has been variously characterised as 'the replacement of the leadership of revolutionary modernisers by that of managerial modernisers', as the replacement of politicians by technicians, and—in the Israeli context—as the transition 'from a natural to a selected elite'.[9] Possibly, the Weberian routinisation of charisma still conveys the meaning best.

The political generation which came to power after the October 1973 war is aware of, and at times overawed by, the significance of the Jewish national revolution which culminated in independence. More particularly, although many do take sovereignty and statehood for granted, they are preoccupied with the primacy of preserving these. This generation feels the emotional burden, as well as the political consequences, of this heritage. Another manifestation of this change of attitudes is an impatience with and even aversion to the highly moralistic political culture of the Founding Fathers. As often as not, this has a contrary effect, namely the idealisation or elevation to the level of principle of improvisations in the affairs of state. This changing mood has now caught on in the political leadership, perhaps by a process similar to that which Frey called 'capillary action'.[10] This delayed reaction at the elite level does not apply, by and large, to matters of concrete public policy, but to two other areas. One is the generalised public sentiments and attitudes towards the style of politics and public life, in which transmission towards the top occurs without a great time-lag. In this respect the Rabin Cabinet reflected the mood of the 8th Knesset, which in turn mirrored changing public opinion.

The situation is different with regard to the socio-demographic composition of the political elite, here taken to include both members of the Knesset and the Cabinet. Lower political echelons, including internal party and local government bodies, were speedier than national level politics to adjust to the changing composition of the population.

From this point of view the 1973 elections—in which the largest switch in terms of the overall support of the two major parliamentary blocs took place—were crucial. Even if not 'critical',[11] these elections should be viewed as part of a 'realigning electoral era'[12] producing a cumulative effect over a number of elections. Perhaps the most appropriate term would be 'converting' elections, since the majority managed to retain its position,[13] and even an impressive shift in the popular vote did not suffice to displace the ruling Israeli Labour Party. Nevertheless, the dominance of that party,[14] or better still, its position as the quasi-majority party, was somewhat shaken, and its position as 'pivotal actor'[15] was threatened. In 1977 this realigning era came to the end with the Labour Alignment badly beaten to second place, which may mean the end of the dominant-party system, at least for the time being.[16]

Really critical at the time was the change of Cabinets in mid-1974, inasmuch as a fairly considerable volte-face within the top echelon of the ruling party took place. This was of even greater import than that signified by Ben-Gurion's resignation as Prime Minister and his ultimate departure from his party (1963-5). Politically relevant in this connection is that the resignation of Golda Meir as Prime Minister was not precipitated, strictly speaking, by the verdict of the 1973 electorate. To some extent it was generated by internal party pressure within the Labour Party and given further impetus by public opinion, which was voiced independently of the parties. This included short-lived but vocal protest and dissent movements. These, in turn, had been primarily formed because, in the view of their former adherents, almost all parties had been compromised by the Yom Kippur War and its antecedents. The Labour Party and its Alignments were accused of being too closely identified with the political status quo, the failure of national policy and military unpreparedness for the war. The Likkud, although it attracted many new voters, was at fault in the eyes of many for missing the chance to come to power under these circumstances and, according to others, for not presenting an unflinching oppositional stance. Both party groups were taken to task for having opposed the opening of the lists before the election, which was seen as an unwarranted shielding of members of the ruling elite. All parties were also criticised for their undemocratic internal processes and, in particular, their nomination procedures. The existing parties were considered by these groups as too inept to mobilise sentiments of urgency and resoluteness. Paradoxical as this may seem, little of this dominated the 1973 elections and almost none of it had an actual impact on the voting behaviour. As a result, the changes of the parliamentary scene were less dramatic than those in the government, although not inconsiderable from the point of view of party composition.

The one party to benefit from these sentiments in 1973 was the Movement for Citizen's Rights. The much-delayed beneficiary of this trend of criticism of all existing parties in the 1977 elections was the Democratic Movement for Change.

Cabinet and Knesset: Common Profile

The foregoing should not give rise to the notion that in Israel any basic variance exists between the legislators and the Cabinet either in terms of policy or social background. As a whole, the parties (or parliamentary factions) of the coalition accept the policy direction of their political leaders who are in the Cabinet. In turn, by way of its collective responsibility to parliament, the Cabinet is considered in general accord with its supporters. If there is any difference between the two, it occurs less frequently over substantive issues than over the standard constitutional division of functions between the legislative and the executive, in which the latter is ordinarily expected to take the lead in policy-making, where it is the more efficacious agent and initiator of policy.

The social profile of Cabinet ministers as a group is not dissimilar from that of the Knesset members, which most of them are concurrently. Perhaps one could say that whatever specifically characterises the Knesset is reflected to an even greater extent in the Cabinet. This refers in particular to the various aspects of sociological misrepresentation of the Knesset, which will be dealt with below.

This can easily be demonstrated by means of recently published data.[17] The average age of ministers on first assuming Cabinet posts is, naturally enough, higher than that of MKs. However, the difference between the average ages of Cabinet and Knesset members has been steady over the years, and so just as the 8th Knesset was younger than previous ones, the average age of the Rabin Cabinet was younger by some five years than previous Cabinets. The educational level of MKs and Cabinet ministers was quite similar, but some 10 per cent more of the latter than of MKs had gone to a university. As to the source of livelihood, a slightly greater percentage of Cabinet ministers than of MKs had owed it to their respective parties before entering remunerative public office. Misrepresentation according to country of origin followed the same pattern: the percentage of those coming from Asia and Africa who sat in the Cabinet was smaller than among MKs, and that of East European origin greater, but in both cases not appreciably so. Knesset membership is not a constitutional requirement for appointment as a minister with the exception of the Prime Minister. Although in recent Cabinets up to a third of the members did not hold parliamentary seats, this is still the exception.

As in most parliamentary democracies, the Knesset has never been either the hub of public policy-making or the centre of gravity of political power. Israeli parliamentarians are aware of the relatively low profile of the Knesset as an institution and of themselves as MKs among other participants in the national decision-making process. Although it is notoriously difficult to provide an objective ranking of the relative importance of the institutions in the political system, in practically everybody's estimate the Cabinet ranks first. An Israeli 'profile of power' would therefore be very similar to that of Britain as presented by Putnam.[18] However, popular rating, at least until recently, would probably have put 'party organisation' at the top of the scale, even above the Cabinet. This would bring Israel closer to the Italian position than to the British; whether this evaluation was ever justified by the factual situation is, however, more than doubtful.

Notwithstanding its rather humble placement, few would deny that it is to the Knesset that one turns primarily when examining the Israeli political elite. With, perhaps, some isolated exceptions of basically non-political people who were brought into the Knesset, any person not considered a part of the elite before his election to the Knesset would automatically be 'elevated' to it on election. On the other hand, however, Knesset members do not *ipso facto* belong to the national leadership. One can even think of a few Cabinet members who cannot be considered as belonging to that group, and this would include not only the three non-partisan ministers who have hitherto each served short interim terms of office. Despite incessant disparagement by the mass media, which in turn take their cue in this matter mainly from popularisers of political science, the Knesset is the only popularly elected, i.e. representative, branch of government which continues to attract the limelight and stays very much in the centre of popular interest. The main reason for this remains the simple fact that although political careers are not made in the Knesset, given a few exceptions, almost everyone having a claim on high elite status gets, or at least tries to get, elected to the Knesset at some stage during his political career. Indeed, there are no more than a very few isolated and exceptional cases of party leaders who have not served for at least one or two terms in the Knesset, and most top leaders have served for longer. In short, in terms of political power the Knesset is what its members make of it, and not the other way around. Were one to add up the sum of power of its members in their individual capacities, taking into account their various organisational affiliations, it would much exceed that of the Knesset as a corporate entity. This is just another way of saying that the Knesset's prestige much outstrips its power.

Election to the Knesset indicates that a person is already well advanced in his political career. Very few, of whom some of the Founding Fathers are the main group, have already reached the acme of their careers, but none is just beginning. Most who enter the Knesset are switching in mid-career, with a considerable advantage. With few exceptions, membership in the Knesset can be described as a reward for service rendered, but in the 8th Knesset there were more exceptions than previously, especially among the youngest members.

The fact that the individual composition of the Knesset can thus be manipulated shows the very tight control which parties (or their respective nominating committees) have over the channels of access to political elite status as here defined, i.e. over the composition of the parliamentary factions of their respective parties. Despite basic differences in the structure and operational code of the various parties participating in the election, the nomination procedures evince far-reaching similarities. Usually these committees are of very restricted membership, somehow balancing the major groups or factions within the party with proper representation of the top leadership. In some parties the leading organ serves as nomination committee as well, but usually this is avoided so that people do not have to nominate themselves. The committees are appointed by top-level party bodies. In some instances the slate of nomination must be approved—usually *en bloc*—by larger bodies, such as a party congress or central committee, which only very rarely makes alterations in their nomination. In any event, in the past, neither the nominating committee nor the nominees themselves were ever elected by the party-wide membership. For the 1977 election a number of parties, and in particular the newly formed DMC, instituted far-reaching democratised procedures.

At least partially these procedures can be attributed to the peculiarities of the electoral system which makes it incumbent on party headquarters to present a slate of up to 120 nominees in an enumerated order. Since the fluctuation of the popular vote is usually within limits of up to 10 and at the most 20 per cent, the rank order on the ticket predetermines who is elected and who is not, i.e. who has and who does not have a 'safe' place. This situation permits the committee to balance the representative character of the list. This balance is obviously subject to the personal and group pressures which are exercised in the process of placing names on the list. Since the election system, however, puts the individual candidate at a discount, the committees develop at the same time a high degree of insensitivity to public opinion so that strong oligarchical tendencies determine more than anything else the representative character of the party leadership.[19]

Inasmuch as prospective Cabinet ministers seek a seat in the Knesset—and almost all do in order to be able (i) to display the legitimacy of having been elected even if only as one of a list, and (ii) to retain a seat in parliament when not holding Cabinet office—the procedure of the nomination committee applies to them as to everybody else. Nevertheless, serving ministers and candidates for ministerial office usually are high up on the list (Rabin was number 20 on the Labour list for the 1973 election, with a firm promise that he would get a Cabinet post).

Indeed, perhaps the potentially most promising way to differentiate between national leaders of a party, including its Cabinet members and prospective ministers, and group representatives is by the nomination committee's determination as to whose candidacy is practically automatic, as contrasted with those who must compete for a place on the party list.

For obvious reasons no such formalised nomination procedure exists for Cabinet appointments, which are made by the Prime Minister designate, who is, however, far from a free agent in his choice from among the *ministrables* of his party and his coalition partners.

The parliamentary career pattern of ministers is also slightly different from that of backbenchers. Quite a number of the Cabinet ministers have made a lateral entrance into the Knesset in the sense of taking up their office soon after election to the Knesset; but then, because Israeli law permits ministerial appointments from outside the Knesset, a lengthy apprenticeship is not necessary. In this respect Israel is one among many parliamentary systems which do not follow what has been called the 'classic picture', according to which, membership in the Cabinet comes after a very long apprenticeship in parliament.[20]

From early on it has been the practice (at least of Labour) to differentiate in the pattern of selection between candidates for a parliamentary career and those considered for executive (i.e. Cabinet) office. Studying the new appointments of Cabinet ministers and deputy ministers of approximately a decade (4th to 6th Knesset), Czudnowski[21] found that half of those were made when first elected to the Knesset. Most of these had at that time come straight from top civil service and other senior appointive positions. More recently there has been a tendency to turn to high-ranking, newly retired army officers, popularly called 'parachutists' (i.e. coming suddenly to high office in the system from outside), who seem to be preferred to loyal party stalwarts and parliamentary backbenchers for Cabinet and other high executive office.

A 1971 study found that the appointment of only four or perhaps five Cabinet members out of a total of 62 who had served since 1948 can be attributed to distinction in parliamentary performance.[22] Obviously, the ministers of the first Cabinets could not have had any parliamentary experience, but the situation has not changed recently. Of the 21-member Cabinet formed by Rabin in 1974, not even one minister had made his career in the Knesset, and the most that could be said is that lengthy service there contributed marginally to the initial appointment of about five of them. Rabin himself was the best example for this: he became Prime Minister only six months after having been elected to the Knesset for the first time, and after having served an apprenticeship as Cabinet minister for about two months. Previously he had been Ambassador to the United States for five years, after a military career of some twenty-five years culminating in a four-year term as Chief-of-Staff of the Israeli army.

Profile of Knesset Members
Over the years, the composite profile of Knesset members—which includes, as we saw, almost all Cabinet members—has been gradually

changing regarding some of its major socio-demographic characteristics. But it is of some interest that from the perspective of group representativeness, other than the obvious and gradual decrease of Founding Fathers, the composition of the Knesset has been remarkably stable. Despite the personnel turnover, the proportion, on the one hand, of national party or factional leaders, and on the other hand, of sectoral or group representatives—spokesmen for the major demographic segments of the population, such as national, ethnic and immigrant groups, women, the young, religious groups, sectors of the economy and their main sub-groups, such as economic interest associations—has not changed much. Part of the explanation for this is undoubtedly that over the years many—but by no means all—of the long-serving members 'advance' from group representation to national party leadership of the first or second rank. At the same time, a small number of newly recruited members can be regarded neither as genuine representatives, i.e. formally designated by their sector or group, nor as pseudo-representatives, i.e. those co-opted by the top leadership in order to gain the support of specific sectors or groups and possibly to serve in the Knesset as spokesmen for them, without having been formally designated by them.[23] These are here called 'second-echelon leaders' who, with the group representatives, comprise the backbenchers of the major party factions; it is among their ranks that the turnover is greatest, i.e. their length of service is shortest.[24]

Taking the Knesset membership as a whole, these generalisations obliterate the quite substantial differences between the various parties.

Table 11.1: Members of 1st, 5th and 8th Knessets, by Representative Status

	1st Knesset (1949)	5th Knesset (1961)	8th Knesset (1973)
Founding Fathers	28	20	6
National and National Party Leaders (not FFs)	18	23	28
Second-echelon Leaders incl. Local Leaders (not group-oriented)	27	31	32
Genuine Group and Sectoral Representatives	27	26	30
Pseudo-group and Sectoral Representatives	20	20	24
Total	120	120	120

The terminology used here further contributes to this. Thus, there are parties such as Mapam, whose Knesset faction, excepting only its urban members, ought to be regarded as an almost monolithic contingent of genuine sectoral representatives of its kibbutz movement, or the NRP which ought to be no more than representatives of the religious sector. In this way, the national status of its top leadership would be unwarrantably disguised. The same applies, *mutatis mutandis*, to the Arab MKs, who represent the various minorities' lists. They come within the category of pseudo-sectoral representatives because no formal machinery of nomination exists within their *de facto* constituency, i.e. the Israeli-Arab community, just as is the case with all other pseudo-representatives.

Of greater consequence to the composite profile is that although every party has its 'national party leaders', those of parties almost continuously in power, and particularly Labour, are likely to be regarded as leaders of the nation. Leaders of smaller parties in addition to those in virtually permanent opposition are less likely to be so regarded. A differentiating factor, however, is the type of party. In sectarian and pluralistic parties formal provisions are made for group representation, whereas in a quasi-populist party such as Herut not quite so many can be counted as sectoral representatives, genuine or otherwise.[25] But more recently, even in Herut group representation has become more prominent, even if—other than for Oriental Jews and working-class people—it is not socio-economic interests around which these groups form. In any event, this structural situation may explain the status of Herut's Begin and possibly one or two others as national leaders.

Table 11.2: Members of the 1st, 5th and 8th Knessets, by Age

Age	1st Knesset (1949)		5th Knesset (1961)		8th Knesset (1973)	
	At Election	At First Entry to Knesset	At Election	At First Entry to Knesset	At Election	At First Entry to Knesset
Under 36	10	10	1	10	6	17
36-45	31	31	23	50	25	54
46-55	45	45	49	45	43	36
56-65	32	32	30	14	39	13
Over 65	2	2	17	1	7	—
Average for Knesset	47.9		53.2		51.3	

Turning now very briefly to some socio-demographic characteristics of the MKs: the rather high age of Israeli MKs has often been discussed, and it is a fact that the average age of MKs has slightly increased for a long time because of the progressing age of the long-service incumbents. More recently, however, average age has actually declined because age at first entrance of new MKs is dropping appreciably. The need for, and the pressure by, young people has been decisive in this respect in almost all parties. The younger entrants include a number of lateral entries designated for executive office, although the ex-generals coming into the Knesset as prospective Cabinet ministers were, for obvious reasons, within the middle-age bracket (46-54). The result of this is that whereas in the 1st Knesset 41 per cent of the MKs were under 45, 60 per cent of the newly entered in the 5th Knesset and 71 per cent of the 8th were of that age group. The very young grew from 10 per cent earlier to 17 per cent in the 8th. The average age of MKs, which had steadily risen from the 1st Knesset to the 7th when it was 54.3 years, was down to only 51.3 in the 8th. Obviously the percentage of older new MKs is steadily declining; in the 8th Knesset the oldest new MK was 63. The image of old age is thus created primarily by the prominent members who are the old-timers in the House.

There has been almost no change over the years in the educational background of MKs. An almost steady 60 per cent had a partial or full university education, and again in the 8th Knesset this has risen slightly to about two-thirds of all MKs. This, incidentally, is also the steady proportion of Cabinet ministers with such a background. One should add, however, that this rather high rate of academically trained persons among the elite is not the result of a determined policy to recruit such people to high political office. Even to the extent that there is a technocratic tendency in Cabinet appointments these cannot be attributed primarily to such background.

Reliable socio-economic background data on MKs are hard to come by; moreover, they are partly quite irrelevant. Perhaps the most interesting concern the main source of livelihood of MKs before their first election. These reveal one of the well-known characteristics of Israeli politics, namely that of the financial interdependence of the party and its functionaries. The index generally used for this purpose, namely that of occupational background, i.e. a person's profession, is much less informative.

About 40 per cent of the members of the 8th Knesset were *asqanim*, i.e. professional politicians who, before election, owed their livelihood

Table 11.3: Members of 1st, 5th and 8th Knessets: Source of Livelihood Before First Election to Knesset

	1st Knesset (1949)	5th Knesset (1961)	8th Knesset (1973)
'Movement'		66	50
Bureaucracy	65	9	24
Military		1	4
Kibbutz-Moshav	23	19	18
Professional	19	12	18
Business and Industry	7	8	4
Agriculture	6	5	2
	120	120	120

to their 'movement', and for whom the movement feels some sort of responsibility once they cease to be MKs. This means that they were employed by a party, labour union or any one of their rather numerous affiliates.[26] This percentage is a slight reduction as compared with over one-half in the 1st Knesset. Most of those had been the leading figures of the *yishuv* (the Jewish community in Palestine) in the last years before independence. For many their election can be described as a reward for their years of public service. Because formal institutionalisation was rather rudimentary during the *yishuv* period, in that the differences between political, bureaucratic and often military functions in the Zionist movement were blurred, no attempt has been made to distinguish among these for the 1st Knesset. It should perhaps not be surprising that over the years the share of movement support for politicians has not fallen appreciably in view of the fact that politics has become well established as a profession with a career pattern of its own, and from which one derives a living. The drawbacks of this situation have been discussed.[27] They do not seem to be detrimental to the independence of judgement and behaviour of individual MKs. To the extent that they feel themselves constrained in action this cannot be attributed to this situation. Conversely, personal financial wealth and independence does not convey any benefits as far as a political career is concerned.[28]

These data on source of livelihood, perhaps in combination with those on education,[29] are the closest approximation we have to indications of class background. In a country which has provided considerable social mobility, partly as an immigrant society, and partly because of socialist motivations and egalitarian policies, it can be argued that the classical notion of class structure has little relevance in analysing the social class composition of Knesset members. Most MKs come from middle and upper socio-economic groups, with only isolated cases from the lower spectrum. The number of MKs with a genuine industrial or service working-class background has always been minimal; in the 8th Knesset perhaps three MKs could be so classified.

The sociological unrepresentativeness of the Knesset, as of other political institutions, has often been discussed,[30] in particular with respect to what is commonly regarded as the politically most salient cleavage in Israeli-Jewish society, namely that between people of European and Oriental origin. To a considerable extent this dichotomy coincides with that of length of residence in the country.

The main elements of Israel's social life and of its political system have been established more or less according to the patterns of a modern Western polity, by the nucleus of the first waves of immigrants most of whom were of Eastern and Central European origin. This Western pattern includes a functioning parliamentary system of government with a multiparty system, an independent judiciary, a professional and effective bureaucracy, deep attachment to human and group rights and a well-advanced welfare policy. As a country of rapid economic development, societal modernisation has been one of its government's main concerns, in particular for those segments of the population which had formerly lived in pre-modern conditions (the Israeli Arabs) or who had immigrated from such surroundings (most of the Orientals). Despite conscious efforts at rapid absorption by the old settlers and of speedy acculturation of the new immigrants, which had considerable success, a time-lag developed. This affected in particular their entry into the upper echelons of politics. The more senior positions reflect the greatest time-lag, which is at its most extreme in the Cabinet, the senior bureaucracy and staff ranks in the army. This can partly be attributed to a deficiency in educational standards. More broadly, the reason is that a new generation with its native-born leaders first had to grow up in Israel, because most of the leaders of the Oriental immigrants found the gap between them and the prevailing system, which was quite alien to them, too wide to bridge.

Concerning representation in the Knesset, the number of members originating from Muslim countries rose appreciably between 1949 and 1973, and the number of Europeans (especially Eastern Europeans) similarly decreased. This is partially vitiated by the numerical rise of second-generation Israelis of Europe parentage (see Table 11.4).

Table 11.4: *Members of the 1st, 5th and 8th Knessets, by Country of Birth and Period of Immigration (Absolute Numbers and Percentages)*

Country of Birth	Period of Immigration*	1st Knesset (1949) seats	1st Knesset (1949) % of votes	5th Knesset (1961) seats	5th Knesset (1961) % of votes	8th Knesset (1973) seats	8th Knesset (1973) % of votes
Palestine/Israel Total	—	*16*	*13.3*	*19*	*15.8*	*40*	*33.3*
Arabs	—	3	2.5	6	5.0	6	5.0
Jews	—	13	10.8	13	10.8	34	28.3
(Parents from Europe or America)	—	(7)	(5.8)	(10)	(8.3)	(30)	(25.0)
(Parents from Asia or Africa)	—	(6)	(5.0)	(3)	(2.5)	(4)	(3.3)
Eastern Europe Total		*86*	*71.6*	*79*	*65.8*	*56*	*46.6*
	2nd Aliya	19	15.8	8	6.7	1	0.8
	3rd Aliya	23	19.2	11	9.1	2	1.6
	4th Aliya	24	20.0	25	20.8	14	11.6
	5th Aliya	9	7.5	21	17.5	21	17.5
	1940-7	10	8.3	11	9.1	7	5.8
	1948 onwards	1	0.8	3	2.5	11	9.1
Central and Western Europe Total		*11*	*9.1*	*9*	*7.5*	*6*	*5.0*
	2nd Aliya	—	—	—	—	—	—
	3rd Aliya	—	—	—	—	—	—
	4th Aliya	5	4.1	4	3.3	1	0.8
	5th Aliya	6	5.0	5	4.1	5	4.1
	1940-7	—	—	—	—	—	—
	1948 onwards	—	—	—	—	—	—
Balkans Total		*1*	*0.8*	*4*	*3.3*	—	—
	2nd Aliya	—	—	1	0.8	—	—
	3rd Aliya	—	—	—	—	—	—
	4th Aliya	—	—	—	—	—	—
	5th Aliya	1	0.8	1	0.8	—	—
	1940-7	—	—	—	—	—	—
	1948 onwards	—	—	2	1.6	—	—
Americas and South Africa Total		*2*	*1.6*	*1*	*0.8*	*4*	*3.3*
	2nd Aliya	—	—	—	—	—	—
	3rd Aliya	1	0.8	—	—	—	—
	4th Aliya	—	—	—	—	—	—
	5th Aliya	1	0.8	—	—	—	—
	1940-7	—	—	—	—	—	—
	1948 onwards	—	—	1	0.8	4	3.3

Table 11.4 (contd.)

Country of Birth	Period of Immigration*	1st Knesset (1949)		5th Knesset (1961)		8th Knesset (1973)	
		seats	% of votes	seats	% of votes	seats	% of votes
Asia and North Africa Total		*4*	*3.3*	*8*	*6.7*	*14*	*11.6*
	2nd Aliya	2	1.6	—	—	—	—
	3rd Aliya	1	0.8	1	0.8	—	—
	4th Aliya	1	0.8	1	0.8	1	0.8
	5th Aliya	—	—	1	0.8	2	1.6
	1940-7	—	—	2	1.6	3	2.5
	1948 onwards	—	—	3	2.5	8	6.7
Overall Total for Knesset		*120*	*100.0*	*120*	*100.0*	*120*	*100.0*

* Periods of Immigration: 2nd Aliya 1904-14; 3rd Aliya 1918-23; 4th Aliya 1924-32; 5th Aliya 1933-9.

An index of representation $\frac{R-D}{(R)}$, where R stands for the percentage of Knesset seats held by each country-of-origin group (here collapsed into a tripartite classification by continents) and D for these groups' share in the population, clearly shows that the rather extreme overrepresentation of Europeans as against the underrepresentation of Oriental and Israeli-born Jews reached its peak in the 1950s after the years of mass immigration and has been very slowly redressed ever since. Were one to add to Oriental Jews (23.2 per cent of the Jewish population in 1973) the Israeli-born children of Oriental parents (also 23.2 per cent), the index of representativeness for them would actually be − 2.03, i.e. as high as in the early years after independence. But most of these additions have not yet reached voting age and should, perhaps, not be taken into consideration. Moreover, if figures for the adult population of voting age (instead of total population) were available the index of misrepresentation would be appreciably lowered. In any event, a capillary action of some sort is at work here, which has increased the representation of Jews from Oriental communities in the Knesset. It has not yet reached the Cabinet. (See Tables 11.5, 11.6 and 11.7.)

Representation by religion among the non-Jewish MKs manifests a similar phenomenon. Whereas the numerical ratio between the three denominational groups of Muslims, Christians and Druze in the

Table 11.5: Jewish Population, by Continent of Birth (in Percentages)

Born	Date		
	8 Nov.1948	31 Dec.1960	31 Dec.1973
Israel	35.4	37.4	49.3
Asia-Africa	19.8	27.8	23.2
Europe-America	54.8	35.0	27.5

Source: *Statistical Abstract of Israel 1975* (Central Bureau of Statistics, Jerusalem), Table II/18, p.43.

Table 11.6: Jewish MKs, by Continent of Birth (in Percentages)

Born	1st Knesset (1949)	5th Knesset (1961)	8th Knesset (1973)
Israel	11.1	11.4	29.8
Asia-Africa	3.4	7.0	12.8
Europe-America	85.5	81.6	57.9

Table 11.7: Index of Representativeness of MKs, by Continent of Birth

Born	1st Knesset (1949)	5th Knesset (1961)	8th Knesset (1973)
Israel	− 2.19	2.28	− 0.65
Asia-Africa	− 1.88	− 2.97	− 0.81
Europe-America	+ 0.36	+ 0.57	+ 0.52

Table 11.8: Non-Jewish Members of the 1st, 5th and 8th Knessets, by Religion

	1st Knesset (1949)	5th Knesset (1961)	8th Knesset (1973)
Muslims	1	3	4*
Christians	2	2	1
Druze	—	1	1

* Including one Bedouin

population has very roughly been: in 1951—8.2:5:1; in 1969—6.5:2:1; and in 1973—9.5:2:1, Muslims so far have always been underrepresented in the Knesset as against Christians and Druzes (see Table 11.8), but in the 8th Knesset this also was largely remedied.

There have always been fewer Arab MKs than the proportion of Arabs in the total population would warrant. Under the proportional representation system operative in Israel, and given the very high voting participation of Arabs, the reason for this low representation was that a considerable number of Arabs voted for Jewish parties and mainly for the Communist Party, so that part of the Arab voting strength actually helped to elect Jewish MKs.

Policy Preferences

MKs constitute the top leadership of their respective parties. Therefore the political views and attitudes of the MKs tend to reflect party policies. However, on the basis of admittedly weak empirical evidence, contradictory interpretations have been set forth to account for the extent to which these vary from each other. One finding has it that MKs are the innovative factor, in that their views no longer correspond to the 'traditional party ideologies'.[31] According to another study, partly using the same data, MKs 'have undergone less ideological change than other groups studied'.[32] In ideological terms, the one finds that the MKs collectively are more moderate than party opinion in general, while according to the other, MKs are more to the left than other groups in the population, who are moving towards the right.

More recently, substantial although selective discrepancies between MKs as a group and the population at large, and also of respective sub-groups on both sides, have been found. These discrepancies relate to ideological and policy orientations, to political attitudes and moods in all the major fields of public policy, but of course are greater on some issues than others. This situation, quite common in representative systems, raises serious questions concerning the relationships between representatives and represented and the mediating role of the political parties, and justifies criticisms of the remoteness of these two from each other. But it seems that no permanent alienation (other than special occasions such as the peak of activity of protest movements) exists between the two sides, even though most MKs do not have a good grasp of the attitudes prevailing in the population. To be more precise: in diffuse issue areas, such as the Israel-Arab conflict, economic affairs and social welfare, MKs seem to sense changes in the public mood—recently more so on the conflict than on the other issues. On the other hand, on specific and concrete policy questions, the political senses of MKs seem to be much better attuned to public opinion.

What is perhaps of the greatest interest in this connection is that all the usual correlations—between background data, such as socio-economic status, party affiliation or role perceptions of the MKs, and the dimensions of these discrepancies—are very weak. The most salient factor in explaining these findings is that the pertinent policy issues at any given time transcend the usual sociological relationships.[33]

The range of ideological viewpoints and policy approaches represented in the Knesset is as wide as in any free parliament. On almost any issue, but particularly on the three crucial dimensions of security and foreign policy, social and economic policy, and the status of religion and national identity, despite a substantial and wide consensus, extreme and nonconformist viewpoints are propagated. From the time of independence to at least the Yom Kippur War the general tendency seems to have been centripetal, i.e. a gradual and slight lessening of radical oppositional viewpoints. The highlight of this development can be seen in the Government of National Unity, in office from the June 1967 war to 1970. During these years the centre of political gravity, viz. Labour as the party then permanently in office, managed to emasculate the more extreme opposition groups mainly by appealing to feelings of consensual national cohesion. Extreme views remained and were actually becoming diversified, but their exponents were small groups, most of them extra parliamentary and rather ephemeral. Since the 1973 war a centrifugal trend has numerically enhanced and intensified oppositional tendencies, in particular in the defence policy area.

Yet, in the 8th Knesset, these developments only slightly eroded the consensus on prevailing status quo positions in the major policy areas, which are here taken in each case to mean the basic trends of governmental policy. Indeed, in a parliamentary system of government the official status quo line must have a formal majority in the legislature, but the individual views of members of both coalition and opposition camps may and do deviate up to a certain degree from their respective party lines. Hence, even in a political system known for stringent party and coalition discipline, where most parties uphold the principle of freedom of discussion but impose unity of action, including that of voting, it is worthwhile to analyse the views of individual parliamentarians in addition to those of parties. The usual roll call analysis becomes meaningless under such circumstances, however, since party factions usually vote *en bloc* in the Knesset.

Instead, the political view of MKs in three policy areas have been determined by a combination of content analysis of their speeches and other public expressions and a reputational technique (utilising a panel of experts). For each policy area views are recorded on a scale ranging from 1 to 5, where digit 3 represents governmental policy at a given time. Almost always this is also the location of the moderate viewpoint on the issue, and may also be the status quo position in this policy area. Digit 1 in security policy represents the extreme dovish and conciliatory line; in social policy a socialist stand emphasising universalistic criteria for welfare policies; and in matters of religion an anti-clerical and extreme secular attitude. Digit 5 is the other pole on each of these axes: in security it is the hawkish and aggressive position; in social policy it represents the anti-socialist policy with an individualist orientation; and a pro-religious or even clerical line. Digits 2 and 4 are intermediary between the governmental line and the extremist positions. The policy profile of every MK (as well as that of every party) is the combination of the digits which represent most closely his (or its) views on each of the three scales.

It is notable that over the years the government or status quo position in all three policy areas has been slightly radicalised in the direction of what is here designated as digit 5. This shift of the centre of the ideological universe may be one facet of the politics of 'normalisation' or perhaps routinisation of a society in which a revolutionary ethos used to prevail.

The composite values of Table 11.9 are the numerical averages of the positions of all (Jewish) MKs in each of the three policy areas analysed. It shows that with one very crucial exception government policy

Table 11.9: Composite Value of MKs' Positions in Specified Policy Areas (in Parenthesis—Percentage of Supporters of Status Quo)

	1st Knesset (1949)	5th Knesset (1961)	8th Knesset (1973)
Number*	124	127	116
Defence	3.07(65.3)	3.13(55.1)	3.39(33.0)
Social	2.96(58.0)	2.95(60.2)	2.95(62.9)
Religion	2.90(54.0)	2.94(52.8)	2.95(52.9)

* Jewish MKs only, including MKs serving only part of term.

(i.e. digit 3) has always been supported, and not merely as expressed by sometimes substantial majority votes in the Knesset, but never by more than two-thirds. The one exception in Table 11.9 is the minority of scarcely one-third of members of the 8th Knesset supporting the government's defence policy. It must be remembered that these figures relate primarily to the personal expression of views, as well as public statements. Factional discipline in almost all divisions in the Knesset will provide the Cabinet with the necessary majority, overcoming even serious conflicts of conscience of individual MKs. Incidentally, in this particular case the term 'status quo' is not quite appropriate, since governmental policy sought incremental changes, whereas most of its hawkish opponents, both outside and inside the then coalition, favoured a status quo policy.

Table 11.9 also clearly indicates that only in security matters has the composite value of MKs' positions throughout been slightly on the hawkish side; in the 8th Knesset this tendency increased. In the two other policy areas the Knesset's overall view was slightly on the 'left' side, but the deviation from government policy positions was minimal.

One of the more interesting aspects of the ideological pattern developing over the years is the gradual reduction of the multi-dimensional character of the political scene, as can be seen from Table 11.10. The index used here is the Pearson Coefficient correlation computed for pairs of the three policy dimensions for every MK.

This reduction has so far only affected the ideological orientation of individual MKs towards greater conformity. Whereas in the 1st Knesset the correlations of the members' views on the three major issue areas was rather low, these correlations have grown ever since, and uniformly so. Early on, a leftish position on social policy was not necessarily combined with secularism and dovishness, and vice versa. More recently, however, this has become the case, and the number of deviants from this pattern is decreasing. Most moderates on one issue

Table 11.10: Pearson Coefficient Correlations of MKs' Positions in Specified Policy Areas

	1st Knesset (1949)	5th Knesset (1961)	8th Knesset (1973)
Defence-Social	0.38	0.60	0.57
Defence-Religion	0.10	0.49	0.54
Social-Religion	0.37	0.57	0.54

are moderates on all, just as extremists on digits 1 or 5 on one issue are most likely to be similarly placed on the others. It may not come as a surprise that over the years the two issues of defence and social policy have shown the highest correlation, indicative of a 'nationalist' politician, although socialist radicalism combined with an activist defence policy has actually been the hallmark of the Ahdut Haavoda Party.

The rather dramatic change over the years in the defence-religion correlation is primarily to be attributed to the reversal in the defence conception of NRP, or at least most of its MKs, from dovishness to hawkishness, as well as to the exclusion from Herut's parliamentary representatives of members with an anti-religious *Weltanschauung*.

This 'streamlining' of the attitudinal profile of MKs of all political camps was an early indication of the growing tendency towards polarisation of the political scene between left and right. The elections to the 9th Knesset (1977) and the Likkud-centred coalition formed in the wake of them seem to have institutionalised these new developments. Ultimately, all this may lead to a realignment of the party spectrum and introduce a regime of alternating coalitions in power in place of the now defunct dominant-party system.

Notes

The author wishes to thank Dan Caspi, Avraham Diskin, Hanan Kristal, Yacov Levy and Yoram Lichtenstein for assistance in various aspects of the research. For very detailed comments on an early draft—my thanks to Frank Tachau and Jacob M. Landau. Research for this chapter was partly financed by a grant from the Levi Eshkol Institute for Economic, Social and Political Research of the Faculty of Social Sciences, the Hebrew University of Jerusalem.

1. W. Bagehot, *The English Constitution* (Oxford University Press, London, 1928), p. 261. Bagehot's contradistinction between gradual transition of leadership and abrupt change can hardly be improved upon, and is very apposite to the Israeli case, even though the popular notion would have denied its applicability to Israel, at least prior to 1977.

2. W. B. Quandt, *Revolution and Political Leadership: Algeria, 1954-1968* (MIT Press, Cambridge, Mass., 1969), p. 20.

3. A. Arian, 'Modernization and Political Change: The Special Case of Israel' in R. W. Benjamin *et al.*, *Patterns of Political Development: Japan, India, Israel* (McKay, New York, 1972), pp. 81-132; Y. Shapiro, *The Formative Years of the Israeli Labour Party* (Sage, Beverly Hills, California, 1976).

4. E. Gutmann and J. M. Landau, 'The Political Elite and National Leadership in Israel' in G. Lenczowski (ed.), *Political Elites in the Middle East* (American Enterprise Institute, Washington, DC, 1975); A. Elon, *The Israelis: Founders and Sons* (Weidenfeld and Nicolson, London, 1971).

5. Y. Shapiro, 'The End of a Dominant Party Regime' in A. Arian (ed.), *The Elections in Israel—1977* (Jerusalem Academic Press, Jerusalem, 1979).

6. S. P. Huntington, *Political Order in Changing Societies* (Yale University Press, New Haven, 1968), p. 14.

7. See, however, I. W. Zartman, 'The Study of Elite Circulation' *Comparative Politics*, vol. 6, no. 3 (April 1974), p. 487; F. Tachau (ed.), *Political Elites and Political Development in the Middle East* (Wiley, New York, 1975), pp. 13-15.

8. A. Arian and S. Barnes, 'The Dominant Party System: A Neglected Model of Democratic Stability', *Journal of Politics*, vol. 36, no. 3 (1974), p. 64.

9. J. H. Kautsky, 'Patterns of Elite Succession in the Process of Development', *Journal of Politics*, vol. 31, no. 2 (1969), p. 383; J. H. Kautsky, 'Revolutionary and Managerial Elites in Modernizing Regimes', *Comparative Politics*, vol. 1, no. 4 (1969), p. 441; Zartman, 'Elite Circulation', p. 471; L. J. Fein, *Politics in Israel* (Little, Brown, Boston, 1967), p. 152.

10. F. W. Frey, *The Turkish Political Elite* (MIT Press, Cambridge, Mass., 1965), pp. 282-4.

11. V. O. Key Jr, 'A Theory of Critical Elections', *Journal of Politics*, vol. 17, no. 1 (February 1955), pp. 3-18.

12. A. Campbell *et al.*, *Elections and the Political Order* (Wiley, New York, 1966), p. 75.

13. G. Pomper, 'Classification of Presidential Elections', *Journal of Politics*, vol. 29, no. 3 (August 1967), p. 367.

14. E. Torgovnik, 'Israel: The Persistent Elite' in Tachau, *Political Elites*, pp. 219-53; Arian and Barnes, 'Dominant Party System'.

15. A. de Swann, *Coalition Theories and Cabinet Formation* (Elsevier, Amsterdam, 1973), pp. 89, 93-5, 290-3, 295n.

16. A. Arian, 'Conclusion' in H. R. Penniman (ed.), *Israel at the Polls : The Knesset Elections of 1977* (American Enterprise Institute, Washington, DC, 1979), pp. 283-7.

17. A. Brichta and G. Ben-Dor, 'Representation and Misrepresentation of Political Elites: The Case of Israel', *Jewish Social Studies*, vol. 36, nos. 3-4 (July-October 1974), pp. 234-52; Gutmann and Landau, 'Elite and Leadership'; Torgovnik, 'Persistent Elite'.

18. R. D. Putnam, *The Beliefs of Politicians* (Yale University Press, New Haven, 1973), p. 13.

19. For a general survey of the nomination procedures in Israeli parties, see A. Brichta, 'The Social and Political Characteristics of Members of the Seventh Knesset' in A. Arian (ed.), *The Elections in Israel—1969* (Jerusalem Academic Press, Jerusalem, 1972), pp. 112-17; for a very detailed study of one party—the Labour Alignment—see H. Kristal, 'The Nomination of Israel Labour Party Candidates for the Seventh Knesset', unpublished MA thesis, the Hebrew University, Jerusalem, 1971.

20. J. A. Schlesinger, 'Political Careers and Party Leadership' in L. J. Edinger (ed.), *Political Leadership in Industrialized Societies* (Wiley, New York, 1967), p. 286.

21. M. Czudnowski, 'Legislative Recruitment under Proportional Representation in Israel: A Model and a Case Study', *Midwest Journal of Political Science*, vol. 14, no. 2 (May 1970), pp. 217-48.

22. S. Weiss and G. Ben-Dor, 'Asqanim, mangenonim u-missud politi be-Israel' (Party officials, machines and political institutionalisation in Israel), *Ha-Rivon le-mehkar hevrati* (Social Research Quarterly), 5 (December 1973), pp. 9-34.

23. For a full analysis of these, see Czudnowski, 'Legislative Recruitment'.

24. Gutmann and Landau, 'Elite and Leadership', pp. 179-80, 188-90.

25. L. G. Seligman, *Leadership in a New Nation* (Atherton, New York, 1964), pp. 58-9; Brichta, 'Characteristics of Members', pp. 118-20.

26. For details see Gutmann and Landau, 'Elite and Leadership', pp. 181, 188-90; Brichta, 'Characteristics of Members', pp. 127-8.

27. Weiss and Ben-Dor, 'Asqanim'.

28. For a different analysis, see Y. Azmon, 'Some Aspects of the Israeli Political Elite' in A. Arian (Ed.), *The Elections in Israel-1973* (Jerusalem Academic Press, Jerusalem, 1975) pp. 41-56.

29. Gutmann and Landau, 'Elite and Leadership', pp. 186-7.

30. By Brichta and Ben-Dor, 'Representation and Misrepresentation'; Torgovnik, 'Persistent Elite'; Gutmann and Landau, 'Elite and Leadership'; and more recently by S. Smooha, *Israel: Pluralism and Conflict* (University of California Press, 1978).

31. Seligman, *Leadership in a New Nation*, p. 56.

32. A. Arian, *Ideological Change in Israel* (Case Western Reserve University Press, Cleveland, 1968), p. 46.

33. D. Caspi, 'Between Legislation and Electors: The Knesset Members', unpublished PhD dissertation, the Hebrew University, Jerusalem, 1979.

12. COMPARISONS

Frank Tachau

We may draw comparisons among the elected elites in Turkey, Lebanon and Israel on three levels. First, we may focus on the role of the parliamentary elites in the power structure of each of the three countries. Second, we may compare the data presented in the three chapters regarding the social and political backgrounds of members of parliament. Finally, we may examine the behavioural patterns, value preferences and policy outcomes of the elected legislative elites in the three countries.

The Role of Parliamentary Elites

In general, one cannot assume that power follows on from position. Such an assumption implies equivalence among political systems in terms of the power position of parliaments and their members. Even if we assume equivalence, it would be necessary to exercise great caution in explaining intersystem differences.[1] On the other hand, our task in this regard is somewhat facilitated by the fact that the three systems we deal with in this volume are all genuinely competitive. In other words, we may take as our starting point Marvin Zonis's hypothesis that 'the less representative (accountable, democratic) a political system is estimated to be, the less the correlation between formal position and actual power is likely to be'.[2] In short, while recognising that 'positional analysis' such as is involved in analyses of parliamentary membership may mislead by including figureheads or rubber stamps and excluding 'informal opinion makers who influence the proximate decision makers', we should also note that to a certain extent power may in fact derive from institutional roles or at least may be reflected by achievement of institutional position.[3]

The precise relation of parliament to the power structure varies somewhat in the three systems under review here. In all three cases, significant power centres are located outside of, and to some extent above, the parliament. Certainly the Cabinet lies closer to the top of the power pyramid in all three countries than does the parliament. In Turkey and Israel the Prime Minister is the highest executive officer. Even in Lebanon, where the President stands at the apex, the prime minister-ship traditionally has been one of the three most highly prized political offices, and has been reserved for one of the two most numerous and important confessional groups, the Sunnite Muslims. In all three countries the Prime Minister and most members of the Cabinet are normally drawn from among the members of parliament. With the significant exception of Lebanon, the Cabinet also depends upon the support of at least the lower house of the parliament (in Lebanon the Cabinet is in the first instance appointed by and accountable to the President, but must also maintain the confidence of the Chamber). Cabinet and parliament thus are constitutionally inextricably linked. Membership in the Cabinet conveys more power; but membership in parliament clearly connotes elite status, and in addition is one of the most frequently utilised routes of access to Cabinet membership.

Aside from the Cabinet, there are other centres of power which over-shadow parliament in fact if not in law. In Lebanon there are the traditional *zu'amā'* or *aqṭāb* whose power, according to Samir Khalaf in Chapter 10, has not been diminished either by passage of time, socio-economic developments, nor yet, perhaps, the bloody fratricide which gripped the country during most of 1975 and 1976. In Israel there are the party organs and certain other institutional power foci, such as the Histadrut, which at least shared with Labour Cabinets in many basic political decisions, if they did not dominate them. In Turkey, too, there are power centres outside of Cabinet and parliament, most prominently the military, although its power is normally manifested only during political crises.

Although our interest in parliaments does not primarily involve their legislative or political functions, but rather their embodiment of political elites as they emerge from competitive elections, we should note one further point which serves to condition the context within which these parliamentary elites operate. Khalaf has commented most directly on the relative impotence of the Lebanese parliament *vis-à-vis* the Cabinet and President. He characterises it as 'more of a "delibera-tive" than a legislative assembly', and attributes its relative impotence to the fact that power lies in the hands of 'the real actors in the political system: clerics, communal leaders, a handful of *aqṭāb,* prominent bankers and businessmen, and of late the various spokesmen of Pales-tinian resistance groups, private militias, and some of the politicised "counter-elite" who are excluded from participation in the formal political system'. Elsewhere, Ralph Crow has suggested that the parliament provides a forum in which 'the executive's need for political support and the society's demands are brought together, meshed, and harmonised'.[4] Regardless of emphasis, it is clear that major political decisions which signify changes in public policy or in the balance among constituent groups in the political system are not worked out within the framework of the parliament, but rather are ratified there after having been agreed upon among the 'real actors in the political system'.

The Lebanese pattern is approximated in parliamentary bodies in other countries. It is generally more efficient if not easier to work out the details of controversial political arrangements in private. Neither Israel nor Turkey are exceptions. As Emanuel Gutmann has noted above, 'the Knesset has never been either the hub of public policy-making nor the centre of gravity of political power'. In Israel, moreover, the system of candidate selection and the electoral system of proportional representation in a single national constituency give central party leaders an inordinate amount of power. In addition, the persistence over many years of governing coalitions dominated by Mapai and the Labour Alignment has further concentrated power in a few hands.

In the days of single-party rule, the Turkish parliament was similarly bereft of power. Especially during the 15-year tenure of the charismatic national leader, Mustafa Kemal Atatürk, the Grand National Assembly hardly ever performed the deliberative function which Khalaf attributes to the Lebanese parliament. Rather it served as a sounding board for the regime; debate and deliberation occurred only to the extent permitted by the national leader, while decisions were worked out within a very small circle of his advisers to be more or less automatically ratified in the public forum of the parliament. This system changed after the advent of multiparty competition. During the 1950s the Democrat Party retained overwhelming majorities in the Assembly, but the deliberations became quite active and often acrimonious. After 1961 the electoral system was changed with the result that opposition parties have achieved much greater strength and parliamentary procedures and processes have become far more meaningful. This has been particularly true during those sessions in which no single party commanded a clear majority of the votes in the Assembly (i.e. 1961 to 1965 and since 1973).

There are thus some differences among the three parliamentary bodies whose memberships have been analysed above. The Lebanese

Chamber appears to be the least salient of the three, with real power exercised outside of it both by formal office-holders like the President, and informally by 'real actors', as indicated by Khalaf. The Israeli parliament is functionally more significant, but also subject to influences above and outside of itself. Finally, the Turkish Grand National Assembly (as opposed to the Senate), particularly in the current context of political fragmentation and polarisation, is the most active cockpit of political activity and decision-making among our three cases.

In another sense, however, the three parliaments occupy similar positions in their respective political systems. As has been noted, none of them automatically confers status in the topmost political elite (e.g. the Cabinet), although all three do provide a means of access to top-level positions, including the prime ministership. In short, all three parliaments are politically significant institutions. Election to membership is by no means merely a formality. On the contrary, seats in parliament constitute significant stakes for competition among organised parties and/or other factions.

Socio-political Backgrounds of Parliamentarians

If the parliaments are indeed meaningful political institutions, what can we learn by comparing the personal attributes of their members? Once again, we must observe certain cautions against facile comparisons between apparently comparable indicators which may in fact have different meanings in differing contexts. It is not enough, for example, to compare the proportions of members of each of the parliaments who have had a university education without also comparing the level of education of both whole populations and elite groups outside of the parliament.[5] More importantly, we should ask: what is the significance of the social-background data we are comparing? As individual authors have noted above, the link between social background on the one hand and value preferences and policy outcomes on the other is highly complex and problematical. Clearly, we must be on guard against simplistic judgements which may turn out to be highly misleading and which are not in fact supported by the data. None the less, hypotheses concerning the link between social backgrounds, values and policy outcomes are widely cited and assume a variety of forms in political literature. Perhaps the least questionable of these hypotheses is one which states that 'the social background of elite members is relevant less as a predictor of individual behaviour than as an indicator of the structure of social power. Background studies may tell us more about the selecting than about the selected.' The argument posited by this hypothesis is simple: 'Because elite composition is more easily observable than are the underlying patterns of social power, it can serve as a kind of seismometer for detecting shifts in the foundations of politics and policy.'[6] In this sense, comparisons among the Israeli, Lebanese and Turkish parliamentary elites are indeed possible and, more significantly, plausible.

In this respect, the most clear-cut example among our three cases is that of Turkey. Turkey has experienced a greater variety of regimes and has undergone more transitions of successive generations of political leaders than either Lebanon or Israel. Moreover, the various regimes (tutelary autocracy 1923-46; competitive one-party dominance 1950-60; competitive multiparty system since 1961) have incorporated different modes of elite recruitment. Thus, changes in social backgrounds of parliamentary deputies can easily be correlated with changes of regime, and both may be taken as indicators of changes occurring in the population at large (see Chapter 9).

In Israel, on the other hand, as Gutmann has argued above, the 'composition [of the Knesset] has been remarkably persistent'. The major change that is observable in this body is a generational shift, particularly as represented by the succession of the Israeli-born Itzhak Rabin as Prime Minister in 1974. Significant as this event is, it did not follow from any sharp or sudden change in the membership of the Knesset. Rather, the shift was the result of the natural ageing process over time, and the concurrent 'capillary action' of new entrants coming into the body with each election. Gutmann shows that while the ethnic composition of the Israeli population has changed remarkably over the 32 years since achievement of independence, the composition of the Knesset has changed much more slowly. Thus, while the proportion of European and American-born Israelis declined from 55 per cent in 1948 to 27.5 per cent in 1973, the comparable proportion of Knesset members declined only from 85.5 to 58 per cent. Significantly, however, almost all of this decline within the Knesset occurred between 1961 and 1973; and, concomitantly, the proportion of Knesset members born in Asia or Africa, or in Israel, increased more sharply during the same period. This is clearly a reflection of changing generations, and suggests that in this respect at least the Israeli Knesset will continue to undergo change, perhaps at an accelerating rate in the future. Notably, however, these changes have not yet manifested themselves perceptibly at the Cabinet level, as Gutmann notes. The prospect, therefore, is for continued gradual change in elite composition and minimal impact on basic policies.[7]

In the case of Lebanon, Khalaf argues that while there have been changes in the social backgrounds of members of parliament, these have neither resulted from nor led to changes in the basic power equation. Nor, it may be added, do such changes as have occurred seem to clearly coincide either with generational shifts or regime changes. Indeed, as socio-economic tensions in the country increased during the 1960s, the composition of the parliament seems to have become more rather than less conservative and oligarchical, with higher proportions of older members and representatives of 'parliamentary families', as well as somewhat lower rates of turnover (see Tables 10.2, 10.7, 10.8 and 10.12).

For reasons stated earlier, comparisons of specific attributes of parliamentarians must be handled with care. None the less, there is no harm in trying.

Table 12.1 shows the occupational profile for the most recently elected session in each of the three countries. There are obvious discrepancies among them. For example, landlords are listed as 'other' in Lebanon, but included among 'economic' occupations in Turkey. Table 12.1 underlines the overwhelming preponderance of free professionals in the Lebanese Chamber, the large representation of party professionals in the Israeli Knesset and the correspondingly small contingent of free professionals in that body. Notably, even if we include 'secondary' occupations, as Khalaf does (Table 10.6) for

Table 12.1: Occupations of Deputies (in Percentages)

	Turkey (1973)	Lebanon (1972)	Israel (1973)
Free Professions	44	69	15
Officials	23	—	23
Economic	23[a]	21	20[b]
Other	10	10[c]	42[d]

Sources: Chapters 9, 10 and 11 above.

[a]—Includes agriculture.

[b]—Includes agriculture and members of collective rural communities (*kibbutzim* and *moshavim*). The latter account for 15 per cent, the former for 1.7 per cent, while business and industry account for 3.3 per cent (see Table 11.3).

[c]—Landlords.

[d]—Political party functionaries.

Lebanon, more than half (56 per cent) of the reported occupations remain in the professional category. It is also noteworthy that the professional contingent in the Lebanese parliament shares two characteristics with its Turkish counterpart: increasing size over the years (from roughly 40 per cent in 1947 to 72 per cent in 1968 in Lebanon; and from 18 per cent in 1920 to roughly 40-45 per cent after 1950 in Turkey) and predominance of lawyers both among the professionals and also in terms of more specific occupational categories for the parliament as a whole. Proportions of members engaged in economic pursuits (including agriculture in Turkey and Israel) are very nearly the same in all three bodies. In no case do they dominate the parliament, suggesting that businessmen, bankers, merchants etc. are less likely to pursue political careers than are free professionals, for example. Lebanon differs from Israel and Turkey in that there were no members with civil service or official employment in their backgrounds. Over time, dominance in the Lebanese Chamber shifted from landlords to professionals with the basic change occurring in the 1950s. In Turkey, officials dominated the Assembly throughout the 1920s and 1930s, while professionals came to dominate during the 1950s. In Israel, professional party officials have lost strength over the years, as did those engaged in economic activities (particularly businessmen, agriculturalists and, to a lesser extent, those from *kibbutzim* and *moshavim*), while bureaucrats gained substantially between 1961 and 1973.

Comparisons of other attributes of parliamentarians are less suggestive. Detailed data on localism have been presented in the above chapters only for Turkey. In Israel, with its single national electoral constituency, this indicator has no place. According to Khalaf, the vast majority of Lebanese deputies are also locally born. In terms of their behaviour during election campaigns and after elevation to the Chamber they manifest a very high degree of local concern. Educational level of deputies appears not to differ significantly among the three countries. In the most recently elected session considered here, university-educated deputies constitute between 60 and 70 per cent of their respective cohorts. If we plot the age curves of the three legislatures, some variation is evident. The Turkish case, again, reflects regime changes, as noted in Chapter 9: a steady rise as the cohort of Atatürk's initial supporters aged over the first fifteen years of the republic; then sharp drops with changes in regime in 1946-50 and 1961, followed by a levelling off of the age curve. Lebanon, by contrast, shows a slow rise in the age curve following an initial decade of slight fluctuation. Israel's age curve reflects the ageing of the first-generation

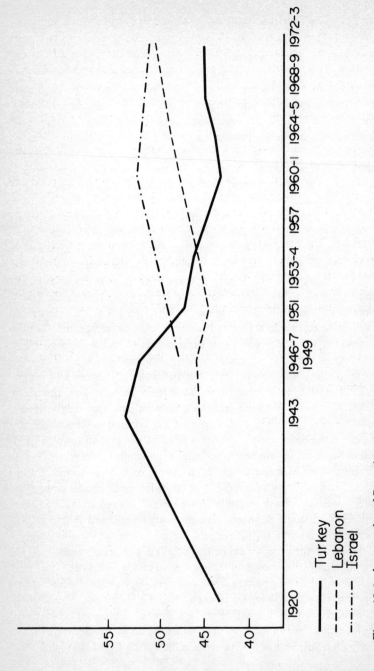

Figure 12.1: Average Age of Deputies

political elite during the first twelve years after independence, similar to the Turkish experience between 1920 and 1946. During the second twelve-year period, the age curve in Israel drops slightly, reflecting younger new entrants into the Knesset. The Israeli and Lebanese parliaments were substantially older than the Turkish Grand National Assembly by 1972-3. In the Turkish case, at least, this is probably a consequence of elite circulation, in particular the relatively high turnover, with rather young new entrants holding down the average age of the entire body. In the Lebanese case, on the other hand, the age curve has continued to rise in spite of a turnover rate which has been relatively high (see Table 10.7).

Let us enlarge the scope of the comparison (with appropriate attention to the caveats noted earlier). It has been suggested, for example, that older Western democracies are characterised by large proportions of lawyers among the members of their parliaments. In fact, data from a variety of countries indicate that, generally, the proportion of lawyers tends to be higher in the parliaments of the Middle East, Africa, Asia and Latin America than in those of the Atlantic region.[8] It would, therefore, be inaccurate to conclude that the high proportion of lawyers in the Turkish and Lebanese parliaments signifies relative modernisation, or even that they resemble the Western democracies in this respect.[9] Quite the contrary: the heavy preponderance of party functionaries in the Israeli Knesset would seem to be a clearer indicator of relative modernisation, if it is taken as a measure of professionalisation in politics. On the other hand, the rise to prominence of lawyers and free professionals in Turkey and Lebanon also indicates tendencies toward modernisation. In Turkey, it should be recalled, lawyers came to replace government officials as the largest group of deputies, signifying greater differentiation and increasing complexity in the occupational structure of the society. Similarly, in Lebanon lawyers and professionals eclipsed landowners, although Khalaf argues that the traditional elite has managed to hang onto its dominant position. None the less, it is probably significant that the replacement of landowners by professionals was more pronounced among more traditional segments of the society, such as non-Christians and the rural hinterland. At the very least, if the traditional elite increasingly finds it necessary or advantageous to acquire professional and technical training for its younger representatives, that in itself may be taken as an indicator of increasing complexity and differentiation in the society, and these, in turn, are indicators of modernisation. In Israel, on the other hand, the drop in proportions of party functionaries in the 1973 Knesset may indicate a loosening of the hold of the founding political elite.

The foregoing discussion should not obscure the fact that, in terms of modernisation, two reference points must be kept in mind. On the one hand, one may compare the three societies in terms of relative degree of modernisation either in general or in terms of particular attributes. On the other hand, one may view the three societies in terms of a scale of modernisation whose reference points are internal. Thus, Israel may have been more modern in 1973 than either Turkey or Lebanon; but Turkey and Lebanon may be moving more rapidly in the direction of greater modernisation as judged with reference to their own past.

Speaking more generally, what do these analyses of social backgrounds reveal about the three societies? In all three cases the changes manifested in the parliament are somewhat reflective of the society at large.[10] Thus, Turkish deputies have in recent years increasingly come to resemble the society at large in terms of such attributes as occupation, place of birth, size of family and even, to a slight degree, educational background. Ethnic cleavages are somewhat obscure in Turkey. Shiite voters do appear to lean toward the RPP, however. In the Lebanese case, there has been some of what Khalaf calls 'proletarianisation', quite aside from the basic structure of the system, which institutionalises confessional cleavages. And, as noted above in the case of Israel, the deepest cleavage in the society, that between the Jewish majority and the Arab minority, is maintained by continuing high levels of tension between Israel and neighbouring states. As a result, Arabs have consistently constituted only modest proportions of Knesset membership. On the other hand, the cleavage between Jews of European and American origin on the one hand, and those of Asian or African origin on the other, seems much more tractable; as the latter begin to achieve higher status in the society at large, they are beginning to appear in greater numbers in the Knesset as well.

Value Commitments and Policy Preferences

As for value commitments and policy preferences, although the three foregoing chapters are uneven in their treatment, some comparisons and general observations are none the less possible. The discussion of Israel in Chapter 11 is more explicit on this point than are the other two, although the data are not broken down by party affiliation, so that it is not possible to draw links between social backgrounds and policy preferences. Gutmann's calculations show that members of the Knesset on balance appear to adhere quite closely to governmental policy in three major issue areas (foreign policy/security, social welfare and religion). Both the government and MKs generally appear to have moved somewhat to the right ideologically in these three policy areas. The greatest divergence between the Cabinet and the parliament appears to have occurred most recently in the foreign policy/security issue area, with the government apparently assuming a somewhat more dovish position than is favoured by Knesset members. Moreover, correlation of MKs' views in these three issue areas appears to have increased over the years. These findings should occasion little surprise, in view of the oft-noted high level of policy and value consensus in the Israeli system—a consensus which in turn is said to derive largely from the country's precarious position in a hostile regional environment. In short, we may conclude that the impact of ideology has diminished in recent years in Israeli parliamentary politics.

Ideology also plays a minor role in the politics of the Lebanese parliament, but for a different reason. By contrast with the high level of value and policy consensus in Israel, Lebanon has been plagued by the very opposite: dissensus. Moreover, this dissensus has coincided with deep-seated social, economic and cultural cleavages as represented by the diverse confessional groups which are the constituent units of the political system. To the extent that consensus has prevailed in this system, it has been a negative consensus—an agreement that the existing system is less undesirable than any foreseeable alternative, given the essential condition that no major group will be deprived of veto power in matters of importance and that none will be allowed to impose its preferences on others. It follows, then, that parliamentarians committed to maintaining this system have an interest in keeping ideological conflict out of the political arena as much as possible. This, in turn, explains two features of the Lebanese system which have been noted by Khalaf: (i) the eclipse of parliament in the face of crisis; and (ii) the prevalence of traditional patronage politics, even among more ideologically oriented parliamentarians. This means simply that the Lebanese parliament is not equipped to deal with sharp ideological or social conflict, nor with strong challenges to the status quo. Hence the virtually complete breakdown of the parliamentary institution in the course of the prolonged and severe crisis of 1975-6.

By contrast, the Turkish parliament and political system have been increasingly characterised by ideological polarisation and social conflict. Moreover, the parliament has come to reflect the political system and society at large in this respect, just as it has in terms of social background attributes of individual members. In fact, in the Turkish case the tenuous link between social backgrounds and policy preferences seems clearer than in either Lebanon or Israel. The evidence for this is to be found primarily in the data presented in Chapter 9 above which highlight some of the differences in personal attributes of parliamentarians of the various political parties. To recapitulate these data briefly: the RPP has generally had the highest proportions of professionals, specifically lawyers; in 1973 the party also elected a sizeable delegation of teachers; the JP had the highest proportions of those engaged in economic activities, particularly businessmen and merchants (rather than agriculturists); the NSP burst upon the political scene in 1973 with an unprecedentedly high proportion of deputies associated with religious occupations and values; and finally, size of family for parliamentarians in general has increased over the years since the advent of political competition, led since 1961 by small parties and independents, and most dramatically in 1973 by the NSP. These characteristics conform quite well to the contrasting ideological and policy tendencies of these parties: the RPP with its commitment to democratic principles and the value of social justice; the JP with its emphasis on rapid economic development within a highly pragmatic context; and the NSP with its commitment to the values of religion. Moreover, the introduction of proportional representation into the Turkish electoral system precludes the possibility of transposing electoral pluralities into overwhelming parliamentary majorities, as was the case in the 1950s. Consequently, the 1973 and 1977 elections produced a fragmented parliament in which no single party commands a majority. Further, the parties are now so divergent that it has proved singularly difficult for them to co-operate in the formation of coalition governments. Significantly, this was also the first time in Turkish history that the parliament cast a vote of no confidence in a government.[11] The Turkish parliament thus served notice that, while it might itself be unable to produce a stable government, it was not about to turn this responsibility over to non-parliamentary forces.[12]

Conclusion

To summarise our findings, it may be said that the parliamentary elites of Turkey, Lebanon and Israel reflect divergent patterns in their respective political systems. The Turkish parliamentary elite reflects the fragmented and polarised nature of politics and society at large. Frey's assessment of more than a decade ago remains valid today:

> No integrated elite offers discipline and direction to Turkish society today. Warring elite elements engage in the intense infighting that produces in Turkey, as in many other nations, simultaneous stagnation and instability.[13]

Stagnation and instability seem to characterise the affairs of parliament as well. In this respect, as with social backgrounds, policy preferences and value commitments, the Turkish parliament manifests a general tendency to mirror the political system and society of which it is a part. What is more, the fragmentation cuts more deeply today than perhaps at any time since the establishment of the republic more than fifty years ago, for it involves not simply competition for power, nor disagreement on specific policy issues, but basic values associated with the process of modernisation. Thus, in place of Atatürk's firm and unyielding commitment to secularisation, even government ministers have openly proclaimed their dedication to religious values and policies. The parliament, in short, is representative and accountable, to revert to Zonis's terminology.

Unlike Turkey, basic cultural and social cleavage in Lebanon are built into the political system in an integral way. The parliament plays a decidedly secondary role in the political system: it is not the forum for either formal or effective processes of conflict resolution, nor are its members important decision-makers. Both formal and effective political power lies outside the Chamber, the former in the hands of the President and Cabinet, the latter in the hands of prominent sectarian leaders (*zu'amā'* and *aqṭāb*). At no time has the ineffectiveness of the Lebanese parliament been more dramatically evident than during the bloody crisis of 1975-6. The Lebanese parliament, in other words, may be representative, but it is not accountable.

And yet, even here, changes over time in the social backgrounds of parliamentarians are evident. Although, as Khalaf argues, the dominance of a small number of leading families seems to have remained intact, the occupational profile of the parliament has shifted from a preponderance of landowners towards a more modern professional bias. If the conflict that broke out in 1975-6 can be resolved in such a manner as to resurrect the basic structure of the political system, one may expect such modernising tendencies to reassert themselves.

In Israel, on the other hand, while the parliament also plays a distinctly secondary political role, we have a political system characterised by a strong value and policy consensus. Moreover, control has been centralised in the hands of a small and (until recently) cohesive political elite. Such changes as are occurring in the personal attributes of members of the Knesset reflect a gradual shift in political generations rather than fundamental social or cultural cleavages. In terms of representativeness and accountability, the Knesset stands somewhere between the Turkish and Lebanese parliaments, probably closer to the Turkish.

Notes

1. Thus, noting the higher degree of professional specialisation among Egyptian Cabinet members as compared to Israel and Lebanon, Dekmejian suggests that in this respect Egypt resembles Third World developing systems, while the other two resemble the more developed Western systems. But an equally valid observation might be that Egypt has had a relatively authoritarian regime, while Israel and Lebanon have been more competitive. Neither observation, however, determines causal relationships. See R. H. Dekmejian, *Patterns of Political Leadership: Egypt, Israel, Lebanon* (State University of New York Press, Albany, 1975), Ch. 5.

2. M. Zonis, *The Political Elite of Iran* (Princeton University Press, Princeton, New Jersey, 1971), p. 5.

3. R. D. Putnam, *The Comparative Study of Political Elites* (Prentice-Hall, Englewood Cliffs, New Jersey, 1976), pp. 15-16.

4. R. Crow, 'Parliament in the Lebanese Political System' in A. Kornberg and L. Musolf (eds.), *Legislatures in Developmental Perspective* (Duke University Press, Durham, N. Carolina, 1970), p. 301.

5. Thus, although the United States has a substantially higher proportion of university graduates among its legislators than Great Britain, Italy or West Germany, it should also be noted that the proportion of the entire American adult population which has graduated from a university is 3½ to 5 times greater than that of each of the three European countries. None the less, for all four countries, the proportion of university graduates among legislators is overwhelmingly greater than among the general population. See Putnam, *Study of Elites,* Table 2.4, p. 27.

6. Ibid., pp. 41-4.

7. Proportions of Arabs and/or non-Jews are subject to special consideration.

8. J. Blondel, *Comparative Legislatures* (Prentice-Hall, Englewood Cliffs, New Jersey, 1973), Appendix C.

9. Dekmejian, *Patterns of Leadership,* puts forward such a suggestion when comparing the cabinets of Egypt, Israel and Lebanon.

10. The fact that less-educated small-scale landowners, peasants, workers and others of low socio-economic status are not represented in any of the three parliaments should occasion no surprise. Membership in parliament, after all, signifies elite status. The only parliamentary bodies in which lower socio-economic status groups have been significantly represented are those of socialist-oriented authoritarian regimes, and in these systems the parliaments are relatively powerless. The early leaderships of labour-oriented political parties in Western democracies constitute another exception. More important than social background in this respect, perhaps, are the policy preferences of

the deputies, and these may be determined as much by professional socialisation and value orientation in adulthood as by social background or childhood experiences. See Putnam, *Study of Elites.*

11. In fact, this occurred twice: in November 1974 and December 1977.

12. The parliament had similarly asserted its political independence by refusing to elect the military officers' candidate for President in the spring of 1973.

13. F. W. Frey, *The Turkish Political Elite* (MIT Press, Cambridge, Mass., 1965), p. 391.

EPILOGUE

Comparative Electoral Politics
in the Middle East

Elections perform several important functions in modern political systems. Among other things, they provide a basis for legitimacy; they assure the recruitment and circulation of political elites; and they play a role in the policy-making process by resolving some political issues. Obviously, the extent to which such functions are performed vary from system to system. The differences between competitive and non-competitive polities are too well known to need further elaboration here, although elections often are held and perform somewhat similar legitimising and recruiting functions in the latter as in the former. Even within the category of competitive political systems, elections may play a prominent role with respect to some of the functions mentioned above, while not significantly contributing to others. For example, elections may have great legitimising value in a certain political system, but their role in elite recruitment or issue resolution may be rather limited. In other words, we observe a substantial amount of cross-national variation with respect to the salience of elections.

The salience of elections should not be confused with the salience of the legislatures, a related but separate concept. In a great many competitive political systems, legislatures have lost, in recent decades, their once prominent role in policy-making to the executives, bureaucracies and political parties. In the Middle East, in general, legislatures have very rarely been the foremost decision-making instrument. 'A Middle Eastern legislature,' observe Bill and Leiden, 'is much less important as a decision-making apparatus than are the more amorphous but powerful informal groups that penetrate it, control it, and, most importantly, survive it.'[1] That the policy-making or 'decisional' role of parliaments has been marginal or has declined does not mean, however, that the importance of parliamentary elections has also declined. In countries where election results determine, by and large, which party or combination of parties will form the government,

315

elections retain their paramount importance. Thus, in Turkey and Israel, the salience of legislative elections is very high, even though the Turkish Grand National Assembly and the Israeli Knesset generally conform to the model of 'weakly decisional' legislatures[2] (see Chapter 12). The Lebanese legislature is also weakly decisional, and the overall salience of elections is lower than in Turkey and Israel, since the composition of the Lebanese executive is only partially related to the outcome of parliamentary elections.

One of the questions to which we address ourselves here is the overall salience of elections in the three political systems treated in this volume. These are the only competitive political systems in the Middle East. Therefore it is fair to assume, and this is supported by empirical evidence, that elections are much more salient in Turkey, Israel and Lebanon than in the non-competitive Middle Eastern states, such as Iran and Egypt, which nevertheless have held more or less regular elections. An Iranian scholar, Mohammedi-Nejad, argues, for example, that 'in Iran, ever since the adoption of a Constitution in 1906 and introduction of a parliamentary system, elections have played neither a legitimacy nor a commitment role in the political system'.[3] Similarly, Binder observed, of the Egyptian elections in the 1960s, that they did not serve to broaden popular political participation, but were considered useful in terms of the requirements of legitimacy and national integration.[4]

With respect to the legitimising (or integrative) function of elections, all three countries studied in this volume can be described as ranking high. To put it differently, in none of these countries do the rulers seem to be able to secure their legitimacy except by way of free and competitive elections. Israel has maintained a parliamentary democracy since its inception under the most challenging conditions. Commitment to free elections also appears to be very strong in Turkey, with the possible exception of some fringe groups on the extreme right and the extreme left. Without taking this commitment into account, one cannot explain the early return to civilian rule after the military coup of 27 May 1960, the suppression of serious coup attempts in 1962 and 1963, and the failure and/or reluctance of the military to take over after their memorandum of 12 March 1971. Even in Lebanon, despite the long and bloody civil war of 1975-6, it is noteworthy that no group or leader demanded the overthrow of the democratic system (see Chapter 6). Indeed, if Lebanon is to maintain its present identity and to restore political order, the only feasible way of doing so seems to be through competitive elections which will ensure some sort of new balance among its many sectarian communities.

While elections thus perform a crucial legitimising function in all three countries, the same is not true for the elite recruitment and issue resolution functions. As stated in detail in Chapter 12 above, the three countries differ significantly in their patterns of elite recruitment and circulation via the electoral process. In Turkey the introduction of free competitive elections resulted in a marked change in elite composition, from bureaucratic domination to domination by free professionals. Israel displays a much less dramatic change in the composition of its parliamentary elite, observed mainly in the form of 'capillary action'. Nevertheless, the fact that professional party officials have lost strength over the years seems politically significant. In Lebanon, despite a shift from landlords to professionals, Samir Khalaf argues persuasively that this is more apparent than real, as evidenced by the persistence of 'parliamentary families'. However, the gap between the parliamentary elite and the 'real' power elite seems to be more pronounced in Lebanon than in the other two countries. The salience of elections as an elite recruitment and circulation mechanism in Lebanon is lower, therefore, than in Turkey and Israel.

The role of elections in the resolution of political issues and, hence, in the making of public policy is more controversial. Admittedly, elections are very rarely fought over a single predominant issue, or even over a set of related issues. Therefore, the outcome of elections can hardly be interpreted as a clear verdict by the electorate for or against a particular position on a single issue. Comparative research on electoral behaviour has demonstrated, moreover, that issue positions of competing parties seldom have a determining impact on voting behaviour. Nevertheless, the policy implications of elections cannot be altogether neglected. Especially under the conditions of the 'responsible party government' model, elections do contribute to the resolution of political issues and provide general directions, if not specific electoral verdicts, in the realm of public policy-making. At the very least, elections help determine which among competing groups of leaders shall have policy-making powers; and these competing groups usually have varying value and policy preferences.

This model, it is well known, requires the existence of clearly distinguishable party programmes and platforms, sufficiently strong party cohesion and discipline, and preferably two-party competition. Distinguishable party programmes give voters a meaningful choice among alternative policies; party cohesion and discipline enable majority parties to carry out electoral promises; and two-party competition makes it possible for a single party to govern without the confusion of responsibility so often encountered in coalition governments.

Turkey and Israel provide examples of 'working multipartyism', which can be described as an adaptation of responsible party government to multiparty circumstances. To be sure, neither country would qualify as a two-party system. However, in both of them, two parties have stood clearly above all others in terms of voting and parliamentary strength: the RPP and the JP in Turkey, Labour and the Likkud in Israel. Furthermore, despite the existence of proportional representation in both countries (actually, the purest version of proportional representation is in Israel), the JP has been able to gain absolute majorities in the Grand National Assembly in two elections (1965 and 1969), and Labour led all coalition governments from the establishment of the State of Israel until 1977. The 1973 elections moved Turkey away from a dominant, or 'one-and-a-half', party model, bringing the two major parties to approximately equal strength. The 1977 elections manifested a pattern much closer to two-party competition, the RPP and the JP both increasing their votes at the expense of the minor parties. A similar, but decidedly less dramatic, change took place in the Israeli elections of 1973, in which Labour lost votes and the major opposition bloc, the Likkud, made significant gains, thus making a non-Labour government a more realistic possibility than it had ever been before. However, multipartyism seems to have been more firmly entrenched in Israel than in Turkey, and a movement toward two-party competition is much less likely in the former than in the latter. Finally, both in Israel and Turkey, parties are generally cohesive and disciplined, and their programmes tend to be clearly distinguishable from each other.[5] Consequently, bargaining for formation of a government coalition can be a long and arduous process in both countries. 'The resulting governmental coalition, however, can depend on the solidarity of each governing party. It is the withdrawal of support by an entire party, not a division in voting within a party, that is the chief threat to stability.'[6]

Thus, under conditions approximating the requirements of responsible party government, elections in Turkey and Israel have had some impact on policy-making or issue resolution. Clearly, this is not to say that elections provide direct mechanisms for the resolution of any specific issues; it only means that they can have an important impact on policy.

The Lebanese case is quite different from the Turkish and the Israeli ones in this respect. In the absence of effective political parties, the typical Lebanese voter decides not among alternative political platforms, but among competing personalities. Whether the depth of sectarian cleavages and the strength of primordial loyalties discouraged the development of strong parties, or the absence of parties contributed to the persistence of such cleavage and loyalty patterns is immaterial for our purposes. What has to be emphasised here is that such a system minimises the policy impact of elections. Indeed, as Ralph Crow observes in Chapter 2, 'Lebanese political institutions are primarily designed and operated for the purpose of preventing communal conflict. Instead of using political institutions to resolve conflict, primary concern is given to preventing conflict from destroying the institutions. [In] this form, "the issues" are not much more than complaints rather than questions to be resolved by the political process.' In Lebanon the underlying political issue of national identity has been carefully and consciously avoided in electoral campaigns for fear of destroying the delicate balance among its religious communities. In other words, Lebanon's electoral process, as well as its other political institutions, is geared not to the open discussion and resolution of basic issues, but on the contrary to preventing them from coming into the open. The failure of the political system to cope with such issues through electoral and parliamentary processes may well be one of the reasons for the collapse of that system in the civil war of 1975-6.

Finally, let us look at the electoral politics of Israel, Lebanon and Turkey within the broader context of comparative Middle Eastern politics. If there is any merit in comparing Middle Eastern political systems with one another (and we strongly believe there is), this should rest on the assumption that the countries of the area share certain common attributes not found (to the same extent, at least) in the other major regions of the world. If so, it is reasonable to assume that such attributes have an impact on the electoral politics of the three Middle Eastern countries under study.

One such attribute is the pervasiveness of informal groups in Middle Eastern politics. As Bill and Leiden observe, 'the crucial units of interest aggregation in the Middle East remain informal groups'.[7] Informal-group politics is characterised by its highly personalistic nature, in that political power within such groups tends to be based on personal loyalty to the group leader. Kinship (family, tribe or clan) ties play an important role in the formation of informal groups. While such primordial ties give some degree of cohesion and stability to Middle Eastern group structure, informal groups still display a high level of fluidity, constantly shifting, fragmenting, reforming, entering into alliances and switching goals. This pattern dominates the Lebanese electoral process, and it is clearly observed in the less developed eastern and south-eastern regions of Turkey, as has been explained above. Predictably, it is least applicable to Israel, the most highly modernised country among the three. Clearly, there is an inverse relationship between the persistence of informal-group politics and the development of strong, effective political parties and associational interest groups.

Another common attribute of Middle Eastern politics is the importance of the religious factor. In Lebanon political cleavages follow sectarian lines. In Israel two religious parties, 'both dedicated to furthering the position of religion in all aspects of public life' (Chapter 3 above), compete in elections and gain seats in the Knesset. Even in Turkey, the most self-consciously 'secular' of the three, an explicitly Islamic party (the NSP) has emerged after a half-century of official secularism. In the first general election it contested (that of 1973), the NSP garnered almost 12 per cent of the total vote, and was a partner in both coalition governments formed subsequently. Despite the pervasive influence of religion in the region, however, it is interesting that in none of the other Muslim Middle Eastern countries have religious leaders been able to organise effective political parties. 'Whatever power is exerted by religious leaders is wielded through ... personal [informal] groups and not through more formal party organisations'.[8] This has been dramatically demonstrated in Iran since the fall of the Shah. Even in Lebanon, where sectarian ties are often the major determinants of political behaviour, the Muslims have lagged behind the Christians in political organisation, the predominantly Christian Katā'ib being about the only effective political party in the country.

Paradoxically, it is in non-Muslim Israel and secular Turkey that religious parties have been able to organise more effectively and to wield greater political influence than anywhere else in the Middle East. This may be a function both of open electoral competition and of a relatively high level of socio-economic modernisation in Israel and Turkey. Electoral competition means freedom to organise for religious (as well as other) groups, while socio-economic modernisation puts a premium on organisation. In a modern society it is extremely difficult for religious groups to compete electorally with the secular ones, unless they adopt the latter's style of organisation and propaganda. Bill and Leiden point out, in this respect, that 'those religious movements that have held political strength (the Muslim Brotherhood, for example) have had to emulate the secular system in organisational style, fund raising, and opinion formation. For all its denunciation of modernity, the Muslim Brotherhood equipped itself with the latest-model printing presses and other gadgetry.'⁹

All three countries under study face the challenge of socio-economic modernisation, like all their other Middle Eastern neighbours. If the forms and substance of electoral politics are associated with the level of modernisation, one should be able to explain a large amount of variation in the electoral politics of the countries involved by modernisation-related variables. We have assumed, at the outset, that such variables have an impact on all three aspects of electoral politics (electoral issues, voting behaviour and parliamentary elites) treated in this volume. This is at least partially borne out by our comparative evidence. Socio-economic modernisation seems to be associated to some degree in all three countries with movement from parochial to national issues, from issues related to centre-periphery cleavages to those related to functional (i.e. socio-economic) divisions, from mobilised and deferential to autonomous and instrumental modes of voting participation, and from parliamentary elites dominated by landlords and bureaucrats to domination by free professionals and party functionaries.

The fact that similar changes have been observed in non-competitive Middle Eastern political systems strengthens the argument that these changes are manifestations of the process of modernisation. The questions that remain concern the basis of electoral politics in these three countries and in particular why competitive politics has survived there and not elsewhere in the Middle East. Our comparative analyses do not provide conclusive answers to these kinds of questions. None the less, some suggestions are in order.

First, as we have already noted, it is probably no coincidence that the electoral systems which have developed in these three countries are patterned very much on the Western model. These three countries are among the most modern and/or Westernised in the region. The politically and socially dominant European-origined elite of Israel brought with it Western political ideas, habits and traditions. Turkey has enjoyed the dual advantage of a long history of governmental and administrative responsibility and immediate geographical proximity to Europe. The former meant that the post-1923 republic came into being with a well-established and highly institutionalised bureaucratic complex ready to assume responsibility for the direction of political affairs. This factor alone goes a long way toward explaining the relative stability of Turkish politics as compared to other countries of the

Middle East. The latter advantage (proximity to Europe) was, of course, a mixed blessing in that the Turks bore the brunt of European political and economic expansion prior to the twentieth century while at the same time this very exposure to European pressure motivated the Turks to undertake basic political reforms which never penetrated in the same degree to the Arab and other non-Turkish parts of the Middle East. Lebanon, finally, is the least modern of our three cases. Yet here, too, it was a Western-oriented group (the Maronite Christians) which led the way towards the development of probably the most unique political system in the Middle East, perhaps in the world.

If orientation toward or contact with the modern West is a common element among our three countries, there are also significant differences among them. Many of these have been discussed in this volume. In this conclusion, we might point out that in terms of the salience and role of electoral politics, these three countries may be viewed as falling at different points on a scale from high to low. Israel would seem to occupy the highest point on this scale. Here, institutionalised parties are deeply embedded in the political culture and there seems little or no question of the continued centrality of electoral politics. Turkey, too, has now developed a highly institutionalised party system, although the level of institutionalisation varies across the country with level of socio-economic development of constituencies or provinces. Although the possibility of a crisis-imposed intervention in the political system cannot be ruled out, competitive electoral politics would seem to be well established here. Lebanon presents the most troublesome tableau. Even when it is functioning normally, the Lebanese electoral system is based on only the most minimal consensus. Its survival depends upon an explicit exclusion of the most basic political and social issues from the formal political arena. Thus, when these issues become critical, as they did in 1975, the political system provides no institutionalised means for their resolution, and violence breaks out. At all times, the real decisions are made in a much more traditional context than in either Israel or Turkey, i.e. by informal groups interacting in highly personalistic fashion. In short, as we have already pointed out, the salience of the electoral system is lower here than in either of our other two cases.

Finally, what can be said about the prospects for the survival of democracy in the Middle East? As the 1980s begin, this rather fragile political system remains under threat in many parts of the world. While democratic regimes have reappeared in several European countries along the northern shores of the Mediterranean (Greece, Spain,

Portugal), no new regimes of this type have emerged among the Middle Eastern countries in this area. Indeed, one of the three societies reviewed in this book has suffered a virtually complete breakdown of orderly political processes (Lebanon), while a second (Turkey) has experienced increasing polarisation and fragmentation and a rising tide of political violence. Our third case (Israel), in spite of the dramatic diplomatic breakthrough on the Egyptian front, remains the object of adamant hostility on the part of most of its other neighbours, with the result that the pressures on the regime remain exceptionally high. Moreover, all countries in the region confront social, economic and political problems (such as rapid socio-economic change, rampant inflation, a destabilised world economy and increased political tension and unrest) which are becoming increasingly intractable.

Notes

1. J. A. Bill and C. Leiden, *The Middle East: Politics and Power* (Allyn and Bacon, Boston, 1974), p. 64.

2. Marvin Weinbaum, 'Classification and Change in Legislative Systems: with Particular Application to Iran, Turkey, and Afghanistan', in C. L. Kim and G. R. Boynton (eds.) *Legislative Systems in Developing Countries* (Sage Publications, Beverly Hills, California, 1975).

3. Hassan Mohammedi-Nejad, 'The Iranian Parliamentary Elections of 1975', *International Journal of Middle East Studies*, vol. 8, no. 1 (January 1977), pp. 103-116.

4. Leonard Binder, 'Political Recruitment and Participation in Egypt', in Joseph LaPalombara and Myron Weiner (eds.) *Political Parties and Political Development* (Princeton University Press, Princeton, New Jersey, 1966), pp. 239-40.

5. The Turkish RPP and the JP became more ideologically distinguishable in the late 1960s and early 1970s, especially as a result of the new social democratic orientation of the RPP. See F. Tachau, 'The Anatomy of Political and Social Change: Turkish Parties, Parliaments and Elections', *Comparative Politics*, 5 (July 1973), pp. 568-72; E. Özbudun, *Batı demokrasilerinde ve Türkiye' de parti disiplini* (Party discipline in western democracies and Turkey) (Hakuk Fakültesi Yayınları, Ankara, (1968), p.185-248.

6. Leon D. Epstein, *Political Parties in Western Democracies* (Praeger, New York, 1967), p. 339.

7. Bill and Leiden, *The Middle East,* p.66.

8. Ibid., p. 52.

9. Ibid.

LIST OF CONTRIBUTORS

Asher Arian is Dean of the Faculty of Social Sciences at Tel Aviv University, formerly Chairman of the Political Science Department, Tel Aviv University, and Professor of Political Science there. His books include *The Choosing People* and *Ideological Change in Israel*. He is editor of the series *Elections in Israel*. In addition, he has published articles in *Comparative Politics, Public Opinion Quarterly, The Midwest Journal of Political Science* and others.

Ralph E. Crow has been, since 1950, a member of the Department of Political Studies and Public Administration at the American University of Beirut. He has served as visiting professor at Indiana University, University of Damascus, Concordia University, Montreal, and as a senior fellow of St. Antony's College, Oxford. His publications include articles in the *Journal of Politics, International Review of Administrative Sciences*, and chapters in the volumes edited by L. Binder, *Politics in Lebanon* and by Kornberg and Musolf, *Legislatures in Developmental Perspective*.

Doğu Ergil, a PhD of the State University of New York in Binghamton, is Associate Professor of Political Science at Ankara University. He has written extensively on questions of political alienation and political modernisation. His books include *Social History of the Turkish National Liberation Movement, Terror and Violence in Turkey, Political Psychology* and *Alienation and Political Participation*.

Emanuel Gutmann teaches political science at the Hebrew University of Jerusalem and is a former Chairman of the Department. He·is also in charge of political science at the Israeli Open University. Books written and edited by him include *State and Society* and *The Israeli Political System*. He writes now on religion and politics in contemporary Europe and on the politics of heterogeneous cities.

Iliya Harik is a PhD of the University of Chicago and serves as Professor of Comparative Politics and International Relations at Indiana University. His books include *The Political Mobilization of Peasants: A Study of an Egyptian Community, Politics and Change in a Traditional Society, The Political Elites of Lebanon* and *Stratification and Poverty in Rural Egypt.* His articles have appeared in the *American Political Science Review, World Politics, Middle East Journal* and *International Journal of Middle East Studies.*

Samir G. Khalaf is Professor of Sociology at the American University of Beirut. He is a PhD from Princeton University and has held teaching and research appointments at Harvard and Princeton Universities. He is currently serving as a member of the Higher Council for Urban Planning in Lebanon and of the Joint Committee of the Near and Middle East of the Social Science Research Council and the American Council of Learned Societies. His publications include *Prostitution in A Changing Society, Hamra of Beirut: A Case of Rapid Urbanization, Persistence and Change in 19th Century Lebanon* and several articles and chapters in American and European journals and publications, including *Encyclopaedia Britannica.*

Jacob M. Landau is Professor of Political Science at the Hebrew University of Jerusalem and has served as a visiting professor at several other universities. His books include *Parliaments and Parties in Egypt, The Arabs in Israel: A Political Study, The Hejaz Railway and the Muslim Pilgrimage: A Case of Ottoman Political Propaganda, Middle Eastern Themes: Papers in History and Politics, Radical Politics in Modern Turkey, The Arabs and the Histadrut, Politics and Islam: The National Salvation Party in Turkey* and *Abdul Hamid's Palestine.* In addition, he has edited *Man, State and Society in the Contemporary Middle East* and has contributed numerous articles to various journals in the social sciences and Middle Eastern studies.

Ergun Özbudun is Professor of Constitutional Law and Comparative Politics at Ankara University and Director of the Institute for Middle Eastern Studies at the same university. He has been a research associate at Harvard University and a visiting professor at the University of Chicago. His books include *The Role of the Military in Recent Turkish Politics, Party Cohesion in Western Democracies* and *Social Change and Political Participation in Turkey.*

Frank Tachau is Professor and Chairman, Department of Political Science, University of Illinois in Chicago. He edited and co-authored *Political Elites and Political Development in the Middle East* and *The Developing Nations: What Path to Modernization?* and has published a number of articles and monographs on Turkish politics.

INDEX